Comparative Elite Sport
Development:
systems, structures and
public policy

KU-546-425

Comparative Elite Sport Development: systems, structures and public policy

Barrie Houlihan
Professor of Sport Policy
Institute of Sport and Leisure Policy
School of Sport and Exercise Sciences
Loughborough University

Mick Green
Lecturer in Sport Management and Policy
Institute of Sport and Leisure Policy
School of Sport and Exercise Sciences
Loughborough University

AMSTERDAM • BOSTON • HEIDELBERG • LONDON • NEW YORK • OXFORD
PARIS • SAN DIEGO • SAN FRANCISCO • SINGAPORE • SYDNEY • TOKYO

ELSEVIER

Butterworth-Heinemann is an imprint of Elsevier

Butterworth-Heinemann is an imprint of Elsevier
Linacre House, Jordan Hill, Oxford OX2 8DP, UK
30 Corporate Drive, Suite 400, Burlington, MA 01803, USA

First edition 2008

British Library Cataloguing in Publication Data
A catalogue record for this book is available from the British Library

Library of Congress Cataloguing in Publication Data
A catalogue record for this book is available from the Library of Congress

ISBN: 978-0-7506-8281-7

For information on all Butterworth-Heinemann publications
visit our web site at books.elsevier.com

Typeset by Charon Tec Ltd (A Macmillan Company), Chennai, India
www.charontec.com

Printed and bound in Great Britain

08   09   10   11   12   10 9 8 7 6 5 4 3 2 1

For my dad ('Tiny' Green), sadly not here to see this book

Contents

List of contributors   xi

List of figures   xii

List of tables   xiii

1 Comparative elite sport development   1
   Barrie Houlihan and Mick Green
      Introduction   2
      Developing elite athletes   3
      Pressures for convergence   9
      Explaining elite sport policy development   14
      Conclusion   20
      References   21

2 China   26
   Fan Hong
      Introduction   27
      The origin and development of the Chinese
      elite sport system   27
      The characteristics of the 'whole country support
      for the elite sport system' (Juguo tizgi)   36
      Elite athlete development   38
      Elite sport system critique   44
      The strategy of winning Olympic medals
      in 2008   46
      Conclusion   49
      References   50

3 Japan   53
   Mayumi Ya-Ya Yamamoto
      Introduction   54
      Current structure of the elite sport system   54
      The development of elite sport policy in Japan   58
      Four dimensions of the elite sport infrastructure
      in Japan   63
      Talent identification system and the
      development of potential athletes   72
      Competition opportunities for young athletes   74
      Distinctive features of the Japanese elite
      sport system   76
      Conclusion   78
      Notes   79
      References   79

4 Singapore   83
   Lionel Teo
      Introduction   84
      Development of sports excellence in Singapore   86
      National sport associations   91
      Dimensions of elite sport policy development   92
      Summary of key issues   104
      Recent developments and future directions of
      elite sport policy in Singapore   105
      Conclusions   108
      References   109

5 Germany   115
   Karen Petry, Dirk Steinbach and Verena Burk
      Introduction   116
      Development and structure of the German
      (top level) sports system   116
      Dimensions of elite sport development in
      Germany   127
      Conclusions   142
      Notes   143
      References   144

6 France   147
   *Emmanuel Bayle, Christophe Durand and
   Luc Nikonoff*
      Introduction   148
      Characteristics of the French model of
      elite sport   151
      Tensions, conflicts, and the future   156
      Conclusions   164

Notes 164
References 165

7 Poland 166
Jolanta Żyśko
Introduction 167
Elite sport in Poland 167
Changes in the system of elite sport
governance 178
Discussion of the elite sport system 184
Conclusions 190
Notes 191
References 192

8 Norway 194
Pål Augestad and Nils Asle Bergsgard
Introduction 195
The elite sport system in Norway 195
The infrastructure of elite sport 198
Focusing events 206
Government and elite sport 208
The Norwegian way 210
Concluding remarks 213
Notes 214
References 215

9 New Zealand 218
Shane Collins
Introduction 219
Current structure of the elite sport system 219
Increasing government intervention 221
The business of elite sport 225
Important dimensions of elite sport
development 232
Conclusion 239
References 240

10 United States 242
Emily Sparvero, Laurence Chalip and
B. Christine Green
Introduction 243
Federal involvement in elite sport 243
Athlete pathways 249
Success of American athletes 253
Research and development 259
Elite sport development amid the chaos 260
Observations and implications 268
References 270

11   Conclusion   272
       Mick Green and Barrie Houlihan
         Introduction   273
         Common pressures for convergence   273
         Mechanisms for convergence and processes
         of learning   278
         An assessment of the three 'explanations'   288
         References   291

     Index   *295*

List of contributors

Pål Augestad, Telemark University College, Norway

Emmanuel Bayle, Burgundy University, France

Nils Asle Bergsgard, International Research Institute of Stavanger, Norway

Verena Burk, Eberhard-Karls Universität Tübingen, Germany

Laurence Chalip, University of Texas at Austin, USA

Shane Collins, Loughborough University, UK

Christophe Durand, Caen Normandie University, France

B. Christine Green, University of Texas at Austin, USA

Mick Green, Loughborough University, UK

Fan Hong, University College Cork, Ireland

Barrie Houlihan, Loughborough University, UK

Luc Nikonoff, Health, Youth and Sports Ministry, Sport Direction, Paris, France

Karen Petry, Deutsche Sporthochschule Köln, Germany

Emily Sparvero, Texas A&M University, USA

Dirk Steinbach, Deutsche Sporthochschule Köln, Germany

Lionel Teo, Nanyang Polytechnic, Singapore

Mayumi Ya-Ya Yamamoto, Loughborough University, UK

Jolanta Żyśko, Jozef Pilsudski University of Physical Education, Poland

List of figures

Figure 2.1   The administrative structure of Chinese
             sport 1952–1996   37
Figure 2.2   The administrative structure of Chinese
             sport 1997–2006   38
Figure 2.3   Pyramid of the selective system   40
Figure 3.1   Organisational structure of elite sport in
             Japan   55
Figure 4.1   Schematic representation of the Sports
             Community and the Sporting Vision
             of Singapore   85
Figure 5.1   The development of the West German
             sports system after the World War II   120
Figure 5.2   Model of training and performance   134
Figure 7.1   The organisational structure of sport in
             Poland   176
Figure 7.2   Historical changes in the naming of the
             central national administrative body for
             the management of physical culture in
             Poland since 1946   181
Figure 8.1   Direct state funding (lottery money) for
             elite sport development in NIF/NOC, the
             income from sponsors of NIF/NOC, and
             total expenditure on elite sport by
             NIF/NOC, 1996–2005   210
Figure 10.1 Key organisations in American sport
             development   252
Figure 10.2 US medal performance in the summer
             Olympic Games   255
Figure 10.3 US medal performance in the winter
             Olympic Games   256

List of tables

Table 1.1   Factors contributing to elite success   4
Table 2.1   China's participation in the summer
              Olympics 1984–2004   35
Table 2.2   China's participation in the summer
              Asian Games 1978–2002   35
Table 2.3   Chinese sports budget 1981–1996   39
Table 2.4   Budget for elite sports teams 1991–1997   39
Table 3.1   Competitive Sports Division Budget
              Allocation regarding the preparation
              for the NTC, JISS, 1998 Nagano Games,
              and 2002 World Cup   65
Table 5.1   Top level German performances in the
              sports of athletics, swimming
              and hockey   128
Table 7.1   Public sport financing: 1989–2006   177
Table 9.1   SPARC actual total funding   230
Table 9.2   Allocation of SPARC investment funds   230
Table 10.1   School and professional system
              support for Olympic sports   254

CHAPTER 1

Comparative elite sport development

Barrie Houlihan and Mick Green

Introduction

In the 4 years prior to the Athens Olympic Games in 2004, the UK government allocated around £70 million in direct financial support to UK athletes. At the Games, the Great Britain and Northern Ireland team obtained a total of 30 medals, 9 of which were gold – an approximate cost of £2.3 million per medal. In the run up to the Beijing Games in 2008, the government has allocated a sum of £75 million in direct financial support. The United Kingdom is far from being alone in providing substantial support for its elite, and especially, Olympic athletes. The poor performance by the Australian team at the 1976 Montreal Olympics prompted a government enquiry which led to sustained and substantial investment of public funds in elite training facilities such as the Australian Institute of Sport and in direct support to athletes and domestic Olympic sports federations. At around the same time, the government of the German Democratic Republic (GDR; former East Germany) was reputed to be spending about 1 per cent of its gross domestic product on elite sport. As Bergsgard et al. (2007, p. 170) note, government resources 'were very much concentrated in high performance training centres in Berlin where there was a substantial "over-employment" of support personnel'. A DSB official reported, following reunification, that 'when we took over, in East Berlin in track and field, we took over 65 physiotherapists. Each individual athlete had his own ...'. Even in free market, non-interventionist and decentralised political systems, such as the United States, draconian government intervention in sport was not unusual if it was deemed necessary to protect elite sport success. For example, in 1978 the US Congress legislated to resolve the long-standing dispute between the National Collegiate Athletic Association (NCAA) and the Amateur Athletic Union (AAU) for control over elite track and field athletes (cf. Hunt, 2007). The Amateur Sports Act marginalised the AAU and gave the US Olympic Committee primary responsibility for the preparation of teams to represent the United States.

There are a variety of explanations why such a diverse range of governments should be so concerned with elite sport success which include international prestige and diplomatic recognition, ideological competition and a belief that international sporting success generates domestic political benefits ranging from the rather nebulous 'feel good factor' to more concrete economic impacts associated with the hosting of elite competitions. In recent years hosting major sports events has been, for a number of countries, an important element in various forms of economic development including tourism promotion (Sydney 2000 Olympic Games) and urban regeneration (Barcelona 1992 and London 2012 Olympic Games). The economic benefits of hosting major sports events are increasingly significant in post-industrial countries where the sports-related service sector is an important engine for growth and employment (Gratton and Taylor, 2000). However, if countries are to be in a position to use sport as a resource, whether for diplomatic, economic or social objectives, they are in a much better position to exploit sport's potential if they possess assets in the form of recognised world-class elite athletes. There are few governments who have not recognised the value of sport as a high-visibility, low-cost and extremely malleable resource which can be adapted to achieve, or at least give the impression to the public/electorate of achieving, a wide variety of domestic and international goals. Such is the flexibility of sport as a policy instrument that it is increasingly difficult for governments, providing of course that they possess the necessary financial resources, not to espouse a commitment to elite sport and competition as illustrated by Canada's agonising over the place of elite sport in public policy following the Ben Johnson doping scandal at the 1988 Seoul Olympic Games. Despite many statements decrying the distortion of values resulting from a commitment to the pursuit of Olympic medals, Canada is now investing heavily in elite sport in advance of its hosting of the 2010 winter Olympics in Vancouver.

Developing elite athletes

There have been a number of attempts to identify the ingredients of successful elite athlete development such as those by Fisher and Borms (1990), Abbott et al. (2002), Digel (2002a, b), Green and Oakley (2001a, b), Oakley and Green (2001), UK Sport (2006). Although the various authors identify a different number of key elements in a successful elite development system, there is considerable overlap between the analyses (see Table 1.1). In particular, it is possible to organise the elements or characteristics into three reasonably distinct clusters: contextual, for example, the availability of funding/wealth; processual, for example, a system for identifying talent, determining the basis on which particular sports will be offered support; and specific, for example, bespoke training facilities.

For Oakley and Green (2001; see also Green and Oakley, 2001a) the 10 characteristics listed in Table 1.1 represent 'common approaches to the problem of enhancing elite sport rather

Table 1.1 Factors contributing to elite success

Factors	Oakley and Green	Digel	UK Sport (SPLISS Consortium)	Green and Houlihan
Contextual	An excellence culture Appropriate funding	Support, especially financial, of the state Economic success and business sponsorship A media supported positive sports culture	Financial support Participation in sport Scientific research	Support for 'full-time' athletes
Processual	Clear understanding of the role of different agencies Simplicity of administration Effective system for monitoring athlete progress Talent identification and targeting of resources Comprehensive planning system for each sport Lifestyle support	Talent development through the education system Talent development through the armed forces	Talent identification and development system Athletic and post-career support Integrated approach to policy development Coaching provision and coach development	
Specific	Well-structured competitive programmes Well-developed specific facilities	Sports science support services	International competition Training facilities	A hierarchy of competition opportunities centred on preparation for international events Elite facility development The provision of coaching, sports science and sports medicine support services

Sources: Digel (2002a, b); Green and Houlihan (2005); Oakley and Green (2001); and UK Sport (2006).

than responses to the social, political and economic elements in each country' (2001, p. 91). Moreover, they suggest 'that there is a growing trend towards a homogeneous model of elite sport development' (2001, p. 91). Digel's analysis (2002a, b) focuses more on the context within which an effective elite sport system can develop, but there is a clear overlap with the analysis of Oakley and Green insofar as he stresses the importance of a culture supportive of elite achievement, adequate financial support, and processes through which talent can be identified and developed.

The joint report by UK Sport, Vrije Univeriteit Brussel, WJH Mulier Institut (The Netherlands) and Sheffield Hallam University, UK (known as the SPLISS Consortium) compared elite development systems in six countries (United Kingdom, Canada, Italy, Norway, The Netherlands and Belgium) in relation to the nine factors (pillars) listed in Table 1.1. The findings were 'inconclusive' insofar as there was no clear relationship between particular factors and elite success. However, the authors did note that the three most successful countries at the Athens Olympic Games, Italy, United Kingdom and The Netherlands, all scored well in relation to the following four factors: funding for national governing bodies (NGBs); coaching provision and coaching development; athletic and post-career support and training facilities. The report also suggested that the similar high scores for the United Kingdom and The Netherlands in relation to 'athletic and post-career support' and 'international competition' might be due to both countries benefiting 'from the learning curve of other nations which might be described as "early adopters" such as Australia' (UK Sport, 2006, p. 15). Finally, the report noted the paradox of

increasing global competition … encouraging nations to adopt … more strategic elite sport policy in order to differentiate themselves from other nations. The net result is an increasingly homogeneous elite sport development system which is ostensibly based around a near uniform model of elite sport development with subtle local variations (2006, p. 16).

However, in an article also published in 2006, by many of the same authors of the UK Sport report they qualify their initial conclusion by stating that

It is impossible to create one single model for explaining international success. A system leading to success in one nation may be doomed to fail in another. Therefore it needs to be emphasised that the combination of the nine pillars may be specific to a given nation's context and that different systems may all be successful'.

(De Bosscher et al., 2006, p. 209)

Although there are some differences in emphasis between the foregoing analyses they have much in common, at least at the general level of specification if not in the detail. The centrality of dedicated training facilities, public sector financial support, an integration of training preparation programmes with competition opportunities and an entourage of specialist support staff was evident across nearly all analyses and received further confirmation by Green and Houlihan (2005) in their review of the Soviet and East German sports systems and their more detailed analysis of the elite sport systems in Australia, Canada and the United Kingdom. Green and Houlihan suggested that there were four common themes: elite facility development; support for 'full-time' athletes; the provision of coaching, sports science and sports medicine support services; and a hierarchy of competition opportunities centred on preparation for international events.

Elite facility development referred to the provision of, and priority access to, specialised facilities for training. While the importance of access to specialised training facilities is widely acknowledged, provision is rarely considered satisfactory. In Australia, for example, elite swimmers complained not about the number of competition size swimming pools, but about constraints on access arising from the lack of ownership and control of pools by the swimming governing body. Attempts to develop a national strategy for the location of pools, crucial in such a vast country, were undermined by the insistence of states in establishing their own priorities regarding elite sport and facility provision. Facility provision for sailing was similarly affected by the state–federal relations, although provision was improved in preparation for the Sydney Olympic Games. Elite facility provision problems were even greater in Canada where the relationship between provinces and the federal government was more fractious thus making the implementation of a national facility strategy extremely challenging. Provincial–federal rivalry was compounded by a pattern of funding which was determined by success in bidding to host major sports events. Thus funding for elite level facilities was allocated to the cities that had been successful in bidding to host events rather than to those that had the greatest need or the greatest long-term commitment to supporting elite athletes. Even in the United Kingdom, which has a much more centralised political system, problems persist with the provision of suitable training facilities although the establishment of the UK Sport Institute (UKSI) network of specialist centres has greatly improved availability and access. However, for many sports there remains an unresolved tension between the facility needs of elite athletes and those of non-elite/club athletes.

With regard to elite facilities, Green and Houlihan (2005) argued that in all three countries swimming and athletics, both heavily dependent on public resources for facility development, found it hard to resolve the tension between support for elite achievement and support for the wider membership of their clubs. With substantial state political and financial support both sports sought to overcome this value conflict by isolating elite facilities from mass access, for example, through the establishment of elite sports centres in Canada and the network of elite sport institutes (UKSI) in the United Kingdom, thus creating separate administrative and financial arrangements to ensure that no elite level funding could be siphoned off for grassroots use. Sailing was an exception largely because its well-established club structure and the financial independence of its membership left it insulated from the competition for scarce resources that featured so significantly in the other two sports. The attempts to meet the acknowledged facility needs of elite competitors were affected by two key factors: first, the resource dependency relationship between the advocates of elite sport and the state; and second, the jurisdictional complexity at both the governmental level and also within their own organisations that most national sports organisations or national governing bodies (NSOs/NGBs) had to cope with.

The standard of competition in most sports makes it extremely difficult for an athlete to compete for medals if they do not treat training as a full-time commitment. Green and Houlihan (2005) found that while the Soviet Union and the GDR funded their athletes indirectly through their armed forces or universities, Australia, Canada and the United Kingdom provided direct financial support to their elite athletes. However, in none of these countries was the subsidy sufficient to enable athletes to be financially independent, even in the United Kingdom where the world-class performance programme is supported by the national lottery. As a result many athletes had to seek additional funding from part-time work or from commercial sponsorship. However, corporate sponsorship of individual athletes, especially in swimming and athletics, encouraged elite swimmers and athletes to compete abroad for prize monies often to the detriment of their long-term development and consequently to their country's medal-winning potential at the Olympic Games. As Slack observed, these athletes 'no longer represent their club, their country, or themselves, they represent the corporations who provide the money for their sport' (1998, p. 3).

The provision of high-quality coaching, science and medical support services also emerged as an important element in the elite development systems in each of the three countries. However, Green and Houlihan noted that

In [athletics, sailing and swimming] across all three countries acceptance of coaching as an important, if not essential, ingredient in elite success … was slow in developing. Until the advent of substantial public subsidy of both swimming and athletics investment in coaching was not possible in the volume that would encourage talented amateur coaches to see the occupation as a full-time career. However, even when public funds became available … [investment in] the supporting services of coaching, sports science and medicine [was] generally an after-thought (2005, p. 175).

Up until the mid-1990s, public sector investment in elite sport was directed towards facility development and direct financial support for athletes. Consequently, with the notable exceptions of the European communist countries, coaching was highly variable in both quantity and quality. Much the same can also be said of the availability of sports science and sports medicine services as, according to Green and Houlihan, 'all sports have been fairly slow to explore the potential of sports science in relation to competitors' (2005, pp. 176–177). Early engagement with sports science tended to focus on equipment rather than the athlete, primarily because the application of science to equipment and apparel design has greater potential to generate profits than research into nutrition, psychological preparation and training regimes.

The final element of the elite sport system identified by Green and Houlihan was the structuring of domestic competition schedules to meet the needs of elite athletes who were preparing for international events. Green and Houlihan concluded that 'the establishment of a competition calendar that met the needs of elite athletes was surprisingly hard to achieve' (2005, p. 177). Part of the explanation lay in the conflict of interests between clubs/grassroots members and elite performers with the interests of the latter providing a poor justification for altering the pattern of competition for the overwhelming majority of club members. A second factor was the frequency with which elite athletes put their own financial interests (or those of their sponsor) ahead of those of their country. In athletics and swimming in particular, it was often the case that athletes would prefer to compete on the commercial Grand Prix circuit rather than in domestic club competitions or international representative events. Third, some NSOs/NGBs have put their need to generate income, for example, through sponsored events, ahead of the needs of their elite athletes to prepare systematically for major international competitions. Fourthly, some countries, Australia and Canada for example, had to overcome the problems associated with the size of their countries and the consequent problems of arranging national events and competitions. Australia faced the further problem of its relative isolation from the main international competition circuits in all three sports. Finally, athletes who rely on scholarships from American universities, such as those from Canada, were regularly required to put the interests of their college ahead of those of their country and their international ambitions.

Pressures for convergence

The extent of similarity and variation between the countries analysed by Green and Houlihan suggests a degree of tension between pressures towards convergence in elite sport systems and factors militating against a uniform approach to developing elite success. Among the pressures towards convergence in elite sport systems are globalisation, commercialisation and governmentalisation.

The assumption that the major determinants of public policy are confined within sovereign state boundaries has, in recent years, become progressively less persuasive as an increasing number of formerly domestic policy issues are now embedded in a series of supranational policy networks. Indeed so significant have supranational actors become that some observers, for example Andersen and Eliassen (1993), argue that the proper focus for analysis should be the global or regional policy arena. In his analysis of welfare policy, Deacon (1997) argues that globalisation has necessitated a revision of the traditional approach to welfare policy analysis. Supranational policy actors, such as the International Monetary Fund, the Organisation for Economic Cooperation and Development, and the World Bank, who have for many years influenced the domestic policy of poorer countries, are now shaping the discourse about the future of welfare programmes in the richer countries of Western Europe. Deacon also suggests that greater account needs to be taken of the 'globalisation of social policy instruments, policy and provision' (1997, p. 20) which takes three distinct forms – supranational regulation, supranational redistribution and supranational provision. Supranational regulation refers to 'those mechanisms, instruments and policies at the global level that seek to regulate the terms of trade and operation of firms in the interests of social protection and welfare objectives' (1997, p. 2). Examples from within the area of sport would include the regulation by international sports federations and the European Union of the transfer market, the role of the World Anti-Doping Agency in shaping national anti-doping policy and the growing importance of the Court for Arbitration for Sport in settling sports-related disputes.

Welfare-related supranational redistribution policies already operate within the European Union and at a much lower level of effectiveness through the United Nations and key agencies such as UNESCO. In sport the closest examples would be the operation of sports development aid bodies such as Olympic Solidarity and the International Association of Athletics Federations (IAAF) sports development programme where the spread of the Olympic diet of international sport is supported with some very modest redistribution of resources. Supranational provision refers, according to Deacon, 'to the embryonic measures ... whereby people gain an entitlement to a service or are empowered in the field of social citizenship rights by an agency acting at the supra-national level' (1997, p. 3). The UN High Commission for Refugees and the Council of Europe Court of Human Rights pro-vide two examples, while in the area of sport the Court of Arbitration for Sport is beginning to fulfil a similar role for ath-letes. At the very least the wealth of research on globalisation requires that any comparative analysis of elite sport development systems is sensitive to the increasing significance of supranational organisations for domestic policy.

Operationalising the concept of globalisation has proved difficult once consideration moves from a simple cataloguing of effects to an analysis of forms (Houlihan, 1997; Hirst and Thompson, 1999; Scholte, 2000), causes (Wallerstein, 1974; Robertson, 1992; Boli and Thomas, 1997) and trajectories of glob-alisation (Robertson, 1995; Hirst and Thompson, 1999; Houlihan, 2007). Despite the eclectic nature of much of the literature on glob-alisation, there is broad agreement that (1) globalisation should not be conceptualised as a coherent and uni-directional process, (2) the analysis of the significance of cultural change must acknowledge the varying depth of social embeddedness and that there is a need to be wary of granting too much importance to shifts in the popu-larity of particular sports or events, (3) the impact of globalisation on policy within individual countries will vary due to the differen-tial 'reach' of global influences and the variability in 'response' in different countries and (4) while the political and cultural dimen-sions have a degree of autonomy from economic processes, it is economic interests that have become much more prominent in sport in the last 25 years as major sports, and sports events have become increasingly a focus for private profit rather than state sub-sidy (see Hirst and Thompson, 1999; Held and McGrew, 2002; Houlihan, 2003; Scholte, 2000).

The second pressure making for convergence, commercialisa-tion, has three dimensions: first, the transformation of many

sports events, clubs and athletes into valuable brands and commodities; second, the growth of sport as a source of profit for
non-sports businesses through, for example, sponsorship and
broadcasting; and third, the growth of sports-related businesses
such as sportswear and equipment manufacture (Amis and
Cornwell, 2005; Slack, 2005). Particularly important is the attitude of government to the sports sector and the extent to which
it perceives sport, not for example as an element of welfare
provision, but as a sector of the service economy. The change in
the perception of sport from being a consumer of public subsidy to a part of the cultural industrial sector (the productive
economy) has been slow especially among some neo-liberal
governments. The commercial potential of sport was recognised most clearly in relation to bids to host major sports events.
For Germany (World Cup hosts in 2006), Canada (winter
Olympic hosts in Vancouver in 2010), and the United Kingdom
(hosts of the 2002 Commonwealth Games and of the 2012
Olympic Games), the economic benefits to the national balance
of payments and to the local and regional economy have
featured prominently in the rationales for government support
of bids.

Commercialisation has also affected the way in which athletes relate to their sport with the most obvious impact being
the increasing numbers who see sport as a significant source of
income. The rapid decline in elite level amateur sport in track
and field, tennis and, most recently, in rugby union, and the
steady increase in the number of national Olympic committees
which routinely give financial rewards to their medallists are
both indicative of this trend. Countries, especially in
Scandinavia, and organisations, such as the European Union,
in which there is a lobby to retain, what the European Union
refers to as, the 'European model of sport' in contrast to the
commercial model typified by the United States, face an uphill
struggle to hold back the neo-liberal commercialisation of
sport. Finally, commercialisation has affected the management
values and practices in sport and, in this respect, overlaps with
governmentalisation.

NSOs in a number of countries including Australia, Canada
and the United Kingdom have experienced rapid change in their
internal organisation, the relationship between professional
management staff and volunteer officers and general management practices often as a result of encouragement or pressure
from government to modernise (become more business-like).
In order to access commercial sponsorship and often public
funding to develop their sports, events and teams as brands and
marketable commodities, NSOs have increasingly been required

to adopt business practices and expertise of the corporate sector. Thus the strong pressures of mimetic isomorphism in relation to commercial corporations are reinforced by some governments through the imposition of targets and performance indicators. Audit and inspection regimes now proliferate, and are supported by sanctions imposed on those organisations that 'fail' to meet these centrally imposed targets (Green and Houlihan, 2006). This form of governmentalisation clearly reinforces and legitimises the value system of commercialisation in privileging the 'the values of self-sufficiency, competitiveness and entrepreneurial dynamism' (Hall, 1998, p. 11).

Although it is clear that governmentalisation reinforces many of the pressures exerted through commercialisation, the most important aspect of governmentalisation is the development of a state apparatus for the delivery and management of sport. In many countries government involvement in sport, particularly elite sport, is a significant and, in some cases, a dominant feature of the sports system and infrastructure. Not only are there many examples of governments working closely with voluntary/not-for-profit sports associations to deliver sports services, but there is also evidence of the steady accumulation of functions by government and the consequent development of specialist administrative departments and agencies, and the allocation of responsibility for sport policy at ministerial level. By the early part of the twenty-first century, concern with elite sport has become so well established within the machinery of government and within the portfolio of ministerial responsibilities that many governments are able to influence significantly the elite sport system.

While the three pressures are evident in many industrialised countries, their impact differs considerably as does the domestic response. Moreover, the response to these pressures will, to varying extents, become institutionalised and form part of the fabric of constraints within which elite sport policy is made. However, it is particularly important to acknowledge the degree to which global pressures are mediated by history. For example, the pressures of globalisation, commercialisation and governmentalisation have been and continue to be mediated in the United Kingdom by a history of sport in which social class and sports participation were intimately intertwined (Mason, 1980; Holt, 1992; Birley, 1995) and a long-standing non-interventionist attitude towards sport. In many respects the initial reluctance of governments, whether Conservative or Labour, up to the 1990s to intervene in order to influence the development of sport gave commercial interests the opportunity to shape substantially the development of elite sport. However, the relatively recent enthusiasm of the government of John Major and those of Tony Blair and Gordon Brown was stimulated less by a desire to temper the excesses of commercialisation than by a desire to harness what was increasingly recognised as a significant political resource that could be deployed to aid the achievement of a series of non-sporting policy objectives such as improved behaviour among the young, community integration, urban regeneration and strengthened national morale. An instrumental perception of sport dominates within government which sees sport as a relatively cheap, yet high-profile tool for contributing to the achievement of a broad range of social policy objectives.

Other countries have similar distinctive histories that affect the impact of global pressures. It would be surprising if the abrupt ruptures that marked German history in the twentieth century had not created a distinctive response to globalisation, commercialisation and governmentalisation. The rise and fall of the Nazi regime and the reunification of East and West Germany were dramatic breaks with the past, both of which have left strong imprints on subsequent developments. Indeed the dominant motif in the history of German sport is the depth of political involvement in sport. In Poland, the 50 years of communist control and the general level of poverty in the country have produced a legacy that cannot be brushed aside, but which will continue to mediate current elite sport policy. In a similar fashion, the geo-political location of Singapore, its colonial history and current prosperity affect how its elite sport policy has been developed just as Protestantism, oil wealth and an intense historical rivalry with Sweden and Denmark have mediated Norway's embrace of elite sport development.

In summary, it is essential to acknowledge the significance of transnational pressures and trends such as globalisation, commercialisation and governmentalisation, but it is equally essential to recognise the significance of national history and the institutional constraints on policy development. With this caveat in mind it is important to examine the attempts to operationalise the concept of globalisation at the level of specific policy. Given that apart from the former communist countries of central and Eastern Europe, most governments have only had an elite sport policy since the early 1990s it is reasonable to assume that policy traditions and institutions have not yet been firmly established and that considerable fluidity remains in the development of policy. It is therefore valuable to explore analytical frameworks and concepts which operate at the meso-level within particular policy areas as a way of understanding the interaction between global pressures and domestic contexts.

Explaining elite sport policy development

Policy learning, lesson-drawing and policy transfer

Implicit in much of the discussion of the development of elite sport systems in the work of Oakley and Green, Digel, De Bosscher et al. and Green and Houlihan discussed above is the assumption that countries learn from each other and that a process of policy transfer is in operation. At a commonsense level, policy learning and policy transfer are attractive. For example, the United Kingdom's main comparators in relation to elite sport success include France, Italy, Australia and Germany and it would be unrealistic and surprising not to expect policy-makers to find out what these countries do and at least ask the question whether their practices could be adapted to the UK context.

The cluster of related concepts of 'policy learning', 'lesson-drawing' and 'policy transfer' has featured prominently in much recent analysis of policy change. Policy learning is rooted in an Eastonian systems model of the policy process where the policy-making cycle is regularly energised by feedback on the impact of existing policy, that is policy learning. While the process of policy learning can therefore be largely domestic and insulated from experience in other countries or even other policy areas in the same country, it is increasingly accepted that policy learning can and often does involve analyses of similar policy areas and issues in other countries.

More recent conceptualisations of policy learning have emphasised the intentional aspect of the process which moves beyond feedback on existing policy and involves the systematic scanning of the environment for policy ideas thus, in part at least, answering the critics of policy learning (e.g., Blyth, 1997; Gorges, 2001) who highlight the lack of clarity regarding the process by which ideas impact upon policy. Often this systematic scanning is undertaken as a routine activity by public officials and is a technical process rather than a political one. Heclo (1972), for example, argues that policy change is often not about the exercise of power but is a more consensual process involving a variety of actors (state, interest groups and political parties) concerned with a particular issue. In contrast, Hall (1986) argues that the impact of an idea is directly related to the strength of the organisation that acts as its sponsor thus challenging the rationalist assumption that ideas are an independent variable in the policy process.

Hall (1986) provides a valuable typology of policy change identifying three levels or 'orders' of policy change which result, potentially at least, from policy learning. First-order changes are alterations to the intensity or scale of an existing policy instrument, such as an increase in an existing funding stream for elite athlete development. Second-order changes are those that introduce new policy instruments designed to achieve existing policy objectives: examples of which would include the introduction of payments to athletes for gold medals where none had previously been given or the psychological and physiological assessment of young athletes as part of a talent identification process. Finally, third-order changes are those that involve a change in policy goals and would include the decision to adopt an elite development strategy where previously the public policy priority had been on mass participation or where the state had previously left elite sport development to the voluntary or commercial sector. However, it is important to bear in mind Pemberton's (2004, p. 189) comment that it is essential to distinguish conceptually between learning and change, and to recognise that 'learning ... does not necessarily lead to change'.

The lack of a necessary connection between policy learning and policy change is a theme developed by Rose who distinguished lesson-drawing from policy learning. Rose (2005, p. 16) suggests that 'A lesson is the outcome of learning: it specifies a programme drawing on knowledge of programmes in other countries dealing with much the same problem'. As Rose notes 'Lesson-drawing expands the scope for choice in the national political agenda, for it adds to proposals generated by domestic experience the stimulus of examples drawn from foreign experience' (2005, p. 23). However, lesson-drawing 'accepts the contingency of public policy' and that what might work in one country might not work in another. In addition, lesson-drawing has the capacity to produce innovative policies only insofar as they are new to the importing country. As Rose notes, lesson-drawing 'presupposes that even though a programme may be new to a government considering it, something very much like it will be in effect elsewhere' (2005, p. 24).

As a result the concept of lesson-drawing avoids, according to Rose, 'the bias inherent in analyses of policy transfer, since the term focuses attention on programmes that can or should be imported from abroad at the expense of giving attention to the obstacles to applying lessons at home' (2005, p. 24). However, lesson-drawing is not a technical or neutral activity as the determination of what constitutes a lesson is a political process. Moreover, it is not always the case that the outcome of policy learning and lesson-drawing is positive as policy-makers may learn the 'wrong' lesson as a result of, for example, lack of analytical capacity or a restrictive ideology.

Green (2007, p. 429) distinguishes policy transfer from lesson-drawing by noting that 'policy transfer is generally conceived of as a broader concept than lesson drawing as it takes account of ideas of diffusion and coercion rather than just the voluntaristic activity of the latter'. In particular policy transfer refers to the process by which lessons learnt are transferred: how lessons are internalised, how lessons are recorded and described and how they are incorporated into a different organisational infrastructure and value system in the receiving country or policy sector. Policy transfer is, in Rose's (2005, p. 16) words, 'action-oriented intentional activity'. An awareness of the extent to which the transfer mechanism facilitates or constrains transfer is crucial. For example, the important role of the armed forces in South Korea in developing elite athletes for the Olympic Games or the role of the high school and especially the university sector in the United States in talent identification and development may be lessons that are clearly understood and learnt but which are difficult to transfer to a country such as the United Kingdom which does not have the institution of conscription and where the cultural values of the higher education system preclude such a heavy emphasis on sporting success at the expense of educational attainment.

The concept of policy transfer needs to be understood as reflecting the degree of ambiguity that surrounds the concept of policy. As a number of analysts have noted policy may be defined in a variety of ways: as government aspiration (Hogwood, 1987, p. 4), government action (Jenkins, 1978, p. 15) or government inaction (Heclo, 1972, p. 85). Consequently, what may be transferred may be an aspiration to achieve elite success without any subsequent commitment of resources or development of programmes. For example, many countries are signatories to the World Anti-Doping Code but have allocated only token resources to support implementation. However, policy transfer might refer to the transfer of a commitment to act supported by the resources necessary for effective action, for example, strategy development, investment in training facilities, the establishment of coach development programmes, and rescheduling of national competitions to better suit the build-up to international competition. Finally, the policy that is transferred might be much more difficult to identify as it is a policy to do nothing, or at least, not to alter current policy perhaps because it is considered to be equivalent to those available elsewhere. As should be clear the analysis of the transfer process is as important as an understanding of the process of policy learning and lesson-drawing. Lessons may well be accurately learned but be imperfectly transferred or transferred to an unsupportive organisational infrastructure.

Despite the attractiveness of the concepts of policy learning and policy transfer, there are some problems, the most obvious of which are the difficulty of explaining how policy-makers learn (Oliver, 1997), what constitutes learning (Bennett and Howlett, 1992) and how learning might be quantified (Pierson, 1993). In addition there are substantial concerns relating to the process by which lessons are communicated and transferred policies recreated in the receiving country (see Dolowitz and Marsh, 1996, 2000).

Path dependency

Underlying much of the discussion about policy learning is the assumption that policy will change as a result of past experience or new information. As Greener notes policy learning 'considers policy legacies to be one of the most significant elements in determining present and future policy' (2002, p. 162). As such, policy learning has much in common with the concept of path dependency which suggests that initial policy decisions can determine future policy choices: that 'the trajectory of change up to a certain point constrains the trajectory after that point' (Kay, 2005, p. 553). Path dependency is also connected to the broader policy analysis literature on the importance of institutions which, for Thelen and Steinmo, are seen as significant constraints and mediating factors in politics, which 'leave their own imprint' (1992, p. 8). Whether the emphasis is on institutions as organisations or as sets of values and beliefs (culture), there is a strong historical dimension which emphasises the 'relative autonomy of political institutions from the society in which they exist; … and the unique patterns of historical development and the constraints they impose on future choices' (Howlett and Ramesh, 1995, p. 27).

As was argued above the relevance of institutionalism within sport policy analysis is clear. A number of authors have identified the organisational infrastructure of UK sport as a significant variable in shaping policy (cf. Roche, 1993; Pickup, 1996; Henry, 2001; Houlihan and White, 2002; Green, 2004) while Krauss (1990) and Wilson (1994) draw similar conclusions with regard to the United States as do Macintosh (1991) and Macintosh and Whitson (1990) in relation to Canada. Allocation of functional responsibility for sport, federalism, the use of 'arms length' agencies, and the presence of a minister for sport are all seen as having a discernible impact on sport policy and its implementation. Similar claims for the significance of cultural institutions are also widespread. Beliefs, norms and values associated with social class (Birley, 1995), gender (Hargreaves, 1994), disability (Thomas, 2007), and ethnicity (Carrington and Macdonald, 2000) have all been demonstrated to have had, and indeed to continue to have, a marked impact on the character of UK sport policy.

Perhaps more significant is the work of Esping-Andersen and his analysis of welfare states which is based on the hypothesis that the socio-economic and cultural foundations of a country will shape policy. Esping-Andersen (1990) identified three types of welfare regime: liberal, conservative and social democratic, using the private–public mix in welfare provision, the degree of de-commodification and modes of stratification or solidarities as dependent variables. Liberal welfare regimes, such as the United States and the United Kingdom, 'reflect a political commitment to minimise the state, to individualise risks, and to promote market solutions' and adopt a 'narrow conception of what risks should be considered "social"' (Esping-Andersen, 1999, pp. 74ff). By contrast the social democratic welfare regime is 'virtually synonymous with the Nordic countries' and is 'committed to comprehensive risk coverage, generous benefit levels, and egalitarianism', the decommodification of welfare and the 'fusion of universalism with generosity' (Esping-Andersen, 1999, pp. 78ff). Conservative welfare regimes, such as Germany and Austria, are characterised by their blend of 'status segmentation and familialism'. Social security systems are based on occupational schemes and corporatist status divisions. The 'accent on compulsory social insurance' means that 'purely private market provision of welfare remains marginal' with the family and non-profit, 'voluntary' associations, frequently affiliated with the Church playing an important role (Esping-Andersen, 1999, pp. 81ff).

Although the tripartite categorisation of welfare regimes has been criticised on a number of grounds (see, for example, Castles and Mitchell, 1990; Liebfried, 1990; Siaroff, 1994), debate has tended to be around methodology and categorisation rather than challenges to the underlying assumption that socio-economic and cultural historical factors constrain contemporary policy development. If it is accepted that socio-economic and cultural history creates policy predispositions, then it is likely that these will be reinforced and compounded by the accretion of policy decisions. Past decisions consequently need to be seen as institutions in relation to current policy choices with path dependency capturing the insight that 'policy decisions accumulate over time; a process of accretion can occur in a policy area that restricts options for future policy-makers (Kay, 2005, p. 558).

In a hard application of the concept of path dependency, one would argue that early decisions in a policy area result in a policy trajectory that is locked on to a set course although one that might, in Esping-Andersen's terms, be particular to a certain type of policy regime. A hard application of the concept in relation to elite sport would lead one to suggest that a prior commitment to a social democratic model of welfare and/or a commitment to mass participation in sport would make the adoption of an elite development sport policy difficult as it would require a break with established values of universalism and non-commodification. A softer application of the concept would suggest that early decisions do not lock a policy on a specific trajectory, but do constrain significantly subsequent policy options (Kay, 2005). As regards elite sport development, it might be argued that while it may be possible to adopt an elite-focused policy the range of policy instruments that could be adopted to achieve its implementation might be path dependent. For example, it might be acceptable to support elite athletes as long as elite development is seen as a by-product of a vigorous commitment to mass participation: by contrast an elite development policy that was disconnected from mass participation, relying for example on early selection of potential high-performance athletes, would be less acceptable.

Does policy determine politics?

In direct contrast to the discussion in the previous section, one of the most significant insights from some, often large n, comparative policy studies was that nationally distinct political characteristics were only very weakly correlated with particular policies and that the dominant developmental process in advanced industrial countries was one of convergence. Freeman (1985, p. 469) summarised the challenge as follows:

The idea that distinctive and durable national policymaking styles are causally linked to the policies of states asserts that 'politics determines policy'. The policy sector approach argues, in contrast, that the nature of the problem is fundamentally connected to the kind of politics that emerges as well as the policy outcomes that result. The policy sector approach shifts our attention away from political inputs to categories of issues and outputs of the political system; it suggests that 'policy determines politics'.

It can be argued that some policy sectors and policy issues within them are less susceptible to domestic politics than others. For example, core welfare services that Esping-Andersen focused on might be much more deeply rooted in the culture of a political system than other services such as sport. Thus while there might be general pressures making for convergence, their impact varies across policy sectors. However, it is not just the relationship of a policy sector or problem in relation to core cultural value that explains the differential impact of convergence pressures, it might also be the intrinsic characteristics of the problem or issue insofar as the particular properties (constraints and pressures) of the problem 'will override whatever tendencies exist toward nationally specific policies' (Freeman, 1985, p. 486). To quote Heinelt, 'the thesis "policies determines politics" would imply – given that a policy sector would be seen as the only relevant variable for explaining politics – that institutions, parties, forms of interest mediation, political culture etc. do not matter, only the policy sector does' (2005, p. 7).

One important, and possibly crucial, indicator of convergence is the extent to which a broad range of countries with different political, socio-economic and cultural profiles adopt similar policy goals. As has already been suggested the proportion of, admittedly more wealthy, countries whose governments have accepted elite sport success as a sport policy goal is high and growing. If it is accepted that there is convergence in policy goals, then the next area for investigation is in relation to the policy instruments that have been selected to achieve that goal and crucially whether the choice of policy instruments is constrained by the nature of the policy objective. In other words it can be hypothesised that there is little scope for variation in instrument selection if a country wants to win Olympic gold medals: either some policy instruments are so much more effective than others that they are selected even though they may jar with deeper cultural values or the repertoire of policy instruments is so limited that there is little scope for variation in policy selection.

Conclusion

The chapters that follow are a response to the conclusions drawn by Green and Houlihan in their 2005 study of elite sport development and summarised above. Each contributor was asked to review the conclusions drawn from the study of Australia, Canada and the United Kingdom and either work within Green and Houlihan's analytical framework or to take it as their point of departure if they considered that their particular country was sufficiently distinct. Each chapter provides an insight into the history and current political and organisational context of elite development policy and will allow firmer conclusions to be drawn about the relationship of elite development to broader sport policy and the extent to which each country's distinctive history and socio-economic and cultural profile affects the intensity with which elite success is pursued and the particular policy instruments that have been selected to achieve policy goals. In particular the nine country studies will enable a fuller debate about the relationships between politics and policy in relation to elite sport goals.

One concern in selecting the countries for inclusion in this analysis was to move beyond the group of English speaking countries often selected for comparison. Other criteria included the concern to select countries that have a history of success in international sport in general, and the Olympic Games in particular, such as the United States and Germany, as well as countries, such as Singapore, which aspire to international sporting success. However, there was also a desire to include examples of countries which had particular characteristics such as Poland (former communist government), Singapore (small and relatively rich country), and New Zealand (small population and strong sporting culture). It is not claimed that the nine countries are representative, but it is suggested that they have been drawn from a sufficiently broad range of institutional, historical and political contexts to allow, at least tentative, conclusions to be drawn regarding trends in elite sport development systems.

References

Abbott, A., Collins, D., Martindale, R. and Sowerby, K. (2002) *Talent Identification and Development: An Academic Review*, Edinburgh: Sport Scotland. GlücksSpirale.

Amis, J. and Cornwell, B. (eds.) (2005) *Global Sport Sponsorship*. Oxford: Berg.

Andersen, S.S. and Eliassen, K.A. (eds.) (1993) *Making Policy in Europe: The Europeification of National Policy-Making*, London: Sage.

Bennett, C.J. and Howlett, M. (1992) The lessons of learning: Reconciling theories of policy learning and policy change, *Political Sciences*, 25, 275–294.

Bergsgard, N.A., Houlihan, B., Mangset, P., Nødland, S.I. and Rommetvedt, H. (2007) *Sport Policy: A Comparative Analysis of Stability and Change*. Oxford: Butterworth-Heinemann.

Birley, D. (1995) *Land of Sport and Glory: Sport and British Society 1887–1910*, Manchester: Manchester University Press.

Blyth, M. (1997) Any more bright ideas: The ideational turn of comparative political economy, *Comparative Politics*, 29(2), 229–250.

Boli, J. and Thomas, G.M. (1997) World culture in the world polity, *American Sociological Review*, 62(2), 171–190.

Carrington, B. and Macdonald, I. (2000) *'Race', Sport and British Society*, London: Routledge.

Castles, F. and Mitchell, D. (1990) Three worlds of welfare capitalism or four? Public Policy Discussion Paper No. 21. Canberra: Australian National University.

De Bosscher, V., De Knop, P., Van Bottenburg, M. and Shibli, S. (2006) A conceptual framework for analysing sports policy factors leading to international sporting success, *European Sport Management Quarterly*, 6(2), 185–215.

Deacon, B. with Hulse, M. and Stubbs, P. (1997) *Global Social Policy: International Organisations and the Future of Welfare*, London: Sage.

Digel, H. (2002a) *Organisation of High-Performance Athletics in Selected Countries* (Final report for the International Athletics Foundation), Tübingen, Germany: University of Tübingen.

Digel, H. (2002b) A comparison of competitive sports systems, *New Studies in Athletics*, 17(1), 37–49.

Dolowitz, D. and Marsh, D. (1996) Who learns what from whom? A review of the policy transfer literature, *Political Studies*, XLIV, 343–357.

Dolowitz, D. and Marsh, D. (2000) Learning from abroad: The role of policy transfer in contemporary policy making, *Governance*, 13, 5–24.

Esping-Andersen, G. (1990) *The Three Worlds of Welfare Capitalism*. Cambridge: Polity Press.

Esping-Andersen, G. (1999) *Social Foundations of Post-industrial Economies*, New York: Oxford University Press.

Fisher, R.J. and Borms, J. (1990) *The Search for Sporting Excellence*, Schorndorf: Verlag Karl Hofmann.

Freeman, G.P. (1985) National styles and policy sectors: Explaining structural variation, *Journal of Policy Studies*, 5(4), 467–496.

Gorges, M.J. (2001) New institutionalist explanations for institutional change: A note of caution, *Politics*, 21(2), 137–145.

Gratton, C. and Taylor, P. (2000) *Economics of Sport and Recreation*. London: E. & F.N. Spon.

Green, M. (2004) Changing policy priorities for sport in England: The emergence of elite sport development as a key policy concern, *Leisure Studies*, 23(4), 365–385.

Green, M. (2007) Policy transfer, lesson drawing and perspectives on elite sport development systems, *International Journal of Sport Management and Marketing*, 2(4), 426–441.

Green, M. and Houlihan, B. (2005) *Elite Sport Development: Policy Learning and Political Priorities*, London: Routledge.

Green, M. and Houlihan, B. (2006) Governmentality, modernization, and the 'disciplining' of national sports organizations: Athletics in Australia and the United Kingdom, *Sociology of Sport Journal*, 23(1), 47–71.

Green, M. and Oakley, B. (2001a) Elite sport development systems and playing to win: Uniformity and diversity in international approaches, *Leisure Studies*, 20(4), 247–267.

Green, M. and Oakley, B. (2001b) Lesson-drawing: International perspectives on elite sport development systems in established nations, paper presented at the *Nation and Sport Conference*, Brunel University, London, June.

Greener, I. (2002) Understanding NHS reform: The policy-transfer, social learning, and path dependency perspectives, *Governance: An International Journal of Policy, Administration, and Institutions*, 15(2), 161–183.

Hall, P.A. (1986) *Governing the Economy: The Politics of State Intervention in Britain and France*, Cambridge: Polity Press.

Hall, S. (1998) The great moving nowhere show, *Marxism Today*, November/December, 9–14.

Hargreaves, J. (1994) *Sporting Females: Critical Issues in the History and Sociology of Women's Sport*, London: Routledge.

Heclo, H. (1972) Review article, policy analysis, *British Journal of Political Science*, II, 83–108.

Heinelt, H. (2005) Do policies determine politics?, *School for Policy Studies Working Paper 11*, Bristol: University of Bristol.

Held, D. and McGrew, A.G. (2002) *Governing Globalisation. Power, Authority and Global Governance*, Cambridge: Polity.

Henry, I. (2001) *The Politics of Leisure Policy*, 2nd edn. London: Palgrave.

Hirst, P. and Thompson, G. (1999) *Globalization in Question. The International Economy and the Possibilities of Governance*, Cambridge: Polity.

Hogwood, B. (1987) *From Crisis to Complacency*, Oxford: Oxford University Press.

Holt, R. (1992) *Sport and the British. A Modern History*. Oxford: Clarendon Press.

Houlihan, B. (1997) Sport, national identity and public policy, *Nations and Nationalism*, 3(1), 113–137.

Houlihan, B. (2003) 'Sport and globalisation', in B. Houlihan (ed.): *Sport and Society. A Student Introduction*, London: Sage.

Houlihan, B. (2007) Sport and globalisation, in B. Houlihan (ed.), *Sport and Society*, London: Sage.

Houlihan, B. and White, A. (2002) *The Politics of Sport Development: Development of Sport or Development Through Sport?* London: Routledge.

Howlett, R. and Ramesh, M. (1995) *Studying Public Policy: Policy Cycles and Policy Sub-systems*, New York: Oxford University Press.

Hunt, T.M. (2007) Countering the Soviet threat in the Olympic medals race: The Amateur Sports Act of 1978 and American athletics policy reform, *The International Journal of the History of Sport*, 24(6), 796–818.

Jenkins, W.I. (1978) *Policy Analysis: Political and Organisational Perspectives*, London: Martin Robertson.

Kay, A. (2005) A critique of the use of path dependency in policy studies, *Public Administration*, 83(3), 553–571.

Krauss, (1990) *Recreation and Leisure in Modern Society*, 4th edn. New York: Harper Collins.

Leibfried, S. (1990) *The classification of welfare state regimes in Europe*, paper, Social Policy Association Annual Conference, University of Bath.

Macintosh, D. & Whitson, D. (1990) *The Game Planners: Transforming Canada's Sports System*, Montreal: McGill-Queens University Press.

Macintosh, D. (1991) Sport and the state: The case of Canada, in Landry, F. et al. (eds.) *Sport … The third millennium*, Sainte-Foy: Les Presse de Universitairé de Laval.

Mason, T. (1980) *Association Football and English Society, 1863–1915*. Hassocks: Harvester.

Oakley, B. and Green, M. (2001) The production of Olympic champions: International perspectives on elite sport development systems, *European Journal for Sport Management*, 8(Special Issue), 83–102.

Oliver, M.J. (1997) *Whatever Happened to Monetarism?* Aldershot: Ashgate.

Pemberton, H. (2004) *Policy Learning and British Governance in the 1960s*, Basingstoke: Palgrave.

Pickup, D. (1996) *Not another messiah: An account of the Sports Council 1988–1993*, Bishop Aukland: Pentland Press.

Pierson, P. (1993) When effect becomes cause: Policy feedback and policy change, *World Politics*, 45(4), 595–628.

Robertson, R. (1992) *Globalization: Social Theory and Global Culture*, London: Sage.

Robertson, R. (1995) Globalization: time–space and homogeneity–heterogeneity, in M. Featherstone, S. Lash and R. Robertson (eds.), *Global Modernities*, London: Sage, pp. 25–44.

Roche, M. (1993) Sport and community: Rhetoric and reality in the development of British sport policy, in J.C. Binfield and J. Stevenson (eds.) *Sport, Culture and Politics*, Sheffield: Sheffield Academic Press.

Rose, R. (2005) *Learning from Comparative Public Policy: A Practical Guide*, London: Routledge.

Scholte, J.A. (2000) *Globalisation: A Critical Introduction*, Basingstoke: Palgrave.

Siaroff, A. (1994). 'Work, women and gender equality: A new typology', in: D. Sainsbury (ed.): *Gendering Welfare States*, London: Sage.

Slack, T. (1998) Studying the commercialisation of sport: The need for critical analysis, Online. Available at: http://www.physed.otago.ac.nz/sosol/home.htm (accessed 4 December 2001).

Slack, T. (2005) *The Commercialisation of Sport*. London: Routledge.

Thelen, K. and Steinmo, S. (1992) 'Historical institutionalism in comparative politics', in: K. Thelen, S. Steinmo and F. Longstreth (eds.): *Structuring Politics: Historical Institutionalism in Comparative Analysis*, Cambridge: Cambridge University Press.

Thomas, N. (2007) Sport and disability, in B. Houlihan (ed.) *Sport and Society: A Student Introduction*, 2nd edn. London: Sage.

UK Sport (2006) *Sports Policy Factors Leading to International Sporting Success: An International Comparative Study*, London: UK Sport.

Wallerstein, I. (1974) The rise and future demise of the of the world-capitalist system: Concepts for comparative analysis, *Comparative Studies in Society and History*, 16, 387–415.

Wilson, J. (1994) *Playing by the rules: Sport, Society and the State*, Detroit: Wayne State University Press.

CHAPTER 2

China

Fan Hong

Introduction

On 30 December 2000 the *China Sports Daily*, the official Chinese sports newspaper, proudly claimed that between 1949 and 2000 Chinese athletes won 1,408 world championships and set 1,042 new world records. Of these, 1,378 world championships were won and 865 new world records were set since 1978 when China began its economic reformation. In addition, between 1984 and 2000, Chinese athletes won 227 Olympic medals (84 gold, 79 silver and 64 bronze) (*China Sports Daily*, 30 December 2000).

At the 2004 Olympic Games in Athens 407 Chinese athletes competed in 203 events and won 32 gold, 17 silver and 14 bronze medals. With these 63 medals in total, China came third in the medal rankings after the United States and Russia. With 32 gold medals, China beat the Russians and came second to the United States. Furthermore, 6 new world records were established by Chinese athletes and on 21 occasions new Olympic records were set. Following the success in Athens, senior Chinese sports officials claimed triumphantly that China, together with the United States and Russia, has become one of the three superpowers in the summer Olympics (Yuan, 2004; Hong et al., 2005).

The triumph of Chinese sport is deeply rooted in China's elite sport system. It is called 'Juguo tizhi' in Chinese and translates as the 'whole country support for the elite sport system'. This system channelled all resources for sport in the country into elite sport and effectively produced hundreds of thousands of young elite athletes in a short time in pursuit of ideological superiority and national status. Its main characteristics are centralised management and administration and guaranteed financial and human resources from the whole country to ensure maximum support (Hao, 2004).

The origin and development of the Chinese elite sport system

The establishment of China's elite sport system began in the 1950s, developed in the 1960s and 1970s and matured with its own character in the 1980s. A close examination of the development of elite sport in China clearly demonstrates that elite sport helps to exploit the implementation of political ideology and is, therefore, vulnerable to political exploitation.

The beginning (1952–1960)

When the Communists defeated the Nationalists and established the People's Republic of China (PRC) in October 1949, sport became a vehicle for expressing Chinese national representation and identity. China's experience at the Helsinki Olympic Games in 1952 stimulated the government's determination to utilise sport as a valuable weapon to help restore the nation's position in international politics. In November 1952, the State Physical Education and Sport Commission (Guojia tiyu yundong weiyuanhui, hereafter the Sports Ministry) was formally established. It is a governmental ministry with the same status as other ministries such as Education, Finance and Commerce, all directly under the leadership of the State Council.

In 1956 the Sports Ministry issued 'The Competitive Sports System of the PRC', which formally laid the foundations for a competitive sports system in China: 43 sports were officially recognised as competitive sports; rules and regulations were defined; professional teams were set up at provisional and national levels and they would compete with each other at regional and national championships; the National Games would take place every 4 years to promote elite sport and to unite the nation through this event. At the same time the Sports Ministry issued 'The Regulations of the Youth Spare-Time Sports Schools' in 1956. The Soviet Union's spare-time sports school model (yeyu tixiao) was adapted to train and foster talented athletes from a very young age. By September 1958 there were 16,000 spare-time sports schools with 777,000 students throughout the country (Wu, 1999, p. 102).

This elite sport system was further developed during the Great Leap Forward (GLF) from 1957 to 1961. From 1957, the goal of the GLF was to accelerate economic development and social progress in order to overtake Great Britain economically within 7 years and the United States within 15 years. Its slogan was 'Go all out, aim high and achieve greater, faster, better and more economic results'. In response to the Party's call, the Sports Ministry initiated the Sports GLF campaign, also in 1957. Its ambition was to catch up with the world's most competitive sports countries in 10 years. It was planned that by 1967, China's athletes in basketball, volleyball, football, table-tennis, athletics, gymnastics, weight-lifting, swimming, shooting and skating were to be among the very best in the world. China would produce 15,000 professional full-time athletes.

At the same time, in order to meet the needs of a healthy labour force, mass sport was also promoted throughout the country. The Soviet model, 'Preparation for labour and defence' (*Laoweizhi*) was adapted. Two hundred million men and women were expected to pass the fitness grade of *Laoweizhi*. One million, seven hundred and twenty thousand sports teams would be formed among 40 million urban workers, and 3 million sports teams among peasants by 1967. It was expected that Chinese sport would develop under the 'two legs walking system': elite and mass sports developing simultaneously (Wu, 1999, pp. 102–106). However, the failure of the GLF and the onset of the Great Famine in 1960 resulted in a change of direction.

Consolidation (1961–1966)

In 1960, the Party changed its slogan to 'Readjustment, consolidation, filling out and raising standards' and, in 1961, the Sports Ministry changed its policy to produce elite sports stars (The Policy Research Centre of the Sports Ministry, 1982, pp. 60, 72). The government determined to use the best of its limited resources to provide special and intensive training for potential athletes in a particular sport so that they could compete on the international sporting stage. Consequently, in physical education institutes, whose major responsibility was to train physical education teachers and instructors for mass sports, reduced in number from 29 in 1959 to 20 in 1960. In contrast, professional sports teams increased from 3 in 1951 to more than 50 by 1961. The Sports Ministry also issued the 'Regulations for Outstanding Athletes and Teams' in 1963 to improve the system. Under the instruction of the Ministry a search for talented young athletes took place in every province (The Policy Research Centre of the Sports Ministry, 1982, p. 102). Meanwhile 10 key sports were selected from the previous 43. They were: athletics, badminton, gymnastics, swimming, football, basketball, table-tennis, shooting, weightlifting and skiing (The Policy Research Centre of the Sports Ministry, 1982, p. 103). The Party concentrated resources on a few elite athletes in order to achieve success on the international sporting stage. It was a key turning point in the Chinese sport ideology and system, changing from 'two legs' to 'one leg' – the elite one.

Development (1971–1979)

The elite sport system came under attack during the Cultural Revolution. For Chairman Mao and his followers, the function of the Cultural Revolution was to prevent China changing its colour from red (communism) to black (capitalism and revisionism). By doing so, the Chinese would transform the ideology, politics, education, culture, literature, media, drama, films and sport – the so-called superstructure realm which had been dominated by the revisionists and capitalists for the past

18 years since 1949 – and embrace Mao Zedong Thought (CCP, 1966). Sport was no exception. It was the place where, 'for 18 years the black line had dominated' (The 'May 12 Military Order', 1968). It should be changed to the red line. However, without criticism and destruction of the black line, the red one could not be established.

A revolution was required. 'A revolution', Mao stated in his famous Little Red Book, 'is not a dinner party, or writing an essay, or painting a picture, or doing embroidery; it cannot be so refined, so leisurely and gentle, so temperate, kind, courteous, restrained and magnanimous. A revolution is an insurrection, an act of violence by which one class overthrows another' (The Quotations from Mao Zedong, 1968, pp. 11–12). Thus, as Johnson described: 'The Cultural Revolution of the late 1960s smashed across China like a violent sandstorm. Its targets were "revisionist" officials who were accused of weakening the philosophies of Mao' (Johnson, 1973, p. 93). In May 1966, the violent political storm, accompanied by intense ideological confrontation, started in the Sports Ministry in Beijing, and then throughout every provincial and local sports commission. This confrontation ultimately concerned the relationship between elite and mass sport. Was sport for a few elite athletes or for the masses? Was sport for medals or for the health of people and defence of the country? The former was regarded as bourgeois ideology and the latter as communist idealism.

He Long, the Minister, was formally accused: 'For the past 10 years he has paid attention not to mass physical education, but to forming professional teams and highly developed activities'. In 1962 he openly advocated that 'The National Physical Education Committee only pay attention to athletic teams and the provincial and municipal levels take care of mass physical education and national defence physical education' (The crime of anti-party and revisionist He Long, 1967, p. 4). He Long was criticised and jailed, and died in prison in 1975. Rong Gaotang, a vice-minister, was labelled a traitor and 'a running dog' of He Long and was also imprisoned. Other heads of departments were criticised and beaten by the Red Guards and revolutionary rebels. One thousand cadres were regarded as untrustworthy and sent to a May Seventh Cadre School in Tun Liu, Shanxi province, an isolated place at the foot of Taihang mountain, to do physical labour.

The training system broke down, sports schools closed, sports competitions vanished, and Chinese teams stopped touring abroad. The table-tennis team that had won 15 medals at the 1965 World Championships disappeared and did not attend the

1967 and 1969 Championships. Provincial and local teams were disbanded. Coaches and athletes were sent to the countryside and factories to do physical labour (Rong, 1984, pp. 262–263). For example, 47 provincial football teams were disbanded, and 1,124 football players and 115 coaches had to find jobs in factories and shops (Guan, 1996, p. 194). Most national teams disbanded except those for table-tennis, gymnastics and athletics. Outstanding athletes were criticised as promising sons and daughters of the bourgeois, and their coaches were criticised, and even beaten up. Less privileged athletes and coaches were encouraged to participate in criticism meetings and to beat the privileged – a sign of revolutionary commitment (Interview, Bi Shiming, Head of the Sports History Commission of the Sports Ministry, 1996).

The situation changed due to the urgent need to establish better Sino-American relations in 1971. At the 31st World Table-Tennis Championships in Japan between 25 January and 3 February 1971 the Chinese used its 'Ping-Pong diplomacy' to open up the political door to the United States and the West. In February 1971, after the World Table-Tennis Championships, China invited table-tennis teams from the United States and five other western countries to visit China and Premier Zhou Enlai received them at the People's Hall on 14 April 1971. He warmly welcomed the American athletes: 'You have opened a new chapter in the relations of the American and Chinese people' (quoted in Qian, 1987, p. 49). The political signal was clear and overt and well received by the US government.

On 11 July 1971 Henry Kissinger, President Richard Nixon's national security adviser, travelled to China to meet with China's Premier Zhou. On 15 July the public announcement of a presidential visit was made on radio and television by Nixon himself in California. On 25 October, Communist China renewed its seat in the United Nations (Nixon, 1978; Kissinger, 1979). On 21 February 1972 President Nixon and Chairman Mao met in Beijing and 7 days later, a 'joint communiqué' was issued in Shanghai. This document marked a major policy shift for both countries. The *People's Daily* proudly announced that China had now come back to the international family (*People's Daily*, 26 February 1972). Richard Nixon commented that the agreement of 1972 had built a bridge across 16,000 miles and 22 years of hostility, and it had changed the world (Nixon, 1978). Sport had played a significant role in bringing the two nations together.

'Ping-Pong diplomacy' not only changed the status of the nation but also the direction of elite sport in China. After the victory of the 'Ping-Pong diplomacy', elite sport became increasingly important, since it could help to effectively break down national barriers and to establish and promote international contacts between different political systems. While the whole country was still in chaos *only* the Sports Ministry was restored. In February 1972 the cadres of the Sports Ministry were liberated from the countryside and returned to Beijing (Wang, 1993, pp. 13–14). In May, the Sports Ministry held a work conference to promote athletic training programmes and restore the training system of sports schools (Guan, 1996, p. 195). In 1973 the Sports Ministry held a national work conference to promote elite sport nationwide (The Policy Research Centre of the Sports Ministry, 1982, p. 112). By the end of 1974, 1,459 sports schools re-opened, and provincial and national teams were restored and began their training for national and international competitions.

Sports competitions took place at regional, provincial and national levels. At the national level, a Five Sports Competition (basketball, volleyball, football, table-tennis, badminton) took place in 1972. The First National Student Sports Meeting took place in 1973 and more than 20,000 athletes took part, and 70 athletes broke 40 national records. The 3rd Sports Meeting of the People's Liberation Army, and the 3rd National Games took place in 1975 and three world records were broken (Guan, 1996, p. 195). At the international level, China renewed its seat on the Asian Olympic Sports Committee in November 1973 and sent a delegation with 269 athletes to attend the 7th Asian Games in 1974 in Iran (Bai and Gu, 1990, pp. 2–3).

From 1971 to 1976 China attended 54 international competitions (People's Sports Press, 1983). China also hosted the Asian and African Table-Tennis Invitational Tournament in 1971, the Asian Table-Tennis Championships in 1972, the Asian, African and Latin American Table-Tennis Invitational Tournament in 1973, the Beijing International Swimming and Diving Invitational Tournament in 1975, the Beijing International Women's Basketball Invitational Tournament and the Shanghai International Table-Tennis Invitational Tournament in 1976 (Cao, 1991, p. 86). 'Sports crazy' became one of the distinguishing characteristics of China during the 1970s (Zhang, 1991, p. 3; Hong, 1999). While there is a great danger in over-emphasising the role of elite sport in the Cultural Revolution it had proved extremely valuable for diplomacy. Elite sport enabled the Communists to make approaches to Western enemies through a medium benefitting from its non-political image. It was also used to strengthen relations between allies, helping China to reproduce and transform its image in order to establish its position as a leader of the Third World.

The Olympic strategy (1980–2006)

In the late 1970s and early 1980s, China initiated a profound economic reformation and made great efforts to integrate with the world economy. The national ambition was to catch up with the Western capitalist world through modernisation. Chinese sport played an important part in stimulating the nation's enthusiasm and motivating people towards modernity (Tong, 1989, p. 114). In 1979, China renewed its membership of the IOC and subsequently other international sports organisations. Many international competitions were now open to the Chinese. Attending the Olympics and other international competitions and performing well became a symbolic means of catching up with and even beating Western powers. The success of Chinese athletes at the 1979 World Volleyball Championships, the 1982 Asia Games and, in particular, the 1984 Olympic Games, raised hopes of the government and the people that China would become a great country again in the near future.

In 1980, Wang Meng, the Sports Minister, stated at the National Sports Conference that forging a relationship between sport and the socialist economy was crucial to the development of Chinese elite sport. On the one hand, China was still a poor country and was restricted in the amount of money it could invest in sport. On the other hand, elite sport was an effective way to boost China's new image on the international stage. Therefore, the solution was to bring elite sport into the existing planned economy and administrative system, which could assist in the distribution of the limited resources of the whole nation to medal-winning sports (Wang, 1980, p. 1). The international success of Chinese athletes would, in return, bring pride and hope to the nation, which were badly needed in the new era of transformation (Rong, 1984).

Following China's participation in the 1984 Olympic Games, the Society of Strategic Research for the Development of Physical Education and Sport (*Tiyu fazhan zhanlue yanjiu hui*) produced the 'Olympic strategy' (*Aoyun zhanlue*) for the Sports Ministry in 1985. This strategy clearly stated that 'elite sport is the priority'. It aimed to use the nation's limited sports resources to develop elite sport to ensure that China would become a leading sports power by the end of the twentieth century. The strategy was the blueprint for Chinese sport in the 1980s and 1990s while the target was primarily the Olympics. Wu Shaozu, the Minister of Sport from 1990 to 2000, claimed that 'The highest aim of Chinese sport is success in the Olympic Games. We must concentrate our resources on it. To raise the flag at the Olympics is our major responsibility' (Wu, 1993, p. 402). To achieve this goal the government must channel the best of limited resources to potential gold medallists in order to provide special and intensive training. Chinese athletes benefitted from both the 'whole country support elite for the sport system' and the 'Olympic strategy' and achieved very satisfactory results.

In 1984, China re-emerged onto the Olympic stage after an absence of 32 years, won 15 gold medals and was placed fourth in the Olympic medals table. Although success in Los Angeles was partly attributed to the absence of the Soviet Union and the Democratic Republic of Germany, it nevertheless excited many in China, from government officials to ordinary citizens. 'Develop elite sport and make China a superpower in the world' became both a slogan and a dream for the Chinese people.

However, for the Chinese, the 1988 Seoul Olympics was very disappointing. When the two sporting superpowers, the Soviet Union and the Democratic Republic of Germany, returned to the Olympics, China's gold medal tally shrank to five and the country slipped painfully from fourth to eleventh in the gold medal table. In 1992, China fought back at the Barcelona Olympics. Although the Soviet Union had split into several countries, it still competed as a unit under the name of the Commonwealth of Independent States (CIS). Germany had re-united and was even more powerful than before. However, China won 16 gold medals and returned to fourth in the gold medal count. The Atlanta Olympics in 1996 did not please the Chinese, for they again won 16 gold medals and remained fourth on the gold medal table. No progress was not acceptable.

Four years later China achieved 'a historical breakthrough' at the 27th Olympic Games in Sydney in 2000, increasing its gold medal count to 28 and was placed third overall. However, some sports officials argued that this result was not a reliable measure of an improvement of Chinese sporting strength, since five of the gold medals came from the newly added events: synchronised diving and women's weightlifting. In 2004, Chinese athletes achieved notable success in Athens: of 32 gold medals, 4 were won in traditional western 'fortress' areas: track and field, swimming, rowing and canoeing. CNN commented: 'In the six Olympic Games they have competed in, China has moved up the medal tally in world record time' (China takes the Olympic limelight, 2004). China is now second in the table and intends to head the medal table at the 2008 Beijing Olympic Games (Hong et al., 2005) – see Table 2.1.

In addition, China won 2 gold, 12 silver and 8 bronze medals at the winter Olympic Games between 1992 and 2002. Between

Table 2.1   China's participation in the summer Olympics 1984–2004

Games	Year	Host city	Gold medals	Silver medals	Bronze medals	Total medals	Gold medal ranking
23	1984	Los Angeles	15	8	9	22	4
24	1988	Seoul	5	11	12	28	7
25	1992	Barcelona	16	22	16	54	4
26	1996	Atlanta	16	22	12	50	4
27	2000	Sydney	28	16	15	59	3
28	2004	Athens	32	17	14	63	2

Table 2.2   China's participation in the summer Asian Games 1978–2002

Games	Year	Host city	Gold medals	Silver medals	Bronze medals	Total medals	Gold medal ranking
7	1974	Tehran	33	46	27	106	3
8	1978	Bangkok	51	54	46	178	2
9	1982	New Delhi	61	51	41	151	1
10	1986	Seoul	94	82	46	222	1
11	1990	Beijing	183	107	51	336	1
12	1994	Hiroshima	137	92	62	276	1
13	1998	Bangkok	129	78	67	274	1
14	2002	Pusan	150	84	74	308	1

1974 and 2002, China participated in the Asian Games eight times and won 1,951 medals. In short, China is firmly established as the sports superpower in Asia – see Table 2.2.

When China achieved extraordinary success at the 2000 Sydney Olympic Games, the term, 'whole country support for the elite sport system' (Juguo tizhi) began to appear regularly in official statements to explain how Chinese sport had achieved so much in such a short time. When Jiang Zemin, the General Secretary of the Party, claimed in 2000 that 'The success of American sport depends on its economic power; the success of Russian sport depends on its rich resource and experience of training elite athletes; the success of Chinese sport depends on

"Juguo tizhi" – "whole country support for the elite sport system"' (Li, 2000), the concept was for the first time approved at the highest political level. Yuan Weimin, the Sports Minister from 1990 to 2004, officially defined the term at the All State Sports Ministers' Conference in 2001. He stated that the meaning of 'Juguo tizhi' was that central and local governments should use their power to channel adequate financial and human resources throughout the country to support elite sport in order to win glory for the nation (Yuan, 2001, p. 364).

The characteristics of the 'whole country support for the elite sport system' (Juguo tizgi)

The distinguishing characteristics of 'Juguo tizhi' include: an embodiment of China's political ideology, as discussed earlier; its administrative and management system is centralised; and it functions only for improving the level of elite sport success through a specialised and selective training system.

The administrative system for sport

One of the significant features of the Chinese elite sport system is its centralised administrative and management structure. The national governmental body, the State Physical Education and Sports Commission (the Sports Ministry) is responsible for the formulation and implementation of sports policy and administration of national sports programmes. It liaises closely with other government ministries including Education and National Defence. Between 1953 and 1954 sports commissions were established at provincial and local county levels to implement the national sports policy and programmes. By the mid-1950s a centralised system of sports administration was in place and has dominated Chinese sport ever since.

Figure 2.1 clearly shows that the Chinese Sports Ministry operated directly under the leadership of the central government. The model of the Chinese sports administrative system reflected the wider social system in China: both the Party and state administrations were organised in a vast hierarchy with power flowing down from the top. Since the 1980s, the Chinese economy has been through a process of change from a planned to a market economy. At the same time, the sports system has been transformed from a centralised system to a multi-level and multi-channel system. In the mid-1990s the Sports Ministry changed its name from the State Physical Education and Sports Commission (Guojia tiyu yundong weiyuanhui) to China

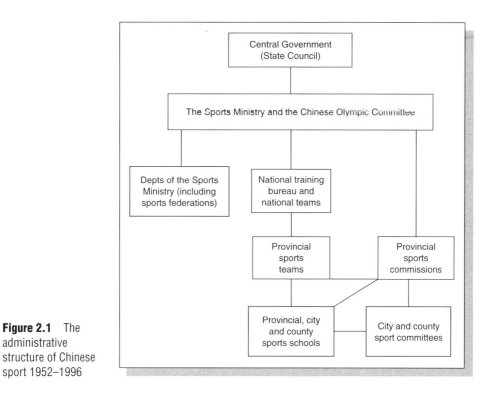

Figure 2.1 The administrative structure of Chinese sport 1952–1996

General Administration of Sport (Guojia tiyu zhongju). Twenty sports management centres were established to manage its training and commercial interests. The change in title and structure was both symbolic and pragmatic. The Sports Ministry's aim was for Chinese sport to now stand more on its own feet and rely less on government support (Hong et al., 2005).

Figure 2.2 illustrates changes in the administrative of Chinese sport since 1997. With regard to the 20 sports management centres, it is evident that except for football, basketball and table-tennis they are far from self-supporting. The centres remain largely dependent on money from central government for survival. With the approach of the Beijing Olympic Games, central government can do nothing but increase its financial support for the 'success' of the Games. Therefore, the reform of the sports management system is in reality old wine in a new bottle. The traditional centralised system remains and still plays an important role in the Chinese elite sport system (Hong et al., 2005).

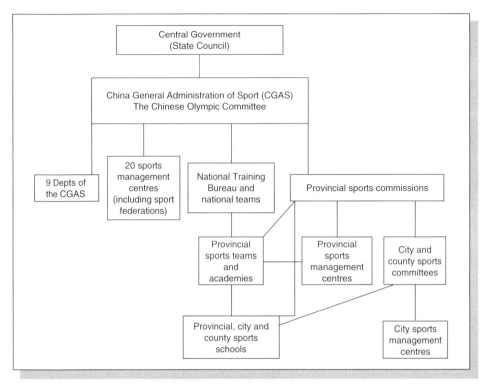

Figure 2.2   The administrative structure of Chinese sport 1997–2006

Elite athlete development

Resources

As discussed, in the 1980s the 'Olympic strategy' stressed that all available resources for sport in China should be concentrated on elite sport. Consequently, in terms of funding, elite sport consumed 80 per cent of the state's sports budget. Table 2.3 clearly shows that Chinese sport still largely depends on governmental funding.

In addition, throughout the 1980s and 1990s there was special funding for Olympic preparation. For example, to secure medal success at the 1996 Atlanta Olympics there was a specific fund of 65 million yuan (US$13 million) for Olympic-related activities (Zhang, 1996, p. 14). In general, elite sports teams were major beneficiaries of the government budget. Table 2.4 illustrates the investment from central and local governments to elite sports teams from 1991 to 1997. Incidentally, the figures do not include

Table 2.3 Chinese sports budget 1981–1996 (unit: 10,000 yuan)

Governmental funding				Commercial Investment		
Year	Central government	Local government	In total	Sponsorship	Commercial profits	In total
1981–1985	305,32	226,112	256,644	0	0	0
1986–1990	56,625	543,166	599,791	0	0	0
1991	13,184	153,392	166,576	0	0	0
1992	14,100	172,400	186,500	0	0	0
1993	18,600	190,800	209,400	2,192.2	76,260.5	78,452.7
1994	15,309	187,045.6	202,354.6	4,185.5	67,394.6	71,580.1
1995	22,567.6	216,235.6	238,806.4	3,664.9	77,820.5	81,435.4
1996	20,945	263,229.2	284,174.2	4,737.3	99,789.3	104,526.6

Source: 'Sports Statistics' provided by the Planning and Finance Department of the Sports Ministry. (In the 1990s, US$ 1 was equivalent to about 5 yuan.)

Table 2.4 Budget for elite sports teams 1991–1997 (unit: 10,000 yuan)

Year	Central and local government funding for elite sports teams	Proportion of sports funds (%)
1991	40,000	22
1992	44,000	24
1993	56,000	25
1994	60,000	30
1995	80,000	32
1996	100,000	34
1997	120,000	30

Source: 'The Research on the Developing Trend of Elite Sport Towards 2010' (Zhan, 2001, p. 12). (In the 1990s, US$ 1 was equivalent to about 5 yuan.)

the budget spent on training facilities and equipment, the cost of national and international competitions and other activities related to elite sport (The Planning and Finance Department, 1994, p. 44).

Selection and training

China has one of the most effective systems in the world for systematically selecting and producing sporting talent from a very young age. As discussed, this system was officially created in 1963 when the Sports Ministry issued the 'Regulations for Outstanding Athletes and Teams'. On the instructions of the Ministry, the selection of talented young athletes took place in every province (The Policy Research Centre of the Sports Ministry, 1982, p. 102). Over the years it has developed into a well-organised and tightly structured three-level pyramid: primary, intermediate and high level. The sports schools at county, city and provincial levels formed the base of the pyramid – see Figure 2.3. After several years of training about 12 per cent of talented athletes from sports schools were selected to go on to provincial teams and become full-time athletes. From there, outstanding athletes progress to the top: the national squads and Olympic teams. The system remains in place today.

In terms of selection procedures, when boys and girls between the ages of 6–9 years old are identified as having some talent in particular sports, they are sent to local sports schools throughout the country. They are trained 3 hours per day and 4–5 times per week. After a period of hard training the promising ones are promoted to semi-professional training: 4–5 hours

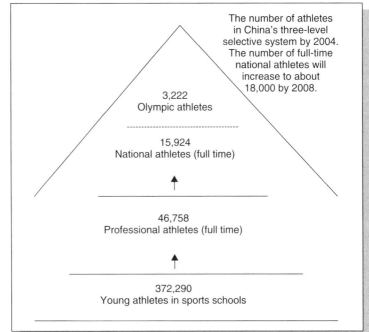

Figure 2.3 Pyramid of the selective system (*Source*: Department of Training of the China General Administration of Sport (the Sports Ministry))

The number of athletes in China's three-level selective system by 2004. The number of full-time national athletes will increase to about 18,000 by 2008.

3,222
Olympic athletes

15,924
National athletes (full time)

46,758
Professional athletes (full time)

372,290
Young athletes in sports schools

training per day and 5–6 days per week. Before the 1990s, the sports schools, which are part of the local sports commission, provided coaching and training facilities and met all costs of training and competition. In addition, the young athletes were provided with a free meal once a day. After 1990, the cost has been borne partially by parents.

After this 'semi-professional' training, young people with potential are selected for the provincial sports academies or training centres. Young athletes live on campus and train 4–6 hours per day and 5–6 days per week. Their aim is to reach the second stage and become full-time professionals in provincial teams and eventually to reach the third stage to become members of the national squads and Olympic teams. The selection system is brutal and is the core of the 'whole country support for the elite sport system'. In 2004 there were nearly 400,000 young boys and girls training at more than 3,000 sports schools throughout China (Dai, 2004). Yet just 5 per cent reach the top and 95 per cent of these young athletes leave their sports schools with no formal primary and secondary education qualifications – only broken dreams.

Athletes in provincial and national teams are full-time professionals and they receive 'wages' from provincial and national governmental bodies. Their average monthly income is 2,000–4,000 RMB (Chinese currency). World champions and Olympic medallists receive additional income from rewards provided by national and provincial governments, and also benefit from sponsorships and advertising. For example, Liu Xiang, the Olympic gold medallist, following victory at the 2004 Athens Games, received rewards of more than 1 million RMB from these sources. However, these full-time athletes receive their pensions only from their provincial sports bodies. Therefore, local governments, especially the local sports commissions, have suffered, and will continue to suffer, from the 'Olympic drainage', a unique system within the elite sport system, as discussed below.

Provincial and local sports teams and commissions have responsibility for nurturing *and* training elite athletes for the national teams and rewarding them when they win medals. Therefore, when the Olympic Games or international competitions are over athletes return to their home teams, and their provincial sports commissions have to reward the winners with huge amounts of money. For those who are not lucky enough to win medals, the local sports authority has a responsibility to look after them and to pay them wages and pensions. Therefore, local sport authorities are constantly short of money for sport, for they have already spent most of their budget on training and have nothing left to pay the rewards, wages, pensions and other costs. For example, in Liaoning Province, where athletes won more medals than any other province, the local sports commission is facing a huge financial burden due to the large amounts of money it has to pay to current Olympic and world champions, and the wages and pensions for those ex-Olympic gold medallists and ex-world champions. 'Able to produce gold medallists but unable to reward and feed them' (duo de qi jinpai, yang bu qi guanjun) is the harsh reality facing local sports governing bodies (Reporter of South China Sport Weekly, 2004; Hong et al., 2005).

Competition opportunities

In order to produce elite sport 'stars' from a young age, local and provincial competitions are held on a regular basis. In general, individual sports have their national championships once every year to provide athletes with experience and to select talented young athletes for the provincial and national teams. There are regional and provincial sports meetings every 2 years and the National Games every 4 years. From the 1980s, in order to train athletes for the Olympic Games, the National Games were re-scheduled to non-Olympic years. Most of the competitive sports events in the National Games are Olympic events. In 1993 the Sports Ministry officially stated that the National Games must directly link to the Olympic Games. In short, the National Games are the training ground for the Olympics. Therefore, when the 8th National Games took place in Shanghai in 1997, the 9th Games in Guangzhou in 2001 and the 10th Games in Jiangsu province in 2005, Chinese athletes competed in all the Olympic sports except Wusu (Martial Arts). The slogans are 'Let the national competitions serve the Olympics' (bian quanyun wei aoyun), and 'Training the athletes in Chinese competitions and preparing them to fight for China at international games' (guonei lianbing, yizhiduiwai). Further more, Chinese athletes regularly participate in international sports competitions. All costs of participation in international competitions are met by the Sports Ministry. The International Relations Department in the Sport Ministry is responsible for facilitating and organising all international competitions.

Coaching and sports science research

Coaches in China, from county to national level, are employed on a full-time basis. To become a coach at a local sports school one has to obtain a higher diploma or bachelor degree in physical education and sports studies, and also pass coaching certificate tests. In 1994 there were 5,926 full-time coaches with bachelor degrees working in sports schools and elite sports teams at provincial and national levels (The Planning and Finance Department, 1994, p. 3).

In terms of training methods, the regime of the People's Army, that is, 'hard, disciplined, intensive training and practice according to real battle', was adopted in 1963. In 1964, however, a new training method was introduced. It included 'three non-afraids': non-afraid of hardship, difficulty and injury; and 'five toughnesses': toughness of spirit, body, skill, training and competition (Hong, 2003, pp. 227–228). This new approach became a legendary Chinese sport method and continues to influence China's training system in the twenty-first century. For example, Wang Junxia, holder of world records from 1,500 to 10,000 metres and recipient of the prestigious Jesse Owens Trophy in 1994, ran 170 kilometres in 4 days in her training sessions. She is not alone. Almost all the girls in her team were trained, and are still trained, under the same methods and routines. Nevertheless, since the late 1980s the emphasis has moved towards advanced scientific training methods including coaching techniques, sports science, sports psychology, sports medicine, state-of-the-art facilities and equipment.

There are 36 sports research centres at provincial level including 29 provinces and the 7 major cities of Beijing, Shanghai, Guangzhou, Tianjin, Xi'an, Chengdu and Chongqin. The National Institute of Sports Science is located in Beijing under the direct leadership of the Sports Ministry. All the sports researchers who work in these research centres are employed as full-time researchers and are required to link their research directly to training athletes to win medals. In addition, there are 9 sports universities and more than 60 sports faculties and departments in Chinese universities. Academics and researchers at universities also contribute directly and indirectly to training gold medallists in the areas of coaching techniques, sports psychology, sports medicine, sports physiology and biomechanics and sports sociology.

Training facilities

All the sports schools have their own training facilities, including gymnasia, football pitch, basketball court, table-tennis court and swimming pool. Historically, they are part of the investment of the local sports commissions. Although the public can share these facilities, the training of young athletes is the priority. At the provincial level, each province provides its sports teams with a training camp, which is normally situated in the provincial capital city and close to the sports research centre. In addition, each provincial team develops its own individual training base outside the capital city of the province. At national level, there are several national training centres in Beijing for different sports such as gymnastics, diving, swimming, synchronised swimming, modern pentathlon, fencing, weightlifting and athletics. In addition, each national team has its own training camp outside Beijing. These training camps have first-class training facilities which are jointly sponsored by local governments and the Sports Ministry, for example:

Haigen camp in Yunnan province: swimming, women's football
Hongta camp in Yunnan province: women's long distance running (It is believed that athletes will benefit from the high-altitude environment in Yunnan province.)
Haikou camp in Hainan province: sailing
Sanya camp in Hainan province: beach volleyball
Zhongshan camp in Guangzhou: table-tennis
Shengzhen camp in Guangdong province: judo, cycling
Guangzhou camp: shooting, softball, baseball, handball, hockey and boxing
Fuzhou camp in Fujian province: athletics (high jump)
Xinzhuan camp in Shanghai: athletics (hurdles)

In general, the national teams spend more than 8 months in their training camps outside Beijing. It is believed that these isolated training bases with first-class training facilities minimise distractions and improve athletic performance. The *People's Daily* reported on 19 January 2007 that during the winter, and when the Chinese New Year (18 February) approaches, Chinese Olympic teams continue their training in the camps outside Beijing (*People's Daily*, 19 January 2007). In summary, through the Olympic medal-oriented policy, the centralised sports administrative and management system, and the selection and training system, the entire Chinese elite sport system is focused on producing a handful of exceptional athletes to win gold medals at the Olympic Games.

Elite sport system critique

Although the elite sport system has been supported by the might of the state, critical voices emerged as early as the late

1980s. In 1988 Zhao Yu's two controversial reports, *Dreaming to be a Superpower* (Qiangguomeng) and *The Defeat in Seoul* (Bingbai Hancheng), revealed the dark side of China's approach to elite sport and criticised the 'whole country support for the elite sport system' (Zhao, 1988a). In 1989, at the height of the pro-democracy movement (the Tiananmen Square Event), there was an intense debate as to whether millions should be spent on the pursuit of Olympic medals or on improving people's physical exercise and health at grassroots level. The debate continued when China bid for the Olympic Games in 1993. Books and articles were published and conferences were held. In 1998 an essay entitled 'The Olympic Movement in China: Ideals, realities and ambitions' was published in the *International Journal of the History of Sport*. It reviewed the development of the Olympic Movement in China from the 1910s to the 1990s and analysed the problems of the Chinese Olympic Movement within which the elite sport system played a major part (Hong, 1998).

Research conducted in 2002 by Deng Yaping, a former table-tennis world champion and Olympic gold medallist, provided an insightful case study. Deng Yaping argued that the elite sport system had a negative impact on those children who began, from a very young age, to play table-tennis and who aimed to become professional players in the future. They spent their first 15 years doing nothing but playing table-tennis and they dreamed of becoming world champions. However, there were nearly 1,000 full-time table-tennis players in China but just 20 could be selected for the national team. The majority had to retire at the age of 25. Deng argued that, because of their lack of a formal education, suitable jobs were difficult to find outside the world of table-tennis. Disillusionment and depression were at least two of the negative outcomes for the many who did not make it to the very highest level (Deng, 2002, pp. 110–111).

In September 2003, the *Xinhua News Agency* reported on the unemployment and poor living conditions of the majority of retired professional athletes in China. Critically, it pointed out that these 'tragedies' were caused by the 'Olympic strategy' implemented by the government at all levels in Chinese society. The elite sport system had not only damaged athletes' bodies but also reduced their opportunities for formal schooling (Tragedy under the pyramid, 2003). In August 2004, a report published in *Looking East Weekly* pointed out that the elite sport system had gravely alienated Chinese sportsmen and women. Its over-consumption of resources had serious adverse effects on mass sport and the 'National Fitness Programme' (Where will the lame Chinese elite sport go?, 2004). In addition, increasingly critics emerged on the Internet where people could express their opinions even more freely.

During the 1990s, the government, under pressure because of rising demands for grassroots sports participation, began to advocate that the 'Olympic strategy' and the 'National Fitness Programme', which was initiated in 1995, should advance simultaneously. However, China's bids, in 1993 and 2001, to host the Olympic Games ensured that elite sport remained the priority. Moreover, the success of the bid to host the 2008 Olympic Games stimulated a new set of Olympic-related objectives. As Jiang Zemin, the General Secretary of the Party between 1989 and 2003, stated: 'The success of the bid will advance China's domestic stability and economic prosperity. The Olympics in China has the objectives of raising national morale and strengthening the unity of Chinese people both in the mainland and overseas' (*People's Daily*, 22 August 2002).

The strategy of winning Olympic medals in 2008

The well-developed 'whole country support for the elite sport system' matches China's Olympic medal ambitions. In July 2002 the Party and the Central Government issued a document titled, 'Strengthening and progressing sport in the new era' (Zhonggongzhongyang guowyyuan guanyu jinyibu jiaoqiang he gaijin xinshiqi tiyu dongzuo de yijian). It emphasised that hosting the 2008 Olympic Games is the priority not only for Beijing but for the whole country. China must grasp this opportunity to display itself to the world and to make Beijing 2008 the best Olympic Games ever. The Sports Ministry immediately drew up two important internal documents: 'The outline strategy for winning Olympic medals 2001–2010' (Aoyun zhengguang gangyao 2001–2010) and 'The strategic plan for winning Olympic medals in 2008' (2008 Aoyun zhengguang jihua). These two documents constitute an action plan to ensure China's successful hosting of the 2008 Olympics. The following actions are some of the key outputs from the two plans.

Selection of Olympic sports

In 2004 China participated in 26 summer Olympic sports and 203 events at the Athens Olympics. Eighteen key events were targeted for medals and these received most of the support in the elite sport system. In order to win more medals in 2008, China is preparing to participate in all the Olympic sports, including 28 sports and 300 events. Strengths and weaknesses have been carefully analysed and the Olympic sports have been divided into four categories:

1 'Traditional Olympic sports', in which China is virtually guaranteed to win gold medals, such as table-tennis, badminton and diving. There are 17 gold medals in these three sports and China won 13 in 2000. The aim is to maintain the country's dominant position in these sports.
2 'Capable Olympic sports', in which China has the ability to win some gold medals, such as gymnastics, weightlifting, shooting and judo. The aim is to win more gold medals in these sports.
3 'Potential Olympic sports', in which China has the potential to win more medals, such as athletics, swimming and water sports. There are 119 gold medals in these sports. China won just 2 gold medals in athletics and 1 in swimming in 2004. These are the sports targeted for more gold medals as China aims to outperform the United States in 2008.
4 'Weak Olympic sports', in which China lags behind, such as boxing, equestrianism, men's soccer, men's volleyball and baseball. These are the sports in which Chinese athletes need to work harder than ever to reach the qualifying standard and ultimately to win medals (The outline strategy for winning Olympic medals 2001–2010 and The strategic plan for winning Olympic medals in 2008; Yang, 2002).

Training of Olympic athletes

In order to train more athletes for the 2008 Olympic Games, the size of the national teams is expanding. National teams consist of experienced team managers, head coaches, and coaches who are appointed by the Sports Ministry and sports management centres, and elite athletes who are selected from the provincial sports teams throughout China. According to Chinese sports custom, when it prepares for international competitions there are two teams for each event: the national team and the resource team. However, for the Beijing 2008 Games, in order to ensure success, 'The strategic plan for winning Olympic medals in 2008' requires an expansion of the number of teams. Therefore, some key events have three teams: the national team, the youth team and the resource team. All elite athletes in China whose age allows them to perform at the 2008 Games are selected and allocated to different teams according to their present ability and future potential.

Each national team is to be given specific targets for the number of medals expected; no team effort is being spared to ensure success but managers, coaches and athletes are working under enormous pressure. One head coach of a national team reveals that he feels that it is like having a sword hanging over his head every day. National teams and youth teams train in their national training centres. The resource teams train in provincial sports commission training centres and at those universities which have superior training facilities. In 2002, China had 1,316 full-time Olympic athletes in national teams. In 2004, an additional 706 athletes joined national teams and 1,200 joined youth teams. In total, by the end of 2004 there were 3,222 full-time elite athletes training for the 2008 Olympic Games, plus others training in resource teams (The outline strategy for winning Olympic medals 2001–2010 and The strategic plan for winning Olympic medals in 2008'; Yang, 2002).

Increasing Olympic resources

The strategy for the 2008 Olympic Games provides for the government to increase financial support – in particular, for those sports in which Chinese athletes have the potential to win gold medals. Wu Shouzhang, Vice President of the Chinese Olympic Committee, argues that 'Our aim is to get more gold medals at the Olympics and everything we do is for this goal' (The cost of gold medals, 2004). Liu Fuming, Deputy Head of the Department of Finance of the Sports Ministry, confirmed that the Ministry received a budget from the central government of 16 billion yuan (ca. US$1.95 billion) in 2000. From 2001, the first year of implementation of the 'The outline strategy for winning Olympic medals 2001–2010', central government increased the budget. Liu Fuming has made this quite clear: 'from 2001 we received more than 16 billion yuan from the central government and the figure is increasing every year as 2008 approaches' ('The cost of gold medals', 2004).

The finance department in the Sports Ministry stated that between 2001 and 2004 the central government is augmenting its budget by 1 billion yuan (ca. US$122 million) each year, and between 2005 and 2008 the figure will be 2 billion yuan (ca. US$244 million) each year exclusively for the 2008 Olympic Games. Therefore, in 2008 the Sports Ministry will receive 27 billion yuan (ca. US$3.29 billion) in total. This does not include additional targeted funding for particular programmes related to Olympic preparation. Liu Fuming confirmed that the total figure would reach more than 40 billion yuan (ca. US$ 4.88 billion) in 2008 ('The cost of gold medals', 2004). It was estimated that 90 per cent of the funds are, and will be, used to pay the wages of athletes and coaches, improve existing training centres, build even more advanced training centres and provide state-of-the-art equipment. Needless to say, the best coaches in China are selected to train Olympic athletes and others are brought in from abroad and the best qualified sports scientists work closely with the national, youth and resource teams to improve athletes' athletic ability.

Preparation for Olympic competition

In order to provide athletes with maximum experience of competition and to prepare them physically and mentally for the 2008 Olympics, national competitions have been restructured. Apart from the National Games, the 5th City Games in China in 2004 added 10 more Olympic sports to its traditional 16 sports and concentration was on the events in which China expects to win in 2008. Rules and regulations mirrored those of the Olympic Games and the other national championships now follow this model. The slogans are 'Let the national competitions serve the Olympics' (bian quanyun wei aoyun) and 'Training the athletes in Chinese competitions and preparing them to fight for China at international games' (guonei lianbing, yizhidui-wai). In addition, young athletes who have the potential to win gold medals in 2008 were sent to international competitions including the Asian Games, the East Asian Games and the 'Universiade' (The World Student Games) in 2006 to prepare them for the Beijing Olympics. China has increasingly exploited its 'whole country support for the elite sport system' to systematically produce more Olympic athletes in order to maintain and hopefully advance its position in the gold medal table in 2008 (Hong et al., 2005).

Conclusion

China's determination to be placed at the top of the Olympic medals table in the 2008 Beijing Olympic Games has resulted in the further strengthening of its elite sport system. There are debates about whether the elite sport system will be dismantled after the 2008 Games. However, China's unique system, which has played such an important role in the country's political life in the form of gold medal ambition, will continue to play a key role in China's ambitions to be one of the global economic and political superpowers in the twenty-first century.

References

Anon (1967) The crime of the anti-party, anti-military, anti-revolutionary, revisionist He Long" (1967) *Sports Battlefront*, (8), p. 5.

Anon (2004) The cost of gold medals [Zhongguo jinpai de chengben] (2004) *Observer* [*Quanqiu caijing guanca*], 13 August p. 2.

Bai, L. and Gu, S. (1990) Yayun huigu [The brief history of the Asian games], *Tiyu wenshi*, (2), pp. 2–8.

Cao, S. (1991) Cong youyi diyi, bishai dire tanqi [On friendship first, competition second], *Tiyushi lunwen ji* [*The Annual Selected Work of Sports History*], (8), pp. 23–35.

CCP (1966) Zhongguo gongchandang zhongyan weiyuanhui tongzhi [The announcement of the centre committee of the CCP], 16 May, 1966. It was published in *Renmin ribao* [*People's Daily*], 17 May 1966.

China takes the Olympic limelight (2004) http://edition. cnn.com/2004/SPORT/08/30/athens.games/

The Chinese Sports Ministry (2001) The outline strategy for winning Olympic medals 2001–2010 [Aoyu zhengguang gangyao 2001–2010]. An internal document.

The Chinese Sports Ministry (2002) The strategic plan for winning Olympic medals in 2008 [2008 Aoyunzhengguang]. An internal document.

Dai, Q. (2004) Zhongguo tiyu yexu yige xinshidai [Chinese sport needs a new era], *Xinwen zhoukan* [*Chinese News Weekly*], 7 September, p. 9.

Deng, Y. (2002) From boundfeet to Olympic gold in China: The case of women's Chinese table tennis, *MA thesis*, Nottingham University, pp. 110–111.

Guan, W. (ed.) (1996) *Tiyu shi* [*Sports History*], Beijing: Higher Education Press.

Hao, Q. (2004) Lun zhongguo tiyu 'Juguo tizhi' de gainian, tedian yu gongneng [The definition, characteristics and functions of the Chinese elite sports system], *Tiyu* [*Physical Education*], (3), 15–19.

Hong, F. (1998) The Olympic movement in China, *Culture, Sport, Society*, 1(1), pp. 149–168.

Hong, F. (1999) Not all bad! Communism, society and sport in the Great Proletarian Cultural Revolution: A revisionist perspective, *The International Journal of the History of Sport*, 16(3), 47–71.

Hong, F. (2003) Women's sport in the People's Republic of China: Body, politics and the unfinished revolution, Iise Hartmannn-Tews and Gertrud Pfister, *Sport and Women: Social Issues in International Perspective*, London: Routledge.

Hong, F., Wu, P. and Xiong, H. (2005) Beijing ambitions: An analysis of the Chinese elite sports system and its Olympic strategy for the 2008 Olympic games, *The International Journal of the History of Sport*, 22(4), 510–529.

Johnson, W. (1973) Faces on a new China scroll *Sports Illustrated*, 39(3).

Kissinger, H. (1979) *The White House Years*, London: Weidenfeld and Nicolson and Michael Joseph.

Li, F. (2000) Li Furong tan ruhe nuli chengwei yi ming youxiu jiaolianyuan [Li Furong's speech on how to become an outstanding coach], *Zhongguo tiyu bao* [*China Sports Daily*], 12(4), 2 [Li Furong is a Vice Minister of Sport in China].

The 'May 12 Military Order' (1968) is jointly issued by the Communist Centre Committee, the State Council and the Centre Military Commission on 12 May 1968. The original document is in the Archives, the Sports Ministry, Beijing.

Nixon, R. (1978) *The Memoirs of Richard Nixon*, New York: Grosset & Dunlap.

People's Daily (1972) 'Editorial', 26 February.

People's Daily (2002) 22 August, 1.

People's Daily (2007) 19 January, 12.

People's Sports Press [Renmin tiyu chubanshe] (ed.) (1983) *Zhongguo yundongyuan zai guoji bisai zhong de chengjiu* [*The Achievements of the Chinese Athletes in the International Sports Competitions*], Beijing: Renmin tiyu chubanshe.

The Planning and Finance Department of the Sports Ministry (1994) *Tiyu shiue tongji nianjian (neibu ziliao)* [*Statistical Yearbook of Sport (Internal Information)*], 1994.

The Policy Research Centre of the Sport Ministry (ed.) (1982) *Tiyu weijian xuanbian 1949–1981* [*Selected Policy Documents on Chinese Sports, 1949–1981*], Beijing: Renmin tiyu chubanshe.

Qian, J. (1987) *Ping-Pong waiao shimo* [*The story of the Ping-Pong diplomacy*], Beijing: Dongfang chubanshe.

The Quotations from Mao Zedong (1968) Beijing: Foreign Languages Press.

Reporter of South China Sports Weekly (2004) Liaoning: duo de qi jinpai, yang bu qi guanjun [Able to produce gold medallists but unable to reward and feed them], *Nanfan tiyu zhoubao* [*South China Sports Weekly*], 30 August(8).

Rong, G. (ed.) (1987) *Dangdai Zhonhguo tiyu* [*The History of Contemporary Chinese Sport*], Beijing: Zhongguo shehui kexue chubanshe.

Tong, Y. (1989) Zhaozhui jiehe dian, liqiu duchuanxin [The combination of the west and the east], *Lunwe ji*, (8).

Tragedy under the pyramid: Investigation of living conditions of retired players [Jinzita xia de beiju: tuiyi yundongyuan chengcun zhuangkuang diaocha] (2003) http://news.xinhuanet.com/focus/2003-09/11/content_1073593.htm

Wang, D. (1993) Marshal and generals, *Tiyu wenshi*, (4), pp. 12–15.

Wang, M. (1982) Wangmeng tongzhi zai 1980 nian quanguo tiyu gongzuo huiyi shang de gongzuo baogao [The report of Comrade Wang Meng in National Sports Conference in 1980], *Tiyu yundong wenjian xuanbian (1949–1981)* [*Collection of Chinese Sports Documents 1949–1981*], Beijing: Renmin tiyu chuban she, p. 150.

Where will the lame Chinese sport go? (Zhuanxiang xiuxian de wanju: bozu zhongguo tiyu he qu he cong) (2004) http://news.xinhuanet.com/sports/2004-08/09/content_1742895.htm; http://edition.cnn.com/2004/SPORT/ 08/30/athens.games/

Wu Shaozu (1993) Olympic strategy and sports reform in China, in Xie Yalong (ed.), *Olympic Studies*, Beijing: Beijing tiyu daxue chubanshe, pp. 402–404.

Wu, S. (1999) *zhonghua renmin gongheguo tiyu shi (zonghe juan)* [*Sports History in the PRC*], Beijing: Zhongguo shuji chubanshe.

Yang, S. (2002) Woguo jingji tiyu de shili xianzhuang, xingshi, renwu ji duice fengxi [The analysis of our elite sport], *Zhongguo tiyu keji* [*Chinese Sports Science*], (1), 3–9 [Yang is Deputy Minister of the Chinese Sports Ministry and the Head of the Department of Competitive Sport in the Sports Ministry].

Yuan, W. (2001) yuan weimin tongzhi zai 2001 nian quanguo tiyu juzhang huiyi huiyi shang de jianghua [Comrade Yuan Weimin's speech at the conference of all-state sports ministers], *Zhanlue jueze-2001 nian quanguo tiyu fazhan zhailue yantao hui wenji* [*Strategitic Plan – A Collections of the Symposium of the National Sports Development Strategy in 2001*], Beijing: Guojia tiwei zhengfa si bian.

Yuan, W. (2004) *Yuan Weimin zai xinwen fabuhui shang de jianghua* [*Yuan Weimin's Speech on the Press Conference in Athens, August 30, 2004*]. http://www.olympic.cn/athens/daibiaotuanxinxi/ 2004-08-30/299251.html (www.olympic.cn is the official website of the Chinese Olympic Committee).

Zhan, J. et al. (2001) Research on developing trend of elite sport towards 2010[Woguo jingji tiyu 2010 nian fazhan qushi yanjiu], *Tiyu* [*Physical Education*], (1), pp. 10–13.

Zhang, M. (1991) Xin Zhongguo jinji tiyu zhenche de fazhan he tedian chutan [The research for the policy on elite sport in new China], *Tiyu wenshi*, (2), pp. 2–4.

Zhang, T. (1996) Di 26 jie aoyunhui ji zhongguo tiyu daibiaotuan cansai qingkuang [The situation of the Chinese delegation at the 16th Olympic games], *Tiyu gongzuo qingkuang* [*Sports Information*] pp. 3–5.

Zhao, Y. (1988a) *Qiang Guo Meng* [*Dreaming to be a Superpower*], Beijing: Zuojia Press.

Zhao, Y. (1988b) *Bing Bai Hancheng* [*The Defeat in Seoul*], Beijing: Chinese Social Sciences Press.

Japan

Mayumi Ya-Ya Yamamoto

Introduction

Success in the 2004 Athens Olympic Games (5th in the medal table) was a significant moment for the Japanese government and national elite sport policy actors insofar as it validated their investment in the development of infrastructure for elite use and legitimated a continued structured approach to the development of elite athletes. The recent re-emergence of Japan as a strong sporting nation in international sport is the outcome of a refocusing by the government on elite sport policy and a number of initiatives including the establishment of the Japan Institute of Sports Sciences (JISS) and the encouragement of its collaboration with the Japanese Olympic Committee (JOC). While the four dimensions identified by Green and Houlihan (2005) are also evident in Japan, the country possesses some distinctive features including the effective way in which information is gathered from other successful elite sport countries such as Australia and the ample evidence of policy learning and policy transfer. This chapter describes the increasing emphasis on elite sport in public policy which emerged in the late 1990s. The analysis is based on the examination of a range of policy documents and over 30 interviews with senior policy actors conducted in 2005 and 2006.

Current structure of the elite sport system

The establishment of a Physical Education (PE) Division in 1928 within the Ministry of Education, which took responsibility for the emerging government interest in sport, coincided with the increasing militarism and authoritarianism within the Japanese government. After Japan withdrew from hosting the Olympic Games scheduled for 1940, the PE Division was restructured as the PE Bureau which took a central role in preparing young males for military services through physical fitness training at school (Nakamura, 1992). The PE Bureau was regarded as one of the major advocates of militarism within the government and was abolished at the start of the Allied occupation in 1945. Prior to the Allied occupation, between 1940 and 1945, the government had established a centralised system of sport administration within the Ministry of Education, elements of which are still evident today. Currently, the Sports and Youth Bureau (renamed from the PE Bureau in 2001) within the Ministry of Education, Culture, Sports, Science and Technology (hereafter MEXT, previously the Ministry of Education, Science, Sports and Culture, MESSC, until 2001, see Figure 3.1) is the lead administrative unit for the promotion and development of sport.

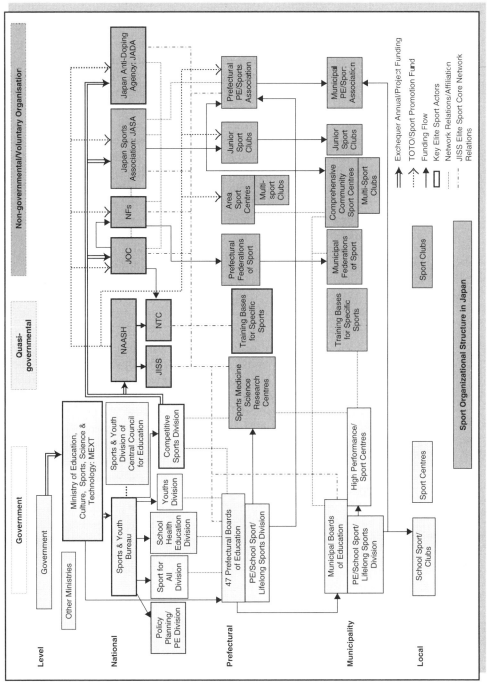

Figure 3.1 Organisational structure of elite sport in Japan

The distinctive features of governmental sport administration and policy-making for sport in Japan are: first, the stronger influence of bureaucrats by comparison with politicians; second, a broad consensus on sport policy among the political parties; and third, that policy on 'sport' is dominated by a concern with 'PE' or 'social PE' which reflects the historic emphasis on the latter within the (social) educational policy agenda. However, this historic priority accorded to PE was challenged, if only modestly, by the creation of separate Divisions for Sport for All and Competitive Sports in 1988 which indicated the growing government interest in separating out the issue of improvement of international medal-winning success from the broader concern with lifelong sporting participation.

Responsibility for elite sport policy is centralised within the Competitive Sports Division of the Sports and Youth Bureau within MEXT (see Figure 3.1). This Division is the primary national policy actor for conceptualising, defining and implementing elite sport policy, and it is from this Division that most of the high-performance-related public subsidies are distributed to sport agencies and to specific programmes and projects. The Exchequer's annual budget allocation to the Competitive Sports Division is divided between: (i) the national sport organisations as direct subsidies and (ii) the research projects or programmes which the Division commissions. One of the distinctive features of the sport policy-making process is the consultative role of the Sports and Youth Division of the Central Council for Education (previously known as the Ministry of Education's Advisory Council of Health and Physical Education, ACHPE) which is influential in developing and overseeing the delivery of sport policy.

The National Agency for the Advancement of Sports and Health[1] (NAASH) is a non-departmental public agency which, in 2001, had its management responsibility expanded to cover: (1) the National Stadium, (2) the activities of JISS, and (3) disaster relief and promotion of school lunch (sic). It is also the distributing body for three major funding streams: (a) the Sports Promotion Fund introduced in 1990 to which the government provided a one-off payment of ¥2.5 billion (as in US billion) principally for the development of elite athletes; (b) toto (the national lottery), which has been allocated for the development of Sport for All since 2001; and (c) the Support for the Development of Sport Project introduced in 2003 with the central aim of winning medals. The influence of MEXT, and its Sports and Youth Bureau, is exercised by means of its budgetary control and its influence over the distribution of subsidies through NAASH which it closely monitors and evaluates.

The inauguration of JISS in 2001 as one of the operational divisions of NAASH can be seen as a landmark insofar as it was the first centralised specialist elite-focused institute. JISS has since become the primary support service provider in sports science, medicine and technical information, and also operates a 'mini-national training centre' located within its facility. Its fundamental aim, as defined in the government document the *Basic Plan for the Promotion of Sport*,[2] 2000–2010 (hereafter *Basic Plan*) is to play a substantive 'supportive role' in relation to potential medal-winning athletes (MEXT, 2000). This quasi-governmental specialised institution is dependent on public money not only for the development of its training centre facility, but also for meeting the cost of human resources and its programme and projects. JISS' scope for innovation in programmes and projects is tightly constrained by the framework of procedure and accountability of government: first, JISS is obliged to obtain explicit approval for projects/activities from its parent organisation, NAASH; second, it is regularly evaluated by MEXT; and third, despite being heavily dependent on government finance, it is nonetheless required to generate money due to its statutory status as an 'independent' administrative body.

The impetus to establish the national training centre (NTC, scheduled to open in December 2007) was the perceived national inadequacy of training facilities and fact that '9 out of 10 countries in the gold medal table at the Athens Olympic Games possess' some sort of domestic NTC (MEXT, 2006a, p. 26). Policy actors within government (especially MEXT) and non-governmental actors (such as the Japanese Olympic Committee, JOC) argued carefully for a government funded elite athlete-centred training facility which will allow 'concentrated, consistent training activities' (MEXT, 2005). The proposed NTC, it was argued, should operate in partnership with JISS and with the already-existing training bases for winter sport events, marine/waterside sports, and high-altitude training (NTC Research Committee, 2004). While the facility itself is to be managed by NAASH, the JOC will be responsible for implementing and facilitating the development of the elite school,[3] the national academy for the development of coaches and management directors, together with the provision of athlete education and second career support.

At the sub-national level, the Prefectural PE/School Sport Division within the prefectural government and the PE (or Sports) Association have considerable influence on the promotion of sport in general and setting performance targets for the annual inter-prefectural National Athletic Meeting (*Kokumin Taiiku-taikai*, known as *Kokutai*[4]) by selecting the best-performing athletes at the respective prefectural levels. It should be highlighted that although success in *Kokutai* remains a policy priority in most of the prefectures, there is growing evidence which suggests that some prefectures developed talent identification programmes to systematically identify, select and nurture 'prefecturally grown' international elite athletes whose interests are incorporated into the overall sport promotion policy. The discernible, though modest, shift of resources at prefectural level towards elite sport development is part of a slowly emerging coalition of elite sport actors, initiated by the JOC and JISS, around a set of values and beliefs that legitimise the systematic identification of potential and talented young athletes and the prioritisation of support for upcoming and elite athletes.

The development of elite sport policy in Japan

Japan gained its political independence in 1951 following the indirect occupation by the United States and from 1952 resumed its participation in the Olympic Games. The participation in the 1952 Helsinki Games was followed by the successful hosting of the 1958 Asian Games in Tokyo. In 1959, the International Olympic Committee (IOC) awarded the 1964 summer Olympic Games to Tokyo, which proved to be the most significant catalyst for the development and definition of national sport policy in Japan (Seki, 1997). The government subsequently enacted the Sports Promotion Act in 1961 which established an organisational and funding framework for sport. What was significant about hosting the Games was that it was seen not just as a Tokyo and sport project, but as a national and multi-purpose project. The government invested a huge amount of money not only to help rebuild the country's devastated infrastructure, but also to help rebuild national morale after World War II. The government recognised the powerful symbolic value both domestically and internationally of hosting a successful Olympic Games. In particular, the government saw the hoped-for success of Japanese elite athletes and the efficient hosting of the Games as opportunities to replace the Japanese name on the world map and to regain national pride for its citizens (Ikei, 1992). Consequently, the pressure to host a successful Games was immense. In relation to the Sports Promotion Act, while it was significant in terms of defining the role of government in sport and that of sport organisations, it was also significant in establishing the balance between elite sport success and Sport for All. However, the Act must be seen in the wider political context of the overriding emphasis on economic growth and industrial development which limited expenditure not only on welfare services, but also on sport, thus delaying until 2000 the implementation of the plan for the promotion of sport.

While the government invested heavily before and during the 1964 Tokyo Games in the development of the infrastructure for sport in order, partly, to satisfy the public concern to win medals, this investment did not stimulate a long-term commitment to the development of elite athletes and to the pursuit of international sporting success. Instead, during the 1970s and at the beginning of the 1980s, a prioritisation of Sport for All over investment in the development of elite athletes gradually emerged. The post-war socio-economic recovery of Japan led Japanese citizens, who were now receiving higher and more stable incomes, to express increasing concern with their quality of life. These new concerns included leisure and sport and led, in part, to the establishment of voluntary sport organisations such as the New Physical Education League of Japan (*Shintairen*) (Uchiumi, 1993; Seki, 1997).

The government's declaration in 1972 of 'the end of the post-war period' and the subsequent commencement of 'welfare policy' in 1973 was indicative of the government considering leisure policy to be part of its policy agenda. The report, prepared by the ACHPE in 1972 on the *Fundamental Policies for the Promotion of Physical Education and Sport* was the first policy document that indicated an active concern with promoting leisure (sport) opportunities for all (ACHPE, 1972; Seki, 1997). Despite the publication of the report, overall government involvement in sport remained low, and such involvement as there was remained oriented to Sport for All rather than elite sport. However, according to Morikawa (1986) from the mid-1970s, and especially following the poor performance by Japan at the 1976 Montreal Olympics, there emerged a growing level of concern within the government and in the media with the country's declining elite performance. Part of the problem was seen as the reliance on the commercial sector to support elite athletes while the weakness in the process of talent identification and development (TID) was also considered partly responsible. The problem became more acute when Japanese business entered a period of economic recession that began in the early 1990s and which led it to reduce its support for elite sport.

The expressions of 'concern' in the mid-1970s developed into an expression of 'crisis' towards the late 1980s due to the decline in the international competitiveness of Japanese athletes. The perception of crisis attracted the attention of governmental committee meetings and the prime minister himself. Although Japan had dominated sporting competition in the Asian region since the 1964 Games, there were consecutive poor performances in the 1982 New Delhi Asian Games, when Japan fell behind China for the first time, and in the 1986 Seoul Asian Games and 1988 Seoul Olympic Games when South Korea gained a total of 33 medals achieving 4th place in the medal table (Japan was 14th). Japan's sharp decline in international sporting success was publicly recognised and criticised by then Prime Minister Nakasone, who established a personal consultation committee on elite sport success but it was only after the ACHPE produced a report on *Strategies for the Promotion of Sports for the 21st Century* in 1989 that the level of elite sporting success began to be established as a significant public policy concern.

The ACHPE report was endorsed in a 1992 White Paper, with the MESSC noting not only the decline of Japanese achievement, but also highlighting the rapid improvement of African and other Asian countries (MESSC, 1992). Consequently, it was not until 1997 that government concern was translated into elite-focused policies. Policy action was prompted by the poor performance of the Japanese national team at the 1996 Atlanta Olympic Games (23rd with 3 gold and 14 medals in total). This and other poor performances in international sport became the key reference point in the *Basic Plan* with its 10-year national objective to regain the level of success in the Olympic Games achieved in the 1964 Tokyo Games (5th position in medal table).

The Sports Promotion Fund, comprising a one-off sum of ¥25 billion from the central government and ¥4.4 billion from the private sector, was established in 1990. The purpose of the Fund was to give more autonomy to MEXT and enable it to use its budget to undertake longer-term strategic planning of the development of elite athletes. Furthermore, the passage of the Sports Promotion Lottery Law in 1998 (the lottery, known as *toto*, was established in 2001) was seen as a major achievement for national sport actors in securing revenue sources with the purpose of building a 'lifelong sporting society' which included money for elite sport (MESSC, 1998). As previously mentioned, the annual decision over the distribution of subsidies from the Sports Promotion Fund and the Sports Promotion Lottery is managed by the quasi-government agency, NAASH. However, both government and *toto* funding have been inadequate for the planned activities for the development of elite sport due to: the severe downturn of the Japanese economy; the persistence of low interest rates (0.5 per cent in 2007) which affected the reserves of the Sports Promotion Fund; and the decline in the popularity of the professional soccer league (J-League) which led to a gradual decline in *toto* sales which are based on J-League results.

The publication of the *Basic Plan* in 2000 which provided political legitimation for the introduction of *toto* was drawn up on the assumption that *toto* revenue would be substantial. The *Basic Plan* identified three fundamental policy objectives: (i) the realisation of lifelong sport participation, (ii) the increase in international sporting competitiveness, and (iii) the development of school PE and sport through (i) and (ii). Its implementation provided the defining moment in the development of a more systematic elite sport policy with four elements being of particular importance. Firstly, it was the first time that the government had announced a target of 3.5 per cent of all medals available at both the summer and winter Olympic Games. The numerical target became more visible in 2003 in the preparations for the Athens Olympic Games, when the Competitive Sports Division produced the 'Nippon Revival Project', which specifically allocated funding to the high-potential medal-winning athletes and sport disciplines. Secondly and importantly, the elite-targeted sports science and medicine specialist institute, JISS, was inaugurated in 2001 as a sub-division of NAASH and its activities were defined in the *Basic Plan*. Thirdly and equally importantly, the JOC published the *Gold Plan* based on, and reinforcing, the government medal target. The JOC indicated its practical responsibility for high-performance development, not only in accrediting national federations for sport (NFs) and sending delegates to the Olympic Games, but also in devising a series of qualitative and quantitative performance indicators based on the results in world championships and the Olympic Games in order to determine the distribution to NFs of the funding that had been received from the Competitive Sports Division (JOC, 2001). Lastly, the construction of the NTC was specified in the initial *Basic Plan* and more explicitly in the revised version of the *Basic Plan* published in 2006 following populist Prime Minister Koizumi's public expression of support for the opening of the NTC in time for the 2008 Beijing Olympic Games (MEXT, 2006a).

It should be reiterated that the policy framework for developing medal-winning athletes only emerged as a systematic programme following the publication of the *Basic Plan*, some 39 years after the passage of the Sports Promotion Act in 1961. Prior to the publication of the *Basic Plan*, sport service expertise related to specialist support for elite athletes and coaches and was dispersed across a large number of organisations and institutions, including sport-specialised universities, NFs' high-performance centres and prefecturally/municipally owned training centres. With the subsequent publication of the JOC's *Gold Plan* and *Gold Plan Stage II: Summer Version* in 2006, which set the even more ambitious target to be third in the medal table by hosting the summer Olympic Games in 2016 (JOC, 2006), the

JOC's responsibility was specified as overseeing the achievement of international success and acting as the mediating and supporting agency for NFs. The role of the JOC was to evaluate the activities and performance of NFs and, on the basis of its assessment, to distribute the annual government subsidy. The assessment criteria used by the JOC emphasised the role of NFs in developing elite success and formed the basis of an implicit contract between the JOC and the NFs in relation to elite sport development.

The JOC's concern with elite success is reinforced by its strong collaborative link with JISS which has focused on: designing a programme of TID; supporting elite athletes through sports science, medicine, and nutrition; and distributing information to athletes, coaches, and support staff within NFs and prefectural/municipal sport agencies. What is significant is the establishment of an organisational and personal network which includes policy actors from local, regional, and national levels that has been facilitated especially by JISS and the JOC leading to the gradual emergence of an elite sport policy community. Furthermore, the importance of constructing a policy community with international contacts is reinforced by the activities of the Department of Sports Information in JISS and the Information Strategy Section of the JOC. Both organisations have been instrumental in using their international contacts to systematically gather ideas and information from successful elite sport countries (discussed more fully below). The concern to develop a domestic elite sport policy community was also reflected in the establishment of the Japan Top League (JTL) in 2005 authorised by the Competitive Sports Division. The objective of the JTL is to establish a collaborative link across the nine leagues of the eight ball sport disciplines not only to provide support with management of each others' professional leagues but also, and more significantly, to produce a solid foundation for achieving medals in team sport at the Olympic Games (JTL, 2006).

The first policy evaluation report commissioned by MEXT on the *Improvement of International Competitiveness* was published in 2006 and was broadly supportive of the current approach to elite sport development (MEXT, 2006b). Part of the reasons for publishing the report may have been to legitimise current government policy and underline the contribution of JISS to elite success in Athens as the report lacked the critical review of policy that would have been provided by an independent third party. The *Basic Plan*, the role of the JOC, and the MEXT review of policy in 2006 all provide evidence of an increasingly structured and long-term approach by the government to the preparation of elite athletes underpinned by a neo-liberal and 'value for money' approach to effectiveness as measured by high-performance achievement in the Olympics and major world championships. The high level of elite success in recent Olympic Games and international championships has been taken as confirmation of the value of the *Basic Plan* and the 2006 review restated the policy goal of 3.5 per cent of medals in future Olympic Games (MEXT, 2006a).

Despite the recent burst of policy-making, the degree of consistency of emphasis on elite sport policy should not be exaggerated as sport remains relatively marginal both within the lead ministry, MEXT, and across the other government ministries that have a more limited interest in sport. However, whether the generally marginal status of sport is a threat to investment in elite sport is debatable, for at the time that the government is privatising public sport facilities managed by local authorities in order to ease the pressure on public expenditure, it is investing about ¥20.2 billion in the construction of the NTC. It should be noted that policy for mass participation and elite sport are the responsibilities of different divisions of MEXT (the Life-Long Sports Division and the Competitive Sports Division, respectively) and that their budgets are not therefore in direct competition. However, the investment in elite sport is partly rationalised by arguing that international elite success boosts enthusiasm for sports participation across the nation (MEXT, 2000, 2006a).

Four dimensions of the elite sport infrastructure in Japan

The development of elite level specialist facilities

The inadequacy of elite training facilities and the incoherence of support for elite athletes have been recurring themes since before the 1964 Tokyo Games, as has been the idea of creating a national training centre and the provision of specialist support services. However, it was only after the 1998 Nagano winter Olympic Games and the 2002 Football World Cup in Korea/Japan that the government felt able to redirect public money towards the establishment of a national elite institute (JISS) which contained a small training facility. Two years later in September 2004, and immediately after the success at the Athens Olympic Games, the most significant facility development for elite athletes was announced as a result of the direct instruction of the then Prime Minister Koizumi to construct an NTC, next to JISS, in time for Beijing Olympic Games. A major reinforcement of this decision was the failure at the 2006 Turin winter Olympic Games, where Japan won just one gold medal. As a result of this poor performance, the development of high-performance facilities designed to meet specific training needs (such as for winter disciplines and high-altitude sports) was argued (MEXT, 2006c). The need for effective and close cooperation between these specialist facilities and the functions of the NTC was highlighted in the revised *Basic Plan* (MEXT, 2006a). When the NTC is fully operationalised at the end of 2007, it is expected to be the hub training base cooperating with the network of regionally based training centres, and collaborating with the existing specialist services provided by JISS.

The history of the development of other specialist services for athletes (sports medicine and sports science) is very similar to that of the development of facilities, namely short-lived enthusiasm around the time of the 1964 Tokyo Olympic Games and then little significant activity until the mid-1990s. Following the decision to host the Olympics and the establishment of the Tokyo Olympic Performance Specialist Committee in 1960, the Sports Science Research Committee and Training Doctor System were launched. The launch of the Sports Science Research Committee was noted as 'one of the most valuable assets' of the Tokyo Olympics (Japan Sports Association, JASA, 1986, p. 154) and, consequently, JASA opened the permanent Sports Science Research Institute in 1967. However, the activities of the Institute were 'small scale' and sporadic (Asami, 2005). Following a review of the importance of sports science and medicine by the President of JASA in 1975, he proposed a plan to construct specialised centres for sports science and medicine at the national and regional levels. The President's view was reinforced by one sports academic who noted that: 'there was confidence in sports science in Japan among scientists … but there was no institution that could provide feedback from the most advanced research results of sports science' (Interview A, 7 April 2005). However, the proposal was not helped by the considerable scepticism towards sports science (but not sports medicine) among athletes during the 1960s and 1970s, many of whom felt they were being used as 'guinea pigs' (Asami, 2005).

The most likely explanation for the institutional shift from scepticism to a willingness to embrace the application of sports science and medicine was the Korean success in the 1988 Seoul Olympic Games where the host nation's medal count exceeded that of the Japanese. However, the combined effect of the economic recession of the 1990s and the construction costs of the facilities for the 1998 winter Olympic Games in Nagano and the Football World Cup in 2002 was to drain the budget of the Competitive Sports Division, and delay or, as Asami (2005) who was the first Director General of JISS claimed, 'hibernate' the construction work on a national sports science centre until 1997.

Retreating from the initial plan to construct national sports service institute with sports science capability, the Competitive Sports Division intended to establish a specialist sports science research institute which would include a small-scale 'mini'-training centre inside the institute. Table 3.1 shows that a large proportion of the budget of the Competitive Sports Division was allocated, from 1997 to 2001, as a 5-year project for the construction of JISS. It is ironic and indicative of the erratic

Table 3.1 Competitive Sports Division Budget Allocation regarding the preparation for the NTC, JISS, 1998 Nagano Games, and 2002 World Cup

Project name	Allocated budget for the preparation of a national sports science institute	Allocated budget for the preparations for the Nagano Winter Games
1994	3,000,000	13,000,000
1995	3,000,000	14,000,000
1996	4,000,000	14,000,000
Project name	Allocation to the development of a national sports centre – 5 year project: (i) preparation to establish National Sports Science Centre (ii) research on a large-scale National Sports Centre	Allocation to the support for the international competitions: (i) preparation for the Nagano Winter Games (ii) preparation for the 2002 World Cup
1997	4,170,000,000	24,000,000
1998	6,679,100,000	22,390,000
1999	3,142,883,000	31,443,000
2000	4,011,000,000	31,443,000
2001	1,690,560,000	n/a
	14,995,000 – a new project on researching for the preparation of establishing NTC	

Note: Up to 1996, the proposal was to have a national sports service institute which would incorporate sports science and research and elite training facilities. In 1996, it was decided to separate these functions and establish a National Sports Science Centre (later renamed JISS) and a National Sports Centre (later renamed NTC).
Sources: MEXT Budget Allocations, 1994–2001.

commitment to elite sport that while the hosting of the Olympics in 1964 (Tokyo) and 1972 (Sapporo) led to increased investment in sports science/medicine and eventually to the establishment of a research centre at JASA (JASA, 1986), hosting the 1998 Nagano Games (despite their perceived success) resulted in priority being given to the construction of facilities over the establishment of a foundation for sports science/medicine, suggesting that hosting the most recent Games did not stimulate the same degree of government interest as the previous two.

However, there seems to be a clear relationship between the increasing acceptance of the application of science/medicine to sport and the growing sense of crisis due to the failure of Japanese elite athletes. Although coaches at the elite level still tend, as they did throughout much of the 1980s and 1990s, to rely on their experience and personal training methods, there was a gradual accumulation of trust and confidence in sports science among elite coaches. The greater willingness to acknowledge the potential of sports science was due to the evident success of the communist/socialist countries, particularly the Soviet Union, and the field research in those countries conducted by Japanese national sport actors who emphasised the value of a centralised approach to developing athletes and particularly a centralised research centre for sport.

After the crisis period of failure in international sport between the late 1980s and mid-1990s, the National Sports Science Centre (later renamed JISS) was planned by following the example of countries such as Australia, Canada, and the United States. However, in the end, downsized from the earlier and much preferred comprehensive training centre, the Competitive Sports Division decided to include only the centralised functions of sports science research and medical support plus a mini-training centre with a limited range of indoor facilities which could be used for training camps. Despite the modest remit of JISS, its significance is that it made available, for the first time, to elite athletes access to specialist support services on a daily basis and particularly free access to medical services (called Total Sports Clinic, TSC). The impact of JISS as shown by the 'success' stories of athletes and coaches at the 2002 Busan Asian Games and the 2004 Athens Olympic Games had already been acknowledged by a number of officers from JISS, JOC, and the NFs (cf. JISS, 2004a, b; MEXT, 2006b).

However, two high-ranking officers at the JOC and JISS were both reluctant to identify sports science/medicine as the sole cause of success in the 2004 Olympic Games partly because the achievement in Athens was also a function of the mini-training centre established inside JISS and because the achievement in high-performance sport had not yet been sustained over the long term (Interview B, 6 April 2005; Interview C, 18 August 2005). Expanding the role of JISS in elite sport development is hindered by the legislative constraints of a fixed budget and a fixed number of permanent employees (researchers) which was seen by some as limiting its long-term impact on the accumulation and utilisation of knowledge. The construction of a NTC, next to JISS, is an acknowledgement that the services and functions provided by JISS are insufficient and that athletes require a more comprehensive support programme.

Athlete support and athlete development

Support for 'full-time athletes' • • •

The two main ways in which athletes and coaches can obtain funding for their activities are from: (i) the government subsidies centrally allocated to the JOC that are distributed to NFs, and then to athletes and (ii) the 'Sports Activities of Athletes/ Coaches' stream within the Sports Promotion Fund established in 1990. The latter provides financial aid to athletes in the JOC's high-performance categories of 'Elite A, Elite B, and Youth Elite' and to the coaches of the designated athletes. The level of funding available to athletes varies depending on their high-performance category. The maximum amount provided for Elite A athletes is ¥200,000, Elite B ¥100,000, and Youth Elite ¥50,000 per month, which is barely sufficient for them to live as full-time athletes even though all funded athletes also receive free access to specialist services such as massage and physiotherapy. Consequently, elite/youth athletes still rely on additional income from sources such as private companies to which most of them belong, part-time employment and/or commercial sponsorship where their image is used for their sponsors' advertisement campaigns or public relations. It should therefore be noted that the introduction of the Sports Promotion Fund did not make a dramatic difference to the income of elite level athletes.

Three weaknesses of the current sporting environment for top athletes were identified by MEXT and its commissioned research team (MEXT, 2000; CSRC, 2005). The first was the dependence of athletes on corporate companies who owned sport clubs and teams and provided athletes with coaching, financial and technical services, and welfare support. The weaknesses arise from the fragility of the financial base of many company sport clubs due to the financial problems of their parent companies with the result that some athletes have lost their income and some been forced to give up their athletic career

(CSRC, 2005). The second weakness is, as a senior JOC official stressed, a sense that the experience of ex-elite athletes is being wasted because they tend to be engaged in non-sporting careers/sectors after their athletic career as there are not enough opportunities to utilise their knowledge and competencies within sport, as coaches for example, and not enough social recognition for sport-related occupations (Interview B, 6 April 2005).

Lastly, it is pointed out in the *Basic Plan* that there is not enough protection (e.g., financial support) when athletes are injured and especially if injury forces early retirement from their sporting career (MEXT, 2000; JOC, 2001). These weaknesses can be seen as a product of the insufficient financial support available for international level athletes. In part, the under-funding of elite athletes is a consequence of the tradition in Japan of relying financially on business for the production and support of elite athletes. While there is a growing awareness of the necessity to increase levels of government support in order to produce a supportive environment in which athletes can train, there are strong reservations, as expressed by a high-ranking NASSH official, regarding the provision of comprehensive financial support due to the association between state support and the system of 'state amateurs' found in the communist and many ex-communist countries (Interview D, 18 August 2005). These reservations notwithstanding the Competitive Sports Division allocated a budget based on the 'Nippon Revival Project' in 2003 and 2004 to prioritised NFs based on performance criteria provided by the JOC. The Project was financed by the Competitive Sports Division as a direct subsidy to the JOC with an increased budget of ¥335 million in order to expand the opportunities for intensive training camps for elite athletes and for the establishment of national team sport leagues in order to prepare for the Olympics and Asian Games. In the same year, the Competitive Sports Division also allocated ¥450 million for the 'Development of Prioritised Disciplines' and distributed additional funding via NAASH to selected Olympic-discipline NFs to maximise their chances of success in the Athens Olympic Games.

The decision to allocate subsidies to athletes based on an identification of the disciplines/events with a 'high potential' for success was unprecedented. It was noted by an officer in the Competitive Sports Division that they intended to demand 'an "immediate outcome" by Athens, by Turin, and Beijing' (Interview E, 18 August 2005). To meet the expectations of 'immediate outcomes' stated in the 'Nippon Revival Project' and the political objective of winning 3.5 per cent of Olympic medals, the above cited interviewee explained that the concept of 'Revival' proved controversial. Although there were those in government who interpreted 'revival' to mean the revival of sports in which Japan had previously excelled, such as gymnastics, the prevailing view was that the objective was to 'revive the level of success achieved in the 1964 Tokyo Games' (Interview E, 18 August 2005) through success in the sports identified by the JOC's evaluation of national federations and the resultant prioritised sports.

There are two categories in the criteria-based evaluation undertaken by the JOC's Information Strategy Section: Category I is a quantitative evaluation, mainly based on past achievement in international championships, Olympic Games, and world rankings (points awarded range between 12 and 20); and Category II, which is a qualitative evaluation of those NFs that have fewer than 12 points but which are recognised by the JOC as having some emergent international quality athletes or having a strong youth/junior development system (NAASH, 2003). It can be observed that the JOC's discretion over the allocation of the performance budget and the identification of prioritised disciplines has strengthened in recent years. The evaluation criteria used by the JOC are consistent with the government's emphasis on the willingness of NFs to establish a long-term structured and planned TID system. The NFs are consequently being pulled in two directions, one to establish a long-term strategic approach to TID and the other to deliver an 'immediate outcome', that is, medals.

Lifestyle support and 'second career' programme • • •

There is a growing awareness of the necessity of constructing a holistic talent identification and nurturing system focused on a national elite academy as perceived to be evident in other countries that have enjoyed elite sport success. As more systematic and scientific approaches to the identification of talent have been promoted, the more the idea of the holistic development of athletes in society has become recognised. However, the desire for the systematic development of talented athletes is challenged by growing criticism of the excessive hours of training that athletes of junior high and high school age undertake and of a 'trade-off' between study and training (Kono, 2003; Saeki, 2006). Kono, a member of the Board and Science/Medical Committee in the JOC and a sports doctor, stressed the necessity of establishing a programme to nurture and develop the character, intellectual and communication skills of athletes (including cross-cultural and presentation skills), and the ability to maintain emotional balance and independent control over their training (Kono, 2003, p. 27; see also Katstuta, 2007). As can be found in such innovative talent identification programmes as the 'Fukuoka Sports Talent Scout Project' (more details below), the objective of the development of physical abilities from an early age is complemented by the holistic approach to young and elite athletes which emphasises the development of conceptual and intellectual skills which have become increasingly recognised as significant for the successful development of young athletes.

In relation to senior athletes, in particular, the career management and career development of young athletes has become more focused in recent years. The JOC established a 'Second Career Project' in 2004 as one of its Athlete Programmes designed to provide 'an environment where athletes can devote themselves to training' (JOC, 2001) and opened a designated website in November 2005 (http://www.joc-athlete.jp/index.php). From 2005, the Competitive Sports Division of MEXT also provided a subsidy of ¥8 million for research to develop a comprehensive support programme for athletes which resulted in the Athlete Career Transition Programme delivered by a specialist recruitment agency. While the term 'second career' implies that it is only concerned with the post-retirement career of athletes, the project is not only focused on career transition, but is also concerned with educational programmes for junior and top athletes. Similar schemes in Australia, the United Kingdom, Canada, and the United States were researched, in particular the 'Athlete Career Education Programme' (ACE) of the Australian Institute of Sport which was seen as a model of good practice (Tanaka, 2004, pp. 54–55). However, although the necessity to investigate the issue of post-athletic career and transition had been recognised, empirical research on athletes' experiences after their retirement remains absent. As Saeki (2006, p. 1) rightly argues, by comparison to the growing salience of early years TID, 'the development of second careers has been marginalised' and the extent to which a sports career is 'socio-culturally valued' remains to be seen.

Developments in coaching

The intention to develop coaches and sport (PE) instructors[5] in an organised and systematic manner at the national level goes back to 1965, a year after the Tokyo Olympic Games. However, progress in turning the 'intention' into practical policy regarding the development of high-performance coaches seemed to have suffered due to the reduction of governmental subsidies to sport during the 1970s (JASA, 1986, pp. 154–155). In 1986, the ACHPE set up by the Ministry of Education emphasised the need to increase the quality of coaches/instructors to meet the 'diversified and sophisticated needs' of sports participation and also 'to obtain social trust' by which was meant increasing the status and quality of coaches in the eyes of the general public (ACHPE, 1986). ACHPE then proposed the establishment of a nationally recognised certification system by setting criteria for competency and 'guaranteeing the knowledge and technical skills of coaches' as well as a national 'data bank for coaches' (ACHPE, 1986). Responding to the recommendations of ACHPE, JASA, in 1988, redesigned and implemented courses leading to government recognised certificates for the development not only of coaches and sport instructors at the community level, but also of coaches concerned with the 'development of international competitiveness' (JASA, 2004a). Because JASA had had a responsibility for the promotion of *both* community sport and elite level success (until its separation from the JOC in 1990) its focus was directed to developing certified coaches/instructors across a broad range of levels of athletic ability.

The need for a sharper focus on elite coach development was highlighted in the 2000 *Basic Plan*. As a result, JASA was required to collaborate with NFs to redevelop the coaching programme so as to 'allow coaches the effective acquisition of knowledge in the athlete development programme' (JASA, 2004a, pp. 5–6) in order to meet the needs of elite athletes. Due to a period of administrative reorganisation within central government, the 'Certified Sports Instructor System' developed by JASA was only given the status of a non-governmentally recognised certificate in 2002. It could therefore be argued that the certificate had been downgraded which prompted JASA to start (re-)conceptualising the profile of the 'desirable sport coach/instructor' to redesign the system yet again (JASA, 2001, 2004b). However, despite the increasing emphasis on elite sport success, JASA continued to stress the goal of realising 'lifelong participation in sport' and the consequent necessity of developing 'a high quality instructor who can develop each individual's skill to enjoy sport culture' (JASA, 2004a, p. 10), namely, a coach with generic skills rather than with the particular skills needed to support elite athletes.

As regards the needs of elite athletes, the Competitive Sports Division recognised not only the unsuitability of the certificate system provided by JASA in 1988 for the development of highly skilled coaches, but also the absence of a structure to systematically develop specialised elite coaches (MEXT, 2002). In 2001, the Competitive Sports Division invested in establishing a training system for nurturing and maintaining coaches with specific experience in working with high-performance athletes. Further investment followed in 2003 aimed at placing two national professional coaches in each national federation (46 coaches had been placed in 30 sport disciplines as of 2005–2006) and to developing 5,000 specialists (coaches, sport doctors, athletic trainers) (MEXT, 2003). The development of specialist coaches is the responsibility of the JOC and it is intended that the process of coach development will take place at the National Coaching Academy which will be located in the new NTC (JOC, 2001, 2002). It is intended that the specialist training system for top-level coaches will enable them to acquire the 'advanced specialised skills' which they can then use within their own sports to 'construct a strategy in accordance with an international competition standard and plan and organise training programmes by applying the knowledge of sports science and medicine' (MEXT, 2002).

Despite recent investment in coach development, it is acknowledged that Japanese elite coaching remains considerably underdeveloped and there is consequently a dependency on importing foreign coaches, especially for ball games. The shortage of 'home grown' elite level coaches was pointed out by one high-performance committee member in the JOC who noted that there are very few Japanese coaches who are 'exported' and internationally recognised (Interview F, 24 August 2005). This point was illustrated by the comment from Masayo Imura, the ex-synchronised swimming national head coach whose team gained medals in all Olympic Games from 1984 to 2004, when she revealed that one of the reasons for accepting the position of coach to the Chinese national team in preparation for the Beijing Games was that: 'it would be the best chance to increase the international status of Japanese coaching' (*Mainichi News Paper*, 24 December 2006). Indeed, a clear secondary objective of the coach development strategy is to produce top-level international coaches who will then gain easier access to globally disseminated information and tactics and also be influential in the decision-making of the international sporting federations (JOC, 2002).

Talent identification system and the development of potential athletes[6]

While the concept and importance of talent identification was recognised prior to the Tokyo Olympic Games in 1964, and has been a constant theme during the latter half of the twentieth century, the operationalisation of a structured TID programme at prefectural/municipal level has only recently been recognised in Japan with the first example of a structured TID programme being introduced in the Fukuoka prefecture in 2003. The acceptance of the need for a systematic approach to talent identification was a result of the criticism of a training and coaching system which was fragmented between schools, universities, and corporate teams and identified as 'one of the causes of the decline of international competitiveness' (MEXT, 2000, p. 15; JOC, 2001). According to MEXT, the dominant pyramid-shaped selection method has limitations, not least because of the rapid decline in the birth-rate and the consequent overall decrease in participation in sport and 'human resources at the national level' which is making it increasingly difficult to find talented young people who can be developed to elite level (MEXT, 2006a).

Overall, the Japanese approach to youth talent identification is fragmented and relies too heavily on private corporations and schools to support potential elite athletes. Neither the corporations nor the schools are systematic with a long-term view or coordinated in what they do. They also tend to act independently of NFs. Furthermore, while a substantial proportion of the annual budget for *Kokutai* has been allocated by municipal authorities to talent identification, the sector remains unsystematic largely relying on school clubs and teachers, especially PE teachers, to take responsibility for coaching school teams and the identification of talented young athletes. PE teachers were also criticised by the project leader responsible for establishing a model of talent development in the JOC for their short term interest in 'winning' (Gamo, quoted in JOC, 2003a, p. 14). Due to the nature of *Kokutai* as an inter-prefectural competition, it is imperative to note the difficulty of achieving cooperation between prefectures and thus contributing to the establishment of a coherent TID system at the regional and national levels.

Following the establishment of JISS, the systematic identification of talented children was seen as the essential basis for sustaining long-term international competitiveness. The 'JISS–JOC Information Strategy Project' played a core role in researching examples of TID programmes developed in other countries and in designing a TID programme for Japan (JISS, 2005, p. 68). The 'Fukuoka Sports Talent Scout Project' was introduced in 2004 as the first example of the systematic selection of children from years 4 and 5 (age 9–11 as 'Fukuoka Kids') and year 6 (age 11–12 as 'Fukuoka Juniors') based on physical testing and scientific and genetic data. Fukuoka Action, the prefectural high-performance sport centre, manages the programme where the selected Fukuoka Kids and Juniors can experience multiple disciplines to develop basic physical skills and later be advised on the one or two 'most suitable disciplines' for specialisation (Tanaka, 2005).

This project is significant for three reasons: first, the initiative came from a prefectural government and may indicate a gradual change in the composition of the elite sport policy community. Earlier comments about inter-prefectural rivalry notwithstanding, it offers the prospect of cross-prefectural/institutional cooperation to complement the cooperation between JISS, JOC, and NFs at the national level. Second, the implementation of talent identification and selection programmes at the prefectural level have to be consistent with the broad policy objective of promoting lifelong participation in sport. As stated in the prefectural policy document, *Basic Plan for Fukuoka Sports Promotion* (2003) and as emphasised by a senior officer of Fukuoka Action, the TID programme needed a mass participation rationale. He commented that terms like 'talent', 'selection', and 'elite' are controversial due particularly to the programme being operationalised by a quasi-governmental agency at prefectural level (Fukuoka Action) and that they needed to be legitimated by connecting with the promotion of citizens' sport participation, educational purposes, and the provisions of opportunities to every child (at the first selection stage at least) (Interview F, 9 May 2006).

Thirdly, and related to the second point, this project is significant insofar as it intends to develop not only the physical abilities of selected children, but also their intellectual abilities and personal competencies, including logical thinking, knowledge of nutrition, and communication skills. This reflects the extent to which the project is based on the development of young talented athletes 'holistically' with a long-term perspective taking precedence over the short-term, thus avoiding the elite athlete 'trade-off' between academic work and sport training. As this project is still in its infancy, its effectiveness in producing medal-winning athletes remains to be seen. However, the accumulated knowledge in TID has already been disseminated to 'interested' prefectural/municipal governments or education departments. Although there are differences in objectives and delivery, the rationale developed for the Fukuoka project appears to have influenced other prefectures such as Wakayama, Okayama, and Yamagata, and the district government of Bifuka in Hokkaido all of which have decided to implement and operationalise a similar TID programme (JISS, 2007).

Competition opportunities for young athletes

The major international competitions to which the JOC sends squads include the summer and winter Olympic Games, the

Asian Games, the East Asian Games, and the Universiade. However, the coordination of the national competition structure in order to provide opportunities for talented and potential upcoming young athletes to prepare for international competitions is proving problematic for the JOC. Although the JOC organises the Junior Olympic Cup, which is part of its Junior Development Programme, and is defined as 'the pinnacle of junior-level sport' (JOC, 2003b), the JOC's proposal to reform the East Asian Games into the top junior athlete competition has been postponed (j-net, 21 June 2006) and overall the domestic competition opportunities and structures for young athletes are fragmented.

The scheduling of domestic (*Kokutai* and inter-collegiate/ school games and events) and international competitions is seen as conflicting in terms of the different interests and values held by the various organisations and agencies. In particular, the policy priority of the prefectural governments and their PE Associations with regard to *Kokutai* is to produce the best set of results and is seen as an inter-prefectural competition rather than a national championship which is part of an elite development strategy. In the absence of a long-term vision of national athlete development, the primary concern within most prefectures was to use the budget to construct facilities and prepare athletes in order to do better than other prefectures.

The different perceptions of *Kokutai* are illustrated by the recurring conflict, from the late 1960s through to the 1980s, between the Minister of Education and JASA on the one hand and the educational organisations and teachers on the other over the criteria for participation. Whereas the former bodies would have liked to lower the age limit in order to raise the level of international performances through *Kokutai*, the educationalists have proved to be unsympathetic due to their perception of participation in *Kokutai* as a distraction from 'students' normal schooling' (Morikawa, 1988, p. 27; Seki, 1997; Takahasi and Takimoto, 1996). A senior member of the JOC identified the issue of 'gypsy' athletes who transferred from one prefecture to the other in order to help the host prefecture to win *Kokutai* as also undermining the contribution of *Kokutai* to national athlete development (Interview G, 12 April 2005).

The absence of a substantial number of elite athletes who prefer to train or take part in the international Grand Prix circuit, the decline in popularity of, and media attention given to, *Kokutai* combined with the expansion in the number of participants and the increased infrastructure costs prompted JASA to propose a reform plan for *Kokutai* (JASA, 2003). Interestingly, the reform plan is intended to make *Kokutai* the highest domestic sport competition with a higher level of competition and focused on the Olympic disciplines combined with a 15 per cent reduction in the number of athletes. With the lowering of the participation age limit to include junior-high students (age 14–15 years), JASA recognised *Kokutai* as the stage to identify and develop junior athletes (JASA, 2003, pp. 8, 18). The most significant element in the reform plan was to allow athletes already competing at international level to participate without preliminary competition and to reschedule the *Kokutai* calendar by integrating the summer and autumn games and thereby enabling more athletes to participate in both international competitions and *Kokutai*. This attempt to resolve the tension between the national and international competition calendars is crucial. In the words of one JOC member, 'it's nonsense to chase the schedule … Japan needs to adjust its schedule to the international one' (Interview G, 12 April 2005). In conclusion, although the reform of *Kokutai* reflects its slow decline it also indicates JASA's concern to maintain its organisational interest in elite sporting success and the development of junior athletes.

Distinctive features of the Japanese elite sport system

While many features of the Japanese elite sport development system correspond to the four dimensions identified by Green and Houlihan (2005), Japan possesses at least one distinctive feature which illustrates processes of policy learning and policy transfer.

The significance of intelligence gathering and the development of a communication network

The establishment of an effective communication network involving actors across all levels of sport and the strategic utilisation of information have become *the* most distinctive features of the Japanese system for developing elite athletes. The facilitation of the sharing of ideas, information, and experience within Japan is organised by JISS and the JOC which are also both responsible for the strategic gathering of information from other countries and its incorporation into debates on elite sport policy. Developed from inter-sport discipline collaborations initiated in the late 1990s,[7] the emphasis given to network-building, the exchange of ideas, information and good practice, and the accumulation of knowledge intensified when JISS formed the Department of Sports Information in 2001, which was encouraged to work closely with the Information Strategy Section of the JOC's Information and Medical Science Special

Committee. These two specialist sections coordinate their work and deal with the technical and strategic aspects of elite sport policy.

One of the most significant features of the work of these sections in JISS and the JOC is that they anchor the ambitious initiative to establish a comprehensive information network which includes local, regional and national sport organisations, academic research organisations and international bodies, through a communication network which relies on email circulations, personal contacts, occasional conferences, forums and seminars, and informal meetings. Effective systematic TID has gradually been recognised as the essential core policy for the long-term success of Japanese elite sport. Crucial to the success of this strategy is the network-building, strategic planning, and analysis through the exchange of information, and sharing of knowledge and resources at the regional and local levels. The data obtained from other countries are analysed by the Sports Information Department to provide not only assessments of Japanese competitiveness, but also details of the different models of talent identification adopted in other counties for specific sports which the JOC then uses to influence both sport-specific policy and national policy (Katsuta et al., 2005b).

The 'information strategy' is perceived as an 'intelligence gathering' activity which according to an interviewee in the JOC can be seen as similar to the services provided by a 'think-tank' or the work of intelligence agencies such as the CIA (Interview F, 1 April 2005). It was also suggested that the function of intelligence gathering was not simply to help set the priorities in elite sport policy, but to influence policy decision-making, particularly at the state level by producing advocates for elite sport programmes who were well informed (Waku, 2005). In addition, the importance of intelligence activities needs to be understood in relation to the geographical position of Japan and the concern that the country is remote from the dominant elite international sport communities located in Europe and North America. This concern was highlighted by one JISS official:

With regard to information, it is more or less borderless. However, … Japan is isolated [from Europe] and also from information. Yet, in the world sporting community, sharing information is taken for granted and from the shared information, [they] consider the next step. Japan had drifted away from this trend, I mean, Japan was way behind this trend (Interview I, 18 March 2005).

There is a strong perception of a world trend in the development of high-performance sport and support provision. However, there is a clear intention to build an international network not only to identify good practice and adapt it to the Japanese context, but also to disseminate selected information from JISS to equivalent bodies in other countries (JISS, 2005, pp. 88–89). This practice of putting 'information' at the core has resulted in, intentionally or unintentionally, stimulating the emergence of a previously latent advocacy coalition for elite sport which, through the intensifying of information exchange, has the potential to develop a view of the preferred elite athlete development system in Japan.

Conclusion

There are three factors that help us to understand the emergence of the priority currently accorded to elite sport policy in Japan. First, the catalyst for policy change and the commitment of government is mainly based on exogenous factors, namely, consecutive poor performances in international sporting events (Olympic Games and Asian Games). Nevertheless, elite sport policy objectives, though of increasing salience to government, need to compete with policy objectives related to improving lifelong participation in sport and PE in school. Indeed, children and young people's participation and their level of physical fitness is steadily rising up the contemporary agenda of the ministry (MEXT) and is prompting some tension with elite sport objectives.

Second, the government maintains the dominant role in shaping and specifying the direction of elite sport policy, in part, through its control over the distribution of financial resources particularly for the construction of elite sport specialist facilities. The role and influence of national elite sport organisations (JISS, JOC, and NFs) is substantially determined by the government due to the fragility of their funding base, their high dependence on public resources, their lack of significant organisational autonomy, and their strict accountability to the state. Although JISS and the JOC can be seen as direct agents of government elite policy, following Sabatier (1993), it should be borne in mind that the elite sport policy subsystem plays a significant role in translating government policy into elite sport policy programmes and in supporting the development of particular sports and individual athletes. In other words, there is still considerable scope to interpret governmental policy at the 'street level'. However, this is not to downplay the dominant role of government in the elite sport policy process. This last point leads to the third characteristic which is the engagement in policy-oriented learning by national elite sport agencies and the transfer and adaptation of good practice from other countries to the Japanese context. The systematic accumulation and analysis of information and data by the specialist departments in JISS and the JOC is particularly designed to improve systems of TID at the municipal/prefectural levels and among national sports federations.

Notes

1 In 1986, the Japan Physical Education and School Health Centre (JPESHC) was created through the merger of three national agencies: the Japan School Lunch Agency, Japan School Safety Agency, and the National Stadium. A further restructuring took place in 2001 with the JPESHC being replaced by NAASH.
2 The *Basic Plan for the Promotion of Sport*, published in 2001, defined the value of sport as to 'realise a bright, fulfilling, and vital society in the twenty-first century' with three objectives to increase lifelong participation in sport, high-performance success in international sport events and opportunity in Pe in schools. The revised *Basic Plan* maintains similar objectives but with a stronger emphasis on children's physical fitness.
3 Whether there will be one or a number of elite schools is yet to be decided.
4 *Kokutai* is the intra-prefectural national sporting competition held annually and coorganised by the host prefecture, JASA and MEXT. It was inaugurated in 1946 and has maintained its status as the premier national competition.
5 Caution is needed in relation to the term '*Shidousha*' which in Japanese can cover 'instructors', 'trainers', and 'coaches'.
6 'Talent identification' or 'talent selection' is used here to refer to the systematic identification of talent from a wider group of young children. The concept of TID in a systematic manner was described as the process of 'identifying, nurturing, and making use of talented human resources' (Katsuta et al., 2005a).
7 The 'Inter-Disciplinary Support Project for Ball Games' (baseball, basketball, handball, rugby union, and soccer) was launched in 1998 in order to share coaching methods and training regimes. The concept was repeated in relation to combat sports (wrestling, judo, and sumo) and artistic sports (synchronised swimming, gymnastics, and figure skating), both of which established their respective support projects in 2000.

References

ACHPE (1972) *Fundamental Policies for the Promotion of Physical Education and Sport [Taiiku-sports no Fukyu Shinkou ni kansuru Kihonteki Housaku ni tsuite]*, Tokyo: ACHPE.

ACHPE (1986) *Certificate System for Social Physical Education Instructor [Syakai Taiiku Shidousya no Shikaku Fuyo Seido ni tsuite]*, Tokyo: ACHPE.

Asami, T. (2005) Reasons behind the Japanese success in Athens Olympics *[Atene Olympic de Nippon ha naze daiyakushin sita no ka]*, *Kojyun Zasshi*, 488.

Corporate Sport Research Committee (CSRC) (2005) *Report on Exploring Partnerships Between Corporate Companies Who Sustain Future of Nippon and Sports [Nippon no mirai wo sasaeru kigyo to sports no partnership wo motomete: Hokokusyo]*, Tokyo: CSRC.

Fukuoka Board of Education (2003) *Basic Plan for Fukuoka Sports Promotion*, Hakata: Fukuoka Board of Education.

Green, M. and Houlihan, B. (2005) *Elite Sport Development: Policy Learning and Political Priorities*, London: Routledge.

Ieki, Y. (1992) *The Politics in Olympics [Olympic no Seiji-gaku]*, Tokyo: Maruzen.

JASA (1986) *75 Years History of Japan Sports Amateur Association [Nihon Taiiku Kyokai nanajyu-go nen si]*, Tokyo: JASA.

JASA (2001) *The Way to Promote Sport for All in the 21st Century [21-seki no Kokumin Sports Shinko Housaku]*, Tokyo: JASA.

JASA (2003) *Searching for a New Kokutai: Kokutai Reform 2003 [Atarashii Kokumin Taiikutaikai wo Motomete: Kokutai Kaikaku 2003]*, Tokyo: JASA.

JASA (2004a) *Development of Sports Instructors in the Future [Korekara no Sports Shidousya Ikusei Jigyo no Suishin Housaku]*, Tokyo: JASA.

JASA (2004b) *21st Century Sports Instructors [21-seiki no Sports Instructor]*, Tokyo: JASA.

JISS (2004a) *Quarterly News Letter Summer 2004*, Tokyo: JISS.

JISS (2004b) *Quarterly News Letter Autumn 2004*, Tokyo: JISS.

JISS (2005) *Annual Report 2004*, Tokyo: JISS.

JISS (2007) *Quarterly News Letter Spring 2007*, Tokyo: JISS.

JOC (2001) *Gold Plan*, Tokyo: JOC.

JOC (2002) *2001 Coach Conference Report [Heisei-13-nen-do Coach Kaigi Houkoku-sho]*, Tokyo: JOC.

JOC (2003a) *Manual for Talent Development Programme [Kyogisya Ikusei Programme Sakutei Manual]*, Tokyo: JOC.

JOC (2003b) *Sports in Japan '02–'03*, Tokyo: JOC.

JOC (2006) *Gold Plan Stage II*, Tokyo: JOC.

JTL (2006) *Cooperative Organization of Japan Top Leagues* (available in PowerPoint), Tokyo: JTL.

Katsuta, T., Awaki, K., Konishi, Y., Waku, T. and Gamo, S. (2005a) The Study of the Talent Detection Programme, *Sendai Daigaku Kiyo*, pp. 50–58.

Katsuta, T., Awaki, K., Kukidome, T., Kawai, Y., Waku, T., Nakayama, M. and Kono, I. (2005b) The Systematic Information Strategy Activities of Japan Olympic Committee, *Sendai Daigaku Kiyu*, pp. 59–69.

Katsuta, T. (2007) The Way to Find and Develop Top Athletes: Challenge for talent identification programme and its meaning *[Top athlete no mitsuke kata, sodate kata: Talent ha-kutsu jigyo heno chosen to sono igi]*, *Taiiku ka Kyoiku*, January, 26–31.

Kono, I. (2003) Sports environment for developing top athletes *[Ima, nozomareru top athlete wo sodateru sports kankyo]*, *Taiiku ka Kyoiku*, January.

Mainichi News Paper, 24 December 2006.

MESSC (1992) *White Paper, Japanese Government Policies in Education, Science and Culture 1992*, Tokyo: MESSC.

MESSC (1998) *White Paper, Japanese Government Policies in Education, Science and Culture 1998*, Tokyo: MESSC.

MEXT (2000) *Basic Plan for the Promotion of Sport: 2000–2010*, Tokyo: MEXT.

MEXT (2002) *MEXT Policy Evaluation of 2001 [Monbu Kagaku-syo Jisseki Hyoukasyo: Heisei-13-nen-do Jisseki]*, Tokyo: MEXT.

MEXT (2003) *MEXT Policy Evaluation of 2002 [Monbu Kagaku-syo Jisseki Hyoukasyo: Heisei-14-nen-do Jisseki]*, Tokyo: MEXT.

MEXT (2005) *National Training Center: Centralized Facility* (pamphlet), Tokyo: MEXT.

MEXT (2006a) *Basic Plan for the Promotion of Sport: 2000–2010* (revised), Tokyo: MEXT.

MEXT (2006b) *Evaluation on Effectiveness of Policy for Increasing International Competitive [Kokutai kyogiryoku koujou sesaku no koka ni kansuru hyoka ni tsuite]*, Tokyo: MEXT.

MEXT (2006c) FY2007 Demand for Budget on National Training Center, Available at http://www.mext.go.jp/a_menu/hyouka/kekka/06091508/089.pdf (accessed 16 June 2007).

Morikawa, S. (1986) Reading 'Sports Charter' *['Sports Kenshou' wo yomu]*, *Taiiku ka Kyoiku*, August, 52–53.

Morikawa, S. (1988) Competitive sports and lifelong participation in sports: With main consideration on the management of *Kokutai [Kyougi sports to syogai sports no aida: Kokumin Taiiku Taikai no arikata wo tyuushin ni kangaeru]*, *Taiiku Ka Kyoiku Zoukan Gou*, November, 26–29.

NAASH (2003) *Selection for Prioritized Sports to Allocate Sports Promotion Fund, 2003 [Heisei 16-nendo Jyutenkyougi kyoka katsudou jyosei ni okeru taisyou kyougi shyumoku no sentei nit suite]* (circulated material), Tokyo: NAASH.

Nakamura, Y. (1992) Public Administration of National Physical Training in the War Period *[Senjika no 'Kokumin Taiiku Gyo-sei': Koseisyo tairyoku-kyoku ni yoru taiiku gyo-sei sesaku wo chyu-shin ni*], *Waseda Journal Human Sciences*, 5(1), 123–139.

NTC Research Committee (2004) *Report on the Establishment of National Training Centre [National Training Centre no secchi tou no arikata ni kansuru cho-sa kenkyu (houkoku)]*, Tokyo: NTC Research Committee.

Uchiumi, K. (1993) *The Establishment of Post-ward Sports System [Sengo Sports Taisei no Kakuritsu]*, Tokyo: Fumaido.

Sabatier, P. (1993) Policy change over a decade or more, in P.A. Sabatier and H.C. Jenkins-Smith (eds.), *Policy Change and Learning: An Advocacy Coalition Approach*, Colorado: Westview Press, 13–39.

Saeki, T. (2006) Project overview *[Project no zentai kousou]*, *Development of Top Athlete Second Career Education*, Tokyo: Tsukuba University.

Seki, H. (1997) *The Post-war Sports Policy in Japan: Its Structure and Development [Sengo Nippon no Sports Seisaku: sono kouzou to tenkai]*, Tokyo: Taishyukan.

Takahasi, N. and Tokimoto, T. (1996) Development of physical education and sport through *Kokutai*: An analysis of speech given by Ministers of Education *[Kokumin Taiiku Taikai ni okeru waga kuni no Taiiku/Sports no Hensen ni tsuite]*, *Sangyo Kenkyu Journal (Takasaki Keizai University)*, 1(32), 52–85.

Tanaka, M.U. (2004) Cases of second career support in major NOCs *[Kaigai syuyo NOC ni okeru Second Career Shien Programme no ji-rei]*, *JOC Olympian*, Autumn, 54–55.

Tanaka, S. (2005) Sports Institute Action Fukuoka: Fukuoka Talent Identification Project *[Chiiki ni okeru Sports Kagaku Center Action Fukuoka: 'Fukuoka Talent Hakkutsu Jigyo' nit suite]*, *Rinsyo Sports Igaku (The Journal of Clinical Sports Medicine)*, 22(4), 381–389.

Waku, T. (2005) Activities of Department of Sports Information in JISS *[Kokuritsu Sports Kagaku Center: Sports Jyoho Kenkyu-bu no Katsudo]*, *Rinsyo Sports Igaku (The Journal of Clinical Sports Medicine)*, 22(4), 367–371.

Singapore

Lionel Teo

Introduction

Throughout the country's short history since gaining independence in 1965, the Singapore government has invariably featured sport in the progress of the island city-state. Sport policy has been utilised as an instrument for fostering social cohesion and national identity (independence to 1970s), and also for the promotion of health and fitness, and national identity objectives (1980s to 1990s), to the more recent effort of nation-building and international recognition (Horton, 2002; McNeill et al., 2003). The People's Action Party's (PAP) pragmatic and paternalistic style of government has guided Singapore from the shadow of colonialism to attain developed country status within just four decades, and it is with this same hegemonic attitude that sport has been used to achieve its various national objectives (Horton, 2002; Soon, 2002).

The omnipresent *Sport for All* policy has recently been eclipsed by a sports excellence strategy that 'embraces the projection of successful sporting individuals as national heroes and heroines' (Horton, 2001, p. 97). From the early 1990s, the government embarked on a vigorous campaign to capitalise on the extensive global value of elite sport to the nation. According to McNeill et al., 'while sport has been instrumental in the process of nation building, it has only recently reached a level of cultural significance as a potential means for highlighting the nation's international status' (2003, p. 39). Within the span of 40 years, elite sport policy in Singapore has advanced from a peripheral pastime to one which today is high on the government's political agenda (Robert, 1998).

Elite sport (or sports excellence) development in Singapore underwent a sea change with the decision by government to appoint a Minister of Sports in April 2000 (Singapore Sports Council, SSC, 2000; Thomas, 2000a). According to the Chief Executive Officer (CEO) of the SSC, 'Singapore may be small but the heart and the appetite is big. When the government wants to move on a project, it is done with logic and with energy' (quoted in Roberts, 2005, p. 4). In what is perhaps *the* defining moment, the decision by government to take the lead was a significant milestone for the sports community (see Figure 4.1), and one that has legitimised the promotion of elite sport to unprecedented levels in Singapore.

The chapter is informed by interviews with senior officers or secretariat staff who have been in post for a number of years and involved with policy planning and decision-making responsibilities. They include one senior management executive from the SSC and two senior-ranking secretariat officials from the Singapore Athletics Association.

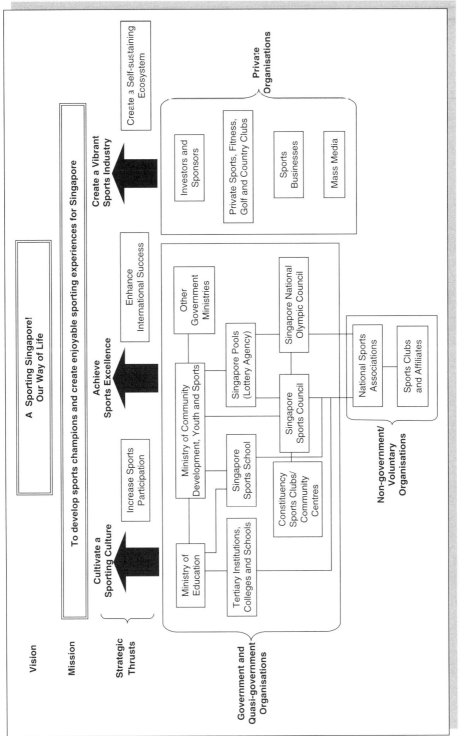

Figure 4.1 Schematic representation of the Sports Community and the Sporting Vision of Singapore

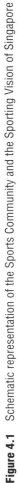

Development of sports excellence in Singapore

The early self-governing years highlighted the government's urgency to establish stability and security amid a period of racial unrest, sectional communalism and uncertainties posed by de-colonialisation (Turnbull, 1982; Chen, 1983). Sport was used instrumentally in the government's effort to endure this turbulent phase with the early establishment of the Sports Division unit within the Ministry of Social Affairs (SSC, 2005a). The unit adopted the 'pyramid model' with the main aim of organising mass, community-based sport and recreational activities, although the then Minister also encouraged it to 'turn out champions of the future' (quoted in Horton, 2002, p. 253).

The emphasis on community level activities reinforced the government's pressing need to build a 'Singaporean identity' owing to the heterogeneous and pluralistic make-up of the population (Chiew, 1983; Perry et al., 1997). Of significance to sport development was the incorporation of Singapore Pools, a wholly government-owned lottery agency, in 1968. Set up to control illegal gambling, the agency had a secondary role of donating surpluses gained from lottery takings 'Towards Community Purpose and Benefit' (its motto) (Singapore Pools, 2005). Lottery funds would prove to be a critical benefactor for elite sport infrastructure, programmes and support in the country.

During the 1970s and 1980s, with economic progress underway, government emphasis turned to providing facilities and activities for mass sport participation and encouraging a healthy and productive society (McNeill et al., 2003). Of significance was the establishment of the Singapore National Olympic Council (SNOC) in 1970 and the SSC in 1973, signalling the government's determination to regulate and provide direction to the promotion of sports in the nation (SSC, 1983).

Coupled with prolonged low sport participation levels was the SSC's discovery of widening competitive standards between local athletes and those from competing countries (Teo, 2002). More alarming was the Singaporean's growing custom with affluence and penchant for social status in the wake of sustained growth in the 1970s and early 1980s (Lim, 1983). In spite of the government's early efforts at promoting the benefits of sport and healthy lifestyles, these benefits remained of relatively low importance to the locals, especially parents, who were more intent on encouraging their children to undertake more conventional careers (Turnbull, 1982). Confronted with these barriers to participation, an Advisory Council on Sports and Recreation was commissioned, and in 1989, it published its report to the SSC 'calling for a concerted national effort to promote constituency sports, enhance sports excellence, improve employment prospects of sports-persons and promote sports that challenge' (SSC, 1994, p. 127).

The 1990s proved to be a significant period for sport in Singapore, marked by the transfer of political power to second-generation PAP leaders, for 'the nature of the discourse of sport used by leading politicians' (Horton, 2002, p. 258) and particularly for a perceptible sea change in emphasis towards elite sport development. Buoyed by 25 years of economic growth, social stability and steady leadership, the country experienced unprecedented levels of affluence and quality of life that stirred expectations of western ideals and political liberalisation from among a growing middle class (Chen, 1983). To a large extent, the government successfully addressed this with a well-managed transfer of political leadership that professed a 'more caring and consultative' style of governing (Perry et al., 1997, p. 84). In his manifesto, *Singapore: The Next Lap*, the new Prime Minister outlined his vision for a more gracious culture 'to make Singapore one of the major hub cities of the world' (Government of Singapore, 1991, p. 6) and, more significantly, reiterated the government's categorical support for Sport for All *and* sports excellence.

The new government advocated a two-pronged approach to sport policy: one centred on the well-being and collective benefits of exercise through mass sport participation and the other based on the perception that local sporting champions would augur well in the next lap with Prime Minister Goh Chok Tong affirming that 'The contribution of sports to nation building and national pride is far-reaching. When Singapore athletes win medals at international sports competitions, they bring immense pride and joy to our people' (quoted in SSC, 1998a, p. 8).

There are several points in the above observations which, it could be argued, were catalytic for elite sport development in Singapore. First, government was eager for the cultural aspects of society to rise in tandem with the nation's economic achievements (SSC, 1998a). Second, sport would play a greater role in the government's aspiration for the island to be a world-class, developed city with positive participation and health rates. Although not a novel strategy per se, the fact that the PAP now regarded it as having 'a national dimension' holds promise for the future of sport development in the country. Finally, the SSC's quest for international sporting glory now had the legitimacy and patronage from the nation's Prime Minister.

In June 1993, Singapore athletes delivered one of the nation's best-ever performances in the South East Asian (SEA) Games winning 164 (50 gold) medals. The *Sport for All* policy remained a central focus but 'the accent on sports excellence was beginning to find a voice all its own' (SSC, 1994, p. 20). A key moment for Singapore sport was the publication of *Sports Excellence 2000 (SPEX 2000): Winning for Singapore* in December 1993 accompanied by a four-fold increase in annual government funding of $SGD10 million from the government, Singapore Pools and sponsors over the next 5 years (Ministry of Community Development, MCD, 1993). *SPEX 2000* was a comprehensive policy document that sets out an ambitious inventory of schemes to advance elite sport in the country, formulated on 'a proactive and focussed approach in promoting sport excellence' (MCD, 1993, p. 7). Pragmatically, the SSC chose to focus on certain sports from which potential for success was greatest, with 'inclusion in the Asian Games or the Olympics, strong medal-winning potential', and 'sound administrative infrastructure' as some of the main criteria for selection (MCD, 1993, p. 11). Seven 'Core Sports' were identified to receive 'intensive development' (approximately $SGD900,000 each annually) while another seven 'Merit Sports' were selected for 'enhanced support' ($SGD400,000 annual cap) (SSC, 1995; Chan, 2002a).

Against this background, supported heavily by lottery funds, the SNOC introduced the *Multi-million Dollar Award Programme* which comprised an attractive range of cash incentives to reward gold medal performances at SEA Games (gold medal worth $SGD10,000) through to Asian, Commonwealth and Olympic levels (where a gold medal was worth an extraordinary $SGD1 million (£330,000)) (MCD, 1993). By the mid-1990s, the SSC had in place a number of financial schemes to support its budding crop of elite athletes. The Sports Aid Fund, which by 1990 had grown to $SGD6 million, was available for disbursement to athletes and coaches to excel in sport (Khoo, 1990; SSC, 1996). There were also significant funding increases for talent assistance awards – from $SGD3,000 to $SGD8,000 in the case of elite athletes – and a surge in applications for grants for loss of wages so that athletes could take time off work to prepare for major competition. The National Coaching Accreditation Programme (NCAP) was launched to cater for coaches from all national sport associations (NSAs) and improvements were made to better equip and expand the central Sports Medicine, Fitness and Research Centre to serve the objectives of *SPEX 2000* (SSC, 1998b).

With *SPEX 2000*, a more active and systematic infrastructure was now in place to identify and nurture talented athletes rather than for them to surface through the pyramid model. Sport was now perceived as having a highly functional social and political purpose while size and population of the country were no longer considered hindrances to the production of champions. The Ministry of Community Development and Sports (MCDS) rationalised the government's rethink on elite sport development in stating that:

The reason we are proposing the creation of an environment for sports excellence is not because others are doing it per se, but because it is one of the missing pieces, that verbalises, illustrates and energises a matter of the heart: national pride and international respect.

(MCDS, 2001, p. 5)

At this point, it is pertinent to point out that Singapore, *as an independent nation*, has yet to win a medal at the Olympic Games. A local-born did win a silver medal in weightlifting at the 1960 Rome Olympics (SNOC, 2005) but the modern generation of Singaporeans, it is maintained, have little or no recollection of that achievement and thus lack the emotional attachment (Sia, 1994; Koh, 1999). On the other hand, Singapore has produced several modern-day, world-class single-sport champions of her own – in bowling, *silat* (a form of martial art), bodybuilding and darts (Yap, 1999) and several more who are notably ranked among the top 20 in their respective sport. The country also boasts a world-record in the 50 metre swimming freestyle event (SSC, 2005a). Yet, it is arguably on the Olympic podium that the public yearn for a champion they can truly call their own, and one that the government expects will inspire more to participate in sport.

The appointment of a Sports Minister in April 2000 was a significant milestone. *SPEX 2000* was re-launched as *SPEX21* to reflect the challenges in the new millennium (SSC, 2001). Still, the elusive triumph on the Olympic platform remained a key objective at the heart of the sport excellence initiatives and prompted the Prime Minister to lay the sports fraternity these challenges: (a) a medal in sailing at the 2008 Olympic Games; (b) to secure qualification in the 2012 Thomas Cup finals for badminton and (c) a place in the Asian Group for the football World Cup in 2010 (Goh, 1999).

The campaign for elite sport development took another considerable step with the establishment of the *Committee on Sporting Singapore (CoSS)*, tasked by the MCDS to formulate a strategic blueprint for the future of Singapore sports policy (Chan, 2000b; SSC, 2002). Chaired by the Sports Minister, the committee's proceedings reflected the familiar PAP hegemony internalised in all aspects of Singapore's development thus far (Horton, 2002). The *CoSS* report centred on the vision of a *Sporting Singapore* culture, to be built upon three strategic thrusts: sporting excellence, Sports for All and a vibrant sports industry (Franklin,

2001; SSC, 2002). Signalling its unequivocal endorsement for sport development in Singapore, the government and Singapore Pools jointly committed $SGD500 million for the next 5 years to implement the proposals (MCDS, 2003). In addition, the Prime Minister identified three specific goals connected to the pillars of sports: (1) to achieve a 50 per cent nationwide sports participation rate by 2005; (2) for Singapore to be among the top 10 sporting nations in Asia by 2010 and (3) to double the value of the sports industry from $SGD680 million to $SGD1.4 million by 2010 (Chan, 2001a, b).

As noted by Green and Houlihan (2005, p. 2), 'governments have shown a considerable willingness to devote significant sums of public or government controlled money to the maintenance or improvement of elite sporting success' and this is clearly evident in the case of Singapore. The new budget represents a substantial financial boost for the NSAs, particularly those managing the 'Core' (up from $SGD900,000 to $SGD3 million annually) and 'Merit' sports (from a $SGD400,000 to a $SGD2 million cap) (Chan, 2002a). The SSC now had $SGD24 million per year to devote entirely to elite sport programmes, up from $SGD8 million in 1993 (MCD, 1993). Approximately $SGD200 million was set aside for the construction of the new Singapore Sports School (SSS) (Foo, 2005b) while other areas to benefit considerably were the fledgling sport industry and *Team Singapore*, the SSC's public relations campaign to get the nation behind the sporting vision (Pok, 2001; SSC, 2002).

Elite sport policy has also influenced the school sports scene. According to McNeil et al. (2003, p. 47), 'as the government began to give sport greater political consideration, schools were identified as the "spawning ground" for future champions and the NSAs were encouraged to make funds, facilities and expertise available for developing school sport'. In his address to policymakers, school principals and physical education teachers, the Education Minister highlighted the significance of identifying sports talent early and the need for schools to 'work in close partnership with all stakeholders, such as the SSC and NSAs … to develop a wider pool of interested students and potential talents' (Shanmugaratnam, 2006). In January 2004, the SSS opened its doors to 141 pioneer student-athletes, representing a determined endeavour by the relevant agencies to address the reluctance shown by Singaporeans to allow their children to choose a career in the sport and leisure industries.

In March 2005, the extraordinary pace and direction of change in elite sport development continued when the government declared an additional $SGD300 million for sports excellence development up to 2010 (Foo, 2005b), and revealed plans of an impending sports hub (estimated to cost $SGD650 million and targeted to be ready by 2010) that would include world-class facilities such as a new 55,000 seat stadium with retractable roof, multi-purpose indoor arena and aquatic centre (Peh, 2005). The fledgling sports industry also contributed with a series of marquee sports events of which the 117th International Olympic Committee (IOC) Session in July 2005, at which London was awarded the right to host the 2012 Olympiad, stood out (Razali, 2006). Mass sports participation levels have also increased from 32 to 48 per cent and the gross domestic product contribution to the local sports industry was $SGD696 million for the year 2004 (Tan, 2006d).

In August 2006, the SSC announced that 'it was very interested to have a Sports Institute in the sports hub ... as part of an integrated plan to achieve high performance objectives and also help Singapore win medals at the Olympic Games' (Tan, 2006b, p. 49). Elite athletes also stood to gain the most when the SNOC announced that it would set aside a $SGD5 to $SGD7 million 'war chest' to fund world-class athletes preparing for the 2008 and 2012 Olympiads (Lim, 2006; Singh, 2006). The government has laid the groundwork for Singapore's elite sport development and has put its steering authority behind the innovative quest for Olympic and international glory. The extent of such political power is evident in the increasingly reciprocal relationships between government agencies, the NSAs, and various other agencies in the sport delivery system in determining the success (or failure) of a sporting culture in Singapore.

National sport associations

One of the main findings to emerge from the *CoSS* report was the idea that strong and effective sport governing bodies played a considerable role in the sports delivery system in Singapore (Chan, 2000a; MCDS, 2001). It acknowledged that NSAs were the cornerstones for raising greater awareness and support for active membership and for the promotion of excellence in their respective sports. On the other hand, it also meant that the relationship between government and the NSAs is expected to become more intense and more significant in shaping the development of sport in Singapore.

The *CoSS* also believed that by strengthening and 'professionalising' the NSAs through management development and accountability, the various sports bodies would be able to better serve their elite and mass participation objectives and thereby help to realise the nation's sporting vision (Ng, 2000). The Sports

Minister emphasised this when stating: 'I urge the NSAs to set clear directions and goals for themselves. I would encourage all the NSAs, especially the leadership, to see this as a challenge to lead your sport and its development to the highest possible level in Singapore' (Ibrahim, 2002). Against this background, the SSC introduced the Code of Governance (COG), essentially a 'planning dictate' (Green, 2004a, p. 377), stipulating the threshold standards of corporate governance with which the NSAs had to comply as a condition for SSC funding (Wee, 2002).

The introduction of *SPEX 2000*, in 1993, marked an increase in government intervention and was a wake-up call for professionalism and rejuvenation in the operations and management of the NSAs in Singapore, including the need for accountability and responsibility for mass and elite objectives. The government's prevailing elite sport aspirations with regard to NSAs were 'to build on the objectives created with *SPEX 2000* but make the NSAs responsible for not only developing elite talent but [also] for administering, marketing and developing the popularity of their sport to the wider community as a measure to achieve the Republic's sporting ambitions' (McNeill et al., 2003, p. 54).

Dimensions of elite sport policy development

Green and Houlihan (2005) argue that four dimensions of elite sport development feature significantly in determining the nature and adequacy of any elite sport system. They are: (1) the development of elite sport facilities; (2) the emergence of 'full-time' athletes; (3) developments in coaching, sports science and sports medicine and (4) competition opportunities for athletes at the elite level (see also Green, 2003). In order to reveal the extent of government intervention in elite sport policy development in Singapore, one of the country's leading NSAs – the Singapore Athletic Association (SAA) – was selected for analysis as it has responsibility for high profile events at Olympic and World Championship levels, factors that help justify its attempts for increased resources and attention from policymakers in Singapore.

Singapore Athletic Association

Organisation and administration • • •

The Singapore Amateur Athletic Association (SAAA) was established in 1934 and is 'responsible for sanctioning, promoting, expanding and strengthening athletics in Singapore' (SAAA, 2005). Currently it has 20 affiliate clubs in its membership and is the national governing body for track and field, cross-country, road racing, race walking and tug of war. According to a senior official in the organisation, track and field has the privileged status as an elite sport under the sports excellence programme, and is also 'the largest participation sport in schools' (Interview, 3 August 2005) in Singapore. Recently, in a determined bid to renew and align itself to the nation's sporting vision, the word 'amateur' was dropped from its title and the NSA is now known as the Singapore Athletic Association (SAA) (SAA, 2006; Tan, 2006a). Yet, it is notoriously weak leadership and poor athlete management that characterises the administration of the SAA.

Subsequent to a review of the *SPEX Programme* in 2000, track and field was removed from the SSC list of privileged sports because the SAAA had not achieved its targets. The SSC leadership argued that 'the SAAA should revamp its management practices and put in place an effective leadership. The SSC hopes that the association and its members will strive to make improvements to revive the sport' (quoted in Thomas, 2000b, p. 75). One of the SSC's main concerns was the failure of SAA to modernise and reciprocate by adopting effective organisational and administrative strategies befitting a Core sport. The tension between the SAA and the SSC was expressed by the SSC's Executive Director when he stated:

We found that they [SAAA officials] were not prepared to listen, not interested in doing any soul-searching. We have nothing in common with them. The SSC is also hoping that the dropping of track and field from the SPEX programme would lead to an injection of new blood into the SAAA's management.

(quoted in Tay, 2000, p. 76)

Of note were the in-house power struggles that ensued in the SAA's leadership, centred on the reluctance of the incumbent to step aside despite a 23 year reign as President. Two tightly contested elections for the top position in 2000 and 2002 provided the SSC with the excuse to intervene and, following the 2002 annual meeting, the SSC's Deputy Director (Sports Excellence) was seconded to the SAA to establish a full-time secretariat and assume responsibility for implementing the development plans (Chan, 2002b). When the incumbent finally agreed to resign in 2004, and after the SAA had submitted its Strategic and High Performance Plans as required by the COG, track and field was duly reinstated to the elite sport status (Chan, 2002a; SAA, 2006).

The newly installed leadership undertook to demonstrate more resolve by aiming 'to provide adequate exposure to athletes at appropriate international competitions and to develop monitoring and support schemes such as sports science and financial support' as its long-term sports excellence objectives for 2005 (SAA, 2006, p. 7). At its 2005 Annual General Meeting (AGM), the new administration declared that its mission was 'to develop the sport of track and field as a preferred choice of sporting pursuit by Singaporeans, while its focus would be high performance management, coaching excellence, sport delivery system and infrastructure' (SAA, 2006, p. 7). Despite these lofty aims, the SAA still has to contend with 'the deficiencies of the previous administration, and help soothe disgruntled stakeholders ranging from athletes to coaches and parents' (Luis, 2004, p. 60) as more controversies ensued.

In July 2005, two Chinese-born athletes sued the SAA for alleged wrongful termination of their contracts and are still awaiting an outcome (Raymond, 2005b). Then, in October 2005, a highly publicised case involving unaffiliated coaches and their athletes broke out over the running sequence for the 4×400 metre relay squad selected for the 2005 SEA Games. The new President blamed 'the lack of control' over athletes and coaches who were not affiliated with the SAA as one of the major reasons for the fiasco (Siow, 2005). Despite efforts by the President to placate all parties, the relay squad missed out on an SEA Games spot and a disciplinary committee was convened to investigate and recommend actions (Siow, 2005). The case drew strong criticism from the media and the SNOC as the affected coaches and runners had irresponsibly put self before country (Fang, 2006b). The President summed up his frustration by stating that 'when I took over athletics last year, I didn't expect it to be so difficult. I was wrong ... because what control do I have over the renegade coaches? None' (quoted in Siow, 2005, p. H10).

In a candid assessment of his 2 year reign as head of the SAA, the President admitted responsibility for the Association's dismal situation: 'To be brutally honest, I've failed. While I've done all right in developing our sports industry and in terms of mass participation, I've failed in terms of sports excellence, in not being able to produce the desired results' (quoted in Tan, 2006a, p. 55). In a strange turn of events, member clubs rallied together to vote in the former leader – the same person who had previously held the position for 23 years – as the new SAA President at the Association's AGM in June 2006 (Foo, 2005b; Wang, 2006). In the victory speech to mark the start of his 24th year at the helm of track and field, the new President stated: 'I am happy with the convincing result. I am also guarded as there is a lot to do, with new programmes to look into and things that need to be revamped' (quoted in Lai, 2006, p. 64).

If history is anything to go by, then it appears that the SAA's 'new–old' administration and secretariat face challenging times ahead in its pursuit of elite sport glory, 'to chart new territories for the future ... and take bold strides to nurture talents, work towards holistic athlete development and making competitive athletics a viable career' (SAA, 2006). While there have been no major achievements that support the SAA's strategies and plans, the organisation realises that it faces the challenging task of rekindling the public's confidence in its management of the sport.

Today, it appears that the SAA enjoys an amenable relationship with the SSC and other stakeholders, having put in place the obligatory systems required of an elite sport. On this issue, a high-ranking SAA official stated that 'There has never been any one period where we do not have problems with anyone' and that policies should be clear and well-communicated (Interview, 3 August 2005). At the heart of these comments are questions relating to the SAA's ability to adjust and cope with the pressures of professional governance and corporate accountability. It will also be interesting to observe how the SAA continues to manage its relationship with the SSC, particularly since funding is contingent upon medal returns at international competitions, and on the SAA's ability to integrate and manage its governance structure for the future of the sport.

Development of elite sport facilities

The responsibility for construction, development and maintenance of most sports facilities in Singapore lies with the SSC. These cater mainly for the masses and are aligned to community and national interest. With the advent of *SPEX 2000*, the NSAs were encouraged to work with the SSC in identifying existing facilities as Centres of Excellence (COE) to facilitate elite sport development in Singapore (MCDS, 2001). In October 2004, the SAA announced (SAA, 2005) that it had obtained priority use at one of the public stadiums as its COE although, due to the multi-disciplinary nature of the sport, athletes and coaches continue to train at various venues. The new COE at Bukit Gombak Stadium was renovated specifically with track and field in mind and includes modern and comprehensive facilities such as a woodchip track for warming-up, sports science testing facilities, fully furnished gym and therapeutic rooms, and laboratories equipped with computers for technique-analysis and biomechanical assessments (SAA, 2005; SSC, 2005b). As observed by an SAA official, 'this is truly a world-class COE that has the facilities instrumental in developing athletic excellence' (quoted in Britcher, 2005, p. 15).

In addition, the SAA also benefits from the Track and Field Academy within the SSS (2005). Equipped with first-rate facilities, modern coaching and sports science services, the Academy's vision is to assist the SAA in improving the standard of athletics and to 'mould world-class youth track and field athletes' (SSS, 2005) in Singapore. Together with the impending world-class stadium to be built in Singapore's new sports hub in 2010, there is no shortage of facilities for athletes to train and compete at the top level. The SAA recently succeeded in attaining accreditation for its COE as an International Association of Athletics Federations' (IAAF) High Performance Centre (SAAA, 2005).

On the other hand, the SSC and the SAA are realistic and acknowledge that facilities and infrastructure are not adequate to host the Olympics or World Championships, although the Commonwealth and/or Asian Games were considered 'not out of Singapore's league' (Xue, 2005). However, it is argued that the lack of facilities for training and competition at the grassroots level is not an issue for the SAA and athletes in Singapore – there are presently 18 public, 'third-generation' (SSC, 1998b, p. 3) sport and athletic stadiums including numerous other synthetic tracks housed within schools, junior colleges, tertiary institutions and military camps throughout the island. Rather, the SAA's chief concern is the sport's lingering negative reputation, tainted largely by management deficiencies over the past 10 years (Yap, 2003a; Luis, 2004). As the President of the SAA argued: 'would athletes and parents be convinced by the SAA's efforts? Would they want to pursue their dreams together with the SAA? So you see, the biggest problem is the SAA's current image' (quoted in Luis, 2004, p. 60). To its credit, the SAA has made attempts to address this concern by recognising its social responsibilities and persuading the public, for example through education and implementing a community outreach programme at the COE (SSC, 2005b).

Although it is dependent on funding and facility support from the SSC, the SAA has steadily provided for mass development through various fund raising and sponsorship efforts. The *New Paper Big Walk* and *Standard Chartered Singapore Marathon*, for instance, are annual focal events on the local sport and tourism calendars that attract many overseas participants and visitors (SSC, 2003). Two points of interest are notable here. The first alludes to the amount of services and resources the full-time secretariat accords to the SAA's mass sport objectives given the secretariat's remit for high-performance athletic development, including the commitment to the terms of the COG and its medal targets as agreed with the SSC. Green and Houlihan (2005, p. 179) describe this practice as 'ring-fencing of elite funding from those responsible for meeting the needs of club and grassroots members'. The second point relates to the fact that revenue from sponsors and donors usually comes at a price, as acknowledged by the SAA President: 'we [SAA] would have to remind ourselves that corporate sponsors would come in only when our Association is well-structured, properly administered and, at the same time, shows reasonable results on the track and field' (SAA, 2005, p. 8).

Fortunately for the SAA, the SSC remains responsible for 'the provision of integrated sports facilities which … cater not only for the needs of Sports For All programmes but also for the specific requirements of Sports Excellence programmes' (Soon, 2000, p. 9). The government's bold plans for a showpiece sports hub is a case in point. Unfortunately for Singapore, sporting glory or a sports culture do not stem merely from the building of extensive stadiums or arenas. As one senior official SAA stated, 'Singapore has more money available than any other country on this earth but is still waiting for acceptable international performances and achievements' (Interview, 21 July 2005).

Emergence of 'full-time' athletes • • •

A range of financial assistance schemes were introduced for athletes as part of the holistic approach to helping talent under the *SPEX 2000* programme. These included funds for training and competition, grants for loss of income, allowances to assist young athletes with training and studies, and assistance to support the athlete for life during and after competition (MCD, 1993). Of significance was the introduction, in 1993, of SportsCOVER (Career Options, Vocational Emplacement and Recruitment) to provide lifestyle support for athletes during and after their high-performance careers (MCD, 1993). This scheme was replaced with Athlete Development programmes by the establishment of the High Performance Management Division (HPMD) within the SSC (2005b). Two prominent HPMD policies that contribute to the appearance of full-time athletes include the ACT (Athlete Career and Training Programme) and *spex*GLOW (Grants for Loss Of Wages). The ACT, launched in 2002, is 'the clearest sign yet of the government's drive to achieve sports excellence that virtually guarantees a top athlete's well-being for life' (Tay, 2002). Under the ACT, individual elite athletes receive carding support up to a maximum of $SGD80,000 a year (Tay, 2002) depending on their standing in the *spex*TEAM (Talented Elite Athlete Management) classification system (SSC, 2005b). These schemes are in line with Green and Oakley's (2001, p. 262) identification of 'lifestyle support programmes' evident in Western elite sport approaches.

A total of 873 athletes, in various classification categories, received carding support from the SSC in the fiscal year 2002–2003 (SSC, 2003, p. 28). *spex*GLOW continues 'to be one of the SSC's popular financial assistance schemes' (SSC, 2000, p. 26) wherein elite athletes are compensated for their full-time commitment at major competitions, perhaps indicative of the perceived general lack of career prospects in sport in Singapore today. According to the SSC's Annual Report 2003–2004, athletes funded through the ACT and *spex*GLOW schemes accounted for 70 per cent of the 30 gold medals won at the 2003 Vietnam SEA Games (SSC, 2004), adding weight to the argument that excellence is contingent on the 'adoption of performance criterion-based funding of elite athletes with subsistence, training, equipment and educational aspects' (Green and Oakley, 2001, p. 261).

The SAA claims to have put in place its own Athlete Support System where, according to one senior official, 'Athletes are constantly monitored for welfare and career planning support' and also benefit from a 'Carding System based on performance benchmarks where athletes can apply for support ranging from training grants to sports science and sports medicine support' (Interview, 3 August 2005). Interestingly, all three SAA athletes presently funded through ACT (two athletes) and *spex*GLOW (one athlete) are foreign-born talents while 54 track and field student-athletes were eligible only for carded training assistance grants from the SSC in 2004 (SAAA, 2005, p. 28).

The local athletics scene has had its share of worthy track and field champions with seven individuals named among 'Singapore's 50 Greatest Athletes' by *The Sunday Times* in 1999 (Yap, 1999). Sadly, all seven have since retired from the elite level, further shrinking the pool of athletes for the SAA. Between 1983 and 1993, Singaporean athletes failed to win a single gold medal at the biennial SEA Games, managing only 17 (3 silver, 14 bronze) medals during that period (SNOC, 2005). With the introduction of *SPEX* incentives, local standards have improved and several athletes were selected by the SAA for Asian, Commonwealth and even World/Olympic level meets (SNOC, 2005). For example, Singapore's track and field athletes won nine (four gold) medals at the 2003 Vietnam SEA Games, and one gold medal each at the 2004 Asian All-Stars Athletics Championships and 2005 Asian Grand Prix Series (Raymond, 2005a).

A local-born sprinter also impressed selectors sufficiently to be picked as a wild card entry for the 2005 Helsinki World Championships. However, despite the large and sustained following at school and club levels, a persistent issue for the SAA remains the dearth of outstanding talent emerging at the national and youth stages. One senior-ranking SAA official alluded to the 'continuation after school issue' (Interview, 3 August 2005) as a major concern, with many promising athletes citing the sense of duty to school rather than personal interest in track and field as their reasons for participating (and excelling) in school meets but not progressing further (Tan, J. 2005). The SAA President again cited the issue of lack of control over a student-athlete's future when he stated that 'I can't control the athletes and coaches because we don't pay them … What can you say when you have no control?' (quoted in Siow, 2005, p. H10).

Another obstacle remains the lack of a sporting culture in Singapore, fuelled by parental reservations about their children pursuing sport at a higher level. These factors, it is argued, accelerated the NSA's search for suitable foreign talent that would fast-track the quest for medals. The Sports Minister provided the government's rationale for endorsing the Foreign Talent Scheme in stating that 'for those medals to be meaningful, they must be Singaporean and they must feel Singaporean … that's where the Sports School gives them a Singaporean home, where they will integrate, where they will pick up our accents and idiosyncrasies' (quoted in Tay, 2005).

The subject of importing foreign talent sparked much debate but the government's unreserved endorsement of the policy has dispelled (for now) the groundswell of public opinion regarding a perceived loss of jobs and the feeling that there is little pride in the achievements as 'medals were being bought' (Yap, 2003b) by foreign imports. A pertinent illustration of the latter is that all 13 medals at the 2002 Manchester Commonwealth Games were won by foreign-born athletes (Yap, 2003b). Today, athletes born in China lead the SAA's medal charge, beginning at the 2005 Manila SEA Games and, subsequently, the Asian and Commonwealth Games in 2006 (Foo, 2005a) although local athletes have recently produced sterling performances at national and regional level (Tan, J. 2005). Still, the objective remains fixed on loftier targets with the SAA's Technical Director asserting, 'the SEA Games is the minimum we should aim at, and a stepping stone towards other things, like winning medals at the Asian level, and hitting the "B" final standard at the Olympics. That is achievable' (Interview, 1 August 2005). The SAA's focus on youth development is also tied in with performance benchmarks, wherein, according to one high-ranking SAA official, the 'SAA has set up a comprehensive monitoring system where we monitor performances at the various levels of competitions [and] … we are beginning to see some "fruits" of that labour' (Interview,

3 August 2005). On the issue of full-time athletes, the same official stated:

Only the foreign sport talents (three of them) are full-time in that they only trained in the sport. A number of athletes may receive some form of financial support and in exchange provide minimal work service in SAA or its projects. The support is tied to their level of performance. Athletes who receive such assistance must be in training for some immediate Major Games or Championships. Otherwise, on a case-by-case basis, any other potential youth athlete may receive the necessary support.

(Interview, 3 August 2005)

Yet, both the SAA and the SSS are quietly confident that the young athletes coming through the school will carry the future hopes for Singapore athletics (Leong, W.K. 2006a). Since its opening in 2004, the school boasts 31 athletes who have represented Singapore at the senior level and who have set more than 30 age-group records in sailing, table tennis, swimming and athletics (Fang, 2006b). Undoubtedly, having a hothouse 'study-sports' environment like the SSS is also a decisive factor in the track and field production line whereby student-athletes undergo 'the strict and disciplined lifestyle in order to become elite athletes' (Wong, 2006).

Developments in coaching, sports science and sports medicine • • •

When *SPEX 2000* was launched in 1993, a total of 23 foreign coaches were hired by the 7 Core (19 coaches) and 7 Merit NSAs (4 coaches), reflecting the shortage of suitable and qualified local coaches at the high-performance level despite the establishment of a National Coaching Plan in 1976 (SSC, 1994). This was replaced by the NCAP in 1995 as the national standard for coaching qualifications (SSC, 2005b) following the concern that 'a significant proportion of the coaching community in Singapore still use traditional methods gleaned from experience in their respective sports' (Lim, 2004). With the NCAP, the SSC aims to capitalise on the synergistic potential of working with the NSAs to ensure that local practitioners are upgraded and kept abreast of the latest coaching developments (SSC, 2005b). According to the SSC's Deputy Director (Coaching Development, Sports Management Division), 'There is a need to make coaching more professional in Singapore' and also 'A knowledge of sports science will help in understanding how the body reacts to training and how rest is just as important as work' (quoted in Lim, 2004).

To cater for community as well as elite groups, a National Registry of Coaches (NROC) was introduced in 2003 with the aim of 'benefiting sports and society by setting the minimum standards of coaching through recognising coaches who have attained a full NCAP certification, committed themselves to a continuing coach education programme, and have agreed to abide by the Coach's Code of Ethics' (Goh, 2003, p. 3). Other coaching development schemes have also been pioneered, following the work of the Coaching Advisory Committee (CAC), an independent professional body tasked to map out the coaching developmental plans for Singapore (Lam, 2002). Led by a consultant from the Australian Sports Commission and the President of the Coaching Association of Canada, the CAC was instrumental in raising the standard and professionalism of the coaching industry with proposals such as the setting up of a Coaches Development Grant, implementing a system of continuing coach education and upgrading of qualifications, and increasing the extent of recognition for coaches (Lam, 2002). According to the SSC, all three initiatives, namely NCAP, NROC and CAC, are key elements in its efforts to increase and promote the professionalism of coaches in Singapore (SSC, 2003).

The hiring of foreign coaches is not without its drawbacks as many do not last long in the system due to their failure to achieve set targets or produce champions (McNeill et al., 2003). Part of the reason why the government intervened in SAA's operations was because it (SSC) had doubts over the Association's 'judgement in the hiring and firing of foreign and local coaches between 1996 and 2000' (Tay, 2000). According to the SSC's Executive Director, 'The association has the right to sack but if it is done too often, then something is wrong. Either you have not done your homework before hiring or else people can't work with you' (quoted in Tay, 2000). Today, as noted by SAA's Technical Director, while foreign coaches are still being employed in specialised areas, the NSAs are increasingly turning to local coaching resources as viable alternatives in their (NSAs') long-term plans to be weaned off foreign experts (Interview, 1 August 2005).

Developments in the local coaching industry recently received a boost with the announcement by the IAAF that it had chosen Singapore to host the Level three Course for senior administrative staff, chief coaches and technical directors in December 2005. The Asian Athletics Association's (AAA) secretariat has been based in Singapore for the past 33 years, and is now considering proposals to move its Asian headquarters to Singapore (Lim, T., 2005), a move that would not only enhance coaching developments, but also provide impetus for the fledgling sports industry in Singapore.

In addition to advances in coaching, the SSC has also recognised the significance of technology, science and medicine in contributing to Singapore's sports policy. Established in 1973, the SSC's Sports Medicine and Sports Science Division (SMSSD) today provides a one-stop, integrated and specialised service 'to the general public and the sports fraternity in terms of evaluation and treatment, prevention, instruction and health education, basic and applied research as well as projects in support of *SPEX21*' (SSC, 2002, p. 34). The SMSSD serves as the central location for sports medicine and sports science support for all NSAs given the size of the country and to prevent duplication of services. Nevertheless, NSAs have also set up individual science/medicine support networks in the various COEs to cater for the specific requirements of their respective athletes: the SAA, for example, has now established a Sports Science and Sports Medicine Committee.

The government's investment in the scientific and medical features of sport reflects the emerging trend of capitalising on technology and research to increase the athlete's technique and mental strength (Coakley, 1998). For example, the SMSSD has added equipment for biomechanical and physiological testing, strength and force analysis, and employed specialists to oversee psychological and dietary aspects (SSC, 1999). The SSS has also invested in a Sports Science Academy which provides services to 'ensure student-athletes perform at their optimum ... while the bar on performance is consistently raised' (SSS, 2005).

In May 1999, the government engaged the consultancy services of a panel of mainly overseas experts to advise the SMSSD on a myriad of issues related to sports medicine, biomechanics, nutrition, psychology and conditioning (SSC, 2000). These governmental initiatives support the argument put forth by observers that many countries are now capitalising on 'strategies for the systematic and scientific pursuit of victory in international sport, supported in large part by the spread of state-sponsored systems' (Green, 2004b, p. 376; see also Green and Houlihan, 2005).

Competition opportunities for elite level athletes ▪ ▪ ▪

Since the launch of *SPEX 2000*, the SAA has taken advantage of the enhanced funding from the SSC to send its athletes to regional and international meets in Malaysia, Thailand, Australia and France (Ho, 1993; SSC, 1994). This is in line with the SSC's objective of encouraging NSAs to expose local athletes to 'opportunities to compete against and train with the world's best' (SSC's Director of Sports Excellence, quoted in Ho, 1993, p. 27). However, it also draws attention to the lack of competitive opportunities for the elite and up-and-coming athletes in Singapore. According to its Training and Selection Sub-committee, a total of 18 local competitions, of which 11 were athletic meets, were organised by the SAA in the competition calendar for 2004; the others being sanctioned for cross-country, race walking and marathon running (SAA, 2005, p. 46).

Although this is by no means indicative of the standard of athletics in Singapore, it does serve to highlight the busy domestic schedule of programmes and activities that the Association has annually committed to its track and field affiliates, schools and the public. For many of these groups, participating in the annual events legitimates the group's existence and offers 'important opportunities for the social contact that helps to bind members together' (Green and Houlihan, 2005, p. 177). Of interest here is the tension between the SAA's broader objectives to meet its membership interests and the Association's obligation to the national quest for sports excellence. As pointed out earlier, the amount of resources available for elite track and field far exceeds that allocated for mass athletic participation, such that the SAA had to resort to fundraising and sponsorship to fund the latter programmes. The priority to set up a competition schedule that would cater for the needs of Singapore's small band of elite athletes remains low, although the SAA did send its athletes to participate in 23 international meets in 2004 (SAAA, 2005) and 27 in 2005 (SAA, 2006). While this situation may not be peculiar to the SAA, it does highlight some of the ramifications for NSAs as a result of a shift towards an emphasis on elite sport.

Aside from costs, the fact that local athletes either have work or academic commitments to contend with supports the SAA's prevailing approach to target specific meets for its athletes to focus on within the year. The main yardstick for local elite athletes remains the biennial SEA Games, indicative of the lack of depth in the SAA's talent pool to compete successfully at higher levels. This point was noted by the local media in its evaluation of track and field's medal hopes (before the SAA sent its athletes to the 2003 Vietnam SEA Games): 'the biennial Games is the only sporting platform where Singapore sprinters have a realistic chance of glory. The prospect of our athletes winning on the track or field is a rare expectation' (Yap, 2003a).

Despite disproving the critics with a nine (four gold) medal haul, the SAA has stuck with its steady approach where, according to a senior SAA official, 'athletes for the 2005–2007 SEA Games' squad were identified immediately after the 2003 SEA Games' (Interview, 3 August 2005). This cautious approach was backed by the SAA's Technical Director when he outlined the Association's priorities for its elite athletes: 'We have set sound subsidy structures that are performance based and targeted at closing the gaps to SEA Games level, to Asian, and finally to reach "B" qualifying standard' (Interview, 1 August 2005). Nevertheless, the SAA's plans to make Singapore a regional athletics hub received a boost with the successful hosting of the inaugural 2004 *Enzer* Asian All-Stars Athletic Championships in Singapore (Lim, M., 2005) and the 2nd Asian Grand Prix Series in June 2005 (SAA, 2006). Having close ties with the AAA, whose secretariat is based in Singapore, also helped the SAA secure regular overseas training stints in China for its athletes to prepare for competitions (SAA, 2006).

The younger generation of athletes continue to be exposed to the rigour of overseas competition with above average performances at the 4th IAAF Youth Athletics Championships in Morocco in July 2005 (SAA, 2006). Two national records were re-written at the 16th Asian Athletics Championships in Incheon, Korea, in September 2005, while the SAA secured another wild card entry at the 11th IAAF World Indoor Championships in Moscow in March 2006 (SAA, 2006). The potential and performances of some of the student-athletes coming through the SSS 'hot-house' could yet prove to be a fertile source of talent as the SAA fine-tunes its athlete support structure to increase its pool of full-time athletes.

Summary of key issues

At first glance, the SAA appears to have overcome its past tribulations as it faces up to the challenges set out by the government's elite sport development policy. For example, its long-term strategies reveal the apparent professionalism and bureaucracy that have characterised its elite focus. In reality, however, the SAA may be undergoing its most challenging phase yet as it pursues the ambitious strategy and targets outlined above. While the future may hold promise for the SAA, events in the past may yet return to blight its aspirations. Today, a young and promising generation of athletes, led by a pragmatic set of coaches, have added confidence to an Association that has achieved stability following the transfer of a government officer to its secretariat and having committed itself to the principles of the COG. However, it remains to be seen how the SAA manages the expectations of its most valuable resource, the athletes.

Singapore's track and field athletes remain highly dependent on the SSC and the SAA's financial support in order to train and compete at the international level. The education- and achievement-centric attitude of Singaporean youths, compounded by the fear of losing out to peers and the lack of national sporting icons, continue to be major barriers for promising athletes to consider full-time commitment to athletics. This has inevitably led to the pursuit of foreign sports talent to enhance Singapore's chances of medal honours. Two (Chinese-born) throwers currently bear the nation's and the SAA's hopes in track and field, particularly at SEA Games level where they have already shown great promise (Yap, 2003b).

In respect of the developments in coaching, the reliance on foreign expertise is realistic given the lack of suitably qualified and experienced local coaches at the elite level. In the NCAP, NROC and CAC initiatives, the SSC and NSAs have a comprehensive framework for enhancing the stature and viability of the coaching profession in Singapore although the SAA is not yet convinced that it can appoint a Singaporean as its Technical Director. With regard to sports science and sports medicine, the support systems and services are in place and available centrally at the SSC, although Core NSAs have established separate networks to cater for their respective specialised sport needs. Of interest here is 'the efficacy of these structures in developing high performance athletes' (Green and Houlihan, 2005, p. 119). For example, the SAA's Technical Director hinted that the Association's sports science services were not geared towards the elite level: 'sports science is a crucial part and linked with the coach's education. However, sports science [personnel] must be prepared themselves for high performance, which they are not for the moment. So both are working towards it [high performance]' (Interview, 1 August 2005).

Recent developments and future directions of elite sport policy in Singapore

Sports Institute

The decision to include a Sports Institute within the sports hub created a buzz among the local sports fraternity with a former Olympian expressing the shared reaction that 'it was time that Singapore caught up with what the leading nations were doing with their sports programmes' (quoted in Leong, C. 2006a, p. 77). A significant development is the Institute's aim to offer athletes holistic support, such as sports science and medicine services, educational and career advice, and lodging and training facilities (Tan, 2006c). Nevertheless, it will be interesting to see how the Institute will complement the positive work already achieved by the NSAs, the COEs and the SSS. In addition, the facilities should be developed with Singapore's sports system in mind and not one that simply duplicates models found at similar institutes in Australia, Japan, or South Korea (Fang, 2006a; Leong, C. 2006a). Questions that require detailed consideration include how the Institute will be managed and staffed, whether it will limit the number and type of sports for support, and how it will integrate the responsibilities of all sports stakeholders. The Chief of the SSC High Performance Group satisfied NSAs that they will retain fundamental roles in the development of their athletes (Fang, 2006a) and reassured them that their feedback and suggestions will be sought:

All NSAs will continue to run their own sports. Ideally, the sports institute will operate in close partnership with them. Responsibility for results at major games will remain that of the NSAs. Their role will be greatly enhanced and supported by the sports institute.

(quoted in Fang, 2006a, p. H15)

The CEO of the SSC also stated that the aim is for the Sports Institute to be a sustainable infrastructure, 'and together with other projects like the Sports School, are vital components towards sports development and excellence, particularly Singapore's aim to win medals at the Olympic Games consistently' (quoted in Tan, 2006b, p. 49).

SSC–NSA relationship and athlete-centred management

Improvements in NSA administration and athlete management remain high on SSC's priority list. The 'half-time' assessment of the *CoSS* blueprint by the CEO of the SSC revealed that there has been 'good progress in the forty CoSS recommendations' (quoted in Tan, 2006c, p. 55). For example, in moves aimed at commercialising NSAs and maximising their limited resources, the SSC abandoned the Core and Merit sport categories and introduced an 'outcome-based and multi-year' funding model in August 2005 (Leong, W.K. 2006b). Based on three strategic thrusts, the new model aimed to 'prioritise and channel resources into critical areas that will create optimum impact and contribute directly to the CoSS objectives' (Oon, 2005).

Essentially, instead of relying on past performances to establish Core and Merit levels of funding for the NSAs, the new model requires NSAs to critically establish 'strong governance and sound management policies' (Leong, W.K. 2006b, p. 54) to attract funds into their sport. According to the SSC, the new system will permit NSAs greater flexibility and empowerment to manage their budget in addition to strategising long-term programmes for sustained benefits. The SSC will also evaluate NSAs' organisational standards when deciding funding allocations. In general, annual funding for the 58 NSAs will increase by 10 per cent – from $SGD28.3 million in 2005 to $SGD31.1 million in 2006 (Leong, W.K. 2006b), although the SSC's CEO reiterated that 'if there are excellent programmes and good associations, we [the SSC] will be flexible and reprioritise if we have to, to ensure that new opportunities will be funded' (quoted in Leong, C. 2006b, pp. 54–55).

The government has now adopted an athlete-centred approach as it tempts more athletes to become full-time performers. The High Performance Athlete Programme was launched to encourage elite athletes to pursue sports excellence without being constrained by the opportunity costs of doing so. The scheme aims to make sure that talented athletes in a particular sport will not lose out, compared to what they might have otherwise earned on a different career path (Lee, 2001). In September 2006, another milestone was reached in Singapore's elite sport development when the Ministry of Community Development, Youth and Sports (MCYS) and the SSC presided over the signing of the Code of Athlete Management (COAM) between elite athletes and their respective NSAs. In an attempt to ensure that the potential of elite athletes is fulfilled, the COAM sets out three obligatory principles – 'to implement a transparent and fair selection policy, to map out what exactly is required from the athlete and NSA and to ensure the target set is met, and to adopt the international doping policy in their respective fields' (Leong, C. 2006b, p. 78).

Moreover, apart from the Core and Merit sports where government intervention is most intensive, the other NSAs' volunteer leadership still lack the 'passion, vision and capabilities to be the driving force behind their sport' at the professional level (Tan, 2000). Building and strengthening the capabilities of local NSAs are the foremost challenges facing the SSC as it endeavours to inculcate best management practices and infrastructure development in organisations reliant on unpaid, elected officials (Robert, 1998; SSC, 2004).

Sports culture

Although the government has given its unequivocal support to the *Sporting Singapore* vision, the lack of international sporting success, and the absence of a sports culture and fledgling NSA structures, have proven to be real challenges for a young and dynamic nation attuned to development of the country's political and economic infrastructure. In October 2006, the SSC announced the establishment of a *Sporting Culture Committee* to 'look at improving Singapore's sporting culture and ensuring its athletes can compete with the world's best' (Tan, 2006c, p. 34). The CEO of the SSC summarised the challenge that his agency faced:

Getting thousands of people on the same wavelength is no easy feat, not to mention that there will always be sceptics. But let us put local and personal differences aside. There is a larger national objective, and we have a very short time, not twenty, thirty years to achieve this.
(quoted in Tan, 2006d, p. 55)

To its credit, the government has been tolerant and staunchly supportive of in-force 'pathways' to foster up-and-coming athletes as it patiently awaits Singapore's first medal(s) at the Olympics. It remains hopeful that the sports sector will equal or better its famed economic accomplishments, buoyed by a vastly improved 13 (4 gold) medal haul (*Team Singapore's* best ever) at the 2002 Manchester Commonwealth Games (SSC, 2004). According to the Chairman of the SSC, 'we have witnessed high-level breakthroughs in policies, mindset changes and initiatives, particularly in key areas of government support for sports, sports management and sports industry and business development' (quoted in Tan, 2006c, p. 55).

To accentuate the pursuit of Olympic and international glory, the SSC and the SNOC jointly announced, in November 2006, funding of $SGD7 million specifically to nurture and prepare elite athletes for the 2008 and 2012 Olympic Games. The Sports Minister, in explaining the *Glory for the Nation* project, stated that 'we're [now] focusing our resources on the precious few whom we think really do have the potential to win an Olympic medal. Now, it'll have to be very individualised and tailor-made for these few' (quoted in Tan, 2006e, p. 55).

Conclusions

Singapore's elite sport development system is still at an embryonic stage of development but the strategies and approaches adopted appear sound and feature many of the best practices apparent in the (tentative) model of Western elite sport development outlined by Green and Oakley (2001) and developed by Green and Houlihan (2005). These include the demarcation of roles and responsibilities for the different agencies involved in elite sport delivery, the provision of systematic and scientific approaches for those charged with the development of elite athletes, and the concentration of resources on selected sports and individuals that exhibit realistic odds of success at international, and especially Olympic, level.

References

Britcher, C. (2005) Built for success, *SportBusiness International*, 104(July), 14–15.

Chan, T.C. (2000a) We're serious about sports, *The Straits Times*, 7 September, 63.

Chan, T.C. (2000b) Committee to chart direction, *The Straits Times*, 7 September, 63.

Chan, T.C. (2001a) PM spells out 3 sports goals, *The Straits Times*, 2 July, 1.

Chan, T.C. (2001b) Three-point strategy for a five-star dream, *The Straits Times*, 2 July, S1.

Chan, T.C. (2002a) Rugby and netball in on merit, *The Straits Times*, 20 March, S1.

Chan, T.C. (2002b) SSC's Song seconded to athletics association, *The Straits Times*, 28 July, 51.

Chen, S.J. (1983) Singapore's development strategies: A model for rapid growth, in P. Chen (ed.), *Singapore: Development Policies and Trends*, Singapore: Oxford University Press.

Chiew, S.K. (1983) Ethnicity and national integration: The evolution of a multi-ethnic society, in P. Chen (ed.), *Singapore: Development Policies and Trends*, Singapore: Oxford University Press.

Coakley, J. (1998) *Sport in Society: Issues and Controversies* (6th edn), McGraw-Hill, Boston, MASS.

Fang, N. (2006a) SSC keen on sports institute, *The Straits Times*, 13 April, H15.

Fang, N. (2006b) Turning out students who lead the league, *The Straits Times*, 14 July, 1–2.

Foo, A. (2005a) Only the best will travel to Manila Games, *The Straits Times*, 5 February, S15.

Foo, A. (2005b) Govt's $300 m carrot cheers NSAs, *The Straits Times Interactive*, 16 March, Available at www.straitstimes.asia1.com.sg (retrieved 26 July 2005).

Franklin, B. (2001) At a glance: The recommendations, *The Straits Times*, 2 July, S2.

Goh, C.T. (1999) Speech by the Prime Minister at the Timesport 50 Greatest Athletes Presentation Ceremony, 18 December, Singapore Government, Available at www.gov.sg (retrieved 28 June 2005).

Goh, M. (2003) National registry of coaches: Shaping the future of sports, *Sports*, 30(15), 3.

Government of Singapore (1991) *Singapore: The Next Lap*, Singapore: Times Editions.

Green, M. (2003) An analysis of elite sport policy change in three sports in Canada and the United Kingdom, Unpublished Ph.D. thesis, Loughborough University.

Green, M. (2004a) Changing policy priorities for sport in England: The emergence of elite sport development as a key policy concern, *Leisure Studies*, 23, 365–385.

Green, M. (2004b) Power, policy and political priorities: Elite sport development in Canada and the United Kingdom, *Sociology of Sport Journal*, 21, 376–396.

Green, M. and Oakley, B. (2001) Elite sport development systems and playing to win: Uniformity and diversity in international approaches, *Leisure Studies*, 20, 247–267.

Green, M. and Houlihan, B. (2005) *Elite Sport Development: Policy Learning and Political Priorities*. London: Routledge.

Ho, S. (1993) SSC approves $640,000 for training, competition abroad, *The Straits Times*, 24 December, 27.

Horton, P.A. (2001) Complex creolization: The evolution of modern sport in Singapore, in J.A. Mangan (ed.), *The European Sports History Review: Europe, Sport, World: Shaping Global Societies*, Vol. 3, London: Frank Cass & Co Ltd.

Horton, P.A. (2002) Shackling the lion: Sport and modern Singapore, *The International Journal of the History of Sport*, 19(2–3), 189–212.

Ibrahim, Y. (2002) Speech by the Minister of Community Development and Sports at the Singapore Sports Awards 2002, 20 April, Singapore Government, Available at www.gov.sg (retrieved 15 July 2005).

Khoo, P. (1990) Almost $6 million in sports aid fund, *The Straits Times*, 5 January, 41.

Koh, T. (1999) A quiet hero and gentleman, *The Sunday Times*, 19 December, 54.

Lai, D. (2006) Landslide win for Loh, *Today*, 30 June, 64.

Lam, S. (2002) A blueprint for coaching excellence, *Sports*, 30(3), 3.

Lee, H.L. (2001) Speech by the Deputy Prime Minister at the Appreciation Dinner for 21st SEA Games participants, Singapore Government, Available at www.gov.sg (retrieved 15 July 2005).

Leong, C. (2006a) Athletes root for sports institute, *Today*, 13 April, 77.

Leong, C. (2006b) New code for elite athletes, NSAs, *Today*, 8 September, 78.

Leong, W.K. (2006a) They're charting new ground, *Today*, 27 January, 46.

Leong, W.K. (2006b) Tell us why you want the money, *Weekend Today*, 11–12 March, 54–55.

Lim, C.Y. (1983) Singapore's economic development: Retrospect and prospect, in P. Chen (ed.), *Singapore: Development Policies and Trends*, Singapore: Oxford University Press.

Lim, M. (2005) S'pore secretary and secretariat to go?, *The Straits Times*, 31 May, H11.

Lim, M. (2006) $7 m kitty to develop Olympic champions, *The Straits Times*, 15 November, H11.

Lim, S. (2004) Eye on Sports: Sport the Paper Chase, 18 March, Available at http://asia1.com.sg\Research%20project\Singapore%20Sport\Eye%20on%20Sports.html (retrieved 17 June 2005).

Lim, T. (2005) Singapore benefits from IOC spin-offs, *The Straits Times Interactive*, 23 July, Available at www.straitstimes.asia1.com.sg (retrieved 24 July 2005).

Luis, E. (2004) SAAA needs image overhaul, *The New Paper*, 15 October, 60.

McNeill, M., Sproule, J. and Horton, P.A. (2003) The changing face of sport and physical education in post-colonial Singapore. *Sport, Education and Society*, 8(10), 35–56.

MCD (1993) *Sports Excellence 2000: Winning for Singapore (December 1993)*, Singapore: MCD and SSC Publication.

MCDS (2001) *Report of the Committee on Sporting Singapore (July 2001)*, Singapore: MCDS.

MCDS (2003) *Annual Report 2002/2003*, Available at www.mcys.gov.sg (retrieved 14 July 2005).

Ng, S.M. (2000) Opening address by the Chairman, Singapore Sports Council at Sports 21@SSC: Towards a Sporting Nation Seminar, 15 January, Singapore Government, Available at www.gov.sg (retrieved 2 June 2005).

Oon, J.T. (2005) Speech by the Chief Executive Officer, Singapore Sports Council at the NSA Networking Session on SSC's New Funding Model, 26 August, Singapore Sports Council, Available at www.ssc.gov.sg (retrieved 12 October 2006).

Peh, S.H. (2005) More cash and space for sports enthusiasts, *The Straits Times Interactive*, 12 March, Available at www.straitstimes.asia1.com.sg (retrieved 26 July 2005).

Perry, M., Kong, L. and Yeoh, B. (1997) *Singapore: A Developmental City State*, Singapore: John Wiley & Sons.

Pok, T.C. (2001) $500 million: A windfall for Singapore sports, *Sports*, 29(5), 5.

Raymond, J. (2005a) Hot zhang: Shot put star looks good for gold in SEA Games, *Today*, 22 June, 44.

Raymond, J. (2005b) 2 Chinese athletes sue SAAA, *Today*, 14 July, 2.

Razali, A. (2006) A future of world stars and events, *Today*, 9 August, 55.

Robert, G. (1998) Isn't it time S'pore had a Ministry of Sport? *The Straits Times*, 1 January, 45.

Roberts, K. (2005) Land of new opportunity, *SportBusiness International*, 104(July), 4–5.

SAA (2005) *Annual Report*, Singapore: SAA.

SAA (2006) Available at www.singaporeathletics.org.sg (retrieved 21 October 2006).

SAAA (2005) Available at www.singaporeathletics.org.sg (retrieved 12 July 2005).

Shanmugaratnam, T. (2006) Speech by the Minister for Education at the 47th Annual General Meeting of the Singapore Schools Sports Councils, 6 January, Available at www.gov.sg (retrieved 2 November 2006).

Sia, C.Y. (1994) Turning top scholars into top sportsmen, *The Straits Times*, 16 March, 26.

Singapore Pools (2005) Available at www.singaporepools.com.sg (retrieved 8 July 2005).

Singh, P. (2006) Singapore forms committee to aim for gold medal at Olympic Games, *Channel News Asia*, 14 November, Available at www.channelnewsasia.com (retrieved 15 November 2006).

Siow, P. (2005) SAA chief laments lack of control, *The Straits Times*, 27 October, H10.

SNOC (2005) Available at www.snoc.org.sg (retrieved 14 July 2005).

Soon, M.Y. (2000) *Sports for All strategies*, Paper presented by the Director (Sport for All) at the Sports 21@SSC: Towards a Sporting Nation Seminar, 15 January, SSC.

Soon, M.Y. (2002) Singapore: Towards a sporting nation with Sport for All, in L.P. Da Cotta and A. Miragaya (eds.), *Worldwide Experiences and Trends in Sport for All*, Germany: Meyer Sports.

SSC (1983) *Singapore Sports Council: The First Ten Years*, SSC Publication by Times Editions, Singapore.

SSC (1994) *On Track: 21 Years of the Singapore Sports Council*, SSC Publication by Times Editions, Singapore.

SSC (1995) *Annual Report 1994–1995*, Singapore: SSC.

SSC (1996) *Annual Report 1995–1996*, Singapore: SSC.

SSC (1998a) *A Nation at Play: 25 Years of the Singapore Sports Council. Leading Sports into the 21st Century*. SSC Publication by Times Editions.

SSC (1998b) *Annual Report 1997–1998*, Singapore: SSC.

SSC (1999) *Annual Report 1998–1999*, Singapore: SSC.

SSC (2000) *Annual Report 1999–2000: Towards a Sporting Nation*, Singapore: SSC.

SSC (2001) *Annual Report 2000–2001: Towards a Sporting Nation*, Singapore: SSC.

SSC (2002) *Annual Report 2001–2002: Championing the Vision*, Singapore: SSC.

SSC (2003) *Annual Report 2002–2003: Spearheading a Sporting Dream*, Singapore: SSC.

SSC (2004) *Annual Report 2003–2004*, Singapore: SSC.

SSC (2005a) *SSC Sports Museum*, Available at www.ssc.gov.sg (retrieved 12 July 2005).

SSC (2005b) SSC Sportsweb, Available at www.ssc.gov.sg (retrieved 26 July 2005).

SSS (2005) Available at www.sss.org.sg (retrieved 15 July 2005).

Tan, B. (2000) *A National Athlete's Perspective of Sports Excellence*, Paper presented by Dr Benedict Tan at the Sports 21@SSC: Towards a Sporting Nation Seminar, 15 January, SSC.

Tan, C. (2005) Two-gold Lay Chi is Best Female Athlete, *The Straits Times Interactive*, 29 July, Available at www.straitstimes.asia1.com.sg (retrieved 30 July 2005).

Tan, J. (2005) Tops in school, yet low in stars, *The Straits Times Interactive*, 23 July, Available at www.straitstimes.asia1.com.sg (retrieved 24 July 2005).

Tan, Y.H. (2006a) I've failed, says Tang, *Today*, 10 May, 55.

Tan, Y.H. (2006b) Sports associations set for review, *Today*, 26 June, 41.

Tan, Y.H. (2006c) Green light for Sports Institute, *Today*, 31 August, 49.

Tan, Y.H. (2006d) Expect an upbeat CoSS report today, *Today*, 2 October, 34.

Tan, Y.H. (2006e) Olympic gold beckons, *Today*, 15 November, 55.

Tay, C.K. (2000) We can't work with Loh, says SSC chief, *The Straits Times*, 18 February, 76.

Tay, C.K. (2002) S'pore's best athletes to be taken care of – for life, *The Sunday Times*, 17 March, 1.

Tay, C.K. (2005) S'pore Sports School should recruit foreign talent, *The Straits Times*, 19 June, S2.

Tay, C.K. (2006) Show us the programme, and we will show you the money, *The Straits Times*, 11 March, S26.

Teo, C.H. (2002) Speech by the Chairman, Singapore National Olympic Council at the XVII Commonwealth Games 2002 Flag Presentation Ceremony, 14 July, Singapore Government, Available at www.gov.sg (retrieved 25 July 2005).

Thomas, L.J. (2000a) The long wait is over for Singapore sports, *Sports*, 28(5), 12–15.

Thomas, L.J. (2000b) Athletics gets axed – and what a blow, *The Straits Times*, 75.

Turnbull, C.M. (1982) *A History of Singapore, 1819–1975*, London: Oxford University Press.

Wang, J. (2006) No fight as Loh romps to SAA hot seat, *The Straits Times*, 30 June, H21.

Wee, S. (2002) Proposed code of governance: Pre-requisite for SSC funding, *Sports*, 30(10), 2.

Wong, G. (2006) Students quit sports school for various reasons, *The Straits Times*, 31 January, H7.

Xue, Y. (2005) Singapore's Mr Olympics, *The Straits Times Interactive*, 22 July, Available at www.straitstimes.asia1. com.sg (retrieved 23 July 2005).

Yap, K.H. (1999) Here's the full list, *The Sunday Times*, 19 December, 52.

Yap, K.H. (2003a) Believe or not, athletics is looking up again, *The Straits Times Interactive*, 1 June, Available at www. straitstimes.asia1.com.sg (retrieved 26 July 2005).

Yap, K.H. (2003b) Tempting scapegoats, these talents, *The Straits Times Interactive*, 12 October, Available at www.straitstimes. asia1.com.sg (retrieved 26 July 2005).

CHAPTER 5

Germany

Karen Petry, Dirk Steinbach and Verena Burk

Introduction

Social relevance and acceptance of top level sport

The social importance of sport is becoming increasingly evident in different sectors such as public health, leisure and competitive sports. Reflecting the increasing social importance of sport the German Olympic Sports Confederation (Deutscher Olympischer Sportbund, DOSB) launched, in 2006, an initiative with the aim of incorporating sport into the German Basic Law as a government objective.[1] The social and political significance of sport is indicated not only by the extent of media interest in competitive sport, but also by the capacity of sports events to regularly attract record attendances. The significance of competitive sportsmen and women as role models and the potential that competitive sport offers as a tool to represent a country internationally are explicitly recognised by the Federal Government and also by the Lander (states)[2] which both offer extensive financial support to promote what has become a quite elaborate and sophisticated competitive sport system.

However, establishing and maintaining the general conditions necessary for an effective competitive sport system is not unproblematic. Creating social conditions that support 'top level' sport[3] calls for political management and intervention which is evident, but only to some extent, in Germany. Neither party political sports programmes nor the government institutions responsible for sport indicate that top level sport has been granted a particular priority which, in part, reflects the deeply embedded principle of the autonomy of sport which is embodied in the differentiated structures that exist for the self-administration of sport. In general, Germany is less interventionist in sport, including elite sport, compared to many other countries.

Development and structure of the German (top level) sports system

In this section the most important milestones in the development of Germany's top level sports system will be outlined. The most important principles of the organisational structures will be derived from the historical perspective discussed below. The features of the state's responsibility for top level sport are then discussed followed by an outline of the support principles governing top level sport.

Historical roots and milestones in elite sport development

Historically, three phases can be identified since World War II, each of which has made a significant contribution to top level sport in Germany in its own way. First, the complete reorganisation of the sports system after World War II; second, the ideological battle between sports systems during the division of Germany; and last, but by no means least, the integration of the sports system developed by the German Democratic Republic (GDR) into the sports system of the Federal Republic of Germany following reunification.

New courses of action were needed to be taken after sport had been subjected, and had succumbed, to totalitarian political indoctrination and exploitation under the National Socialists between 1933 and 1945. When Directive 23 of the Allied Control Council entered into force on 17 December 1945, all fascist organisations and all branches of the Nazi sports system right down to club level were disbanded and any activities by sports organisations were banned. The German sports system was subsequently reorganised from scratch between 1945 and 1950 (Grupe, 1990, p. 18; Nitsch, 1990, pp. 21ff). In the course of this reorganisation, against the backdrop of the previous experience of the misuse of sport by a totalitarian state, the key principles governing support for sport including top level sport were developed and remain deeply enshrined in the federal German sports system to the present day. These are, specifically, the autonomy of sport, the principle of subsidiarity and the principle of cooperation between sports and the state based on the spirit of partnership. Furthermore, the distinct federal organisational structure of sport also originates from this phase of reorganisation.

In the years when Germany was divided, top level sport was mainly characterised by ideological principles and resulted in two very different elite sport systems. The GDR's (East German) sports system was marked, in particular, by party ideology and top level sport offered a means of expressing an alleged socialist superiority over the capitalist enemy. As such, the system used by the GDR was characterised by a strict and clear decision-making and competency hierarchy. The GDR's top level sports system was organised along very strict lines. Schools and sports clubs were used in a targeted way to identify talented children and young people. These talented youngsters were further monitored at training centres, were trained at children's and young people's sports academies and were then promoted into top level squads. This meant that the party and the state were able to influence the children's and young people's academies via the central sports federation, the German Gymnastics and Sports Federation of the GDR. Scientific institutions such as the Research Institute for Physical Culture and Sport, the Institute for Research and Development of Sports Equipment, the German University of Physical Culture and Sport and the Sports Medical Service were also under the influence of the party and the state (Büch, 2002a, p. 10).

In the Federal Republic (West Germany), efforts were made to avoid the imposition of ideologically derived guidelines for sport. Nonetheless, in the West, the state also developed a major interest in national representation through top level sporting performances, particularly in the form of Olympic medals. Consequently, during this period, nationwide structures for supporting top level sport were also created at considerable expense in the Federal Republic. Even now, the training centre, squad and coach systems constitute key pillars of the top level sports system in Germany (see below). During this period, both systems aspired to join the ranks of the most successful sporting nations in the world and both rose to the challenge.

With reunification, the German top level sports system faced the challenge of integrating the GDR's centralist and totalitarian system into the top level sports system of the Federal Republic, which was characterised by great openness and by the fact that it took federal structures into account. Some extraordinarily successful structures of the GDR's top level sports system had to be eliminated as part of this process for political, economic or ethical reasons, only to be reintroduced later in a changed or similar form. In relation to the role Germany plays in international sports competition, the aspiration for success that developed during the previous phase has been maintained. This also manifests itself in the publicly stated requirement that Germany be one of the top three nations at the Olympics (DSB, 2003, p. 3). Objectives are much more rigidly and accurately defined in the all-German top level sports system than in the former federal German sports system. Medal guidelines have become customary in a large number of sports federations and the weighting of Olympic successes according to their representative value in society appears to have increased, particularly over the past 10 years.

In addition to these historic events such as reunification, which have affected the whole of society, individual Olympic Games naturally represent important milestones in the development of top level sport in Germany. However, not all Games are considered of equal consequence. Of especial significance are the Games that were rated as failures measured against their highly ambitious targets. Here too, it is possible to identify three phases or periods. The first phase included the Olympic Games of 1964 and 1968 and the successful bid for the Olympics in 1972, and was identified by Emrich (1996) as being the trigger for much more systematic support for top level sport in the Federal Republic of Germany. A large number of structural changes and trends occurred during this phase especially between the end of the 1960s and the early 1970s. They included the establishment of the first federal training centres, the introduction of the coach system with federal coaches working full time, the introduction of central training courses by the sports federations and the establishment of the German Sports Aid Foundation (*Stiftung Deutsche Sporthilfe*, DSH) in 1969. To these can be added the establishment of the Federal Performance Committee to coordinate the development of top level sport, also in 1969, and the founding of the Federal Institute of Sports Science in 1970 and of the Coaches' Academy as the central venue for initial and advanced training for top level coaches in 1974 (Emrich, 1996, p. 61ff). Figure 5.1 illustrates the establishment of new structures within the German top level sports system since World War II.

The second phase was set against the background of the 1984 Los Angeles Olympic Games. In the context of the absence of Eastern European countries owing to their boycott of the Games, the 59 medals won in Los Angeles were nonetheless interpreted as a failure and as a warning sign of a loss of competitiveness. Immediately afterwards, with an eye on the successful sports clubs in the GDR, the model of Olympic training centres, which had been judged a success up to now, was developed for the Federal Republic. The Olympic training centres were intended to facilitate 'holistic coaching close to the athletes homes' for top level sportsmen and women (cf. Emrich, 1996, p. 66ff).

Finally, missing the target set prior to the Games in Sydney and Athens can be identified as the third phase in Germany's recent Olympic history. Senior officials both at state level and in the federations interpret the results from these two Games as evidence of fundamental change in the international top level sports system in the form of increasing competitiveness on the part of other nations which have significantly increased their spending on the development of top level sport. The merger of the National Olympic Committee for Germany (NOC) and the German Sports Confederation (DSB), which was completed in May 2006, can be seen as a reaction to the poor results achieved in Sydney and Athens, even though there were a number of other reasons for the merger as well. With a view to other sporting nations, stronger centralisation of top level sports organisation was called for following the two Games and was also partially achieved with the establishment of the German Olympic Sports Confederation (DOSB).

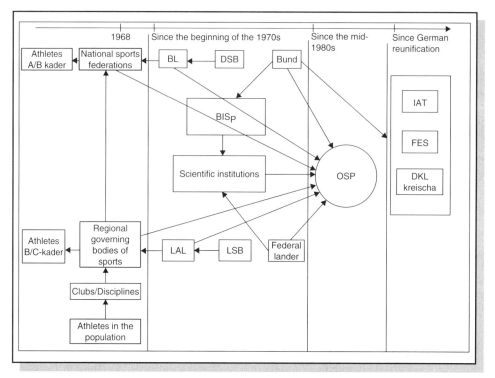

Figure 5.1 The development of the West German sports system after the World War II: BL, Bundesausschuss Leistungssport (Federal Top Level Sports Committee); DKL, Anti-Doping Laboratory Kreischa (Doping Control-Laboratory Kreischa); DSB, Deutscher Sportbund (German Sports Confederation); Bund, Federal Government; BISp, Bundesinstitut für Sportwissenschaft (Federal Institute of Sports Science); FES, Institut für Forschung und Entwicklung von Sportgeräten (Institute for Research & Development of Sports Equipment); IAT, Institut für Angewandte Trainingswissenschaft (Institute of Applied Training Science); LAL, Landesausschuss für Leistungssport (Regional Top Level Sports Committee) (*Source*: Büch (2002b, p. 137))

Furthermore, a number of milestones can be identified within the different disciplines in elite sport development. In the disciplines chosen for this chapter, hockey and swimming, for instance, they involve innovative changes to the rules or extending key officers' authority to make decisions and to act in relation to top level sport. It is not possible, however, to make generalisations at the level of individual sports in relation to the top level sports system in the Federal Republic.

Principles and structures of top level sports development

The organisation of sport in Germany is oriented to the previously mentioned principles of the autonomy of sport, subsidiarity and cooperation based on the spirit of partnership.

These principles, like the federal structure of the state and administration, are the result of historical learning processes that extend beyond sport. They are firmly embedded in the political thinking of the German people and are therefore extremely resistant to all types of reform endeavours. It is important to know this if one wishes to understand where the limits to the reform or restructuring of the German top level sports system lie. The organisational structures of the sports system are also shaped, to a large extent, by the federal structure that is characteristic of the Federal Republic and which is a feature of both public sports administration and the structures of autonomous civic or self-administered sport.

Reduced to their core elements, these general organisational structures of sport can be described as follows: beyond the local, regional and national level, it is possible to make a distinction between a pillar of public administration of sport and a two-tier pillar of autonomous or self-administered sport. In the public administration of sport, both the Federal Government (through the Ministry of the Interior) and the 16 federal regions (for instance, via their Ministries of Culture or the Interior) have joint responsibility for sport in their area. There are consequently no independent specialist ministries of sports. However, at local government level sport issues would be the responsibility of specialist sports offices. Owing to the country's federal structure and the associated distribution of competencies, these public structures do not constitute a hierarchically integrated, top-to-bottom system, as in other countries. Rather, the individual ministries operate largely independently within the framework of their competencies, although at the regional level they coordinate their activities as part of the Conference of Ministers of Sports of the regions. The situation is different with regard to the self-administered autonomous sport sector where approximately 88,000 sports clubs form the basis of an integrated sports system. As has already been indicated, the clubs are organised both at the level of specific disciplines (into governing bodies) and at the level of multiple sports (into sports confederations). Integration at all levels is via voluntary membership, in other words, from the bottom up. Since the merger of the DSB and the NOC in May 2006, the German Olympic Sports Confederation (DOSB) has represented the interests of its member organisations as the sole umbrella body.

The structures of elite sport development are embedded in this framework. The DOSB's Performance Division and the equivalent structures at regional level (Regional Performance Committee/LA-L) play a guiding and coordinating role in elite sport development. The Performance Sports Division is responsible for managing and coordinating top level sport within the DOSB. It launches initiatives for the development of strategic plans and makes declarations of principle regarding performance sport for young athletes and top level sport. Currently, the main strategy papers in this area are the National Top Level Sports Concept, the Support Concept 2012 and the Concept of Top Level Sport for Young Athletes 2012. However, these strategy papers have not yet been combined into a single, comprehensive development plan. At the regional level the criteria for promoting talent are laid down by the Regional Committees for Performance Sport (LA-L).

The main bodies involved in the top level sports system are the clubs and the sports federations. The clubs form the basis of top level sport. They admit children and young people, introduce them to sport and spot talent. In particular, however, the clubs act as a social system which creates security for the athletes and in which their daily sporting activities are embedded. This inclusive role is extremely important in a system which is otherwise unconditionally focused on selection. This occasionally causes problems when, despite a lack of infrastructure and support options at their local club, talented athletes are not redirected to better equipped clubs or training centres.

As each discipline in Germany can only be represented nationally by a single sports federation, the latter have a representative and organisational monopoly for their discipline. At present, there are 33 Olympic and 27 non-Olympic national sports federations. The federations organise the German championships and also nominate and send national teams to world and European championships. In addition, they are responsible for preparing athletes and teams for these major events and also establish squads of talented young athletes and top level athletes for this purpose. All the federations have their own more or less differentiated development concepts for top level sport. In addition to these specialised development plans and concepts, elite sport development in Germany is characterised by a comprehensive support system which is based on three interlocking subsystems or pillars: the squad system, the training centre system and the coaching system. The combined system of top level sport and science and the combined system of schools, universities and other establishments of higher education, the Federal Armed Forces and the Federal Police, all work across the three pillars.

The squad system plays a key role in this regard and constitutes the formal basis for the various sub-aspects of support for top level sport. As in many other countries, athletes in the

German top level sports system are classified according to a hierarchical model in which a distinction is made between different squads (A, B, C, C/D and D). The criteria for allocation to a particular category are the athlete's age as well as his/her performance and performance potential. The support provided is not confined to the purely financial aspect. In the training of young athletes, it is focused, in particular, on providing the required age-related support for a successful sporting career, based on performance development. The squad system constitutes the organisational framework for this support and is linked to the different development levels on the way to reaching the top of the international ladder (DSB, 1997, p. 18).

The talent support groups are the first level in the selection of talent at schools and clubs. The next group up is the so-called D squad, which comprises talented young athletes. The youngest competitive athletes in the top level sports system are organised in this squad. It relates to the regional structure of the top level sports system and comprises the largest number of athletes. Via two further squad levels, the best athletes reach the respective A squads. Based on their performances and their potential, the A squad athletes compete at world level in their sport or discipline. In order to be named in the top level squad, athletes need to achieve success at international competitions and meet performance standards that are in line with world standards. Special squad levels, the so-called Olympic squads or world championship squads of the individual sports federations, are organised via this squad level and they relate to upcoming major events.

The training centre system aims to make available to all athletes nation-wide performance-oriented training groups, qualified coaches and suitable coaching and training facilities for performance-oriented training. With the exception of the 20 multi-sports Olympic training centres, this involves sport-specific training centres at municipal, regional or national level, which are recognised by the national sports federations. This training centre system is complemented by the schools with a sports focus and the elite sports schools which cooperate with the sports federations' training centres.

In order to ensure that the quality of coaching and training is consistent throughout the country and across all performance levels, initial and advanced training for coaches in all the sports federations is structured in a four-tier coaching system, the uppermost tier being the training course at the DOSB's Coaches' Academy in Cologne leading to the qualification of state-certified 'qualified coach'. Both voluntary and full-time coaches work at the training centres. In addition, regional and national coaches employed on a full-time basis normally coordinate the training process at regional and national level and also coach the relevant selections and supervise training courses run by the federations.

State responsibility and competency in respect of top level sport

Under Article 30 of the Basic Law, the 16 federal regions are generally responsible for subsidising sport in the Federal Republic of Germany. The main focus in this regard is on the area of subsidies for school sport, university sport, sport for all and leisure sport within and outside the federations, and on the construction of sports facilities. Responsibility for top level sport, however, lies with the Federal Government, with the Federal Ministry of the Interior operating as the specialised department. The latter plays the leading role in the area of state support for top level sport. It also coordinates the activities of the other federal ministries that have specific responsibilities in the area of top level sport, such as supporting top level sport in the Federal Armed Forces. As in other countries, the state's primary interest in top level sport lies in its potential for enhancing the country's international reputation. This is shown, in particular, by the fact that the more prestigious Olympic sports are given priority over all other sports in terms of state support for top level sport (BMI, 2005, p. 10).

Adhering to the principle of the autonomy of sport, the state interprets its role as that of a sponsor who merely creates the framework that enables autonomous sport and its athletes to perform at the highest international level. For this reason, the government does not become involved in dealing with issues through its own programmes or initiatives, but rather by participating in the different bodies involved in the self-administration of sport. The Federal Government is represented, in particular, on the commissions and committees that have high-level competencies in the area of top level sport. Representatives of the Federal Government are present, inter alia, on the boards, commissions and committees of the DOSB, the national sports federations, the German Sports Aid Foundation and on the boards of trustees of the federal training centres. However, even if the state overtly orients its role in the area of elite sport development according to the principles of the autonomy of sport and subsidiarity, it has used federal funds as a covert control instrument. It recently demonstrated this by clearly rejecting the demand made by organised sport for blanket financing and allocation of funds by the DOSB.

To sum up, we can say that the relationship between the DOSB and the Ministry of the Interior is characterised by the following features:

1 The Federal Ministry of the Interior provides the financial subsidies and lays down the support principles. The focus of support is on the Olympic sports and the allocation of funds is based on the performance principle. The 4-year Olympic cycle is critical in this regard.
2 The DOSB tries to influence the support principles by developing strategy papers and sees itself as the sole policy adviser in respect of top level sport.
3 However, the actual capacity of the DOSB to determine elite sport policy is, in practice, moderated by its relationship with the Federal Government.
4 The Federal Ministry of the Interior (BMI) refuses to transfer sole responsibility for implementing support for top level sport to the DOSB primarily due to an unwillingness to surrender control.

State financing of sport • • •

Top level sport in Germany is characterised by a complex mixed financing system. Probably the most important contribution results from payments that athletes make themselves together with their families. This applies, in particular, to top level sport for children and young people. In quite a few disciplines, however, this applies to all the classes of top level sport. The second most important contribution results from citizens' tax contributions. The taxes paid by the population are invested directly or indirectly in sports funding at municipal, regional and national level. As such, the contribution made by the population at municipal level is particularly high, as it ensures the construction and maintenance of sports facilities. The population also makes another important contribution. This one is, however, a voluntary contribution made by participating in toto and lotto (national or regional lottery) competitions or by being willing to participate in games of chance.

Almost all budgets of public authorities in Germany – from municipalities and counties to the federal regions and the Federal Government – contain expenditure for high-level sport. Financing by the state is characterised by a complex division of labour. The Federal Ministry of the Interior (BMI) finances, in particular, projects involving top level sport and top level sports measures initiated by the national sports federations in the form of competitions, training courses and instruction. The individual sports federations receive support from the Federal Ministry of the Interior based on their sporting success and on the national and international importance of the sport represented by the federation. The support they receive is thus performance-related; in other words, it is based on a particular sport's record of success. Furthermore, the Federal Ministry of the Interior partially finances (operating and maintenance costs) the federal training centres and Olympic training centres, pays the full-time managerial staff and the federal and voluntary coaches and subsidises the sports medicine and performance diagnostic facilities provided to top level athletes.

In 2005, a total of €133 million was allocated to sports funding in the federal budget. Of this, €0.4 million was earmarked for the National Anti-Doping Agency (NADA) and €0.7 million for 'international sports projects'. Approximately €10.65 million was listed in the 2005 appropriation for the launch events and the security arrangements at the 2006 World Cup. The figure shown in respect of financial subsidies for key measures in sport was almost unchanged in comparison with previous years at €71.4 million. An allocation of €3 million was made to the special support programme entitled 'Golden Plan East'.[4] In addition, allocations for top level sport can be found in the budgets of the Federal Ministry of Defence and of the Federal Ministry for Family Affairs, Senior Citizens, Women and Youth (cf. BMI, 2004, o.S.).

With regard to Germany, it should also be taken into account that because of the country's strong federal structure, the federal regions also make a significant (financial) contribution towards sports funding. It amounted to approximately €668 million in 2002, with the municipalities covering the remainder (approximately €3.1 billion (UK billion)) (cf. Statistisches Bundesamt Deutschland, 2004, o.S.). At regional level each government has a department that has overall responsibility for top level sport. The competent regional ministry controls and is responsible for all budgets relating to top level sport in the D/C squad.

Sport is a major beneficiary of the revenue that the state receives from games of chance. Most of the net proceeds from all state betting and lotteries flow into a betting fund which is earmarked for the provision of subsidies to the areas of sport (44 per cent), the arts and culture (25 per cent), heritage conservation (20 per cent) and selected social areas (11 per cent). A special arrangement applies in respect of the game of chance called 'GlücksSpirale' (Lucky Spiral). The surplus generated by the GlücksSpirale goes in equal shares of 25 per cent, respectively, to the Federal Association for Voluntary Welfare Work, the German Olympic Sports Confederation, the German Foundation for Monument Preservation and to conservation and environmental protection (cf. Staatliche Lotterie, 2002, o.S.). In 2001, sport in Germany received grants from the GlücksSpirale amounting to approximately €30 million (of which 40 per cent was allocated to the Land (state) sports confederations, 30 per cent to the DSB, 25 per cent to German Sports Aid, 5 per cent to the NOC). Further funds are provided for sport at regional level; these funds come from the revenue generated by all state betting and lotteries, with all the 16 German regions having their own state lottery boards.

Dimensions of elite sport development in Germany

In Germany, the following are regarded as major dimensions for assessing the support structures of top level sport:

1 The state of development of the national strategy for sport and for the development and promotion of young athletes.
2 The quality of talent spotting and talent support programmes.
3 The quality of coaching qualification programmes.
4 The state of development of the coaching and competition system.
5 The sports science support in the area of coaching, including the sports medical support system.
6 The scope of public and private sector support programmes for top level sport. A prominent status is ascribed to the concept for the development and promotion of young athletes (Krug et al., o.J.).

These dimensions essentially match those identified by Green and Houlihan (2005, p. 170). The first dimension, the quality of the national strategy, is reflected across all the other dimensions and the coaching qualification system is considered as part of the sports science support. Hence, the key features of elite sport development in Germany can be described along the dimensions of sports facility infrastructure, talent spotting and support, support for full-time athletes and the importance of sports and training science.

The description in respect of all the dimensions refers first of all to multi-sports structures and concepts before dealing with specific features in selected sports in greater detail, where applicable. As such, the selected sports (hockey, swimming, athletics) represent a good cross-section of the German elite sport environment. The sports examined[5] also boast a differentiated elite

Table 5.1 Top level German performances in the sports of athletics, swimming and hockey

	German athletics federation	German swimming federation	German hockey federation
Number of members	906,541	607,421	67,695
Sydney Olympic Games (2000)	2 × Gold 1 × Silver 2 × Bronze 3rd in the national ranking	3 × Bronze 14th in the national ranking	Women: 7th Men: 5th
Athens Olympic Games (2004)	2 × Silver 13th in the national ranking	1 × Silver 4 × Bronze 13th in the national ranking	Women: Gold Men: Bronze
World championships	*Helsinki 2005* 1 × Gold 1 × Silver 3 × Bronze 7th in the national ranking	*Montreal 2005* 1 × Gold 3 × Silver 2 × Bronze 7th in the national ranking	*Madrid 2006* Women: 8th *Mönchengladbach 2006* Men: world champions
European championships	*Göteborg 2006* 4 × Gold 4 × Silver 2 × Bronze 2nd in the national ranking	*Budapest 2006* 6 × Gold 4 × Silver 2 × Bronze 2nd in the national ranking	*Dublin 2005* Women: Silver *Leipzig 2005* Men: Bronze

sports structure, are included in the canon of the Olympic sports[6] and are among the top 10 sports federations in Germany. Table 5.1 illustrates the sporting successes achieved in the three sports between 2000 and 2006.

Sports facilities for top level sport

The basis for coaching competitive sportsmen and women in Germany is the coaching and training facilities that are available in the relevant club. However, as the clubs are not able to provide all the structures that ensure high-quality development from a potential sporting talent into a top level sportsman or woman, coaching facilities at local level are augmented by coaching provided at regional and national levels. Therefore, a distinction can be made between *decentralised* and *centralised* coaching. From a certain performance level upwards, athletes are integrated into coaching and training squads and consequently they participate in regional, national and international training camps. Besides the training camps, coaching courses are also important, where talented athletes receive further higher-level instructions from specialist elite coaches, particularly in the area of technique.

Through the system of decentralisation in the German top level sports system, athletes have different coaches who need to coordinate with one another: in some cases, a local coach, the federation's coach or the national coach is available to assist the athletes. This means, therefore – particularly in swimming, for instance – that athletes mostly train at their home clubs and that only a few athletes make use of coaching available through the training centre system.

Overall, the provision of sports facilities in Germany is rated as good by international standards[7] (cf. DSB, 2002). There are adequate coaching facilities in swimming, even if indoor swimming pools are continually being closed down as a result of the restructuring of public swimming pools. This makes it clear that the commercialisation of leisure sport and Sport for All is having an indirect impact on top level sport: not only are training areas being lost but top level sport will also lose talented young athletes in the long term. However, the lack of swimming time for school sport is far more serious than in top level sport: 20 per cent of schools have no in-the-water time at all and, consequently, no swimming sports as part of school curricula. The situation with regard to sports facilities in hockey is slightly different: most hockey clubs have their own pitches which they own themselves.[8] In this regard, the top clubs point to a lack of training facilities, which could be solved by building a second pitch. The investment required for building pitches is mostly borne by the clubs themselves and is, for instance, financed via sponsorship funds.

Besides the decentralised training facilities at the clubs, squad athletes can also use the training centres: as such, the regional training centres are the foundation, the Olympic training centres form the umbrella and in between are the federal training centres. These training facilities run by the national sports federations enable both club training and high-quality training for the federal squad and, in some cases, also for the squads of young athletes. The sportsmen and women train several times a week in homogeneous training groups using facilities available locally or in the surrounding area. The development and provision of federal training centres began as early as the 1960s. The principles governing the planning, construction, use, maintenance and administration of the federal training centres are laid down by the Federal Ministry of the Interior (BMI). The federal training centres are sports facilities that are recognised by the Federal Ministry of the Interior and approved by the DOSB and the sports federations, where training and training courses as well as advanced training courses for coaches are held. Although, it is mainly top level sportsmen and women who train in these centres, depending on capacity available at the centres, top level sportsmen and women at regional level and club and school athletes can also gain access. Depending on the discipline, the federal training centres have all the sports facilities that are required for the relevant training. Normally, accommodation and catering facilities are also available. The centres are designed either as combined training centres for several disciplines or for a single discipline. Currently, there are five federal training centres in Germany: Kienbaum (summer sports); Duisburg (canoeing); Hennef (boxing and wrestling); Warendorf (equestrian); and Wiesbaden (shooting) (cf. DOSB, 2007, o.S.).

The concept of Olympic training centres was approved by the then German Sports Confederation in 1985 as part of the 'Guidelines for top level sport'. The structure of the individual Olympic training centres varies and is determined by the following criteria:

- requirements of the sports or disciplines coached;
- physical size (centralised, decentralised coaching facilities);
- sports science facilities, equipment and staff;
- number of athletes coached;
- sponsorship.

There are a total of 20 of these service facilities for the national sports federations of Olympic sports in Germany. However, the individual sports pursue different centralisation approaches: for the winter sports, the 2 Olympic training centres in Bavaria and Thuringia are the central facilities, while there are 12 Olympic training centres for the sport of athletics, 8 training centres for swimming and 4 for hockey. The track records of the different sports vary greatly; however, centralised training of top level athletes appears to work very well as most of the Olympic winter sports have proven over the past few years.

The Olympic training centres are financed by the Federal Ministry of the Interior, which shoulders the lion's share of the cost as part of its support for top level sport, the respective federal Land (state), the respective regional sports confederation and the relevant municipality. In addition, financial support is provided by sponsors and by marketing activities (cf. DSB, 2000,

p. 64f). Some Olympic training centres have so-called *houses for athletes* comprising a school/boarding school, residential group and educational supervision and represent the most comprehensive support for young athletes. The aim is to create these houses for athletes at all the Olympic training centres (BMI, 2002, p. 15).

Talent spotting and talent support

The influence that talent spotting and talent support have on the success of top level sports systems is undisputed. A look at the demographic trends also makes it clear that in Germany, as in other Western European countries, a decline in potential talent attributable to demographics has set in, which makes it all the more important to improve the efficiency of talent spotting and talent retention.

Representatives of the public sports administration, the federations and the sports science community have up to now regarded talent support, and talent spotting even more, as a relative weakness in the German sports system compared with other areas of support for top level sport. In this regard, a key point is, among other things, the fact that the federal nature of the German sports system in the area of talent spotting and talent support comes into play even more strongly than in other areas of elite sport development. Support for young athletes, including the relevant D squad structure, falls within the scope of the competent ministries, sports confederations and national sports federations at regional level. As a result, the approaches used for talent spotting and support for young athletes in some cases vary significantly according to the federal Land (state) and the specific sport. In this regard, the German Sports Confederation's concept of top level sport for young athletes is merely a framework concept which sets out "the range of common features" in the area of support for young athletes (cf. DSB, 2006, p. 5). Given the large number of institutions involved, however, with independent competences in the planning and strategy area, a major coordinating effort is required. Emrich and Güllich (2005) illustrate the problem in an analysis of the policy for top level sport for young athletes when they identified 405 necessary coordination procedures in 49 areas of support for young athletes.

Talent spotting

The organisation of talent spotting in Germany varies according to regions and specific sports. There is no uniform nationwide or even multi-sports talent spotting system. While it was possible to adopt approaches and structures used in the GDR system in the area of talent support or sports science support for top level sport, it was neither appropriate nor possible to adopt the uniform talent spotting and selection system, 'Einheitlichen Sichtung und Auswahl für die Trainingszentren und Training-sstützpunkte des DTSB der DDR (ESA)',[9] which had proven its worth in the GDR. The aim of ESA was to have PE teachers record the physical features and current capability of all pupils in classes 1 and 3. This was followed in a multi-stage process by verification of system-compliant behaviour and by psychological and discipline-specific tests and finally the pupil would be admitted to the children's and youth sports academy system. This recruitment system contributed in no small measure to the GDR's sporting success; however, it was impossible to integrate it into the Federal Republic's top level sports system following reunification not least because the system was cost-inefficient owing to the high staff costs, but also because it was incompatible with a social and sports system that was distinguished by multiple opportunities for the use of time by children as well as by personal freedom in terms of choices. Only in a totalitarian sports system like the GDR's, talented children could be tied to top level sport regardless of their personal preferences or individual socio-economic circumstances.

In the Federal Republic of Germany, the search for talent therefore continues to be based on school and club sport. As such, proving one's worth in competition is considered the key criterion in practice-oriented talent spotting as it most closely corresponds to the complexity of the relevant sport's requirement profile and to the required ability on the part of young athletes. For this reason, searching for talent via the standardised and traditional system of competition operated by the clubs and federations is the most widespread method. Specific talent spotting measures and talent spotting courses implemented by the sports federations are other common recruitment methods.

In addition, the reason why cooperation between schools and clubs plays such an important role in terms of the effectiveness of the talent search and talent support system is that the stages of top level sport for young athletes mainly occur during the latter's school years and that the institution of school includes almost all children. However, the institutionalisation of cooperation programmes between schools and sports clubs did not occur in the Federal Republic of Germany until recently. In the 1980s, only two large regions had state-wide cooperation programmes. Since the mid-1990s, however, the other regions have followed suit and introduced similar initiatives. The programmes are generally in the area of after school sport and, for instance, take the form of training groups and action days. As a rule, these programmes are sport-specific and regionally oriented and they frequently rely on the personal commitment of volunteers.

The representatives of the sports federations see deficiencies in, among other things, the training provided to PE teachers and the tension within the school sport curriculum between core sports and competitive and performance-oriented sports on the one hand and new content (e.g., newly fashionable sports) and new objectives (e.g., health) on the other.

Both at clubs and in school sport, the search for talent is mostly based on visual inspection. In other words, it depends on the experienced eye of a coach or teacher to determine whether, in a group of children or young people playing sport, those young people who are particularly well suited to a specific sport are identified. This process depends on the coach or teacher possessing the relevant expertise. However, this expertise is not always sufficiently evident, particularly among PE teachers and voluntary youth coaches at clubs. The federations therefore have explicitly stated that the development of objective and valid testing procedures with sound, discipline-specific predictor features is high on their sports science research wish list. Even the two school sports competitions, *Federal Youth Games* and *Youth trains for the Olympics*, which are held on a nationwide basis in different sports, do not meet this requirement. They are fairly unsuitable for talent spotting as both competitions are focused more on broad participation in sport than on the systematic selection of talent. Overhauling or expanding *Youth trains for the Olympics* should improve matters in this regard.

If the talent spotting strategies in the sports of swimming, athletics and hockey are compared, it becomes clear that the German Hockey Federation relies very strongly on a central talent spotting system with four talent spotting tournaments. Consequently, it is assumed that 90 per cent of future internationals have already passed through the talent spotting system between the ages of 10 and 12. By contrast, talent spotting in swimming and athletics is carried out on a decentralised basis via different programmes and competitions organised by the regional federations.

Talent support

Talent spotting is followed by targeted talent support. It is an important prerequisite for subsequently achieving the highest international performance level. In this regard, sport and

133

discipline-specific requirements need to be reconciled with requirements outside sport. The overall system of talent support consists of several subsystems which aim to make it possible for young and adult top level sportsmen and women to pursue a dual career within and outside of top level sport. Training stages, squad membership and competitive and support systems need to be coordinated in a targeted way as part of talent support. The model of long-term training and performance development (see Figure 5.2) is used here for orientation purposes (DSB, 2006, p. 10).

Institutionalised coaching and support begins at an early stage when young athletes are accepted into the D/DC squads organised by the national sports federations. According to a survey of squad athletes conducted by Emrich and Güllich (2005), this occurs on average at the age of 14½ years. Being nominated to join a squad is linked to a comprehensive package of support and coaching.

From an analytical point of view, in line with the advocacy coalition framework (Sabatier, 1998, 1999), at the level of secondary beliefs, different ideas on the effectiveness of various

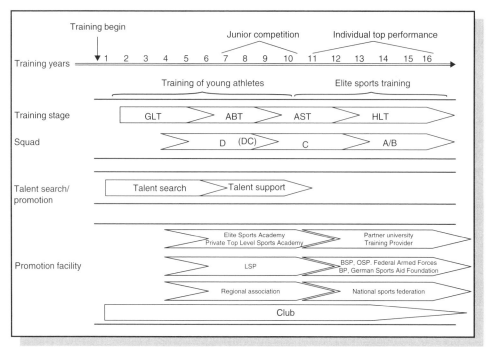

Figure 5.2   Model of training and performance: GLT, Basic training; ABT, Advanced training; AST, Subsequent training; HLT, Elite sport training; LSP, Regional training centre; BSP, Federal training centre; OSP, Olympic training centre; BP, Federal police

talent support measures in top level sport can be identified. According to Emrich and Güllich (2005, p. 74), the majority of participants have a framework of unquestioned assumptions, which they describe as follows:

It is assumed that successful sportsmen and women train in a sport early on for lengthy periods in a continuous training process, receiving ongoing support from the sports support system, and that performances or successes achieved at an early age are a valid predictor of long-term success in top level sport.

In conjunction with the existing structures (see below), this belief system contributes to a scenario where early specialisation and early successes are, in some cases, given precedence over long-term career development, particularly because squad membership, the extension of coaches' contracts and also the level of budgetary appropriations for the federations are generally decided on the basis of current capabilities. Besides a change in beliefs, there is, therefore, also a need to create structures that reward long-term training strategies and successes, and investment in basic training and the willingness to facilitate the transfer of talent to other sports. The Performance Division (BL) endeavours to play a controlling role in this area by issuing planning specifications.

Support for full-time athletes

The squad system which has already been described constitutes the formal basis for selecting sportsmen and women for targeted support. Athletes receive financial and non-material support during the course of their sporting career based on being members of the relevant squad.[10] This reward system is performance-based and the payments vary considerably in the individual sports. If one looks at the institutions that are involved in the payments, it is noticeable that the state does not provide *any* financial rewards to athletes. The state is merely involved in facilitating sporting performances. The performances are, however, rewarded by private individuals, institutions, commercial companies and sponsors and also via the sports federations themselves and the German Sports Aid Foundation (*Stiftung Deutsche Sporthilfe*, DSH).

Based on the acknowledgement that increased internal and external demands made a special, comprehensive style of support indispensable, the 'German Olympic Society' and the then 'German Sports Confederation' in 1967 established the DSH. The DSH exclusively and directly serves the charitable objective of supporting sportsmen and women who are preparing for, are producing or have produced, top level sporting performances, by way of compensation in material and non-material ways. Those athletes in receipt of support are not only aided in their endeavours to develop and maintain their sporting capabilities, but also receive social support to enable them to develop their abilities in their initial and advanced vocational training. The prerequisite for being accepted into a support programme is first of all membership of a federal A, B or C squad organised by the national sports federations which are supported by the German Sports Aid Foundation. Since its establishment in 1967, the Foundation has supported a total of 38,000 athletes to the tune of almost €350 million. The Foundation also rewards the international successes of Olympic disciplines at world and European championships as well as at Olympic Games. In addition, there are separate arrangements for team sports, the junior division and non-Olympic sports (cf. Stiftung Deutsche Sporthilfe, 2006, p. 4f).

A large number of federations have developed their own reward systems for their national teams, which involve a payout to athletes at the end of a season based on participation and performance. In addition, it is standard practice to pay appearance fees and winner's bonuses at competitions, particularly in sports such as athletics or swimming. Reward systems, which are sometimes applied in a highly non-transparent manner in the different disciplines, enable many athletes to make a substantial part of their living through their involvement in sport. Even at intermediate level, this creates a semi-professional system for a certain length of time. However, non-transparent reward systems can hardly be described as an appropriate foundation for an efficient high-level sports system. The risk in the reward system that is applied in German top level sport lies in the fact that it is possible to earn enough money even with mediocre performances, as there is no incentive and no need to make the effort to achieve better and greater performances.

The system of dual development • • •

One of the principles of support for top level sport in Germany is the dual development of sportsmen and women; in other words, they receive support not only in the area of sport but also in regard to their schooling and their career. This principle applies to all age groups and to all sports. In the debate on support for athletes, the entitlement to a dual career is a constant and major area of conflict as it places an enormous time burden on sportsmen and women. The call for a second career track alongside the sporting career stems from the aim underlying the German top level sports system of humane top level sport which has the athlete at its centre.

Essentially, there are a variety of support options for children and young people who are involved in top level sport. In addition to supportive systems of competition, there are, in particular, supportive training schemes that make it possible to help children and young people systematically improve their performance. At the same time, there are support measures (e.g., timetable arrangement, homework supervision) aimed at linking the double burden between school and the club, school and top level sport, studies and top level sport or vocational training and top level sport.

Where problems with talent support do arise, they relate to the fluctuation aspect and the fact that children's and young people's interests inevitably change. Moreover, talent support measures are only geared to a limited extent to meeting the needs of children and young people whose performance stagnates or declines in the short or medium term. The risk here is that they may drop out, and in the existing talent support structures it is a major risk. The transition from junior level to top level sport, in particular, points the way forward in an athlete's life: when facing such decisions, athletes should receive advice from the career advisors who work at the Olympic training centres.

Extremely successful talent support is provided at the so-called elite sports schools. The elite sports schools programme has its origin in the former sports schools for children and young people in the GDR. Since 1997, the Savings Banks Finance Group has provided a total of approximately €3 million as financial support to the programme. There are approximately 40 elite sports schools nationwide. Approximately 11,200 talented athletes are coached at these schools and their coaching is managed by approximately 480 full-time coaches – including 75 national coaches. In the regional distribution of schools, it becomes clear that the northern part of Germany has rather a backlog of demand in comparison with schools in the eastern part of Germany. However, cooperation between the school supervisory authority and the sports organisations urgently needs to be improved and the special status of pupils who are involved in top level sport needs to be regulated by law by the relevant Land (state) ministries of education.

Besides the elite sports schools, there are also the 'top level sport partner schools': these sports-friendly schools are mostly located in the vicinity of regional training centres or Olympic training centres and give athletes a special status in day-to-day school life, which allows them to train, attend competitions and fulfil school requirements. The so-called top level sport partner universities pursue a very similar approach: budding academics often face a very difficult balancing act between pursuing a sporting career and gaining professional qualifications.[11] How well students cope with their studies, however, depends on what sport they are involved in and hockey is a particularly positive example in this regard because a very large number of top athletes successfully complete a course of study.

In addition, support structures still vary from region to region: in Baden-Württemberg, for instance, the federal Land and the company OBI established the foundation 'Squad Support Perspective Baden-Württemberg' in 2000. The scheme ensures that approximately 60 top level sportsmen and women in Baden-Württemberg receive targeted support while they are preparing and qualifying for the Olympic Games (Ministerium für Kultus, Jugend und Sport Baden-Württemberg, 2001, p. 14f). Initiatives of this type launched by the business community and sponsors are becoming increasingly important as regards the provision of support to top level athletes. The establishment of collaboration between the sports federations and partners in the business community varies from sport to sport and depends mainly on the initiative of those in charge. The state would like to see these funding collaborations expanded but finds that there are too few partners in the business community willing to become involved in providing financial support to sport.

It is also a German tradition that the relevant military system plays a major role in the development of top level sport in Germany. This applies not only to the German Reich, the Weimar Republic and the period of National Socialism, but also to the Federal Republic of Germany since the establishment of the Federal Armed Forces in 1956 and to the GDR with its People's Army. In the late 1960s, the establishment of the so-called sports support companies began in Germany. Approximately 740 sports soldiers are supported there under high-quality training and competitive conditions. Following basic training, athletes are transferred to these sports support groups which have been set up near Olympic training centres and training centres run by German sports organisations. This enables athletes to use up to 70 per cent of their duty hours for training and competitions. The athletes generally train at the training centres run by the sports federations or at their clubs (Bundesministerium für Verteidigung, o.D., p. 6).

In addition, since 1978, the Federal Border Police (BGS) has supported top level sportsmen and women in different winter sports and set up a training centre at the Federal Border Police Sports Academy in Bad Endorf for this purpose. In 1999, as part of a top level sports support project, the support was expanded to include different summer sports, although the sportsmen and women are coached mainly at the Cottbus/Frankfurt (Oder) Olympic training centre. The focus is on both vocational training as a law enforcement officer in the Federal Border Police and the provision of support to young, highly talented athletes. During periods of vocational training, the athletes have adequate training facilities at their disposal. Sportsmen and women who have completed their police training can devote the whole year to top level sport (cf. Bundesgrenzschutz, 1998, p. 12). Olympic winter sports athletes are the main beneficiaries of this arrangement: '80 per cent of the Turin Olympic team was employed in the Federal Armed Forces, the Federal Police and Customs. That indicates where one of the key success factors lies' (Schwank, 2006).

Incorporating sports and training science

In the competitive battle between the two German sports systems between 1964 and 1989, a great deal of sports science research was carried out in both East and West Germany. In both systems, training science and sports medical research contributed significantly to overall success. When the GDR's sports system collapsed following the peaceful revolution of 1989, although the type and scope of scientific services provided for top level sport changed, the great importance of sports science research and the know-how acquired in both systems remained. It was also possible to retain some of the structures of the GDR's sports system, albeit in an adapted form. The former Research Institute for Physical Culture and Sport, which once had over 600 employees, was spun off into the Institute for Applied Coaching Science and the Institute for Research and Further Development of Sports Equipment, both of which play a key role in scientific monitoring.

This combined system of science and top level sport is based on four pillars: basic research; application-oriented research; practice-oriented research; and coach training. Specific tasks can be allocated to the structures of these four pillars, although some overlapping and competency-related disputes have occurred.

The least clearly defined task area is that of basic research. The approximately 60 sports science institutes at universities and the German Sport University Cologne implement a large number of basic research and application-oriented research projects in cooperation with the Olympic training centres and the sports federations. They are financed from different sources but funds appropriated by the Federal Institute of Sports

Science for research into top level sport represent a key resource in this context.

Application-oriented research into top level sport in Germany is closely linked to the Institute for Applied Training Science in Leipzig (IAT) and the Institute for Research and Further Development of Sports Equipment in Berlin (FES). The IAT has approximately 90 staff and offers, among other things, direct scientific assistance to the federations in developing training concepts, in discipline-specific training and competition research and in evaluating the results in the form of world ranking analyses. Furthermore, the IAT conducts research in the area of aptitude and talent diagnostics and into the development and adaptation of specific measurement technologies and evaluation and management software. For example, the German Hockey Federation is one of the most innovative federations in German sport, also in terms of using scientific monitoring. In the area of game analysis and video observation, in conjunction with the IAT, among others, hardware and software solutions as well as equipment for sports facilities have been developed which represent the current gold standard internationally. Besides the IAT, the Olympic training centres also play an important role in the area of application-oriented research. They assist the federations, coaches and athletes primarily in the area of performance diagnostics and training management.

The FES in Berlin is responsible for dealing with engineering problems in top level sport. Practice-oriented research in disciplines that rely on materials, implementation in the form of equipment and measurement engineering prototypes and the testing and adjustment of such equipment in training and competitions involving national teams form the basic idea behind the institute. The aim is to optimise the 'athlete–equipment' system. All in all, the FES cooperates with around 15 German federations in developing, optimising and building new sports equipment (e.g., boats, bicycle frames, skates) and in researching new materials (BMI, 2002, p. 59).

The Federal Institute of Sports Science (BISp) has overall responsibility for managing and coordinating all research for the benefit of top level sport and for awarding research contracts. The overriding task and key goal of the Federal Institute's work is to ensure that top level sport is always humane. The BISp performs consulting and support tasks, including, among other things, supporting applied sports science research, ensuring that doping analyses are carried out, supporting research into sports facilities, developing concepts for the construction of sports facilities and running a central federal documentation and information office. Approximately €6.28 million every year is allocated to the Federal Institute from federal funds for this purpose (BMI, 2002, p. 51f). In addition, universities can support sports science research for the benefit of top level sport on the basis of an application and appraisal system, particularly for research activities in the field of sports medicine, training science and biomechanics.

In order to ensure that there is a sustainable transfer of know how into practical training, the sophisticated system of coaches' training can be mentioned as the fourth pillar. The DOSB's Coaches' Academy serves as a central initial and advanced training centre for top coaches in Germany. The task of the Academy is to further enhance coaches' technical expertise, taking into account the very latest sports science findings in relation to sports performance factors. As such, admission to a course of study depends not just on educational requirements but also, primarily, on having the preceding coaching licences and, in particular, on the specific endorsement of the relevant national sports federation. The diploma obtained at the Coaches' Academy builds on the C, B and A licences issued by the national sports federations and is thus the highest coaching licence in Germany.

The German Hockey Federation distinguishes itself by a tightly woven control system to guarantee a comprehensive transfer of current knowledge and coaching concepts between coaches of different age groups as well as federation or club coaches. Special club coaches, for instance, participate in coaching sessions of the federation and also work as co-coaches in select teams of the federation.

Despite this infrastructure, which as a whole is well developed, and the proven efficiency of the combined scientific system, criticism has also been voiced. In 2004, in its 'Augsburg Theses', the Spokespersons' Committee of the Coaching Science Section of the German Society of Sports Science, for instance, criticised the scientific support provided to top level sport in Germany (cf. Lames, 2004). Collectively, the theses imply, first of all, that top level sport in Germany is dependent on stronger scientific support in order to maintain its competitiveness, attesting that other nations have something of a head start. Second, they state that scientific support needs to be provided in a balanced ratio of basic research and applied research, involving all scientific institutions. And the third and final point is that scientific support requires competent management and coordination at the highest level. In concrete terms, this position paper calls for improved financial resources, more stringent coordination of top level sports research and more active involvement on the part of the national sports federations as the purchasers of the research results.

All three selected sports cooperate closely with the scientific support system. Projects supported by the Federal Institute for Sports Science are generally implemented in cooperation with different university institutes and Olympic training centres. Worthy of mention in this regard is the initiative launched by the German Swimming Federation, which, from 2007 onwards, will be formulating its knowledge requirements and advertising the individual projects in the universities and other institutions of higher education. This approach meets the requirements of the Augsburg Theses and could also serve as an example to other federations of a model approach for improving scientific monitoring in top level sport.

Conclusions

The German system of top level sport is characterised by the strong autonomy of sport and by the federal structure which is a feature of the political system in Germany as a whole. As a result of these two factors, the structures of top level sport are very heterogeneous and, consequently, a uniform picture emerges only to a very limited extent. Expressed in positive terms, the system provides openness to individual solutions that differ from discipline to discipline. This openness is both an advantage and a disadvantage of the German top level sports system as, on the one hand, there are well-developed substructures, while on the other hand, however, these substructures are not connected and have a tendency to take on a life of their own. The existence of these many different competencies and areas of responsibility calls for an enormous amount of coordination and young talented athletes are often lost in this complex system. Traditional control mechanisms via hierarchically integrated and centrally controlled structures do not work in German top level sport. In this area, the Performance Division is looking for new control mechanisms (e.g., incentive structures, model-based learning).

Yet in regard to deep core and policy beliefs, hardly any differences can be identified between governmental and non-governmental players. All the players acknowledge the principles governing the organisation of sport and declare their support for humane top level sport and the principle of the dual career. Yet, this is not just lip service, but real conviction! The essential congruence of the policy beliefs of different players is also manifested by the fact that in Germany no fundamental changes occur in sports policy when there is a change of government. At the level of secondary beliefs, some distinctions can be made in relation to the following questions: when should systematic training and systematic support begin? and to what extent can and should the organisation of top level sport be centralised?

Overall, it is certainly important when examining the German system of top level sport that during the existence of the former GDR, the system was characterised for many years by the competitive battle between the two German systems. If relevant differences are found, they will more than likely be between players with 'socialisation' in the former eastern and western systems. However, as the last generation of eastern athletes and coaches has now left (or has been requested to leave) the system, the two systems have become strongly aligned. Nonetheless, there are still considerable differences in mentality between East and West regarding the acceptance and importance of top level sport in society. For instance, elite schools and schools that focus on sport are much more readily accepted in the eastern part of Germany.

It becomes clear that the Performance Division (BL) and the federations, clubs and coaches (particularly at regional level) pursue different inherent interests. As a rule the federations and coaches at local and regional level benefit from early successes and are no longer involved in these athletes' success when they are adults or indeed in any success they may have if they switch to a different discipline. This is where solutions need to be found that reward cooperative behaviour and the long-term development of athletes. Objectives for the future are to strengthen the grassroots level (i.e., the clubs), for instance, via the possibility of direct support by the business community and to reduce bureaucracy and increase transparency in relation to competencies and the distribution of tasks.

Notes

1 The Basic Law defines a number of so-called national objectives, such as the principle of a social state, equal rights for women and men and achieving a united Europe. 'The national objective of sport should be incorporated into a new paragraph 2 of Article 20a of the Basic Law together with the national objective of culture. The wording could be as follows: 'the state shall protect and promote culture and sport' (DOSB Positionspapier, 2006, p. 2). However, whether sport does actually become a national objective depends primarily on the stance of the German Bundestag and the 16 federal regions which are involved in the decision-making process under the principle of Germany's federal structure.

2 Germany is divided into 16 federal regions called 'Länder'.

3 'Top level' sport is the terminology used for elite or high-performance sport in some European countries.

4 The 'Golden Plan East' is a special support programme that grants subsidies from federal funds for the construction of sports facilities aimed at delivering Sport for All in the federal regions of former East Germany and in the former eastern part of Berlin.

5 It was possible, based on a guideline interview with a representative of each sport (employee in the relevant sports federation, coach and/or official), to verify the information in regard to quality.

6 'The rapid commercialisation occurring in sports that attract major media interest is not reaching many Olympic sports and, as a consequence, the state remains the main sponsor of Olympic sport' (BMI, 2002, p. 8).

7 In 2002, the Federal Government reduced its capital expenditure on building projects to approximately €18 million. In 1998, financial subsidies had amounted to €34 million. By contrast, capital expenditure requirements amounted to €132 million in 2002 (cf. Deutscher Bundestag, 2002).

8 Field hockey is now played almost exclusively on astroturf pitches by the top clubs in Germany. The game is faster, more precise, more varied and, consequently, also more attractive to spectators.

9 Uniform talent spotting and selection for training centres and training bases.

10 Honouring athletes in a non-material way has a long-standing tradition and is in some cases still important today. An example is the Silver Laurel Leaf, which is presented by the Federal President, or other honours that may be awarded to athletes at municipal, regional and national level. Reward systems of a non-material nature also include sportsmen's elections, fair play awards and the like.

11 Academics constituted the second largest group in the 2004 Olympic team after Federal Armed Forces personnel (cf. Gernandt, 2006).

References

BMI (2002) 10. Sportbericht der Bundesregierung. Berlin o.V.
BMI (2004) Schily: Bund sichert Sportförderung auf hohem Niveau. Zugriff am 1 März 2007 unter http://www.bmi.bund.de/nn_338278/Internet/Content/Nachrichten/Archiv/Pressemitteilungen/2004/11/Sporthaushalt__2005.html

BMI (2005) Programm des Bundesministeriums des Inneren zur Förderung des Leistungssports sowie sonstiger zentraler Einrichtungen, Projekte und Maßnahmen des Sports auf nationaler und internationaler Ebene mit Rahmenrichtlinien.

Büch, M.-P. (2002a) Die Entwicklung des Leistungssports in Deutschland unter besonderer Berücksichtigung der Rolle der Sportwissenschaft. o.O.: o.V.

Büch, M.-P. (2002b) Elite sport, in R. Naul and K. Hardman (eds.), *Sport and Physical Education in Germany*, London/NY, pp. 132–152, S. 137.

Bundesgrenzschutz (1998) Bundesgrenzschutz-Sportschule Bad Endorf. Bonn: o.V.

Bundesministerium der Verteidigung (o.D.). Sport in der Bundeswehr. Köln: J.P. Bachem GmbH & Co. KG.

Deutscher Bundestag (2002) Antwort der Bundesregierung auf die Große Anfrage der CDU/CSU Fraktion. Drucksache 14/114.

DOSB (2006) Staatsziel Sport. Positionspapier des Deutschen Olympischen Sportbundes.

DOSB (2007) Bundesleistungszentren. Zugriff am 1. März 2007 unter http://www.dosb.de/de/leistungssport/materialien/bundesleistungszentren.

DSB (1997) Nachwuchs-Leistungssport-Konzept. Frankfurt/Main: o.V.

DSB (2000) 50 Jahre Deutscher Sportbund: der Sport ein Kulturgut unserer Zeit. Frankfurt/Main: Umschau Braus GmbH.

DSB (2003) Sportpolitische Konzeption des Deutschen Sportbundes – Sport tut Deutschland gut. – Das Leistungsspektrum des Sports und die politischen Konsequenzen.

DSB (2006) Nachwuchsleistungssportkonzept 2012. Leitlinien zur Entwicklung des Nachwuchsleistungssports. Frankfurt.

Emrich, E. (1996) Zur Soziologie der Olympiastützpunkte. Eine Untersuchung zur Entstehung, Struktur und Leistungsfähigkeit einer Spitzensportfördereinrichtung. Niedernhausen: Schors.

Emrich, E. and Güllich, A. (2005) Zur Produktion sportlichen Erfolges. Organisationsstrukturen, Förderbedingungen und Planungsannahmen in kritischer Analyse. Köln: Sport & Buch Strauß.

Gernandt, M. (2006) Duale Karriereplanung: Spitzensportambitionen und Berufsperspektiven in Einklang bringen. In Olympisches Feuer 6/2006, pp. 16–19.

Green, M. and Houlihan, B. (2005) *Elite Sport Development: Policy Learning and Political Priorities*, London: Routledge.

Grupe, O. (1990) Der neue Weg im Sport. Über Sinn und Organisation des Sports. In Deutscher Sportbund (Hrsg.), Die Gründerjahre des Deutschen Sportbundes. Wege aus der Not zur Einheit. Schorndorf: Hofmann, S16–S24.

Krug, J., Hoffmann, B., Rost, et al. (o.J.) Das Fördersystem im Leistungssport der Bundesrepublik Deutschland. Leipzig.

Lames, M. (2004) Augsburger Thesen zur wissenschaftlichen Unterstützung des Spitzensports. Online-Zugriff unter http://www.sportwissenschaft.de/fileadmin/pdf/download/Augsburger_Thesen_lang.pdf am 07.01.2007

Ministerium für Kultus, Jugend und Sport Baden-Württemberg (2001) Förderung des Leistungssports im Nachwuchsbereich. Stuttgart: o.V.

Nitsch, F. (1990) Traditionslinien und Brüche. Stationen der Sportentwicklung nach dem Zweiten Weltkrieg. In Deutscher Sportbund (Hrsg.), Die Gründerjahre des Deutschen Sportbundes. Wege aus der Not zur Einheit. Schorndorf: Hofmann, S29–S64.

Sabatier, P. (1998) The advocacy coalition framework: Revision and relevance for Europe. *Journal of European Public Policy*, 5(1), 1998.

Sabatier, P. and Jenkins-Smith, H.C. (1999) "The advocacy coalition framework: An assessment". In: P. Sabatier (ed.), *Theories of the Policy Process*. Westview Press: Boulder.

Schwank, B. (2006) Wir tun alles, um 2008 und 2012 erfolgreicher zu sein. Interview FAZ vom 29.11.2006.

Staatliche Lotterie (2002) Erträge. Zugriff am 6. März 2002 unter http://www.toto-lotto-bw.de/index1.html

Statistisches Bundesamt Deutschland (2004) öffentliche Ausgaben für den Sport: 47 Euro pro Kopf in 2002. Zugriff am 1. März 2007 unter http://destatis.de/presse/deutsch/pm2003/p2580061.htm

Stiftung Deutsche Sporthilfe (2006) Presseunterlagen. Frankfurt/Main: o.V.

CHAPTER 6

France[1]

Emmanuel Bayle, Christophe Durand and Luc Nikonoff

Introduction

Thirty-six million French people practice a physical or sporting activity, and approximately 15 million of these do so as licensed members of France's 175,000 sports clubs. Up to 350,000 jobs in France are associated with sports development; over 200,000 of these (in the public and private sectors combined) are in sport itself. In total, sports-related spending in France amounts to an annual €24.6 billion, or 1.7 per cent of gross domestic product (GDP) (Andreff and Nys, 2001); of this total, more than €10 billion is public money, mainly at the level of the *commune*.[2] In the light of such statistics, sport in France has evidently become a significant economic sector in its own right. It also plays a strategic role in France by virtue of its public service functions with regard to education, civic associations (*la vie associative*), health, social integration (especially in cases of social deprivation), tourism, regional, and local development, the international identity and image of France, and supporting French diplomacy, particularly France's relations with developing countries. These are roles that have grown in significance over time and, in a national political culture that prizes public service, it is no surprise that they have benefited from large-scale state intervention dating back to the beginning of the 1960s.

The first major legislative activity in relation to sport dates back to the Sports Charter (*Charte des Sports*) of 1940, a period marked by its very specific political context.[3] The next phase of French state activity in terms of its 'annexation' of sport – in particular of elite sport – came in the early 1960s. In this equally specific international climate of Cold War, it became a symbolic importance that nations were represented at the highest levels of sports competition; in the case of France, no medals were brought home from the 1960 Rome Olympic Games. Sport had become a matter of state, and France's machinery for centralised economic planning ensured a raft of legislative measures which constituted France's first public sports policy.

France's sports federations became subject to new regulations: framework laws (*lois* programmes) were adopted in 1961 in relation to the building of new sports facilities; a system of aid to federations was put in place; a corps of sports technicians was created (paid by the state and made available to federations); and a National Council for Sport (*Conseil national des sports*) was set up in 1960 with the aim of facilitating relations between the government and those responsible for sport in France. Sport in schools and universities was also overhauled, with the intention of bringing school/university and club sport closer together; the idea here being to channel more sportsmen and women into competitive sport. The 1960s also saw the state embarking on the regulation of the various professions linked to sport, and extending the state financing of sports federations across the country.

One effect of these measures was to rationalise for the first time the way in which France's sports federations functioned, the declared aim being to improve French performance in top international sports competitions. In effect, the federations were 'nationalised' in the name of the general interest, and as a clear manifestation of the state's desire to play, effectively, a supervisory role (*tuteur effectif*) vis-à-vis the federations (Lachaume, 1991). This trend reached a peak in 1984 with the passing of legislation (*la loi generale sur le sport*) concerning the organisation and promotion of sports and physical activity. Here too, sport was clearly defined as belonging to the state's sphere of competence; nevertheless, the law also provided for the delegation of this public service provision to the federations themselves, which historically had had the responsibility for the organisation, promotion, and development of sport.

In order to fulfil this role, the national sports federations receive sizeable direct and indirect state aid; thus, 80 sports federations in 2006 shared between them two types of resource totalling €227 million. Roughly half of this takes the form of the 1,700 technical experts (all civil servants) made available to the federations (representing approximately 23 per cent of the total staff numbers of the French Ministry for Health, Youth and Sports (*le Ministère de la santé, de la jeunesse et des sports*). These specialists act as technical advisors to the federations and report both to their parent Ministry and to the sports federations themselves which underwrite the bonuses and expenses paid to this seconded personnel. The civil servants are involved with the formulation and implementation of federation-level policy; the scouting and coaching of elite athletes; and the training of the federations' own technical experts. The other half of the state funding takes the form of direct subsidies to federations and clubs and to local authorities for the building of sports facilities.

This 'French model' of sport is thus characterised by a very high level of intervention by public authorities, which makes France very distinct, in particular in relation to northern European countries where the state is traditionally far less interventionist. Even so, the state in France only accounts for 12 per cent of national spending on sport (of which a mere 2.7 per cent comes from the sports secretariat within the Ministry for Health, Youth and Sports); 52 per cent of total spending comes from households, and 29 per cent from local authorities. Although the state has arrogated a number of prerogatives in regard to elite level sport, and thus operates as a significant regulatory body, local public authorities (the regions, *départements*,[4] inter-*commune* bodies (*intercommunalités*), and towns have a constitutional right to self-administration. Indeed, there has not, to date, been a clear set of mechanisms for the division of powers between these different levels of public administration, with the result that a number of sub-national authorities intervene in elite sport (at the level of both clubs and individual sportsmen and women), giving rise to significant regional disparities. The French model was therefore built in the 1960s and 1970s, and its first results in elite sport came through in the 1990s and 2000s at the Olympics and World Championships.

In this chapter we make an important distinction between 'elite' and 'professional' athletes. Elite athletes certainly benefit from specific structures and systems put in place by the state and by their respective sports federations but at the same time, their official status is not without its ambiguities. Professional athletes, on the other hand, are defined by their exercise of a salaried activity governed by an increasingly well-defined regulatory framework, which guarantees their status as professionals.

The professional might well be of elite standard (e.g., when selected for, or eligible for selection for France's national teams), but more often than not this is not the case. For example, a professional boxer is not acknowledged as an elite athlete, because only amateur boxing (AIBA – The International Amateur Boxing Association) is recognised as an elite sport discipline. In France, there are approximately 1,500 professional football players but only 318 qualify as elite athletes. And elite sport is not necessarily professional (Bayle, 2002). For example, there are 206 elite kayakists and 176 rowers in France, very few of whom make a living from their sport.

Finally, we must also make the distinction in the French case between individual and teams sports (elite and/or professional) at both the Olympic and non-Olympic levels. In team sport, the professional disciplines are as follows: football (leagues 1 and 2); basketball (Pro A and Pro B); rugby (Top 14 and Pro D2); handball (D1); volleyball (Pro A and Pro B; and ice hockey (the Magnus league). In these professional team sports, France has created a professional league which comes under the responsibility of the federation. In individual sports, the viability of professionalism often depends on the existence or not of an international professional circuit (possibly, but not necessarily, answering to international sports federations). This is the case for athletics, cycling, golf, tennis, snow-boarding, sailing, windsurfing, surfing, boxing, motor sports, motorcycling, and figure skating (Bayle, 2002). We do not cover professional sport in this chapter, other than indirectly insofar as it feeds elite athletes to the national teams.

Characteristics of the French model of elite sport

In this part of the chapter, we first outline the basics of the organisation of elite sport in France; second, we analyse the different forms of assistance for elite athletes in France; and third, provide an examination of the forms of financial support for elite sport in France, and in this context evaluate the strategic role of the Ministry for Health, Youth and Sports.

The organisation of elite sport in France

In 1984, the French government created a National Committee for Elite Sport (*la Commission nationale du sport de haut niveau*). Sixteen of the Committee's members are state representatives; three are from local authorities; and another sixteen are from the sports movement. The Chair of the Committee is the Minister for Sport. A key role of the Committee is to determine the criteria for the definition of 'elite' for the following, in each of the sports disciplines accorded elite status for 4 years: athletes, trainers/coaches, referees and judges; sporting young talent; and training partners. The Committee also pronounces on the number of individuals, thus defined, eligible to feature on the ministerial lists and to benefit from the policies and support systems that constitute the pathways to elite sport; and it defines the selection criteria for competitions organised under the auspices of the International Olympic Committee. The status of elite athlete, discipline, federation strategy, and support system recognised as such therefore bear the stamp of the state.

In France in 2007, there were 7,080 elite athletes: 753 with full elite status; 2,652 at 'senior' level; 3,491 juniors, and 184 'partners in training and coaching' in 54 recognised disciplines. A further 8,507 elite young sporting talent athletes (*sportifs espoirs*) aged 12 years and above also qualified for elite status. In total, nearly 16,500 individuals constitute the elite sport environment in France. The access pathways to elite sport in France come under the responsibility of the relevant sports federations,[5] and are organised on the principle that there are two fundamental aspects to an elite athlete's experience: the first is to develop sporting excellence and the second is to develop a professional career. In order to achieve these goals, the pathways to elite sport are composed, essentially, of Centres of Elite Excellence and Centres of Elite Excellence – Young sporting talent (*Pôles France* and *Pôles Espoirs*, respectively).

To gain state recognition (the 'stamp of approval' of the Ministry of Health, Youth and Sports), these Centres of Excellence have to fulfil conditions set by the national technical director nominated to the sports federation. These conditions will have been approved, at the beginning of an Olympiad, by the National Committee for Elite Sport, and these pathway bodies are checked by the state on an annual basis to ensure that they are fulfilling their conditions and are operating properly. In 2007, there were 133 Centres of Elite Excellence and 369 Centres of Elite Excellence – Young sporting talent, making a total of 502 of such state-approved centres for elite sports development.

In France, three types of public body, coming under the responsibility of the Ministry, house 45 per cent of these Centres. The first of these is the National Institute for Physical Sport and Education (INSEP), based in Paris, whose role is to meet the educational and sports development needs of elite athletes. It houses 29 of the 133 Centres of Elite Excellence which range across all the traditional Olympic disciplines, including athletics, judo, gymnastics, fencing, and swimming. Three national schools exist for, respectively, horse riding, skiing and alpine sports, and sailing. They train the coaches in these disciplines, offer advanced level training for the athletes, and also conduct research in their respective field. Two of these schools house Centres of Excellence.

France has 24 centres for sports education (*Centres régionaux d'éducation populaire et sportive* – CREPS), of which 22 are in mainland France. They are polyvalent (multi-sport) centres of regional excellence, and their principal functions are to accommodate regional centres of coaching and training; the Centres of Excellence – Young sporting talent; and in some cases, the Centres of Elite Excellence. Some of these structures house centres of research and excellence designed to support the work of national coaches. Here, France's elite athletes develop not only their sport, but also their careers, thanks to the training and educational programmes on offer on a one-to-one basis.

The 2006–2008 National Programme for the Development of Sport featured a number of sports facilities which also figured in the Paris 2012 Olympic bid. These include the Plaine Commune Aquatic centre; the Saint-Quentin velodrome, the Versailles shooting centre; the nautical sports centre; and the extension of the Roland Garros stadium. In all these cases, the Ministry made additional building funds available. INSEP also put in a €115 million bid to upgrade its facilities between 2004 and 2008.

All these projects, funded largely by the French taxpayer, demonstrate the commitment of the French state to its elite sport development.

At the 2000 Olympic Games, 59 per cent of the selected French athletes had trained in the Centres described above, and 78 per cent of them had spent at least some time in the facilities. Furthermore, 77 per cent of the medal-winners had been trained in the facilities. In 2004, 16 of the 33 medallists at the Athens Olympics were INSEP athletes. Most of France's elite athletes and performances today are thus 'products' of these state-supported elite sport pathways, contributing to France's 5th place ranking in the world for its results in the highest level international sporting competitions – the Olympics and the World Championships. Those elite athletes who feature on the ministerial lists have access to support for both their sporting and professional lives.

Support structures for elite athletes in France

With the status of elite athlete comes certain entitlements and flexibility in respect of schooling, as well as priority access to certain competitive entry examinations, for example, to train as a physiotherapist, podiatrist or sports/PE teacher. Since the law of 16 July 1984 and in order to address the difficult social and financial positions that some elite athletes find themselves in, particularly in the non-professional individual sports (including rowing, wrestling, and kayaking), the French state has created a range of contracts guaranteeing elite athletes access to the labour market. These are contracts signed by the elite athlete, his/her sports federation and his/her employer, and are explicitly designed to help the elite athlete balance the demands of their sporting career and the need for a professional activity at the end of that career. In 2007, 643 elite athletes took advantage of this type of contract which benefited their employer to the tune of €1,389 of state aid. In 70 per cent of cases, the employer is a state (national level) or local authority.

Medallists at the Olympic Games receive a one-off, tax-free bonus payment from the French state: €40,000 for a gold medal; €20,000 for a silver medal, and €13,000 for a bronze. For the 2008 Olympics, the gold medal amount has been raised to €50,000 and the bonuses for Paralympic medal-winners is to be the same as for Olympic medallists. France is one of a number of countries that now awards its Olympic athletes in this way. This policy of support for elite athletes contains further measures relating to work, earnings, and pensions. Thus, in order to help elite athletes to save, the government plans to give salaried athletes access to various public pensions savings schemes and benefits. This particular measure – the opening of pensions savings schemes to elite athletes – is part of government policy to provide better social insurance cover in general for elite sportsmen and women. Thus, by way of further example, it is the government's intention that in the medium term the state takes over national insurance contributions for low-earning athletes from the age of 18 years. A final set of measures has been proposed by the Ministry for Small and Medium-Sized Enterprises (SME) to complement those described above: any SME that hires an elite athlete will be able to describe itself as a 'citizen-partner in elite performance'.

Supporting these state-level measures, towns, departments, and regions offer support to elite athletes living in their locality. In the individual, non-professional sports, elite athletes can benefit from a range of income streams (from their club, federation, local authority, and sometimes from sports equipment manufacturers) and from different types of other financial assistance (e.g., salaries, bonuses, training, and competition grants). Although the state retains overall responsibility for elite sport in France, the direct and indirect contributions made by sub-national authorities are far from negligible. They own most of the 250,700 sports facilities and 65,300 sports grounds that exist in France (MJSVA, 2006), and their cooperation is therefore vital for the successful implementation of public policy for sport. In 2003, the 45 largest towns and conurbations alone generated 35 per cent more funds than that provided by the state for sports – a figure of €981 million. In 2005, moreover, local authorities in France employed over 47,500 local public agents in sports-related activities, according to the National Centre for Local Public Service (*Centre national de la fonction publique territoriale*).

The financing of elite sport in France, and the strategic role of the Ministry for Health, Youth and Sports

As a complement to the Ministry budget for sport, the National Development Fund for Sport (*le Fonds national pour le développement du sport* – FNDS) was created in 1979. Its budget is one-third of that of the Ministry, namely in the region of €250 million per year. This fund increases by roughly one-half the total of state funding dedicated to sports policy in France. Originally, the Fund's resources came solely from lottery revenues (horseracing and the national lottery) but since 2000, 5 per cent of the revenue from TV rights at sports competitions has also been added to the Fund's resources, amounting to an annual figure of approximately €40 million. By means of this tax revenue, the Ministry has set itself the task of organising and regulating a symbolic link between elite sport on the one hand, and professional sport on the other. This is a link operated at the national level between the federations, and at the local level between the professional clubs and/or supporting associations. The aims of the policy are to strengthen the redistributory mechanisms within French public policy for sport as outlined above. We note here that this particular strategic aspect of the 'French model' for sports development has not been affected by changes in government – it has survived sports ministers from both sides of the political spectrum.

In 2006, the FNDS was replaced by the National Centre for the Development of Sport (*Centre national de Développement du Sport – CNDS*) which has taken over the bulk of FNDS' activities. Expenditure of these funds is divided between the national and the regional level. Nationally, the funds are spent primarily on investment in large-scale facilities; regionally, the money is redistributed in the form of subsidies to the sports associations and is not, in theory at least, part of the assistance given to the pathways to elite sport. The rationalisation of public intervention in sport as in other sectors has come about in France as a result of the 2005 public finance law (*la loi organique relative à la loi de finances – LOLF*) which supports the concept of objective-setting and contractual evaluation indicators. Following a period from 2003 to 2006 marked by negotiations and change, by 2007 the objectives and indicators of the Ministry's 'Sport' programme had more or less stabilised. Of the six objectives, three relate directly to elite sport. The objectives are to:

- Promote the practice of sport, especially within clubs, with specific attention to target groups (women; disabled people; inhabitants of priority urban zones (*zones urbaines sensibles* – ZUS).
- Promote the financial probity and efficiency of the sports federations.
- Devote particular attention to a balanced spread of sports facilities throughout France.
- Adapt the supply of sports training to the evolution of sports jobs and careers and to contribute to the professional prospects of the elite athlete. In the case of this objective, a specific indicator relates to elite athletes, namely 'the professional qualification and prospects of the elite sportsmen and sportswomen'. This objective is composed of two indicators: the rate of economic and social integration of athletes two years after leaving their sport; and the rate of high level athletes in training or in employment.

- Maintain France's rank in world-level sports competition. This objective is composed of three indicators: ranking in summer and winter Olympic Games; ranking on an annual basis across a range of twenty-five Olympic and non-Olympic sports; and ranking by a panel of sports journalists.
- Reinforce the respect for ethics in sport, and protect the health of athletes.

Two indicators relate specifically to elite sport:

1 The number of elite or young sporting talent-elite athletes having complied with all medical regulations in the course of a year compared to the total number of elite or young sporting talent-elite athletes.
2 The number of athletes testing positive in drugs tests compared to the number of athletes tested. France operates an interventionist anti-doping policy initiated by the law of 1999, and by means of the National Laboratory for Drugs Testing – a public body in Chatenay Malabry accountable to the Ministry.

The 'French model' of sport is subject to a number of tensions and conflicts which will have an impact on its future development.

Tensions, conflicts, and the future

Over the past 20, years a number of changes have occurred in the European sports environment that will undoubtedly lead to significant developments in the years to come. Here we underline two of the most significant of these changes. The first is the emergence of private bodies from outside the world of sport. These new actors operate principally according to commercial logic and, although to date they have had most impact in 'classical' professional sport, they are starting to reach the world of elite sport. The second phenomenon is in part an explanation of the emergence of these new actors. Here we are referring to the extraordinary growth in interest in sport over the course of the past 20 years. Rising living standards, growth in leisure time, and technological progress, particularly in the media, are at the roots of this phenomenon. Faced with this increase in demand for sport, the supply of sport has increased, and considerably so. Elite sport may well be primarily about *sports* competition, but by the same token it has also become the focus of intense *economic* competition amongst new and old actors. The trend is most notable between, on the one hand, the 'historical' actors such as sports federations and, on the other, the more recently arrived private operators. But the trend can also be seen *within* the 'historical' sports movement itself, in conflict between the different levels of the hierarchy of France's sports organisations.

Conflict number 1: Between governing bodies within the same sport over 'market shares' in time; in particular the competition between athletes' time spent in national team competitions in relation to their employers' duties and rights regarding insurance and financial indemnities.

Numerous questions are raised under this point: insurance cover; the distribution of income; and in time, the appropriate significance granted to different types of competition over the course of the annual sporting calendar. The first of these questions concerns elite athletes' insurance coverage when competing for their national team. The athlete's club is collectively responsible under the regulations governed by the federations to insure the players made available for the entirety of the international competitions in which the national team is participating. This question became an issue in professional sport in 1997 when Rome's Lazio football club demanded that the Italian football federation pay the sum of €6.3 million following an injury sustained by one of Lazio's players, Alessandro Nesta, during a period when Nesta had been made available to the Italian national squad. In September 1998, the club asked to be reimbursed the €3 million transfer fee it had paid for a player to replace Nesta, as well as the €29 million for this player's salary, and the €1 million that the club had paid to Nesta when he was not able to play for them.

In March 1997, Barcelona FC had invoked the Bosman ruling in order to avoid making its players available to their national teams. The University of Saragossa issued a statement critical of the club's action, stating that 'The obligation of the players to make themselves available to their national team cannot be deemed a barrier to the free movement of workers, in that the status of an international player is neither permanent nor immutable.' Ten years later came the Oulmers affair. This was the case of a player for Charleroi (Belgium), Abdelmajd Oulmers, who was injured while playing for Morocco in a friendly international, and whose club demanded substantial financial compensation from the federation in question (the world football governing body, International Football Federation (FIFA)). The case marked a clear departure in terms of rulings potentially favourable to the clubs.

In the case of basketball, the participation of Tarik Abdul-Wahad in the 2001 World Championships had raised a similar problem for the FFBB (the French Basketball Federation – *Fédération française de basketball*). The FFBB is the biggest European basketball federation, with over 450,000 members – but the player had just signed a contract for seven seasons with the NBA (National Basketball Association). Had he sustained an injury playing for the French national team which subsequently made him unavailable to play in the United States, the compensation due to the NBA would have been in the order of €75,000 for each match missed during the season. Multiplied by 82 matches per season, and by 7 years, this would have amounted to a huge figure which eventually brought the two bodies, the NBA and the FFBB, to an agreement to share the costs. While these examples clearly pertain first and foremost to team sports, it is not hard to imagine a similar scenario in individual sports where the athletes answer to private bodies (see above).

Furthermore, we can envisage two other potential issues likely to arise. The first is that both athletes and their employers, in some cases clubs turned private companies, may well demand compensation when the athlete is selected for their national team, injury or no injury. Indeed, in the case of athletes selected for the national team who receive bonuses, the question arises as to what happens to their salary, in these cases paid by a private company (Bayle and Durand, 2000). The significant growth in the financial implications of sporting events associated with the traditional organising bodies (such as the International Rugby Board (IRB) in rugby; FIFA and Union of European Football Associations (UEFA) in football; the French Tennis Federation (FFT) in the case of Roland Garros) effectively opens the door to significant demands on the part of the employers who have released their best talent for selection by the national team. It will become harder and harder to justify the notion that competitions generating such vast financial income are unable (or unwilling) to offer substantial compensation to the private bodies who provide the athletes and pay their salaries. This is already a sensitive area in those sports readily acknowledged to be 'professional', and is becoming equally so in disciplines hitherto considered as having 'amateur' status.

In this context, the arrival on the French elite sport scene of Group Lagardère, a highly influential business in European industry and media,[6] had already marked a turning point. Part of the group, 'Team Lagardère', presents itself as an 'innovative research platform working for the sporting elite' (http://www. teamlagardere.com/va/), offering cutting-edge technical support to certain elite athletes in targeted disciplines. Thus, agreements have been reached with the national federations for tennis table, athletics, rugby (the physical preparation of the members of the French national team); Paris Judo Club; and contracts signed with 19 professional tennis players. On the face of it, this is not a development that automatically conflicts with the activities of the traditional sports federations in France. However, Lagardère also proposes to find partners who will sponsor the athletes in its team, and in this respect demonstrates that its ambitions go beyond its initial objectives of providing technical and technological expertise. The link between Team Lagardère and its parent media group provides a glimpse of the sort of vertical integration that might come to characterise sports structures in the future. For example, if the media arm of Lagardère was to buy the French events rights for tennis – or even to take over certain competitions in their entirety – what would stop the group from also ensuring that the sporting stars of Team Lagardère were guaranteed participation in the events in question?

This approach is typified by Team Lagardère's buyout of Sportfive (European leader in sports marketing) for the sum of €865 million; in 2005 Sportfive had an annual turnover of €550 million and has signed contracts with 270 clubs, including the FFF (French Football Federation) and the Olympique Lyonnais Football Club. Team Lagardère has also bought up Newsweb, a leading sports content website; it owns 25 per cent of Amaury, the sports organisation company which owns the sports newspaper *L'Equipe Magazine* as well as events such as the Tour de France and the Paris–Dakar rally. Lagardère has a minority holding in the TV channel Canal+ which owns football and professional rugby TV rights. This private operator is thus attempting to bring together under one roof TV/audiovisual rights, the management of athletes' careers, and the organisation of sporting events. In late 2006, it bought the Racing Club de France, the biggest European all-sports club (18 different sports sections and 20,000 members). Leading figures in France's sports movement are wary of the possible excesses of such an exclusively commercial strategy. Arnaud Lagardère himself is open about his strategy, stating in an interview with *L'Equipe Magazine* on 16 December 2006 that 'I am not doing this because I like sport, but because it is important that the Lagardère group expands its business.

The signing in March 2007 of a partnership contract between the French swimmer Laure Manaudou and the Artemis group (itself part of the Pinault finance conglomerate) is part of a rather different phenomenon. In this case, Artemis will pay the swimmer €1 million per year for five seasons without, it would appear, any explicit guarantees in return. According to Artemis, their involvement is a form of sponsorship akin to its patronage of the contemporary arts. Manaudou already has contracts with Aréna, Electricité de France, LastMinute.com, the luxury goods firm Lancel, Sporever, and the *Société de bains de mer de Monaco* (operator of luxury hotels, casinos, and spas in Monte Carlo). Given these multiple contractual, commercial obligations, future conflicts of interest regarding the swimmer's availability for certain sporting events cannot be ruled out.

Above and beyond the matter of financial flows and trans-actions, therefore, the question of the sporting calendar will inevitably raise its head. It is only a matter of time before clashes of interest occur over 'ownership' of the athletes' time, with the sporting calendar potentially being carved up between the different bodies involved in organising the competitions. The sports federations on the one hand and the private organ-isations on the other may well end up disagreeing over when an athlete is available. We could even envisage the different organisations – clubs, national teams, and national, regional, and world organising bodies – keeping a tally of the number of dates that accrue to each.

Ice hockey and basketball illustrate perfectly what the future might hold in these respects. The major North American leagues, the National Hockey League (NHL) and the NBA, respectively, are and always have been private bodies that have complete discretion over whether or not to release players for the Olympics, World and European Championships. In 1998, for example, the NHL had rearranged its own calendar to fit with the Nagano Winter Olympic Games, so that for the first time ever, the Olympic tournament was able to bring together all the world's elite ice hockey players. The Olympic ice hockey event, however, made very little impact on the professional championship, with the consequence that in the 2002 Salt Lake City Games, the Olympics merely represented a week's break in the NHL's Stanley Cup. The Cup's organisers, moreover, let it be known that they only agreed to the interruption of their tournament because the Olympics were also being held on the North American continent. The very next day after the Olympic final (between Canada and the United States), the players resumed their club competition in the NHL.

This question of the sporting calendar is all the more crucial now that the calendar is so overloaded, with the result that even by staggering competitions across the year, the problem of the athletes' preparation is far from resolved. In the case of swimming, for example, the participation by top athletes in the French Championships is at the express request of the swim-ming federation which understandably wishes to maintain the profile of the competitions for which it is responsible. Yet not only do the swimming coaches on occasion view the champi-onships as of secondary importance; so do some of the sponsors and other commercial partners of the swimmers, with the result that swimmers are either absent or put in a merely symbolic appearance. Furthermore, the top athletes are heavily in demand to make public relations appearances to which they are contractually obligated and which pay extremely well, but which are costly of their time. The federations have no significant sanctions to bring to bear on individual athletes in these one-to-one negotiations, and so certain national competitions could well find themselves deprived of the best athletes who will have chosen to earn their living elsewhere.

Where tennis is concerned, the time spent by athletes in their national teams in competition for the Davis Cup and the Fed Cup (known as the Federation Cup until 1995) is seen by certain players themselves as interruptions in the only sporting calendar which actually matters, namely the tournament circuit, where rankings are everything. Only those federations in a position to offer substantial financial bonuses manage to persuade the best players to participate in their competitions. The Athletics League, created in 2007 by the French federation in partnership with Lagardère, is now attempting to restructure the calendar by offering players guaranteed payments if they agree to compete in four of the seven annual meets that are planned for the sport.

Conflict number 2: Between federations and governments and between governments, over the definition of 'sporting nationalities'.

The second point of tension between the bodies involved in the organisation and development of elite sport concerns the definition of 'sporting nationalities'. The organising principle of sport in Europe has, since its beginnings, been nationality. The Olympic Charter may well stipulate that the Games are a competition between athletes and not between nations, but it did not take long for the ambassadors of Olympic values *in* their respective countries to become the ambassadors *of* their country within the Olympic movement.

The political importance accorded to sports performances soon raised the stakes of international sports competitions. One side-effect for several decades has been for rich countries to drain poor countries of their best sporting talent. France has not been immune to these pressures, notably in athletics and weightlifting. These powerful countries fall over themselves to attract the best athletes, at best by supporting their sports development within the structures available in their country of origin, at worst by poaching them at an advanced stage in their sports careers. Since the Sydney Olympics, the trend for athletes to seek naturalisation in another country for their personal, economic gain has risen; the highly symbolic and memorable image of this phenomenon being the sight of the six

Bulgarian weightlifters parading the Qatar flag following a fast-track naturalisation process, and the exchange of some million dollars.

Nowadays, each international federation sets its own conditions for the eligibility of its athletes, but in all cases the athlete must have lived for a certain period of time in the host country, and must have been eligible for selection in the 'sending' country. For rugby, selection for the national team does not depend on political nationality, but on the length of time the athlete has been resident in the country in question. Thus, a South African player is a frequent member of the French national team and a number of players originating from the Pacific Islands are to be found lining up for the New Zealand All Blacks in international competitions. In a similar fashion, UEFA is currently considering making clubs' eligibility for European competition football dependent upon the presence in the squad of a significant number of players (8 of 25) who are nationals in the sense of having been trained in the club (at least 4) or in a another club in the same country (the remaining 4).

The international governing bodies find themselves on a knife-edge in these respects, since there are serious moral objections against discriminating between citizens of the same country on the grounds of their nationality, however recently citizenship was granted. To date, no serious complaint has made it all the way to the courtroom, but the number of litigation disputes is multiplying nevertheless. The related problem of nationality with regard to clubs participating in competitions deemed hitherto as strictly 'national', or using sports facilities that must be in their own country, will inevitably also rear its head. Certain top clubs have already requested the right to take part in competitions organised in third countries, or to have access to play in stadiums outside their own country. At a time when internal European borders are becoming increasingly irrelevant, we can expect these various aspects of the problem of 'sporting nationality' to give rise to ever more serious debates.

The French position on this issue is somewhat schizophrenic. On the one hand, the very principle of a 'market' in the nationality of elite athletes is seen to go against the founding principles of sport. On the other hand, some French sports federations (athletics, weightlifting, gymnastics, figure skating, short track speed skating, and badminton) do not hesitate in practice to look abroad to recruit potential medallists in order to enhance the international ranking of their sport, which is the key factor determining the partnership between the French government and its sports federations.

Conflict number 3: Between athletes, employers, and federations over rights ownership.

Elite sport today serves significant commercial purposes. Sports events can now be viewed remotely in real-time, or virtually real-time – via live telephone links, for example. Conversely, coverage of these events is archived and can be viewed long after the competition itself. These are controversial developments, since they pose the question of ownership of the rights to sports events and competitions. Producers of sports video games who in any way personalise their product – featuring identifiable players or organisations, real-life stadiums or sponsors, or a ball that is identical to the original – find themselves dealing with any number of rights-holders; yet the payment of royalties in such a complex situation is far from easy. Several years ago, a number of British footballers claimed the rights over goals they scored that were played and replayed as part of the introductory sequence of a TV programme about football! Their argument was that the broadcaster only had the right to play the footage in the form of highlights of the game itself, not as archive material disconnected from the game, that is, showing the 'work', as the claimants described their goal sequence. The basic question here is that of the ownership of the rights to sports events at the time of the event itself and thereafter. In the case of team sports, French law has recently specified how these rights are to be divided between the clubs and the leagues.

Technological progress has complicated the matter even more. Clubs are claiming rights, for example, over the high-quality digital transmission of their competition images and the amounts generated from the rights to digital re-transmission are creating rivalries and envy. Some athletes in individual sports disciplines have decided to produce and sell DVDs of their competition footage which in theory belongs to the organisers of the events in question, which in some cases have produced materials of their own. This has led to contradictory statements by the various interested parties regarding rights to their image in all its forms. Who, for example, owns the overall rights to competitions and the images that they generate?

What emerges from this overview of recent developments is a picture of a rather fragmented sporting world. In the long term, these controversies will be resolved, either because of pressure from market forces and private operators or through government intervention, as in the case of France, via legislation intended to safeguard the specific public service function of sport. These debates and conflicts between interested parties will very soon constitute pressing questions for the organisation and development of elite sport in France. There is an urgent need for the formulation of an overall doctrine, setting out the rules and terms of engagement to be followed by specific legal instruments. The French system has already demonstrated its capacity to generate a specific model of its own along these lines. France's anti-doping legislation and its laws governing the financial regulation of professional leagues (such as the creation of the *Direction nationale du contrôle de gestion*, the body overseeing the finances of France's professional football clubs) were in their time showcases for the potential of specific regulatory regimes for sport.

Conclusions

Our analysis of the organisation of elite sport in France has demonstrated the dominant role played by the state and the Ministry for Health, Youth and Sports; this is a role which has led some foreign commentators to characterise this system as the 'Soviet model' of French sport. France can boast exceptional sports performances by virtue of having developed early on a number of critical factors of success, although this has not made France immune to growing international competition, despite the collapse of the Soviet bloc. Former Sports Minister J.-F. Lamour announced the objective of 40 French medals at the Beijing Olympics in 2008. The specificity of the French model of elite sport is also a question of a relative maturity in terms of the support mechanisms available to the elite athlete. It is not a case of 'success at all costs' as indicated by the concern to provide the sorts of opportunities described above in terms of an athlete's overall career and lifestyle, and the system's anti-doping policy. French elite sport also maintains strong links with amateur sport, particularly in the team sports, that are widely practised in France.

Despite all this, the growth of commercial pressures on elite sport, and the pressures of globalisation itself raise questions regarding the future direction of the French model of elite sport, in particular regarding the best regulatory mechanisms. France has succeeded in being a pioneer in the foundation of the World Anti-Doping Agency but new threats, as seen above (the 'market' in nationality and privatisation), call for a renegotiation of the regulatory principles of elite sport, and this is a process that can only realistically take place at the European and world level.

Notes

1 Translation by Helen Drake, Department of Politics, International Relations and European Studies at Loughborough University, UK.

2 The *commune*, or municipality, is France's smallest administrative unit; there are over 36,000 of them on mainland France.
3 This was at the time of the Vichy regime in France, established in June 1940 after the fall of France.
4 The *département* is France's principal unit of territorial administration; there are 96 of them on mainland France.
5 Since 1992, 'objectives contracts' exist between the Ministry for Health, Youth and Sports and the sports federations. These are annual contractual agreements between a sports federation and the Ministry. The specific purpose of the contract is to specify the objectives of the federation in relation to the development of both elite and mass sport. On the basis of these objectives, the Ministry sets out the amount and type of financial aid and technical support that it will make available in order to reach the agreed objectives.
6 The biggest press conglomerate in France, with a turnover of €13 billion.

References

Andreff, W. and Nys, J.-F. (2001) *Economie du Sport*, Paris, PUF, Que sais-je?, 4th edition, Paris.

Bayle, E. (2002) Le sport professionnel et les structures marchandes associées au spectacle sportif, in *L'emploi sportif en France: situation et tendance d'évolution*, Eds. J. Camy and N. Leroux, Co-édition Afraps–Runopes, pp. 45–64.

Bayle, E. and Durand, C. (2000) Sport professionnel et représentation nationale: Quel avenir?, in *Reflets et perspectives de la vie économique*, no. 2–3, Vol. XXXIX, J.-J. Gouguet and D. Primault (coordinator), Special issue Sport et Mondialisation: Quel enjeu pour le XXIème siècle? Bruxelles: De Boeck Université, pp. 149–168.

Lachaume, J.-F. (1991) Du contrôle de l'État sur les fédérations sportives, *Revue juridique et économique du sport*, 16, 3–20.

MJSVA (Ministry of Youth, Sport and Associative Life) (2006) unpublished internal document, Paris, MJSVA.

Poland

Jolanta Żyśko

Introduction[1]

This chapter provides a discussion of the elite sport system in Poland, including an overview of policy and the role of the state (central administration) in the Polish sport system. The key issue is the division, within social policy, of responsibilities between the state (governmental sector), business (commercial sector) and civil society (voluntary sector). This overview is followed by an account of the influence of politics on elite sport structures and financing in Poland. The review of sport structures and financing is presented in the context of ongoing systemic transformation (since 1989), and also in the context of changes in the system of elite sport development. The next section discusses the Polish elite sport system including infrastructure, employment, financing of athletes, sports competition systems, education and professional training of coaches and instructors, and finally scientific support to the process of sport training. Examples for this chapter are taken from the following sports: basketball, football, swimming and sailing.

Elite sport in Poland

Today, sport, including elite sport, has become a vital factor of social development. It plays an important role in maintaining lifelong health and fitness, preventing the formation of social pathologies and is a crucial educational influence. In its broadest sense, sport has become a truly general phenomenon. The widespread social participation in institutionalised sporting activity as well as growing media coverage of sports events gives it economic importance high enough to generate growing interest on the part of the state. By virtue of these factors, sport has been gaining importance as part of the state's social policies. Acknowledging such social needs, for example, the requirement for physical activity, achievement and belonging, places sport among the crucial domains of social policies in modern democratic states.

Responsibilities of the governmental, commercial and voluntary sectors

The state's interest in sport is not an altogether new phenomenon. Indeed, since the end of World War II, the structure of the sport sector in Poland has been based on a mixed state-civic model. As in the elite sport management systems in other European countries, this model assumes coexistence and cooperation of two sectors: public (governmental) and private; the latter encompassing the commercial and voluntary sectors. However, unlike in other European countries, when it comes to shaping sport policies, in the Polish system it is the extent and depth of state intervention that stands out.

According to the criteria and definitions adopted by Chaker (2004) in research conducted for the Council of Europe, the Polish elite sport management system should be termed interventionist, centralised and bureaucratic. In the light of Chaker's findings, it is typical of the interventionist model to create field-specific legal regulations and to follow their legal-formal procedures, while non-interventionist models rely on the legal frames of the financial and logistical environment of sport activities.

Current sport policy in Poland displays unmistakeable features of the interventionist model, with its multiple field-specific normative acts and the dominant and intervening role of public sports administration, notably of the central administration body – the Ministry of Sport.[2] State sport policy is formalised and regulated by the Act established by the Polish Parliament on 21 January 2005 regarding the development of sport in Poland (M.P. No. 6, Item 75), and by *The Strategy of the Development of Sport Until 2012*.[3] Both documents illustrate the state's interest in devising policy and structures for the execution of tasks related to sport. In this approach, *The Strategy of the Development of Sport Until 2012* (The Ministry of Sport, 2003), states that 'The objectives the state aims at achieving through sport require concrete tasks to be fulfilled not only by clubs and sports associations but also public administration structures developed especially for this purpose'. This statement stresses the role of the state and state administration in shaping sport policy in Poland. The strength of the state is also emphasised in legal acts regulating the operation of the sector.

When discussing the legal framework of sport's structure and organisation in Poland (Cajsel, 2006) distinguishes two basic approaches: positivist, in which legal sources can be arranged hierarchically into a pyramid; and sociological, which essentially turns the pyramid upside down. In the former approach, at the top of the pyramid is the Constitution of the Republic of Poland, the fundamental legal Act defining Poland's legal framework. At the level below, there are legal codes and other legal acts, such as international conventions ratified by Poland. The third level is composed of normative executory provisions, that is, government directives based on legal acts. Under Article 87 of the Constitution of the Polish Republic, only the legal acts listed above represent formal sources of law originating from legislative activities of the governing bodies. The Article reinforces the strong normative role of the state in Poland by formally restricting legislative authority to the public administration. Cajsel (2006), however, distinguishes another crucial element in the realm of sport, namely, the norms established by sports organisations, the most important of which are: the internal statutes and regulations of Polish sport associations, and then, at the base of the legislative pyramid for Polish sport, there are the statutes and regulations of sport clubs. As Cajsel (2006) notes, 'When viewed from the sociology-of-law perspective the pyramid should be reversed' since, in practice, the statutes and regulations of basic units (i.e., sports clubs) are the most universally applied. Of second level importance, there would be the normative acts drawn up by sport associations, followed by decrees, acts, codes and conventions ratified by the Polish Parliament, with the legal act – the Constitution – being of little significance.

Although the Polish Constitution does not include direct regulations concerning sport, there are a number of documents, with the power of legal act, regulating sport activities. Among the most important are: the Physical Culture Act of 1996 (Journal of Laws No. 25, Item 113); the Championship Sport Act of 2005 (Journal of Laws No. 155, Item 1298); the Associations Act of 1989 (Journal of Laws No. 20, Item 104); and the Safety of Mass Events Act of 1997 (Journal of Laws No. 106, Item 660). The organisational–legal system in Polish sport is undoubtedly interventionist in character and similar to the French system of sport management. Interventionism of state administration structures is exemplified by the obligation to secure the approval of the Minister of Sport in order to establish a sport association and to pass its statutes, in the supervision of the state over Polish sport associations, as well as in the fact that a formal approval is required to participate in a professional league from sport clubs operating under a legal form other than a joint stock company.

The legal foundations of the central administration body regulating sport (the Ministry of Sport) are specified in the Championship Sport Act. Furthermore, under Article 23 of the Act, the Minister of Sport, as the supervising body, has the right to take the following measures: suspend the activities of a Polish sport association and appoint a commissioner until a new governing body is elected; ask the courts to dissolve the association; or withdraw his consent to the founding of an association. Dissolution through the appointment of a commissioner was recently exercised towards three associations: the Polish Skiing Association, the Polish Biathlon Association and the Polish Football Association, upon discovering irregularities in the functioning of these bodies. In the case of the Polish Football

Association, this measure brought about the threat of penal reaction from the International Football Federation (FIFA). This amounted to possible exclusion, under the statute of FIFA, to exclude the PFA and its members from all international competition for 5 years (Rapkiewicz, 2006). The strong position of the state administration bodies, described in state policies and expressed in the normative acts listed above, is reflected also in the structure of Polish championship sport.

Organisational structure of elite sport

The organisational structure of Polish elite sport reflects a division of authority and responsibilities between the state (represented by the governmental sector), civil society (the voluntary sector) and business (represented by the commercial sector).

Governmental sector

At the central (national) level, Poland has a governmental body dedicated exclusively to sport. No other European state can boast a similar entity. Since 2005, Poland has had a Ministry of Sport – a central administration body created by the Championship Sport Act. The Ministry was established by a merger of sport departments of the former Ministry of National Education and dissolved Polish Confederation of Sport. As stated by its founders, the rationale behind the establishment of the Ministry was to 'create one decision centre for the entire [field of] championship sport (including professional sport) capable of bringing Polish sport out of crisis and stimulate it towards the maximum growth' (The Ministry of Sport, 2003).

The Ministry of Sport comprises nine departments, three offices, an internal audit unit, and supervises the activities of Polish sport associations as well as the training and recruitment for Polish national representation in all disciplines of sport. Responsibility for these tasks falls within the remit of the Departments of Top Sport and Youth Sport. The Ministry also supervises the sectors of youth and children's sport and sports infrastructure. The Minister of Sport has under his direct control the Main Sports Centre, the major training base for Polish national athletes. Common access to sports, talent identification and youth training serve to produce strong national sport representation to enable success on the international sporting stage. In order to achieve this aim, the Ministry cooperates with non-governmental entities, especially the Polish Olympic Committee (POC) and national-level physical culture associations.

At the regional-level, elite sport structures in Poland are supported by dedicated bodies in 'voivodeship' (regional) offices, usually departments dealing with sport and physical culture as a whole, and frequently in combination with other spheres of social activity, such as tourism, education and social affairs. Voivodeship offices vary and depend on current policy and the overall strength of public administration at this level. Part of the authority is shared by regional self-government structures – voivodeship self-government with regional councils and management boards plus special sport councils cooperating and sharing their sport governance competence with non-governmental organisations (NGOs) in the form of interdisciplinary physical culture associations.

At the local-level public administration bodies, that is, *poviat* (district) and *gmina* (commune) administration offices have units or officers for the management and coordination of sport activities in their respective district or commune. However, their responsibilities focus on youth and children rather than elite sport. Nevertheless, with the recently passed Championship Sport Act, there are now possibilities for linkages with elite sport structures with arrangements at regional and national levels. In line with Article 7, Section 1, Item 10 of the Act on Municipal Government of 8 March 1990 (Journal of Laws of 2001 No. 142, Item 1591) satisfying the collective needs of local communities is among 'tasks proper for each commune'. The Championship Sport Act expanded the competence of central and local administration bodies in this respect. Under current legal regulations, it is the responsibility of central and territorial administration units to create an environment conducive to the development and growth of championship sport (by assisting, for example, its organisation, financing and in-kind support) which, prior to the Act, was reserved for amateur sport (Cajsel, 2006).

Moreover, every local government body has a 'sports council' consisting of representatives from local organisations and institutions active in the fields of physical culture and sport – in brief – sports clubs. Their task is to design strategies for the growth of sport activity in a given area, sport infrastructure programmes, sport and recreation events, as well as to draft physical culture acts and budgets for their respective communes and districts. Members of sports councils perform their duties on a voluntary basis. Finally, there are also basic-level public units such as sport and recreation centres which operate (in legal terms) as state-owned enterprises or budgetary entities. However, such entities hardly ever deal with elite sport development and, in normal circumstances, usually supply access to recreation or mass sport facilities and services.

Voluntary sector ● ● ●

The voluntary (or third) sector of the sport organisation model in Poland could be termed non-consolidated,[4] since there is no single umbrella organisation at the national level, for both sport and Olympic organisations. The POC emerges as the leading nationwide NGO active at the central level. The POC is defined as a federation of associations and legal persons acting to forward the goal of 'ensuring the participation of Polish national representatives in the Olympic games, promote Olympism, represent Polish sport in the international Olympic movement and among other national Olympic committees' (Article 27 of the Championship Sport Act). Similarly, the Polish Paralympics Committee was established in order to ensure the participation of Polish athletes with disabilities.

At the central level of the Polish NGO sector, there are two types of associations dealing with elite sport: (a) sports federations (multi-discipline) and (b) Polish sport associations (mono-discipline). Central-level 'sports federations' are multi-discipline associations such as the Academic Sports Association of Poland, Federation of Popular Sports and Athletics Clubs, School Sports and Athletics Association, Polish Sports Federation *Gwardia*, Army Sports Federation and a new phenomenon in the sector, religious sports organisations, such as Salesian, Christian Orthodox, IMCA and MAKABI. Most of these are remnants of the 1970s and 1980s vertical sports structures, that is, academic, school, folk/rural, police and army.

The key tasks of sports federations are listed in their statues and codes. Among the most popular are:

- to conduct activity within the domain of sports and physical recreation;
- to organise tournaments as well as sports and recreational events;
- to conduct educational and promotion activities for the benefit of physical culture;
- to train and develop coach and instructor personnel;
- to grant support to youth sports clubs.

The highest sport potential (from the federations listed above) was identified for academic organisations, notably the Physical Academy Clubs (*AZS-AWF*). At the 2004 Olympic Games in Athens, representatives of five *AZS-AWF* clubs gained approximately 50 per cent of all points won by the Polish Olympic representation. A similar situation happened at the winter Olympics in Torino, where the athletes from one club, *AZS-AWF*

Katowice, won approximately 48 per cent of the points awarded to the Polish representation. Almost the same high-level performance is recorded for academic athletes at World and European championships in senior as well as junior categories. In 2005, there were five *AZS-AWF* clubs in the top 10 of Polish sports clubs (Sozański, 2006).

Polish sport associations are nationwide mono-discipline organisations, acting along the lines of law-enforced national monopoly since, under Polish law, one association alone is allowed per discipline and the foundation of an association is possible only upon securing the approval of the minister responsible for physical culture, that is, the Minister of Sport. Currently, there are some 60 Polish sport associations. The number is not fixed and varies between years. The key tasks of a Polish sport association include:

- to organise or maintain sport competition;
- to prepare Polish representatives to participate in international competitions;
- to conduct educational, socialising and popularising activities in the field of sport;
- to represent its respective discipline in international sport organisations and to organise Polish participation in international sport competitions;
- to propose candidates for national representation to the minister responsible for physical culture and sport;
- to educate and train coaches, umpires and referees;
- to determine the terms and procedures for athletes' membership in sports clubs for their discipline;
- to conduct activities involved in granting licences to sports clubs, athletes, coaches and referees/umpires;
- to take disciplinary measures in accordance with the rules of the Polish sport association.

Polish sport associations do not enjoy the autonomy similar to that available to sport organisations outside Poland. Although the Championship Sport Act states that 'A Polish sport association has the exclusive right to make any decisions concerning its proper discipline', it emphasises the dependence of Polish sport associations on the central administration (the Minister of Sport) who has the sole capacity to license the formation of new associations, supervises those that already exist, and can accept or reject an association's statues. In the event of illegal actions conducted by an association, the Minister of Sport has the right to suspend the execution of a questionable resolution or demand it to be withdrawn and suspend the activities of the management of the association and appoint a commissioner (this is the case in the ongoing proceedings into the Polish Football Association). The Minister can also withdraw his consent to the founding of a new association or press for the dissolution of an association. The above measures, available to the Polish state authorities and courts of common law, allow interference with Polish sport associations, but are incompatible with the rules of some international federations, such as FIFA's statutes which state that national football associations have full autonomy and which allow only for the intervention of the Court of Arbitration for Sport (CAS). Under Article 61 of the Statutes of FIFA, recourse to ordinary courts of law is prohibited and may cause penal measures on the part of FIFA. This is a somewhat strange approach considering the fact that by its very nature common law should not be denied to anybody (Rapkiewicz, 2006).

In the structure of NGOs at the regional level, many sport associations have developed intermediary structures. Polish sport associations as well as multi-discipline federations have their own voivodeship agents. There are also 16 voivodeship multi-discipline federations of sport associations. In the past, these organisations had eight macro-regional counterparts in the shape of federations of physical culture associations. The task of these structures is to create conditions conducive to the growth of out-of-school children's and youth sport activity. At the local level, basic functions are fulfilled by approximately 87,000 sport clubs. Both field research and theoretical studies depict a clear segmentation of sport clubs along the lines of needs and expectations of various social groups: children and youth (school sport); academic community (academic sport); rural communities (folk clubs); military (sport in the army, police and other military units); and athletes with a disability. Polish sport theory terminology, with regard to this chapter's concerns, distinguishes the notion of elite sport which, as specified by Sozański (2006), 'encompasses all forms adopted and executed towards achieving maximum results in the process of long-term structured training'. In this notion, the author distinguishes four major areas: youth sport, championship, Olympic and professional sport.

The sport club is the basic unit for the achievement of the objectives and tasks of elite sport. Traditionally, most sport clubs in Poland exist in the legal form of associations, that is, non-profit entities. At present, a sport club can take the form of a legal person (including association or partnership) or an individual entrepreneur, as stated in the Freedom of Economic Activity Act (Journal of Laws No. 173, Item 1807). Thus, the Act allows for a sport club to operate along the organisational–legal provisions of the commercial sector.

Commercial sector • • •

Until 1989 the presence of sport entities in the business sector was a marginal phenomenon, although in the early 1980s proposals emerged for the transformation of sport clubs from associative to commercial bodies. This was largely due to the failure of the legal status of an association to cater for the needs of professional sport. Currently, as stated in *The Strategy of the Development of Sport*, professionalisation and commercialisation are natural development directions for elite sport. The legal–organisational framework for the development of professional sport set out in the Physical Culture Act initiated this process. It has regulated not only the foundation of sport joint stock companies, but also the issuing of permits for professional competition to Polish sport associations. The Championship Sport Act takes this issue further by eliminating the economic fiction in which the formal status of Polish sport associations (association or federation of associations) prevented them from conducting any for-profit activity.

Article 13 of the Championship Sport Act introduces a new rule under which, in order to manage the commercial use of its tangible and intangible assets, a Polish sport association is allowed to create a corporation operating under the provisions of commercial law. Similarly, league structures emerge in those league-type disciplines in which over half of competing sports clubs have the legal status of joint stock companies. A professional league of this kind is managed by a legal person not belonging to any Polish sport association, acting in the form of a commercial company, either a limited liability company or a joint stock company. Similar governance patterns are observed at the local level in professional leagues in which only the clubs with the status of joint stock companies are allowed to enter competitions, which limits the group of participants to the commercial sector. In those disciplines where competition is not arranged in a league pattern, a respective Polish sport association can transfer full or partial management of the sectoral competition to a legal person or individual qualified as entrepreneur under the Freedom of Economic Activity Act (Journal of Laws No. 173, Item 1807). The regulations listed above (notably the Championship Sport Act) have largely steered the course of the development of Polish professional sport in the future to focus on the commercial sector.

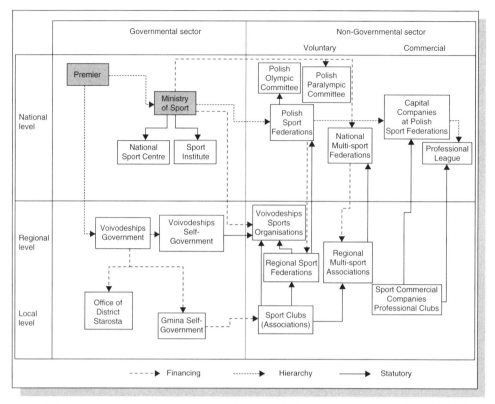

Figure 7.1 The organisational structure of sport in Poland (*Source*: Adapted from Tokarski, Steinbach et al., 2004)

Figure 7.1 illustrates the organisational structure of sport in Poland, including the three sectors discussed above.

Financing of elite sport

The ongoing dispute concerning the financial model for sport, including public sports infrastructure such as stadiums, primarily involves a choice between public financing or the state providing mechanisms for investing private capital along commercial lines. The Polish model of sport financing currently relies largely on public interventions. The state interventionist approach discussed above refers also to the financing of sport, which by no means implies that the Polish state invests heavily in the development of the sport sector. In 2006, public funding for physical culture and sport constituted as little as approximately 0.09 per cent of total budgetary expenditures and amounted to PLN 731,550: just 0.075 per cent of gross domestic product. Some 30 per cent was paid directly from the state budget, 68 per cent from the

Table 7.1 Public sport financing: 1989–2006

	1989	1991	1993	1995	1997	1999	2001	2003	2005	2006
Physical culture and sport expenditure in millions PLN	18.70	81.40	64.10	203,100	548,80	566,000	687,800	603,400	713,430	731,550
Physical culture and sport expenditure in total state budget (%)	0.55	0.34	0.13	0.13	0.17	0.14	0.12	0.08	0.09	0.09

Source: *Statistical Yearbook of the Republic of Poland*, GUS, Warsaw (2006).

Physical Fitness Development Fund (PFDF) and 1.5 per cent from the Youth Sports and Recreation Fund. As illustrated in Table 7.1, public sport financing dropped from 0.55 per cent of total state budget in 1989 to as little as 0.09 per cent in 2006.

Similarly, provisions for physical culture and sport in the Draft Budget for 2007 are not much higher. Total outlays assigned for this purpose amount to PLN 772,420 including PLN 232,030 from the state budget, and the remainder from non-budgetary state purposive funds including: PLN 517,750 from the PFDF and PLN 22,630 from the Youth Sports and Recreation Fund. These provisions are listed in Section 25 of the Draft Budget – physical culture and sport, with the Minister of Sport responsible for the disposal of the funds.

Regarding public sector financing, territorial administrations emerge as the largest contributor, with 70 per cent of total public outlays on sport coming from territorial budgets. In local budgets, outlays on sport constitute approximately 1.5 per cent of total spending. The remaining 30 per cent of public funding comes from the central state budget and surcharges on lotto rates. According to the state strategy, the share of outlays on sport in local administration budgets is to double from the current level of 1.0–1.5 to 2.5–3.0 per cent. Public sources discussed so far fail to satisfy the financial needs of Polish sport. Furthermore, they are extremely sensitive to the fluctuations in central and local public budgets. Other sources of financing include membership fees, sponsoring, patronage, earnings from sport and recreational services and events, and the income from economic activity of physical culture associations and sport public companies.

Some disciplines, such as football, attract funding from private investors: share capital (ITI, Inter Groklin Auto, ComArch, Tele Fonika, Kolporter, Amica and others); income from broadcasting contracts with the media; and sponsorship funding, such as in the case of Orange sponsoring *Ekstraklasa* (PLN 9.2 million for distribution among all premier league clubs) (Gąsiorowski, 2006). Unfortunately, since no systematic and consistent updates on non-public funding of sport are available, it is impossible to provide a comprehensive account of financing structures for Polish sport (Pastwa, 2000).

Changes in the system of elite sport governance

The structure of elite sport in Poland discussed above resulted from changes over many years. Indeed, it has always been a very dynamic field, displaying a considerable tendency for frequent change. The most stable period occurred in the 1960s and 1970s, which was also the time of the greatest successes of Polish athletes on the international sporting stage. Among the key rationales and motivations behind the ongoing organisational changes in the structure of Polish sport are:

- political factors – internal (e.g., public administrative reform) and external (e.g., EU policies);
- economic factors (resulting from changing socio-economic conditions, notably the transition from a centrally planned to a free market economy);
- legal factors (resulting from changing general and sport-specific regulations – factors from this group are especially numerous due to state interventionism as well as the use of law as an instrument for the state's interference in sport);
- aspirations to raise the prestige of sport in general and of organisations in the sport domain in particular;
- motivations resulting from perceived threats, especially on the part of the central administration, as well as other organisational units;
- benefits to specific interest groups;
- personal motivations;
- rational motivations objectively aiming at improving the system.

The process of systemic transformation which commenced in Poland in 1989 impacted upon the Polish elite sport system as well as in other domains of social life in so much as to render them far more thorough, dynamic and extreme than in other European states. Much like other spheres of life, sport and sport structures have undergone multi-faceted change resulting directly from the transition from central governance to a decentralised self-governing democratic system. According to Doktór (1996), this process will take much longer and assume a more complex form in the physical culture system than in other spheres of social life. While describing various forms of resistance to this process appearing in Central European countries, Krawczyk (1995) points to their intense, even acute character and similar, although complex, transition mechanisms in many post-communist states under systemic change. A report on the condition of physical culture, issued in 1989, shortly before the systemic transformation, listed the following major defects and gaps in the system:

- proliferation of national decision centres;
- over-centralisation of the system;
- disunity of the sport management and financing systems;
- lack of independence and self-governance of basic organisational units;
- lack of responsibility for the execution of statutory activities;
- no space for elite sport activity (Krawczyk et al., 1989).

After nearly 20 years of continuous transformation, analyses of the sport governance system in Poland reveal similar problems. The following section therefore provides a brief account of the changes in three sectors of the sport system in Poland – governmental (public), commercial and voluntary.

Changes in public sport governance

Any change occurring in Polish public sport institutions is usually planned and enforced by law. The organisational structure of physical culture in Poland has been characterised by the associative status of its basic units since the beginning of the twentieth century. For years, the system was termed 'state-civil', not so much because it relied on associative structures but rather because of the construction of the central administrative body responsible for this domain (a collegial entity referred to as the 'committee'). The institution was usually named the *Committee for Physical Culture* although it could temporarily assume various additional sub-units (e.g., physical culture was sometimes associated with tourism or the youth services). However, the crucial factor was the collegial nature of the committee, representing various social groups which would benefit from physical culture and its application to their needs. Committee members represented the sectors of healthcare and welfare, education, national defence, internal affairs, trade unions, sport unions and other groups. Sub-committees developed temporarily, when the body was also responsible for tourism, and its decisions were made collegially as resolutions. The committee chairman was appointed by the Prime Minister. However, the Committee of Physical Culture ceased to exist in 1991 but left a team of officials, and was renamed the Office of Physical Culture and Tourism – *Urząd Kultury Fizycznej and Turystyki (UKFiT)*; a change that failed to register with either the wider public or those closely involved with the sector. This restructuring was one in a long series of administrative reforms that began in 1946, see Figure 7.2.

The dissolution, on 30 June 2002, of the Office of Physical Culture and Sport (*Urząd Kultury Fizycznej and Sportu, UKFiS*), the successor to UKFiT, brought an end to a 75 year history of having a central public administration body responsible for the management of physical culture. Since 2002, responsibility for the sector has shifted between three ministries: Ministry of National Education, Ministry of National Education and Sport and currently Ministry of Sport. Figure 7.2 illustrates the historical changes in the naming of the central national administrative body.

Most of the administrative bodies mentioned in Figure 7.2 acted as an independent central office, with the exception of *PUWFiPW* and *UKFiS*, of which the first was subordinate to the Ministry of National Defence and the second to the Ministry of National Education. Most assumed the form of collegial bodies or committees, which were popular in those times. Jaworski (1993) claims that it is through the committees that the state-social model of physical culture was realised in Poland. Unlike the committees, offices and ministries are monocratic bodies within which all power rests in the hands of the president or minister. Under socialist rule, sport, notably elite sport, was one of the top priorities in the politics of many socialist states, to which it offered the only opportunity to mark their presence on the international stage. Hence the crucial importance of the central state administration body responsible for this domain.

Changes similar to those described for the central administration also occurred at the regional – voivodeship – level, and resulted from changing state policies and the role of regional-level public administration. The changes in state administration structures also applied to the governance of physical culture. In the sport domain, state administration bodies were to promote and supervise the latter through monitoring the

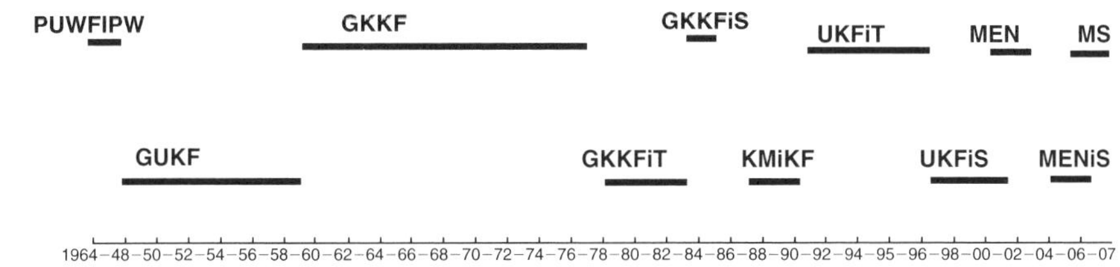

PUWFiPW — State Office for Physical and Military Education (*Państwowy Urząd Wychowania Fizycznego i Przysposobienia Wojskowego*)

GUKF — Main Office of Physical Culture (*Główny Urząd Kultury Fizycznej*)

GKKF — Main Committee for Physical Culture (*Główny Komitet kultury Fizycznej*)

GKKFiT — Main Committee for Physical Culture and Tourism (*Główny Komitet kultury Fizycznej i Turystyki*)

GKKFiS — Main Committee for Physical Culture and Sport(*Główny Komitet kultury Fizycznej i Sportu*)

KMiKF — *Committee for youth and Physical Culture (Komitet do Spraw Młodzieży i Kultury Fizycznej)*

UKFiT — Office of Physical Culture and Tourism (*Urząd Kultury Fizycznej i Turystyki*)

UKFiS — Office of Physical Culture and Sport (*Urząd Kultury Fizycznej i Sportu*)

MEN — Ministry of National Education (*Ministerstwo Edukacji Narodowej*)

MENiS — Ministry of National Education and Sport (*Ministerstwo Edukacji Narodowej i Sportu*)

MS — Ministry of Sport (*Ministerstwo Sportu*)

Figure 7.2 Historical changes in the naming of the central national administrative body for the management of physical culture in Poland since 1946 (*Source*: Adapted from Jaworski, 1993)

activities of sport associations in their respective territories. Their responsibilities also included supervising regional structures of medical care for the sport sector and managing sports infrastructure, most importantly, the development and modernisation of sports facilities.

At this point, it should be noted that the structural links between voivodeship physical culture governance units and their local (*gmina*) counterparts were rather limited. The latter were governed by boards appointed by local councils (local self-government bodies), which had considerable autonomy from state administration in their territory.[5] Meanwhile, the subordination of voivodeship physical culture departments to the central state administration body (UKFiT) was purely functional, since they reported to the Prime Minister via their respective voivods.

One of the major changes in the systemic transformation was the transfer of authority from central administration bodies to the lowest level, that is, to local communities, which translates into increasing the role of local communities in the activities of bottom-level territorial administration in various domains of social life. Territorial self-government is a basic form of civic activity in communes – *gminas* – and is represented by community councils elected by community members. At the bottom level, administrative tasks, which include provision for physical culture and recreational and sports facilities, are conducted by two structures: local state administration (local offices) and territorial self-government.

Local territorial self-government units are also obliged to organise and monitor the physical education of pre-school and school children. This issue has grown in importance since 1 January 1994, with the mandatory transfer of secondary schools under the authority of district self-governments. Reinstating extra-curricular sport or recreational activities should be among the priorities arising after schools came under the control of local administration, as well as forming good physical culture habits to last for life. And school gyms should be available to children and young people from their respective local communities. The strengthening of territorial self-governments appears to be a necessary precondition to any systemic transformation, in particular, in the context of decentralisation and self-governance. Although strictly necessary, the process of transferring competence, rights and responsibilities from the central to local level is proceeding at a very slow pace. This is due to the fact that, along with legal and organisational change already initiated, it also requires a revamping of organisational culture and a new approach by local officials and all community members to governance and management strategies.

Changes in the commercial sport management sector

Developments in the Polish commercial sport sector primarily relate to sports products and services, most notably sport–recreational services. In this domain, the fitness market emerges as a thriving segment. In elite sport, professional sport is the evolving sector. First attempts at transforming sports clubs, functioning on the associative basis into commercial entities, were made in the early 1980s but it was not until the early 1990s that commercialisation began to gather momentum.

It was the Physical Culture Act of 18 September 1996 that provided a formal basis for professional sport and its growth within the organisational–legal framework of the commercial sector. At that point, the legislator assumed the existence of professional clubs only in the form of sport joint stock companies. The moment when the Act took effect initiated slow but consistent growth of the number of sport public companies in Poland (Żyśko and Smoleń, 2003). Statistical analysis of the sport joint stock companies currently present on the Polish market reveals their concentration in football and basketball (approximately 85 per cent), with the remainder operating in volleyball, handball, hockey and cycling. Research conducted by M. Stachurska[6] reveals that 62.5 per cent of all *Ekstraklasa* ('Premier League') football clubs in Poland are sport public companies. Financial potential of shareholders is a key issue for the functioning of sport joint stock companies. Research conducted among Polish *Ekstraklasa* clubs revealed that only 13 per cent of their equity is in the hands of their parent clubs. The financial difficulties experienced by sport public companies make it difficult for them to produce the necessary financial guarantees for admittance to the league competition (Cegliński, 2003) and/or cause them to become heavily indebted (Łopatko and Borakiewicz, 2003).

Changes in the voluntary sport sector

Transformations in the non-profit (voluntary) organisations are the least evident due to considerable stability of the sector as well as because of the tendency for strong resistance to change in this area. The organisational structure of entities representing this sector has thus not undergone major change. Most enjoy considerable stability and a strong societal position. What has changed is the mechanisms of functioning, and above all financing, with the ongoing commercialisation process bringing about the arrival of hybrid forms.

According to a report (Jawor/Klon, 2005) sport organisations represent the most numerous group in the non-governmental sector and constitute about 40 per cent of all registered organisations. In 2003, the annual revenues of 19 per cent of all sport NGOs did not exceed PLN 1,000 (about 40 per cent came from community funding and only just over 17 per cent from membership fees, while in other NGOs the latter figure constitutes over 22 per cent). Sixty-nine per cent of sport NGOs do not employ paid staff and rely on voluntary work contributions from their members. Moreover, sport NGOs are the most well organised sub-sector, with over a half of their total number admitting to a membership in a union of associations or a sectoral federation, which is not surprising in the case of sports clubs participating in sport competitions organised by Polish sport associations.

Discussion of the elite sport system

Growth of infrastructure

The sports infrastructure for elite sport in Poland is undoubtedly one of its weakest links in the sports system. In 1996, the sports infrastructure in Poland amounted to slightly under 20,000 sports facilities, which translates into one sports facility per 2,000 people. The most numerous were team sport pitches, which constituted 20 per cent of all facilities, followed by gymnasia, multi-sports pitches and tennis courts. The sports infrastructure in Poland is owned primarily by territorial administrations, sports clubs, academies and the Central Sports Centre. Sports facilities are very unevenly distributed across voivodeships. In 1992, in an attempt to improve the highly unsatisfactory condition of sports infrastructure in Poland, the government established the PFDF. The Fund is financed from surcharges on lotto rates and is currently managed by the Minister of Sport. Since its creation, the Fund has been instrumental in distributing a total of over PLN 3,000 million to 956 infrastructure projects, with a further 690 planned. Detailed instructions on granting financial support from the Fund are listed in the directive issued by the Minister of Sport on financing projects from the PFDF. Financing limits vary depending on the character and objectives of the project as well as the entity executing the project. Financing of up to 33 per cent of all costs is available for modernisation, renovation or construction of sports facilities.

There are exceptions to this rule, for example, when a project is executed by a community without a comprehensive sports centre the funding can amount to 60 per cent of all costs, while for reconstructing or renovating facilities destroyed in a natural catastrophe the Fund can cover up to 95 per cent of total costs. Financial support is also available for projects aimed at fostering sport activity among children, youth and for people with disabilities. In such cases, the state can cover up to 50 per cent of the costs. In this category, state funding can amount to 95 per cent when the facilities constructed for the project have the capacity to host high-profile international events, or when the project is executed by one of the bodies listed in the directive. Projects conducted by the Central Sports Centre can be financed up to 99 per cent, and up to 70 per cent of total costs for those executed by Polish sport associations, national physical culture association, Academies of Physical Education or other higher education institutions, as well as territorial self-government bodies supporting athletic schools. Institutions and organisations apply for a place on the list of sport infrastructure projects directly to their respective marshal's office, who then passes the applications to the Ministry of Sport. Applications for financing special-purpose projects are submitted directly to the Minister of Sport. Every year a national financing plan is drawn up on the basis of voivodeship plans and investment plans of strategic importance to national sport. Up to 65 per cent of PFDF funds are directed towards voivodeship sport infrastructure development, while the remaining 35 per cent is spent on the development of strategic projects such as those for elite sport.

Introduction of a system of surcharges on lotto rates opened a source of stable financing of the construction and modernisation of facilities of special importance to sport. Adopted financing rules have a mobilising effect on local governments stimulating them to secure other sources of financing for their share of the costs. The strategy for the future is to search for new solutions optimising the conditions for further growth of sports infrastructure, managed by local authorities, with special emphasis on neighbourhood, city and district sports and recreation centres as well as facilities for championship sport. Among the most numerous projects are gymnasium halls, indoor swimming pools, stadiums and ice rinks. Of the total annual outlays on sports infrastructure, up to 70 per cent is to be directed towards local projects, according to voivodeship sports infrastructure development plans, and up to 30 per cent is to be spent on the development of strategic infrastructure.

Athletes: their rights and responsibilities

Strong state intervention is also apparent in the domain of athletes' rights and responsibilities, as well as in the way the term 'athlete' is defined. Under Article 3, Item 5, of the Championship Sport Act 'an athlete is a person participating in a sport discipline and licensed to participate in sporting competition by a suitable Polish sport association'. A club athlete is an individual fulfilling any of the conditions below:

- is a member of a sports club (applies to clubs functioning on associative basis);
- is bound to a club by contract (applies to clubs functioning on commercial basis);
- manages or participates in the management of a sports club.

Athletes with the status of sports clubs members, who are de facto and de jure amateurs and are not paid for their sport activities, may receive sport scholarships.

The Polish system of financial support for amateur athletes offers three types of scholarships:

1 Scholarship paid by a club under a contract stipulating at least the rights and responsibilities of the athlete and the club as well as the amount of scholarship.
2 Scholarship paid to national representatives participating in preparations for the Olympic Games or achieving top positions in international sport competitions (e.g., in World Championships and European Championships) or those who have signed a commitment to participate in the preparation programme for the Olympics or World Championships. This type of scholarship is independent of club scholarships. It is financed from the part of the state budget at the disposal of the minister responsible for sport (currently the Minister of Sport). Earmarked scholarships guarantee the participation of the best athletes in the national sport representation (Cajsel, 2006).
3 Scholarship paid by territorial self-government units, granted to athletes achieving superior results in international or national competition but not receiving any payments for their sport activity or any of the scholarships listed above.

The period during which an athlete is officially entitled to a scholarship is recognised as employment in the light of workers' rights and benefits, such as paid leave, disability or retirement pensions.

Athletes bound to a club by contract are entitled to payment under the terms of their contract. In the Polish championship sport practice, two types of contracts are applied to regulate the relationship between professional athletes and clubs: contract of employment or contract for sport services. Due to the absence of specific labour law for professional athletes, most contracts are signed on a civil-law basis. Research conducted by Kabała (2006) among athletes participating in the Polish Basketball League *Polska Liga Koszykówki S.A.* substantiates this claim since it revealed that just one athlete participated in the league in the 2005–2006 season under a standard contract of employment. Most contracts signed by professional athletes are sport contracts under civil law (e.g., contract for professional football performance). A contract between an athlete and a sports club must comply with the standards and terms determined primarily by the respective Polish sport association.[7]

The third type of athlete is defined as a person managing or participating in the management of a sports club. This is an option new to the Polish sport law system. It was introduced in Article 4, Item 3, of the Act on Championship Sport. According to Cajsel (2006), this practice is mainly to be found in individual sports, such as athletics, in which one individual can combine two functions, that of a professional athlete participating in a sport competition, and of the president of a limited liability company conducting championship sport activity.

Structure of sport competition

Under the Championship Sport Act, sport competition is defined as: 'individual or collective competition towards achieving results appropriate for the respective discipline'. In the light of this legal regulation, and in particular according to sport practice, sport competition is conducted at two levels: club and individual, with the former being the consequence and reflection of the competition between individual athletes. In order to enter a competition, both clubs and individuals require a licence issued by their respective Polish sport association.[8] Detailed rules, procedures and conditions for the issuing or withdrawal of a licence, as well as the terms of participation in sport competition, are determined by the statutes and regulations of Polish sport associations.

Sport competition differs considerably between disciplines, which is a direct consequence of the specific features of these disciplines but also results from the way competition is organised for a given discipline. Two basic types of sport competition patterns are: (a) a league or (b) a regatta or series of races. In those disciplines within which sport rivalry takes the shape of a league competition, a Polish sport association may establish a professional league, and in those disciplines, in which over half of all clubs participating in top-level league competition have commercial status, the appropriate Polish sport association is obliged to launch a professional league. A professional league is managed by a legal person independent of the Polish sport association operating as a capital company: either joint stock or limited liability. The operation of any professional league is regulated by a contract between the managing commercial body and the appropriate Polish sport association, signed upon the approval of the Minister of Sport. The Minister's consent is also required for the participation in a professional league of a non-commercial sports club.

So far only a few professional leagues have been established in Poland, including the Polish Basketball League, *Polska Liga Koszykówki S.A.* (since 1997) and Polish Women's Basketball League, *Polska Liga Koszykówki Kobiet Sp z o. o.* (since 2001), Polish Volleyball League, *Polska Liga Siatkówki S.A.* (since 2000) and Polish Premier League *Ekstraklasa S.A.* (since 2005 – earlier entities were the Autonomous Polish Football League, *Piłkarska Autonomiczna Liga Polska* – since 1999, later as the Polish Football League, *Piłkarska Liga Polska*). In those disciplines, in which sport competition does not assume the shape of a league, Polish sport associations sign contracts for the organisation or management of sport competition with other organisations.

Growth of sport sciences and personnel training

The education of personnel for Polish sport is regulated by the Directive of 27 June 2001, issued by the Minister of Sport and National Education concerning the qualifications, degrees and professional titles in physical culture and detailed regulations on obtaining these qualifications (Journal of Laws No. 71, Item 738; Journal of Laws of 2003 No. 8, Item 93). This represents enabling legislation aligned to Article 44, Section 3; of the Act on Physical Culture of 18 January 1996 (Journal of Laws of 2001 No. 81, Item 889 and No. 102, Item 1115 and Journal of Laws of 2002 No. 4, Item 31, No. 25, Item 253, No. 74, Item 676, No. 93, Item 820 and No. 130, Item 1112). The above directive recognises three types of professional titles in the Polish sport system: instructor (including sport instructors, physical recreation instructors, instructors for people with disabilities and biological regeneration instructors); coach (three-degree system); and manager (including sport manager, discipline manager and event manager). A person is officially recognised as an instructor, coach or manager only upon fulfilling the appropriate conditions stated in the directive.

State policy in training physical culture and sport personnel was expressed in the programme developed by the Ministry of National Education and Sport and accepted by the Council of Ministers: *The Strategy of the Development of Sport Until 2012* (The Ministry of Sport, 2003). According to this document, a priority for the near future is to modify the personnel training system for Polish sport. The programme assumes that physical education academies continue to train personnel for Polish physical culture, while adapting their structures to state-of-the-art knowledge and the changing environment. In current projects implementing the Strategy's goals, personnel training for elite sport is among the priorities.

The Minister of Sport is the supervising body for the training and development of personnel for Polish sport, in the broad understanding of the term. In this domain, the Minister conducts legal normative activities, and in many cases also issues

documents certifying coach, instructor or sport manager qualifications (as is the case with institutions licensed to train sports
recreation instructors and instructors for people with disabilities). An advisory body – the Council for Coach, Instructor and
Manager Training – operates within the structure of the central
state administration office responsible for Polish sport. The key
tasks of the Council are to review applications and provide recommendations for personnel training projects, special case professional qualifications in physical culture, promoting coaches
to Class I and Master Class, and conduct upgrade examinations
for coaches. The Council also supervises courses for Class II
and Master Class coaches. Its activities are conducted in two
sub-divisions: (a) reviewing upgrade applications submitted by
coaches and instructors and (b) dealing with dissertations on
sport training by graduates from qualifying courses.

In the academic education system, specialist training for elite
sport is conducted primarily by the universities of physical culture. There are six such universities in Poland (in Warsaw,
Gdańsk, Katowice, Kraków, Poznań and Wrocław) and two
external faculties (in Biała Podlaska – the faculty of Warsaw
University of Physical Culture and in Gorzów Wielkopolski –
the faculty of the University School of Physical Education in
Poznań). Graduates from the physical education departments
at these universities and individuals who completed postgraduate studies in the same area constitute over 90 per cent of the
annual training personnel output. Nearly 40 per cent of all
sport discipline instructors hold physical education degrees. As
a result of the dynamic diversification of physical education
training, the number of educational institutions providing education in this area has grown to around 35 in number.

Under the regulations listed earlier, specialist training for
sport and physical culture can also be provided by units other
than academic institutions, provided they are licensed by the
Minister of Sport. Until now, these licences have been issued to
130 institutions. However, not all have actually opened courses.
Despite the existence of state strategy and policy in personnel
training for sport and physical culture, some informal trends can
be observed. Some sport associations (Polish Skiing Association,
Polish Sailing Association, Polish Flying Club) prefer to apply
the legal codes of their international umbrella federations and
introduce their own professional classes and titles (e.g., assistant instructor, junior instructor). This fact again confirms the
existence of a conflict in Polish elite sport, caused by the strong
role of the state and the state administrative model generating
problems in confrontation with the regulations of non-governmental sports federations.

On the basis of existing professional titles, the system of personnel development and training for sport and physical culture distinguishes approximately 10 training programmes for various specialities: coaches (including separate programmes for Class II, Class I and Class M coaches); sport instructors; active recreation instructors; biological regeneration instructors; umpires; sport managers; sport event managers and physical education teachers. For the above, professional qualification is achieved through obtaining a university degree in physical education, with various specialities. Meanwhile, professional development training is conducted through:

- specialist courses, organised by academic institutions of physical education;
- specialist courses, conducted by institutions other than physical education universities, and certified by the Minister of Sport;
- postgraduate studies also organised by academic institutions.

Scientific research for sport

Results are the essence of elite sport. These are achieved through a combination of many factors, one of which is supporting sport training with scientific knowledge, research and the implementation of scientific findings into sport practice. Although the use of scientific research has a long tradition in Polish elite sport, currently the practice of supporting sport with scientific findings is largely neglected. As a result of the changes in the financing of science in Poland, the Institute of Sport – central research and development unit for Polish sport – despite its long experience, has ceased to conduct programmed research and implementation activities. Meanwhile, as well as the statutory contribution of the Institute of Sport, an increasing number of independent research initiatives have appeared on the market, established by research teams or individual researchers recruiting primarily from the universities of physical education, which is a sign at least of a developing 'research market' (Sozański, 2006) and one which is not dependent on the Ministry of Sport or any national research centre.

Conclusions

The Polish elite sport system is strongly interventionist, centralised, bureaucratic, intensely formalised but unstable. The key role of state structures in managing elite sport in Poland stands in contrast to European sport policies described by the Council of Europe in the 'European model of sport', as well as to one of the key principles of European Union policy – the subsidiarity principle. Conflict is also to be observed in the vertical dimension (transfer of power to the lowest level of management), as well as in the horizontal dimension (transfer of competence to non-governmental structures in all domains of state agency is not strictly necessary). The Polish elite sport system appears to be moving in the reverse direction, towards greater centralisation and a strengthening of the state administration's grip of the management of sport. The creation in 2005 of the Ministry of Sport, with very broad supervising and controlling powers over sport organisations, conflicts with EU policy and also with strategies adopted in other European states, where the dominant model is based on autonomous NGOs.

Moreover, the current Polish sport system is a combination of traditional and contemporary elements – voluntary activity of non-profit organisations with centralised state administration management. Moreover, the ceaseless changes in the system compromise its efficiency. Between 1990 and 2006, the central administration body experienced five major overhauls and frequent unjustified management replacements, more often than not for political reasons. It is, however, to be noted that some of the changes introduced in the period in question were of a regulating character (such as providing legal grounds for professional sport and elimination of pathologies resulting from the formerly unregulated status of professional sport).

Notes

1 This study was conducted with the financial support from the Ministry of Science and Higher Education – project Nr Ds. – 101.
2 The conflict between the Polish Football Association and the Minister of Sport, continuing for several years and intensified in January 2007, is evidence of the authority of the Ministry of Sport.
3 The weakness, instability and lack of persistence in the execution of the strategy is made evident by the fact that a new strategy 'The Strategy of the Development of Sport until 2015' has already been drafted by the Ministry of Sport, Warsaw 2006.
4 A similar term was used in the research by Chaker (2004). However, Chaker's research did not include the Polish sport system.

5 Relationships between these bodies are regulated by the Act on Territorial Self-Government of 8 March 1990 (Journal of Laws No. 16, Item 95).

6 Unpublished data by courtesy of M. Stachurska of Heidelberg University.

7 See the regulations and decrees of Polish sport associations such as Resolution No. II/11 of 19 May 2002 issued by the Board of the Polish Football Association on the status of Polish footballers and the change of their club status and the Resolution No. II/39 of 14 July 2006 issued by the Board of the Polish Football Association on the change in the above Resolution (www.pzpn.pl/a/statusPP.doc), as well as the regulations of Polish Basketball, *League Polskia Liga Koszykówki S.A.* (www.media.pl/dokumenty/regulaminy2006_2007.pdf)

8 Similarly, umpires and coaches require licensing by their appropriate sport association, although in the case of coaches this is a new practice.

References

Cajsel, W. (2006) *Ustawa o sporcie kwalifikowanym*, Warszawa: Wydawnictwo C.H. Beck.

Cegliński, L. (2003) Dziesięć dni. Koszykówka. PLK bez Legii? *Gazeta Wyborcza Stołeczna*, 10 September.

Chaker, A.-N. (2004) *Good Governance in Sport*, Strasbourg: Council of Europe.

Doktór, K. (1996) *Dylematy współczesnego sportu*. I Ogólnopolska Konferencja Menedżerów Sportu, Warszawa: Polska Korporacja Menedżerów Sportu.

Gąsiorowski, D. (2006) Kto rządzi polską piłką? *money.pl*, Available at www.money.pl (accessed 31 July 2006).

Jawor/Klon, S. (2005) Podstawowe fakty o branżach sektora organizacji pozarządowych w Polsce, Raport z badania, Kondycja sektora organizacji pozarządowych w Polsce 2004, Stowarzyszenie Klon/Jawor.

Jaworski, Z. (1993) Struktury organizacyjne w skali makro, *Trening* 3.

Kabała, M. (2006) Funkcjonowanie profesjonalnej ligi zawodowej na przykładzie Polskiej Ligii Koszykówki, *Katedra Nauk Społecznych*, Warszawa: Akademia Wychowania Fizycznego. praca magisterska: 55.

Krawczyk, Z. (1995) *Społeczne przesłanki przeobrażeń kultury fizycznej w krajach Europy Środkowo-Wschodniej*. Międzynarodowej Konferencji Naukowej na temat: Przeobrażenia kultury fizycznej w krajach Europy Środkowej i Wschodniej, Warszawa.

Krawczyk, Z., Przewęda, R. et al. (1989) *Raport o kulturze fizycznej w Polsce*, Warszawa: Wyd. AWF Warszawa.

Łopatko, M. and Borakiewicz, W. (2003) Areszt za lewą kasę, *Gazeta Wyborcza*, 3 October (z dnia).

The Ministry of Sport (2003) *The Strategy of the Sport Development Until 2012*. Warszawa: MSport Warszawa.

Pastwa, M. (2000) *Zarządzanie finansami instytucji sportowo-rekreacyjnych*. Warszawa: Polska Korporacja Menedżerów Sportu.

Rapkiewicz, M. (2006) O naprawie futbolowej Rzeczypospolitej Warszawa, raport Instytutu Sobieskiego.

Sozański, H. (2006) O potrzebie niektórych działań modernizacyjnych w polskim sporcie, *Kultura Fizyczna*, 9–12, 15–22.

Tokarski, W., Steinbach, D., Petry, K. and Jesse, B. (2004) *Two Players – One Goal? Sport in the European Union*. Oxford: Meyer and Meyer Sport.

Żyśko, J. and Smoleń, A. (2003) Geneza i rozwój sportowych spółek akcyjnych, in T. Rychta and J. Chełmecki (eds.), *Wkład nauk humanistycznych do wiedzy o kulturze fizycznej*, Warszawa: AWF Warszawa.

CHAPTER 8

Norway

Pål Augestad and Nils Asle Bergsgard

Introduction

Since 1992, Norway has experienced almost unprecedented success in the field of sports. During the four most recent winter Olympics, Norway has won 42 gold medals and 96 medals in all. In comparison, during the previous four winter Olympics, the numbers were 7 and 31, respectively. Progress has also been made in the summer games. A total of 13 gold medals, and 30 medals in all, have been won since 1992. The corresponding figures for the four preceding summer Olympics were 5 and 14, respectively.

In this chapter, we describe the Norwegian system for elite sport development to which this success can be attributed. First we provide a short overview of the main features related to the elite sport system, and then, second, examine more thoroughly the four elements that constitute the infrastructure of elite sport in Norway: the facility structure, the emergence of full-time competitors, the emphasis on sports science and medicine, and competition opportunities. Third, we will discuss some factors behind this model for elite sport and for the governmental involvement in elite sport. Finally, we highlight some national characteristics of the Norwegian model. Despite striking similarities between the various national models for the organisation of top-level sport, there are also distinguishing national features which result from different cultural and political traditions.

The discussions and findings presented in this chapter are a result of an ongoing research project on the elite sport development system in Norway carried out in the period from 2004 to 2007.[1] We have collected data from two primary empirical sources. First, we analysed documents related to the development of Norwegian elite sport since 1970.[2] Secondly, we conducted interviews with 68 informants. Twenty-four interviews were with centrally placed informants in the sport system, bureaucrats in the Ministry, and employees in the central elite sport unit in Norway called Olympiatoppen. We selected informants on the basis of their position in the sport policy system and/or as experts, especially in the medical–scientific area. The remaining interviews were with leaders, trainers, and athletes in three selected national federations, canoeing, track and field and cross-country skiing.

The elite sport system in Norway

Olympiatoppen (OLT) is the fulcrum in the Norwegian elite sport system, especially regarding the Olympic sports. Olympiatoppen is formally the elite sport division within the voluntary umbrella organisation – the Norwegian Olympic Committee and Confederation of Sports (NIF/NOC). NIF/NOC has a monopoly on organising the Olympic sports, while the actual sporting activity takes place in the national and specialised sports federations (SFs) that are members of NIF/NOC.[3] Olympiatoppen was established in 1988–1989 as a central coordinating organisation for the development of elite sport. It was set up to improve conditions for the development of elite sport in Norway. Specifically, this involves: granting scholarships to talented performers in all the Olympic sports, providing medical support to all the national teams and operating a well-equipped national training centre. It also implies offering professional competence in the various types of support that are important for improving the athlete's performance, such as training experts, physiologists, sport psychologists, nutritionists, physiotherapists, and masseurs.

However, it is the SFs that have the main responsibility for the elite sport activity in their sport. In a recent policy document published by NIF/NOC, covering 2003–2007, the following comments describe the division of labour between the SFs and Olympiatoppen (NIF/NOC, 2003, p. 33):

OLT has an overall responsibility for the results of the elite sport in Norway. In addition OLT has a responsibility to implement the Norwegian participation in the Olympic Games. OLT is – under the supervision from the Sports Board [of NIF/NOC] – to follow up the General Assembly's decisions regarding elite sport. The SFs have the total authority within their sport. As follows the SFs have the responsibility for all elite sport activity and all results in their field, and thus have the decision-making authority on all questions regarding their sport.

The division of labour between Olympiatoppen and the SFs is thus not clear cut and has, on several occasions, caused quite intense discussions. The establishment of Olympiatoppen alongside the Elite Sport Centre in Oslo represents in many respects a centralisation of the Norwegian elite sport system. Besides the medical and technical elements mentioned above, Olympiatoppen has also administrative responsibilities such as the distribution of funding to the SFs and the selection of athletes to take part in the Olympics. Several of these elements had previously been the responsibility of specific SFs (or the board of the former and separate National Olympic Committee consisting of representatives from SFs). However, Olympiatoppen's aim is to be close to the individual athlete and her or his trainer, and consequently the organisation's experts and consultants work in close collaboration with the national teams and the SFs.

Further, from the mid-1990s, several regional centres have been established in Norway that collaborate with, or are under the authority of, Olympiatoppen.

It was the sports organisations themselves that initiated, implemented, and completed the process by establishing a separate organisation for elite sport. High performance goals are almost invisible in public sport documents in Norway because elite sport is considered to be primarily the domain of the sports organisations. The Ministry states that 'High performance sport is an important priority for organised sport' (St.meld. nr. 14, 1999–2000, p. 54). However, the government recognises its responsibility for providing a solid basis for an elite sport system, and the main arguments for involvement are that 'The Government will support Norwegian elite sport financially so that the basis for an ethically and professionally qualified elite sport environment is secured, and so that elite sport may still be considered as a means of cultural identification in Norwegian society' (St.meld. nr. 14, 1999–2000, p. 37).

Public funding is the major source of income for Olympiatoppen. Public funding also constitutes an important proportion of the cost of elite sport development for many SFs, and was also crucial in contributing up to 50 per cent of the total capital cost of the construction of the Elite Sport Centre and several national facilities for elite sport. To some degree, commercial income is also of importance to Olympiatoppen, although income from sponsors fluctuates and there has been a decline in recent years with the result that public funding has constituted nearly all of Olympiatoppen's financial resources (Bergsgard, 2005; Augestad et al., 2006). On average public funding amounts to around one-fifth of a SF's income, while for one-third of the SFs, public funding amounts to 70 per cent or more of their income (Enjolras, 2004, p. 53, 2005, p. 16). In 2005, direct support from Olympiatoppen to the SFs, including grants to athletes, was 11 per cent of the total public funding of SFs through the NIF/NOC system (NIF/NOC, 2006, p. 33). In 2001, the direct support from Olympiatoppen was 5 per cent of the total income for SFs, while in 2003 the figure was around 3 per cent.[4]

Income from sponsors and from the sale of the rights to broadcast events and leagues is important for the larger and more popular sports (and thus the SFs concerned) constituting, according to Enjolras (2004, p. 53), 28 and 10 per cent respectively in 2001.[5] On average the commercial income amounted to around 50 per cent of the total income for the SFs in 2001 and, for one-third of the SFs, more than 70 per cent.[6] The money spent on elite sport by SFs is not easy to identify, but the figures appear to be between 20 and 40 per cent, depending on whether the cost of personnel and management of elite sport development is included (Kearney, 1998, p. 19; Enjolras, 2005, p. 20; see also Augestad and Bergsgard, 2007). In addition, the proportion of income allocated to elite sport development varies considerably between SFs, from 2 to 60 per cent. It is, however, very difficult to link the different items of expenditure with different sources of income, especially when most of the public funding is not earmarked but is received as block grants (Enjolras, 2004, p. 62, 2005, p. 20). Nevertheless, it is clear that a substantial portion of the public funding distributed by NIF to SFs is spent on elite sport development, especially among the smaller and less commercialised federations.

The infrastructure of elite sport

In order to be competitive at the international level in sport, a number of structures specific to top-level sport have been established over the past 20 years in Norway. The initiative for these developments has come from a range of actors including SFs, NIF, and sports clubs. Here, we focus on four major elements and some of their implications: facilities, the lifetime support programme, the role of sports science, and athletes' competition opportunities.

Facility development

The founding of the Toppidrettssenteret (the elite sport centre) in Oslo in 1986 was an important move in the direction of a coordinated policy for top-level sport in Norway. In this centre, elite athletes train together, receive medical treatment, and take advantage of a range of physical tests. The idea behind the centre was to concentrate the sports science and medicine competences related to elite sport in one location. The range of services, the number of staff, and the budget have gradually increased, and today the centre is divided into four different sections: testing and training; health; laboratories for endurance; and nutrition. From 1990, the Toppidrettssenteret has been an integral part of Olympiatoppen.

The section for training at the Toppidrettssenteret/Olympiatoppen is occupied with physical testing and training. Here we find experts in areas such as strength, jumping, speed, flexibility, and coordination. In addition, there are well-resourced departments with the equipment and apparatus to plan, implement and evaluate exercise, and testing regimes. The health section provides a range of services, especially relating to the treatment of, and rehabilitation from, illness and injuries. The health section also provides advice for athletes and coaches on medical issues and initiates research projects related to sports medicine. Further the health section offers a 24-hour phone service for top-athletes concerning questions about doping and related issues. The nutrition section at Olympiatoppen focuses on the relationship between nutrition and performance and how to optimise the shape of the athlete's body and, more specifically, the regulation of weight and issues related to clinical nutrition and eating disorders. The nutrition section disseminates research-based knowledge and provides advice to athletes from different sports, providing written guidelines, factual information, and individual advice concerning athletes' diets.

In the 1980s, the government began to improve conditions for the development of elite sport in Norway. The government established a funding arrangement for the so-called 'Riksanlegg' with the goal of meeting the need for facilities in order that Norway could host international championships (Bergsgard, 2002, 2005). Using lottery funds, the government covered up to 50 per cent (maximum 25 million NOK) of the capital cost to (re)build such facilities in each sport. This arrangement was costly however due to its open and wide set of rules, and many facilities were built that were not, in practice, used as facilities for international championships. Consequently, a new arrangement termed 'Nasjonalanlegg' was established in the mid-1990s. Under the new arrangements, the number of sports to be included was limited to a maximum of 10 and it was agreed that there should only be one facility for each type of sport. Specific guidelines were drawn up to determine what constituted a national facility – both in terms of which sports and which facilities for each sport. Obtaining status as a national facility conferred about the same economic benefits as the Riksanlegg arrangement, namely the receipt of up to 50 per cent of approved costs from the lottery for development, reconstruction or rehabilitation of the facility in question. Moreover, status as a national facility meant that facilities were 'to be used for presentation of national elite sport in Norway, and as arenas for international championships and competitions in Norway' (Ministry of Cultural Affairs, 1997).

The legacy of facilities for elite performance from the Lillehammer Olympics in 1994, the construction of new arenas for the 1997 Skiing World Championships in Trondheim, and the famous Holmenkollen ski facility in Oslo for the 1952 Olympics and the 1982 World Championships provided the foundation for the debate regarding which arena was to become the national facility for skiing (Bergsgard, 2002, 2005). Thus, there appears to be a surplus of elite level ski facilities in

Norway. The latest funding from the Nasjonalanlegg arrangement was 100 million NOK allocated to Holmenkollen in Oslo to prepare for the hosting of the 2011 Skiing World Championships, which could be interpreted as indicating a desire by the government to concentrate the national facilities for skiing to the Oslo area. Furthermore, the government turned down NIF/NOC's application to bid to host the winter Olympics in 2014 in Tromsø. However, the government has recently indicated that it may support a new application for the 2018 Olympics. Of the possible locations (Oslo/Lillehammer, Trondheim, and Tromsø), the Sports Board of NIF/NOC decided to promote Tromsø's candidacy for the 2018 winter Olympics and the final decision is now in the hands of the government.

The facility strategy is complemented by a technology strategy intended to ensure that athletes not only have state-of-the art facilities in which to train, but also that they have access to equipment (skates and skis for example) that most effectively supports the practice of their sport. Thus, developments in sport are achieved not only through technologically advanced facilities, but also through innovations in, or modifications of, the micro-physics of sport. For example, since 1989 Olympiatoppen has spent more than 15 million NOK on the Gliding project to test everything that may have an influence on the friction between ski and snow. This has, first and foremost, an impact for the different ski sports, but some of the conclusions can also be of benefit for sports like kayaking, sculling, and sailing. The research project also illustrates some of the difficulties of using money on sport-related research. National innovations will flow not only between different sports in Norway, but also between different nations. The motivation for equipment-oriented research is driven by Norway's aspiration to win more medals in international competitions in the future. However, the professionalisation of coaches and experts around the national teams implies that knowledge flows across national borders as coaches/experts move to other nations, researchers need to present their findings in international publications, the media investigate and publicise innovations, and the technicians involved sell their abilities to other nations.

The emergence of full-time competitors

The opportunity to train and compete on a full-time basis in order to help realise elite sport ambitions depends not only on time and money, but also, for many, on the possibility of combining top-level sport with education. The goal of the lifetime support programme in Norway is to enable the athlete to fulfil a 'double career', to gain an education or vocational training at the same time as he or she is involved in elite sport. Lifestyle support is an explicit aim in the Norwegian sport system; it implies a focus on educational plans and on athletes' careers after retiring from sport. At the junior level, Norway has developed some sport-oriented secondary schools where young talented athletes are given the opportunity to combine top-level sport with a school education. These schools are called gymnasia and are meant for boys and girls between 16 and 19 years old that choose a particular sport – such as golf, football, cross-country skiing, and volleyball – as their major area of study. In some cases the young athletes move away from home in order to attend these schools (Slettemeås, 2005, pp. 93–97; Eriksen, 2006, pp. 84–90). In these institutions, promising young athletes 'learn' a lifestyle that includes training, education, and social life, which is essential if they want to win medals in international competitions in the future. It is argued that their identity as top-athletes is developed not only through training, but also by daily interaction with other students who have the same focus and aims. It is further argued that the hard work of training will only be meaningful if they are part of a community that shares their aspirations.

According to Bergsgard (2003), in a study of athletes in their late teens in cross-country skiing and football who either attended an elite sport gymnasia and/or were a part of a national team at junior level, the majority viewed their sporting activity both as a lifestyle and as a hobby. Fewer saw their athletic career as a job. Moreover, nearly all the athletes were studying or had plans to study alongside their athletic career. Thus, while some of the most talented athletes are selected for one of the national teams and a few also receive a grant to prepare for elite sport after graduation from the gymnasia, a large proportion of athletes have to prepare for a career and must therefore try to combine an education with high level sport. This implies that some athletes finance their sport career by living on money from their student loan. In the study referred to above, the student loan was listed as the second most important source of finance, after support from parents/family (Bergsgard, 2003, p. 23) and, for 12 per cent of the top-level athletes that are a part of Olympiatoppen's programme, the student loan was their main source of income (Gilberg and Breivik, 1997).

Athletes' access to a university or a university college is independent from their sporting performance. However, there is an agreement between the sport system and some universities that enables athletes to combine training and competition with university study. In practice, this means lengthening the period of study and rescheduling examinations if they conflict with training camps. Olympiatoppen has specialist support staff that help athletes on matters that we might term, non-sporting development plans. These staff collaborate with schools to provide education plans tailored to the needs of athletes as well as helping athletes to find part-time jobs. According to the study of talented athletes in their late teens, a flexible study curriculum and/or special arrangements at universities are the most important factors when combining elite sport and study (Bergsgard, 2003, p. 26). Despite this flexibility, more than half of these young athletes planned to follow a normal progression of the curriculum.

Olympiatoppen also provides grants for national elite athletes. In 1976, the NIF applied successfully to the government for a fund to subsidise elite level athletes and, from 1978, NIF was allocated 300,000 NOK for distribution to elite athletes.[7] The distribution of grants to athletes is now the responsibility of Olympiatoppen. Over the period 1985–1988, government funding increased to about 2 million NOK per year[8] and, by 1998, 4.3 million NOK was allocated in grants to elite athletes.[9] From 1999, this funding was included as a specific element and later as a non-specific element of the lottery-funded bloc grant from the government to NIF/NOC for elite sport. Up to the last 3–4 years, the size of the grant has increased considerably. In 2003, Olympiatoppen distributed 12.8 million NOK and in 2005 10.7 million NOK in grants to athletes. Olympiatoppen currently divides the grants into three different categories: A-stipend (100,000 NOK), B-stipend (50,000 NOK), and U-stipend (50,000 NOK).[10] In addition, some athletes also receive grants from their local authority (municipality) and from private sponsors. More than half of the athletes included in Olympiatoppen rely on their sporting activity, which includes elite sport grants, as their main source of income, while 32 per cent rely on other types of work and, as previously mentioned, 12 per cent rely on student loans as their primary source of income (Gilberg and Breivik, 1997).

The provision of opportunities for athletes to train and compete on a full-time basis is essential for Norwegian success in international competitions. This means the opportunity to train twice a day (or for about 4–6 hours), the opportunity to relax between training sessions, and the possibility of being away from home for more than 100 days per year for training camps and competitions. To enable this lifestyle, athletes need time and money. The concept of the 24-hour athlete (24hrA) is a central element in the Norwegian sport system, and the concept is used to build up structures around athletes. 24hrA indicates that top-level sport is a way of living, and that athletes need plans not only for the 4–6 hours of training, but also for the remainder of the day. In addition, athletes have to plan for a life after their sport career ends. Indeed, Thor Ole Rimejordet, one of the founders of the Norwegian model for top-level sport, explains that 'As a serious athlete you have to consider that you are an athlete in [a] cycle of 24 hours, so that you get [a] balance between strain and rest … and between sport, education and social life' (Rimejordet, 2002). The national federations (SFs) and Olympiatoppen help athletes to balance their sport-related activity with other areas of their lives, and also to realise their educational plans. In the Norwegian sport system, it appears to be taken for granted that it is important for athletes to focus on things other than sport. But the issues of 'when' and 'how often' athletes should concentrate on performance are always related to the perspective of improvement. In short, the discussion on 24hrA is not only about balancing elite sport and education, but also about finding practical and mental techniques in order to realise maximum improvement in a specific sport.

Sports science and medicine

Over the past 10 years, Olympiatoppen has invested in enhancing the availability of scientific knowledge in elite sport, especially in the area of nutrition where work focuses primarily on providing athletes with a diet to aid their performances. In order to achieve this goal, Olympiatoppen has initiated a number of measures aimed at providing relevant information for athletes. The organisation publishes brochures providing general advice regarding nutrition and training, and also more specialist advice concerning the selection of dietary supplements for athletes in a range of specific sports. The organisation publishes free books about healthy food and prepares guidelines for the intake of liquids in connection with competitions as well as offering individual guidance concerning diet. In this manner, Olympiatoppen attempts to distribute knowledge to elite athletes concerning the relationship between nutrition and physical activity. The task of providing information is dependent on having a team of professionals who can assist in the dissemination of the relevant knowledge: trainers, doctors, physiotherapists, and other support personnel who can undertake the 'missionary work' in spreading 'the word' concerning the 'right diet path' to follow.

Knowledge concerning diet is not only improved by spreading information, but also through establishing new arrangements which directly or indirectly influence the athletes' dietary habits. For example, food might be brought to national team meetings abroad to ensure that athletes have the correct diet; a specific regime concerning the intake of liquids during training sessions might be introduced to make training sessions more effective (e.g., drinking liquids such as Nutridrink directly after a training session is designed to reduce the recovery period); and blood samples might be taken to determine whether athletes have an iron deficiency and DEXA measurements (dual-energy X-ray absorptiometry – measures fat mass) conducted to establish if athletes have an optimal relationship between their fat and muscle mass. Olympiatoppen has a number of such 'routines' for the various national teams, which ensures that the relevant scientific knowledge becomes part of an elite athlete's daily life.

Olympiatoppen's task not only consists of knowledge dissemination, in the form of information and science-based routines, but also concerns extracting knowledge concerning nature and human beings: for example, What do elite athletes eat? How much do they eat? When do they eat? and How often do they eat? Olympiatoppen consequently initiates research projects in order to map out and oversee the elite athletes' dietary habits. However, it is not only of interest to collect data which describes the status quo, but also to attempt to gain knowledge concerning what happens when new knowledge is brought to athletic practice. For example, what happens to selected indicators when athletes eat more fruit or take the maximum dosage of iron supplements? And what is the difference between those who take iron supplements and those who do not? This represents experimental method taken out of the laboratory and used in a practical sport situations. The methodological challenge consists of keeping the effect of all the so-called irrelevant variables constant. An improved diet should result in fewer cases of sickness, improved well-being, and more energy for training. However, the pedagogical challenge of such a project lies in convincing elite athletes to participate, that is, to change their diet. Therefore, it is important that the national team works in conjunction with a doctor who can ensure that diet plans are implemented, and at the same time ensure that individual athletes keep to the planned routines.

Highly competent professionals within the field of nutrition and training confer legitimacy on the dietary regimes, thus transforming theoretical scientific knowledge into concrete practices. Olympiatoppen's health team consists of professionals and researchers working in close cooperation with other researchers, thereby enabling them to develop a network of contacts working within their respective expert environments. Diet is only one of many variables in the web of factors that need to be controlled in the daily lives of elite athletes but nevertheless it is one that Olympiatoppen considers highly significant and thus one in which it invests considerable resources.

The squad system and competition opportunities[11]

The home club is the cornerstone of the Norwegian sport system. Athletes have the club as their initial sport context and training location until they are about 16 years old and, for some, even longer. In the clubs, young athletes learn to practice their particular sport and it is here that they experience their first competition. Moreover, the club constitutes their social milieu, it is where they have their coaches and, together with their peers, take part in their first training camp. The clubs in the Norwegian sport system are primarily based on voluntary work and operate with very small budgets and only very modest payment to coaches. The club members and the athletes' parents are the clubs' main contributors, both in terms of money and effort (Enjolras and Seippel, 1999; Skirstad, 2002, pp. 242–245; Seippel, 2003, p. 14).[12] Therefore, 'the family' appears to be the most important contributor to athletic improvement for young athletes, followed by 'the club' and 'the trainer' (Bergsgard, 2003; see also Gilberg and Breivik, 1998).

In many sports, the best youngsters are selected for what is called 'kretslag' (the county team).[13] In cross-country skiing, selection takes place when the athletes are around 14 years old, and selected skiers come together at training camps led by skilled coaches. The aim is to develop the best skiers through exercises and by training at a more sophisticated level. The county team also takes part in training camps together with other county teams at regional camps based on the underlying assumption that the best will improve when they train with and compete against the best athletes in the region. The Norwegian Ski Federation also arranges a ski school in the summer for athletes between 12 and 15 years old. Here, the 'young talents' meet athletes from the national teams who act as coaches and with whom they train. When the athletes are between 12 and 16 years old, they participate primarily in their own county competitions and against skiers from different clubs in the county. But some of the most eager also travel to different counties to compete. In addition, an unofficial national championship is arranged, called 'hovedlandsrennet', which is designed for young skiers.

When the skiers finish their 10 years of compulsory schooling, some choose to move to sport gymnasia while others choose to go to an ordinary school and stay with their home club. Every year, the National Skiing Federation selects six boys and six girls for the junior national team (17–19 years old). The team is organised and supported by the Federation and has its own coach, assistant coach, equipment keeper, and medical practitioner. The team members are selected solely on the basis of their performances during the previous season. If the athletes do not show progress measured by performance in national and international competitions, they lose their position in the national team. The team meets at different locations for training camps every month but between camps athletes continue to train with their home club and their home coach. Members of the national team compete against junior athletes in national competitions, including the 'Norwegian Cup' with some of the best athletes being selected for championships in Scandinavia and other countries. Some of the athletes also compete against senior athletes in national competitions. If results decline, the young athletes lose their place on the national team for the next season and, if they decide to continue, will do so only with help from their home club and the home coach.

In the Norwegian sport system, the next 'level' in the centrally provided support infrastructure is the senior national teams. In cross-country, these teams are run by the national federation with support from Olympiatoppen.[14] The teams are led by five full-time coaches, with a physiologist and a doctor connected to the teams. The team members are selected entirely on the basis of their performances during the previous season and very few skiers move directly from junior national team to senior national team. Normally the athletes are about 25 years old before they are selected for one of the senior teams. This implies that many athletes face a difficult and uncertain transition period. In this period, most of the promising skiers will be connected to different racing teams financed by the county level of the Ski Federation and private sponsors, and they attempt to qualify for international competitions and for national teams through their performances in the extensive competition infrastructure in Norway.

Focusing events

The description above indicates the institutionalisation of the Norwegian elite sport model with Olympiatoppen at its centre and supported by increased governmental support for elite sport. But what facilitated these changes? Several focusing events enhanced the growing acceptance of elite sport development in the sport environment and in the political milieu. Oakley and Green (2001) include both 'traumatic events', such as poor performance in the Olympics, and significant 'focusing events' such as hosting the Olympic Games. We can identify at least three such events in the development of the Norwegian elite sport model: one traumatic and two significant focusing events.

The first event was of a traumatic character and changed the way the sports organisations thought about the organisation of elite sport. After the poor performance of athletes at the summer Olympics in 1984 (Los Angeles), the need for an independent elite sport organisation became a pressing topic for discussion within the sport system (Hanstad, 2002). As a result, NIF and NOC established 'Project 88' (*Prosjekt 88*). The basis for the work of Project 88 was reflected in slogans such as 'athletes in focus', 'holistic development', and 'knowledge-based elite sport'. Despite the disappointing results at the Olympic Games in 1988, and especially the winter games in Calgary where Norway did not win any gold medals, the evaluation of Project 88 was almost entirely positive. The model – with its unified, centrally located organisation and resources, and competence to support athletes and various sports associations – was appealing and considered by many to be the way to go in the future (Olsen, 1988). Thus, a system with a separate and centrally located elite sport organisation was created in 1988 but under a new name, Olympiatoppen. In 1990, the NOC was given operational responsibility for elite sport and Olympiatoppen. These changes also indicated a shift in how the organisation was managed: out went the 'cheerful amateurs' and in came the professional trainers and leaders (Hanstad, 2002; Bergsgard, 2005).

The decision in 1988 that Lillehammer should host the winter games in 1994 was the first of the two significant focusing events that contributed to an increased commitment by the sports organisations to the Norwegian elite sport model, and particularly to Olympiatoppen. The award of the Games helped Olympiatoppen achieve a strong position within the sport system, indicated in part by a large increase in its budget. Part of its strength was due to the growing acceptance within the sport policy community of the need for an independent and strong elite sport organisation (Olsen, 1988; Hanstad, 2002). Moreover, Norway's subsequent success in Albertville in 1992, and especially on home ground in Lillehammer 1994, appeared to confirm the appropriateness of a model centred on a strong, central sports organisation: the medals 'spoke for themselves'. Norway's success then in the 1990s can be seen as a third and positive focusing event that contributed to the legitimation of elite sport both in the political milieu and among the general public in Norway.

While focusing events are important, there are deeper structural forces to consider in understanding the increased focus on, and willingness to support, elite sport development. The deeper question was whether Norway should participate in the expensive and intensifying 'arms-race' of international elite sport (Augestad and Bergsgard, 2007; Bergsgard et al., 2007). The positive answer to this question must be seen in the light of the changing political discourse discussed below, and also against the generally positive image of sport in Norway and the close relationship between the sport sector and the government (Bergsgard and Rommetvedt, 2006; Bergsgard et al., 2007).

Government and elite sport

The attitude of successive governments towards elite sport in Norway is somewhat ambiguous as governmental support for elite sport is evident but government takes no active part in its development. In the last government report on sport, elite sport is not mentioned among the principal challenges in the years to come, and no explicit performance objectives in international competition were set as this is considered to be the responsibility of the sports organisations (St.meld. nr. 14, 1999–2000). This ambiguous view towards elite sport stems, on the one hand, from the egalitarian values in Norwegian society from which sport policy discourses are not immune and, on the other hand, from the fact that Norway, as a relatively young country, has a strong focus on elite sport in order to foster national pride and self-esteem by winning international sport competitions (Bergsgard et al., 2007). Moreover, this ambiguity is not only evident in the government's relationship with elite sport, but also within the NIF/NOC.

From the 1970s onwards, elite sport was placed higher on the agenda of the NIF/NOC, and also in the political arena (Augestad et al., 2006; Bergsgard et al., 2007). Several proposals to establish a coordinating unit for elite sport development were discussed inside the sport movement but the public authorities were reluctant to become involved in elite sport, emphasising Sport for All as their main objective. Gradually, however, this reluctance changed. Even if the 1981 White Paper on cultural policy reaffirmed Sport for All as the priority, it also stated that 'elite sport must, at the same time, be provided with good and sound conditions' (St.meld. nr. 23, 1981–1982, p. 116). The subsequent White Paper in 1983 stated that 'Elite sport has a legitimate and important function in the Norwegian society' (St.meld. nr. 27, 1983–1984, p. 27). These comments notwithstanding, scepticism towards elite sport in the political milieu was extensive and deeply rooted.

The focusing events discussed above changed attitudes among politicians who, as a result, became more positive towards the development of elite sport. The growing acceptance of elite sport led to the next step in the direction of increased government involvement. As noted, from 1978 the government provided state grants to elite athletes, although distributed by NIF and later by Olympiatoppen. In 1985, the government supported the building of Toppidrettssenteret by granting half the necessary funding. In the same year, the government also provided a guarantee for Lillehammer as a possible future venue for the winter Olympics. And, when Lillehammer was awarded the 1994 Olympic Games, the government agreed to cover most of the costs, which were eventually calculated at around 7 billion NOK.

It was the sports organisations that took the leading role in the process that resulted in the establishment of Olympiatoppen in 1988–1999. Most significantly, the major part of Olympiatoppen's funding in its early phase of development was from the share of the sale of Olympic rights that accrued to the Lillehammer Olympic Organisation Committee and from increased sponsorship income (Hanstad, 2002). The government's initial direct contribution to elite sport involved subsidies and grants for participation in the Olympics. It was only when income from sponsors decreased in the late 1990s, in the period following the Lillehammer Olympics, that government's contribution to elite sport increased considerably, exceeding Olympiatoppen's own income. Figure 8.1 shows the government's direct support for elite sport development, the income from sponsors to NIF/NOC, and NIF/NOC's expenditure on elite sport.

Although government contributes to elite sport in various ways, including supporting the building of an elite sport centre, providing funding to host the Olympics and, more generally, by supporting Olympiatoppen and the national sports organisations, it is fair to say that direct involvement in the development of a Norwegian elite sport system has been limited compared to many other Western countries (Augestad et al., 2006; Bergsgard et al., 2007). As we saw earlier, central government is reluctant to link explicit achievement objectives to their support for elite sport. Consequently, Olympiatoppen is a product of voluntarily

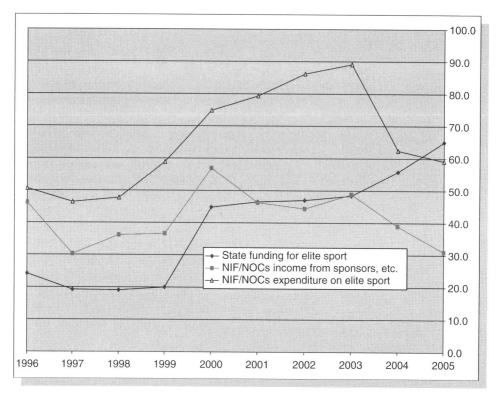

Figure 8.1 Direct state funding (lottery money) for elite sport development in NIF/NOC, the income from sponsors of NIF/NOC, and total expenditure on elite sport by NIF/NOC, 1996–2005 (million 2005 NOK.)

organised sport, which however enjoys close ties with the Sports Department in the Ministry (Hanstad, 2002; Bergsgard, 2005).

The Norwegian way

There are several factors associated with the Norwegian sport system that differ from international trends. These distinctive national characteristics may be called 'local variations' in the context of various elite sport development systems. While other countries, including Australia, the United Kingdom, and Canada, are proactively exploring formal systems of talent identification, Norway has shown a fair amount of resistance towards the establishment of such a system (Oakley and Green, 2001; Bergsgard et al., 2007). In 1987, the *Regulations for Children's Sport* were established and they are still valid although slightly revised in 2000 and 2007 (NIF/NOC, 1987/2000). These Regulations placed considerable restrictions on talent identification concerning children younger than 13 years old. The Regulations require that a child should avoid specialisation in *one* sport at an early age (before 10 years old) and, from 10 to 13 years old, specialisation should be limited. The Regulations also insist that all exercise between competitions must be play-oriented, that all activities be suited to the physical and psychological development of the child, and that learning is more important than achievement. In Norway, sport for children is meant to stimulate the child's physical, psychological, and social development. Play and socialisation are assumed to be more important than competition, and the aim of the Regulations is to ensure that all children are included regardless of their level of knowledge and skill. These rules might be said to reflect an important idea and tradition in Norway, namely that sport is for everyone, as well as emphasising the pedagogical and psychological aspects that children's sport should first and foremost be play-oriented. Also important in this context is the idea that the purpose of sports activity is not to be an end in itself, rather it is to fulfil a function for society as a whole. It is especially important to note that it is the sports organisations and not government that proposed and implemented these rules for children's sport. However, the political environment strongly reinforces the values on which the Regulations are based. The *Regulations for Children's Sport*, and the thinking they represent, may partly explain why Norway does not achieve success at international level in sports such as gymnastics, figure skating, and rhythmic sports gymnastics, as international success in these sports demands a huge investment in special training during an athlete's early years.

While international developments demand that the Norwegian sport system implements procedures to identify young talent, Olympiatoppen must appear to be legitimate according to Norwegian norms and values in the field of sport. It is not only a question of identifying the optimal solution to a perceived problem, but Olympiatoppen also has to identify a solution that is supported by dominant actors inside the field of sport. The *Regulations for Children's Sport* limit Olympiatoppen's room for manoeuvre in this respect but they do not 'paralyse' the organisation. The organisation implements initiatives that indirectly modify the consequences of the rules for children. Olympiatoppen's strategy is to assist different national federations in developing a plan for their work with young athletes, and to be an important contributor to the development of sport for children and young people in Norway (NIF/NOC, 2002).

A former consultant at Olympiatoppen observed that 'We don't have a system for identification of talented athletes, but we have tried to increase the interest in training among the children, and this has partly been a success ... The specific sport doesn't have a good system to pick talents. They don't evaluate the milieu, mental process, the parents' motivation, the trainers' motivation and so on' (Interview, 30 April, 2004). Moreover, the present head of Olympiatoppen wanted to 'soften' the Regulations and explained the ambiguity of thinking in this area by arguing that 'The Assembly [of NIF/NOC] said "no" to softening up the "Regulations for Children's Sport" where the potential for future high performance sport lies. They only voted unanimously in favour of the goal to become among the best in the world' (Aambø, 2005, p. 168). The former consultant argued that Norway should be better at talent identification, a view confirmed by the former head of Olympiatoppen who was even more explicit in arguing that '[I] am quite certain that we have to select or choose athletes at an earlier stage than today. We should not be afraid of, especially in technically demanding sports, that the athlete, maybe as young as nine or ten years of age, should pick the sport so he or she learns the necessary technical training in the golden age of motory' (quoted in Dette sa Stensbøl, 2002). Although Olympiatoppen does not strongly press for the modification of the *Regulations for Children's Sport*, it is acutely aware of the problems that adherence to the Regulations pose for achieving elite success. Consequently, some Olympiatoppen members are among the voices supporting amendment of the Regulations.

The nature of the discussion of sport for children also reveals the presence of strong democratic tendencies in the Norwegian sport system. There are two channels whereby democratic control may be exerted in relation to sport. First, since sports organisations and Olympiatoppen receive much of their funding from government, politicians can develop guidelines regarding how these funds should be spent. Second, the sports organisations also have a democratic system which can exert control over the elite sport development system. In most cases, democratic institutions, such as the Sports Board in NIF, do not exert power over the elite sport development system in any noticeable way. A significant example to the contrary, however, is the ban on using high altitude chambers in Norway. Despite the fact that the use of high altitude chambers is not illegal according to international rules, the General Assembly of the NIF/NOC, that meets every fourth year, decided in 2003 that the use of high altitude chambers should be prohibited in Norwegian elite sport. The General Assembly has the highest authority in the NIF system and a resolution accepted at this level is binding for all members of the organisation.

In the debate prior to this decision, both the International Olympic Committee (IOC) member Gerhard Heiberg, and the former President of NIF/NOC, Arne Myhrvold, argued that at the international level the use of high altitude chambers was not a subject of controversy and that a Norwegian ban would weaken the competitive situation for Norwegian athletes (Toppidrettens etikkseminar, 2001). The Olympic 800 metres gold medallist in Atlanta 1996, Vebjørn Rodal, holds an opposing view, however. As reported in the Norwegian newspaper, *Dagsavisen* (Høydehus ekstremt, 2001), Rodal argued that 'I would like to keep the sport as natural as possible. It has become more and more "chemical", high altitude chambers might be said to be a kind of chemical manipulation. Ethics and morals concern personal choices and these should be as simple as possible'. The image of Norwegian elite sport as being clean and fair, and the legitimacy that this provides in respect of public opinion, is of great importance in understanding the decision of the General Assembly to prohibit high altitude chambers.

This self-imposed norm could reduce the nation's chance of winning medals in many different sports and Olympiatoppen has to acquiesce to the decision. Yet, it accepted this resolution because it had already conducted extensive research into altitude training and therefore had sufficient competence and confidence to substitute the use of high altitude chambers with more expensive training in the natural environment (Hem, 1990; Olsen, 1993). This means the comprehensive use of a more expensive method. One national coach argued that 'The ban to use high altitude chambers is acceptable in the situation today. Currently we have [a] good economy and ... we can spend enough days in the mountains' (Interview, 14 October, 2004). The cost to Olympiatoppen was low since acquiescence enabled it to maintain political and popular support. Norwegian elite sport has voluntarily imposed restrictions on the use of methods that have implications for performance (rules and regulation for children's sport and the ban against high altitude chambers). By means of democratic channels, the general public's influence has ensured that norms governing healthy sport should also apply to elite sport.

Concluding remarks

The elite sport development system in Norway exhibits a number of features which are commonly found in other countries. First, the Norwegian elite sport model is similar to that found in many other countries insofar as it has a centralised structure, with Olympiatoppen, including the Elite Sport Centre, at the hub. However, this centralisation needs to be qualified by an acknowledgement of the extent to which the national federations retain a high degree of independence in the Norwegian sport system. Consequently, some of the strongest federations have resisted Olympiatoppen's dominance which might indicate a more fragmented system in the future. A second feature that Norway has in common with many other leading sports countries is the emphasis given to medical and scientific approaches to elite sport. A third common feature is the focus, not only on the sport elements of an athlete's life, but also on the whole situation surrounding the athlete, that is, the so-called '24-hour athlete'.

Despite the extent to which Norway possesses a sports system that has many features in common with other countries, it does exhibit two distinctive features. The first is the central government's ambiguity towards elite sport, providing financial support and general legitimacy on the one hand while, on the other, maintaining an arm's length relationship with the major sports institutions and being apparently content to let the national sports organisations formulate the specific objectives for Norwegian elite sport. A second, and arguably more significant, distinctive feature of the Norwegian model is the strong norms and democratic structures that provide the institutional context for elite sport development which moderate the enthusiasm for an emphasis on elite sport objective at the expense of Sport for All.

Notes

1 The project is a collaboration between the University College of Telemark and Telemark Research Institute, and the main document from this project is a book to be published in 2007 in Norwegian: *Toppidrettens formel – Olympiatoppen som alkymist*.
2 The documents were collected from the archive of the Norwegian Olympic Committee and Confederation of Sports (NIF/NOC), with supplements from a private archive.
3 National federations is the translation of the Norwegian 'Særforbund', and resembles National Governing Bodies of sport in the United Kingdom and National Sports Organisations in Canada and Australia.
4 32 million NOK was distributed by Olympiatoppen to SFs in 2001 and in 2003 (NIF/NOC, 2001, 2003), while the total income for the SFs was 666 million NOK and 1002 million NOK, respectively (see Enjolras, 2004, 2005).

5   In 2005, TV companies paid around 1 billion NOK (one thousand million) for a 4-year deal on Norwegian football, almost eight times more than 8 years earlier.

6   Besides income from sponsors and TV rights, 'commercial income' includes money from competitions, sales, and rental income.

7   300,000 NOK in 1978 is equivalent to approximately 998,000 NOK in 2005.

8   2 million NOK in 1988 is equivalent to approximately 2.99 million NOK in 2005.

9   4.3 million NOK in 1998 is equivalent to approximately 4.95 million NOK in 2005.

10 This was the amount for 2007. In 2007, 146 athletes were awarded scholarships from Olympiatoppen. 'U' is the first letter in the Norwegian word 'utvikling', which means development in English. The U-stipend is a talent scholarship.

11 This section is based mainly on the pattern found for cross-country skiing in Norway but the competition structure and squad system for skiers is much the same for all individual sports in Norway.

12 In 70 per cent of all teams in Norway, the work in clubs is undertaken by volunteers, and in a further 19 per cent of teams at least 90 per cent of the labour contribution is voluntary (Seippel, 2003, p. 15).

13 In opposition to golf, for example, which has no county team structure, and consequently talent development takes place primarily in the local clubs.

14 The cross-country national team is organised into three different subgroups: one all-round team for men, one all-round team for women, and one sprint team for men.

References

Aambø, J. (2005) Hvem vil egentlig ha toppidrett?, in D.V. Hanstad and M. Goksøyr (eds.), Fred er ei det beste. Festskrift. Hans B. Skaset 70 år, Oslo: Gyldendal.

Augestad, P. and Bergsgard, N.A. (2007) Toppidrettsformelen – Olympiatoppen som alkymist, Preliminary manuscript, Telemark University College.

Augestad, P., Bergsgard, N.A. and Hansen, A.Ø. (2006) The institutionalisation of an elite sport organisation in Norway: The case of 'Olympiatoppen', *Sociology of Sport Journal*, 23.3, 293–313.

Bergsgard, N.A. (2002) National facility for ski sport – 'Yes please, all three'. From rational and sequential to open an ambigous dicision-making process. Paper presented at the *XV World Congress of Sociology*, Brisbane.

Bergsgard, N.A. (2003) Fornuft og følelser. Unge lovende idrettsutøvere på spranget til en toppidrettskarriere, Bø: Telemarksforsking-Bø, arbeidsrapport 2/2003.

Bergsgard, N.A. (2005) Idrettspolitikkens maktspill. Endring og stabilitet i den idrettspolitiske styringsmodellen, Dissertation, Dr. Polit., University of Oslo, Rapport 228, Bø: Telemarksforsking-Bø.

Bergsgard, N.A. and Rommetvedt, H. (2006) Sport and politics: The Case of Norway, *International Review for the Sociology of Sport*, 41/1, 7–27.

Bergsgard, N.A., Houlihan, B., Mangset, P., Nødland, S.I. and Rommetvedt, H. (2007) Sport policy: A comparative analysis of stability and change. Oxford: Butterworth-Heinemann/ Elsevier.

Dette sa Stensbøl (2002, 19 desember) NRK. Hentet den 20. des. 2002 fra: http://nrk.no/redskap/utskriftsvennlig/2401591.

Enjolras, B. (2004). Idrett mellom statlig styring og selvbestemmelse. Idrettens bruk av spillemidler, Rapport nr. 2004:7, Oslo: Institutt for samfunnsforskning.

Enjolras, B. (2005). Idrettens økonomi og effektivitet, Rapport nr. 2005:8, Oslo: Institutt for samfunnsforskning.

Enjolras, B. and Seippel, Ø. (1999). Frivillighet, kommersialisering og profesjonalisering. Utfordringer i norsk idrett, Oslo: Institutt for samfunnsforskning, Rapport 9/99.

Eriksen, A.G. (2006) Hvordan skapes en toppidrettsutøver? Bø: Telemark University College (HiT).

Gilberg, R. and Breivik, G. (1997) Gjennom slit til stjernene. Første rapport fra prosjektet Toppidrettsutøvernes levekår og livskvalitet, Oslo: Olympiatoppen, NIH and Ministry of Cultur Affairs.

Gilberg, R and Breivik, G. (1998) Hvorfor ble de beste best? barndom, oppvekst og idrettslig utvikling hos 18 av Norges mestvinnende idrettsutøvere, Oslo: Olympiatoppen and NIH.

Hanstad, D.V. (2002) Seiern'n er vår. Men hvem har æren? En bok om det norske idrettseventyret, Oslo: Schibsted.

Hem, E. (1990) Høydeprosjektet 1990 – langrenn, Oslo: The Norwegian School of Sport Science (NIH).

Høydehus ekstremt (2001, June 7) Dagsavisen, Retrieved June 7, 2001, from http://dagsavisen.no/sport/2001/06/ 576932.shtml.

Kearney, A.T. (1998) Norges Idrettsforbund og Olympiske Komité (NIF) Analye av pengebruken I særforbund go idrettskretser, Oslo: A.T. Kearney.

Ministry of Cultural Affairs (1997) Tilskuddsordningen for nasjonalanlegg, Etablert 15. jan., 1997 [Government grants for national facilities, Established 15 January 1997], Oslo: Ministry of Culture Affairs.

NIF/NOC (1987/2000). *Barneidrettsbestemmelsene*. [Regulations for children's sport]. Oslo: Norges idrettsforbund.

Norges Idrettsforbund og Olympiske Komité (NIF/NOC) (2002) Årsrapport 2001 [Annual report 2001], Oslo: Norges idrettsforbund og Norges Olympiske Komité.

Norges Idrettsforbund og Olympiske Komité (NIF/NOC) (2003) Idrettspolitisk dokument. Tingperioden 2003–2007, Oslo: Norges idrettsforbund og Norges Olympiske Komité.

Norges Idrettsforbund og Olympiske Komité (NIF/NOC) (2006) Årsrapport 2005 [Annual report 2005], Oslo: Norges idrettsforbund og Norges Olympiske Komité.

Seippel, Ø. (ed.) (2002) Idrettens Bevegelser, Oslo: Novus Forlag.

Oakley, B. and Green, M. (2001) The production of Olympic champions: International perspectives on elite sport development systems. *European Journal of Sport Management*, 8(1): 83–105.

Olsen, E. (1988) Rapport fra evalueringsgruppa for Prosjekt 88 [Report from the evaluations-group of Prosjekt 88], Oslo: Norges idrettsforbund og Norges Olympiske Komité.

Olsen, S. (1993) Høydetrening, Oslo: The Norwegian School of Sport Science (NIH).

Rimejordet, T.O. (2002, September 27), www.skiforbundet.no.

Seippel, Ø. (2003) Norske idrettslag 2002, Oslo: Institutt for samfunnsforskning.

Skirstad, B. (2002) Norske idrettslag: Oversikt og utfordringer, in: Ø. Seippel (ed.), Idrettens Bevegelser, Oslo: Novus Forlag.

Slettemeås, K.T. (2005) Sosialisert til å konkurrere, Bø: Telemark University College (HiT).

St.meld. nr. 27 (1983–1984) Nye oppgåver i kulturpolitikken. Tillegg til St.meld. nr. 23 (1981–82) Kulturpolitikk for 1980-åra, Oslo: Kultur- og vitenskapsdepartementet.

St.meld. nr. 14 (1999–2000) Idrettsliv i endring. Om statens forhold til idrett og fysisk aktivitet, Oslo: Kulturdepartementet.

St.meld. nr. 23 (1981–1982) Kulturpolitikk for 1980-åra, Oslo: Kyrkje- og undervisningsdepartementet.

Toppidrettens etikkseminar, Oslo Plaza (2001, June 6) Retrieved 29 May 2006, from http://www.idrett.no/t2.aspx?p=24703.

CHAPTER 9

New Zealand

Shane Collins

Introduction

New Zealand consists of two main islands and a number of smaller coastal islands. Given the land area of 268,000 square kilometres and a population of 4,098,300 (Statistics New Zealand, 2007), New Zealand's geography is defined by large areas of open land which are sparsely populated. Despite its relatively small population, New Zealand prides itself on its performance on the international sporting stage. The early influence of England and its sporting traditions and activities are still evident today in the popular sports of rugby and cricket; however, New Zealand's elite athletes now participate on the world stage across a wide range of winter and summer sports.

Despite New Zealand's strong sporting history, government intervention in sport has been sporadic. Although early debates regarding state involvement in sporting matters centred upon whether government should indeed be involved at all, towards the latter part of the twentieth century this debate was accompanied by a new tension, the role of government in supporting and resourcing elite and/or recreational sport. This chapter explores the relatively recent changes to the (elite) sport policy landscape, the growing salience of sport to the New Zealand government and the increasingly targeted prioritisation of Olympic sport as an area of elite sport policy. Consistent with the findings of Green and Houlihan (2005) the four dimensions of specialist elite level facilities, support for full-time athletes, development of sports science and coaching support, and the existence of a domestic competition structure designed to support elite athlete success have all, to varying degrees, been identified as areas for attention and investment. Along with these four dimensions, the development of an effective talent identification system has also been emphasised as a key variable for the success of elite sport. The chapter provides an overview of the changing emphasis on and in elite sport policy in New Zealand, highlighting the impact of recreational sport, changing political and socio-economic values, and the increased recognition of elite sport's ability to contribute to achieving stated national government goals. Research for this chapter was based upon a review of academic, government and national sport organisation (NSO) documents and a series of semi-structured interviews conducted with senior staff in NSOs and the government sport agency SPARC (Sport and Recreation New Zealand).

Current structure of the elite sport system

Responsibility for the development of sport policy in New Zealand resides with the crown entity SPARC. Established under the Sport and Recreation New Zealand Act (2002), and located under the Ministry of Culture and Heritage, SPARC has responsibility for developing and balancing the areas of elite sport, recreational sport and physical recreation. Under the initial structure of SPARC, each of the three areas operated as a distinct group: (a) the New Zealand Academy of Sport (high performance); (b) Sport Development and (c) Physical Recreation. However, in an effort to meet the sector's changing needs and to better integrate the areas of high performance and participation, all three areas now operate under the Sector Development Division. The other business areas within SPARC include organisational development, corporate services, marketing and communications, and research, policy and planning. More significantly, SPARC allocates funding to NSOs, Regional Sports Trusts (RSTs), local government and strategic partners with regard to delivering particular outcomes relating to elite and recreational sport. Within SPARC, the High Performance Unit (HPU) is the group primarily responsible for the development and delivery of elite sport policy.

The HPU works directly with NSOs to improve high performance plans and programmes and directs its elite sport investment through its NSOs and its high performance services network, the New Zealand Academy of Sport. Established in 2000, and funded directly by SPARC, the New Zealand Academy of Sport network delivers services to athletes in the areas of coaching, sport science, sports medicine, athlete career education and training facilities. The network also delivers coaching support, coach education and coach professional development. Initially a three region network, north (top half of North Island), central (bottom half of North Island) and southern (South Island), this was refined to a North Island and South Island model in 2007. Each academy has a variety of partners who assist in delivering the support services required by the NSOs, elite athletes and coaches.

Funding for SPARC is received from two key sources, Vote Funding (allocated direct from the Crown) and New Zealand Lotteries Commission, with additional funding received from other government departments, although this is frequently allocated to specific programmes. Funding is distributed by SPARC according to established priorities and allocated to organisations/agencies within the sport sector that are able to assist SPARC in achieving its organisational goals. The rapid increase in funding of SPARC and the subsequent allocation of resources to NSOs and other sporting bodies have resulted in SPARC attaining an influential position in the elite sport sector due to its increasing level and control of resources. Nevertheless, SPARC is reliant upon other organisations to achieve its outcomes and has moved away from being a provider of programmes to being a strategic partner providing funding, information and other support services to its partners (SPARC, 2002a, p. 9). Key groups which assist SPARC in achieving and developing elite sport policy include National Sports Organisations (NSOs), the New Zealand Academy of Sport network, New Zealand Olympic Committee (NZOC) and Drug Free Sport New Zealand (DFSNZ), while local government plays a key role through the provision of sport facilities and, together with RSTs, the development of recreational sport in the community.

The NSOs are responsible for the development of their sport both in respect of increasing participation levels and developing elite performance. Funding is provided direct to NSOs from SPARC for the purpose of achieving both increased participation levels and improved elite performance, with the achievement of key priorities and targets a key aspect. The New Zealand Academy of Sport network works closely with NSOs in the areas outlined earlier to assist in improving elite level performance. Since 2001–2002, funding for NSOs has increased significantly (see Table 9.1), with funding targeted specifically at high performance within NSOs increasing from NZ$7,123,440 in 2001–2002 to NZ$11,491,300 in 2004–2005 (SPARC, 2002b; 2005a).

The NZOC assists SPARC and the NSOs in the preparation and selection of athletes for the Olympic and Commonwealth Games. An autonomous organisation, the NZOC operates independently from SPARC, despite the level of funding received from SPARC steadily increasing from NZ$100,000 in 2002–2003 to NZ$500,000 in 2005–2006 (SPARC, 2003a, 2006a). DFSNZ is the independent Crown Entity responsible for the testing for banned drugs in New Zealand sport. Drug testing is a key activity (644 conducted in 1994–1995, 1,602 in 2005–2006), which has grown considerably due to the increasing significance placed upon ensuring New Zealand sports comply with the World Anti Doping Code (New Zealand Sports Drug Agency, 2005). Moreover, there is a dual and equally important emphasis placed on providing education to athletes with regard to drug taking. The education of athletes is an area of increasing focus which has recently been raised due to infractions that have occurred within New Zealand sport, most noticeably in respect of recreational cannabis use (DFSNZ, 2006).

Increasing government intervention

As Watson (1993) noted, for much of the twentieth century government involvement in the sport sector fluctuated between sporadic and non-existent (quoted in Collins and Downey, 2000). Early government involvement in sport in New Zealand was characterised by the desire to control undesirable leisure activities such as gambling and prostitution. However, it was concern for the low level of fitness amongst young New Zealanders, and the implications for defence that was a key driver for the establishment of the Physical Welfare and Recreation Act in 1937 (Hindson et al., 1994). More significantly, this legislation provided a structure that enabled state involvement in sport, as it provided a mechanism for central government to grant sport facilities money to local government and allowed local government to spend money on these facilities (Ministerial Taskforce, 2001). Despite the hosting of the 1950 Empire Games (now known as the Commonwealth Games) in Auckland, public sector involvement remained focused upon using sport as a tool to address urban social problems throughout the 1950s and 1960s.

The 1970s were characterised by growing pressure for government to become involved in both recreational and elite sport. Most noticeably, pressure was growing for the government to become more involved in elite sport due to mounting recognition that New Zealand needed to keep pace with sporting developments in other countries, particularly in respect of Olympic Sports, if New Zealand wished to remain competitive (Stothart, 2000). However, prior to the 1972 General Election, a clear divide became evident between the two major political parties with regard to the extent and level of government involvement in sport. Whereas the Labour Party supported the idea of a new sports agency, the National Party made it clear that the national government should not become involved as this would be detrimental to sport itself (Stothart, 2000). In 1973, under a Labour government the Ministry of Recreation and Sport and the Council for Recreation and Sport were established under the auspices of the Ministry of Internal Affairs. Although there were a number of criticisms regarding the inherent problems of a bifurcated structure, more significantly both the Council and Ministry signalled to sports organisations the need to professionalise and become more efficient if they were to receive funding. Through the provision of direct funding, the Ministry was able to exert pressure on NSOs to adopt more effective management techniques and processes; for NSOs unable to provide evidence of increased efficiency, grants were either delayed or withdrawn (Stothart, 2000).

It was during this period that an underlying tension between elite sport and mass participation began to emerge as the Ministry and Council faced criticism for an over, emphasis on recreation and mass participation rather than (or at the expense of) elite or competitive sport, and the perception that the needs of sports organisations were not being met (Stothart, 2000). This signalled the first overt signs of competing coalitions of interest within the New Zealand sport sector. While the government agencies invested in mass participation and recreation, an equivalent structure or emphasis was not established for elite sport. In 1978, the New Zealand Sports Foundation (NZSF) was established by a group of businessmen who believed that elite sport was not being given the emphasis it deserved (Ministerial Taskforce, 2001). A private organisation, the NZSF linked elite sporting success with the enhancement of 'national pride, unity, morale, and confidence in New Zealand, both economically and socially' (Collins and Stuart, 1994, p. 49). Despite being a private entity, the NZSF was funded directly by government with an expectation that these funds would be matched by the corporate sector.

Despite the government providing limited funding to elite sport, interest remained evident with the instigation of the government-initiated enquiry, *Sport on the Move* in 1985. This report highlighted the continuing dual approach of the government towards sport, with the development of elite and recreational sport being the focus of the report. Among the range of issues identified were a crisis in sports funding, inherent structural problems and a misleading impression that sport received adequate resources, in part due to its international success. Unsurprisingly, in addressing elite sport, the *Sport on the Move* report argued for increased funding if New Zealand was to succeed on the international stage. Among the challenges facing New Zealand were a small participation base, geographic isolation and a lack of support for athletes. To overcome these obstacles, the 1985 report identified the need to develop effective coaching along with effective talent identification, higher levels of support to athletes, and better application and use of science and technology (Sports Development Inquiry Committee, 1985). The *Sport on the Move* report provided the blueprint for the establishment of the Hillary Commission in 1987, which was to have the key purpose of promoting a more active lifestyle for all New Zealanders.

During this period, external events impacted upon the development of not only NSOs, but also the developing area of elite sport policy. It was during the 1980s that New Zealand underwent sweeping economic reforms. The revolutionary changes, based upon free market reform, were considered more radical than anywhere else in the world (Quiggan, 1998). As part of the extensive economic changes, there was a systematic programme of commercialisation within the public sector. This period of rapid economic, political and social change impacted directly upon sport, acting as a catalyst for sports organisations to become more professional as well as increasing the commercialism of sport (Collins and Downey, 2000). The impact of these reforms was also reflected in the *Sport on the Move* report. Calls for higher levels of support for elite sport in the *Sport on the Move* enquiry reinforced the need for 'very hard-headed, cost effective, non-egalitarian policies' (Sports Development Inquiry Committee, 1985, p. 128).

A reluctance for government or community funds to be invested in elite sport was however still evident during the 1980s for, despite a call for increased support of elite sport, this was tempered by a recognition that funding of a small number of international athletes from community and government sources was 'hard to justify in a democratic society – to do so challenges the principles of social equity' (Sports Development Inquiry Committee, 1985, p. 130). Significantly, the 1985 report recommended the establishment of Lotto with the intention of providing funding to sport and recreation along with other activities and programmes. Lotto was to provide guaranteed future funding of 20 per cent of the lottery commission profits to sport, and for the first time a regular stream of revenue was secured (Collins and Stuart, 1994; Stothart, 2000). Yet there remained an apparent reluctance on the part of the national government to invest in sport. Although funding to the Hillary Commission increased between 1987 and 1992, perhaps of more interest was the change in the funding sources, with government funding decreasing – from 79 per cent of the Hillary Commission revenue in 1987 to 4 per cent in 1992 (Collins and Stuart, 1994). In contrast, funding from the Lotteries Board increased steadily, and became the major source of funding for the Hillary Commission.

Despite hosting the 1990 Commonwealth Games in Auckland, by the mid-1990s concern was growing regarding the level of support and funding of high performance sport in New Zealand prompting a government-initiated review of high performance sport, the *Winning Way Review* in 1996. At the same time, the awarding of the 2000 Olympic Games to Sydney placed additional pressure on the government to maximise the opportunity of having an Olympic Games so close to New Zealand. Again, despite recommendations for a one-stop shop to deliver high performance sport support and funding, the outcomes of the review were less than hoped for. Importantly, it did manage to increase government funding for elite sport, with increased resources provided for the development of elite level sport in the build-up to the 2000 Olympics Games in the hope of winning more medals. But again there was no long-term or ongoing commitment to provide support for elite sport (Collins and Downey, 2000).

Although previous enquiries had failed to bring about considerable government involvement or investment in (elite) sport, the report of the *Sport, Fitness and Leisure Ministerial Taskforce* in 2001 (also known as the Graham Report) was conducted during a period when both sporting organisations and the government were ready to accept change. The Graham Report had a major impact upon the structure and development of elite sport policy in New Zealand. Not only did the Graham Report act as catalyst for the establishment of a new government entity, but it also signalled the growing recognition of the benefits of sport (elite and recreational) to the New Zealand government. The report was instigated 3 months before the 2000 Olympic Games as a result of a Labour Party promise to provide leadership to the sports sector (Sam, 2004). New Zealand's performance at the 2000 Olympic Games was disappointing, with just four medals won, making it the country's poorest performance since the 1976 Montreal Olympics. As a result, there was significant criticism of elite sport from both the public and politicians. As Cumming (2000) noted, criticism was also directed at the NZSF funding policy which was considered short sighted as well as risky in its approach to targeting and funding likely winners (quoted in Knight, 2005). Recognition that problems identified in the 1985 Sport Development Inquiry had still not been addressed and acknowledgement that the sport sector had been largely ignored by successive governments created an environment where it was accepted that there was a need for change (Ministerial Taskforce, 2001, p. 9). The 2001 *Ministerial Taskforce on Sport, Fitness and Leisure*, which commenced in June, therefore developed its findings in the midst of considerable public interest.

The business of elite sport

The invitation for government to become more involved in sport signalled a significant shift in thinking from the previous 30 years. The establishment of the crown entity, SPARC in 2002 marked a significant change in the sport policy landscape of New Zealand. Key reasons for the creation of a single government agency included sector fragmentation, which resulted in a lack of integration, poor coordination and leadership, insufficient direction and resourcing from government, and an identified need to change the organisation of the sector and delivery system at both national and regional levels (SPARC, 2002a).

The new quasi-government agency had a clear purpose to drive a 'clear and cohesive' vision for the sport sector and to take responsibility for providing leadership to the sector (SPARC, 2002a). While a large number of the recommendations of the Ministerial Taskforce were adopted, most notably the recommendation that the new agency should achieve excellence in sport, high performance was not included as a function of SPARC under the Sport and Recreation Act (2002). Despite this, SPARC took a leading role in clearly identifying elite sport as a key area of focus. SPARC identified three objectives around which its services, policies and investments would be targeted:

1 Being the most active nation.
2 Having athletes and teams winning consistently in events that matter to New Zealanders.
3 Having the most effective sport and physical recreation systems (SPARC, 2002a).

Achievement of national government outcomes was a clear motivator for increased investment, particularly in relation to elite sport, as stated by the Minister of Sport and Fitness, 'building national identity is a key goal for this government. Elite sport and participation in international competition gives us a sense of who we are as New Zealanders, not only this, it lets the rest of the world see who we are' (quoted in Anon, 2001, p. 19).

This was to be a period of rapid change. From the outset, SPARC established an environment where accountability, performance targets, governance issues, annual and strategic planning, and return on investment were all to become essential in an effort to achieve SPARC's goals. As stated in the initial strategic plan, SPARC would make funding decisions based on the 'likelihood of achieving a return on investment' and will fund and support NSOs that 'demonstrated they can assist us in achieving our mission' (SPARC, 2002a, p. 10). The increasing emphasis on return on investment was not exclusive to elite sport however and was also to be applied to the area of recreational sport participation. Most noticeably, in 2006 sport development funding to Athletics, New Zealand was withdrawn due to its inability to impact upon participation levels in the sport.

Alongside the introduction of business concepts/processes, an increasing prioritisation of Olympic sports became evident as part of elite sport development. Clear targets were set to achieve the mission of having athletes and teams winning consistently in 'events that matter' to New Zealand. Funding was prioritised and sports were separated into four categories: recognition, development, participation and performance. Seven sports were identified as priority sports: cricket, equestrian, golf, netball, rowing, rugby and yachting, with athletics, cycling and swimming named as 'revitalisation sports'. The goal was to ensure that these 10 sports would be on a sustainable footing by 2006 so that SPARC could then focus on another group of sports. For the revitalisation sports, a concerted effort was required to explore how these sports could be rejuvenated and re-established on a sustainable basis. What became evident was that funding of sport was now to 'be focused on ensuring that in exchange for funding, sports and physical recreation bodies deliver performance – both in participation and results' (SPARC, 2002a, p. 10). This signalled a significant change for New Zealand sports organisations as no longer were sports organisations 'entitled to support'; they were now required to show what the 'investment' would return to SPARC.

The rationale for the selection of the initial seven priority sports was based on four criteria: levels of participation; links to industries and infrastructure; an ability to be world leading and achieve recognition for New Zealand; and the ability to stop New Zealanders in the street when we are doing well (SPARC, 2002a). For those sports that had greater financial independence, such as rugby and cricket, the partnership with SPARC was to be built around developing opportunities for juniors, talent identification and athlete career education.

A 4 year funding plan clearly sets out the expectations of SPARC in respect of return on its investment in sporting organisations. Investment in NSOs was at times accompanied by an expectation that governance and administration concerns would be addressed in an effort to increase efficiency and effectiveness. Resources were developed to assist NSOs in achieving more effective governance, such as SPARC's *Nine Steps to Effective Governance, Building High Performance Organisations*. The importance of a strong governance structure and system was clearly considered a crucial component of an effective NSO as indicated with regard to funding arrangements; SPARC would commit funding for more than 1 year where an 'organisation can demonstrate they have a sound structure and good governance system' (SPARC, 2002a, p. 9). For revitalisation sports, funding from SPARC also required governance issues to be addressed. As one senior NSO official stated:

The big boost that we got, and possibly what aided the vote [to change the governance structure], is that SPARC declared us a revitalisation sport ... and they gave us some money, quite a lot of money; half a million a year for three years if we restructured ... Yes, they were pretty clear on what it had to be ... we'll give you some money if you can get this thing through.

(Interview, 23 October 2006)

Key performance targets included not only the development of a strong governance structure, but also the achievement of publicly stated medal targets at the 2004 Athens Olympics, Paralympics and 2006 Melbourne Commonwealth Games. A target of 3 to 8 medals was set for the 2004 Athens Olympic Games and 18 to 24 medals at the 2004 Paralympics. At the 2006 Melbourne Commonwealth Games, a target of 40 or more medals was identified as the goal for the New Zealand Team (SPARC, 2003b). The setting of these targets increased public pressure for New Zealand's elite athletes to perform along with greater public examination of reasons for failing to achieve the stated targets. Despite what was considered a successful 2004 Olympic Games for New Zealand athletes, a total of five medals, the inevitable review of the Athens Olympics resulted in increased calls for NSOs to continue improving their management systems and achieve targets set by SPARC.

As part of the post-Athens review, it was recommended that where NSOs 'cannot show the ability to manage and operate their high performance programmes effectively, the NZAS (New Zealand Academy of Sport) will provide the necessary short-term support in order to protect its investment, most likely through the prescriptive involvement of an NZAS Performance Director' (SPARC, 2005b, p. 10). This move signalled the growing preparedness of SPARC to become more closely or directly involved in the management of elite sport in NSOs; if NSOs were unable to demonstrate effective elite sport systems, more direct forms of intervention were now to be considered.

In the wake of a disappointing 2006 Commonwealth Games, SPARC was criticised and questions were asked as to why New Zealand did not achieve the medal targets set. The media and public asked questions regarding where and how funding had been allocated. In the resulting review of the 2006 Commonwealth Games, a lack of depth among New Zealand sports, along with too many part-time athletes, combined with coaching deficiencies, were highlighted as the primary areas of concern. The theme of government intervention into NSOs that were unable to demonstrate effectiveness continued as 'SPARC would protect its investment in at-risk high performance programmes by assuming a role in management of the at-risk programme or withdrawing its investment support' (SPARC, 2006c, p. 11).

Learning and adapting polices and programmes from other sporting systems was also recognised as a method through which New Zealand could improve its elite sport system. As part of the review of the Melbourne Commonwealth Games, the gap between New Zealand and other nations (Australia and United Kingdom among others) was identified as widening with regard to the establishment and performance of their respective elite sport systems. Attempting to compete against countries with larger resources and population bases highlighted the need for New Zealand to learn from other elite sport systems, SPARC identified the need to be smart, innovative and adapt quickly (SPARC, 2006c). The establishment of reciprocal arrangements with other international high performance training institutes has also been identified as an area of focus by SPARC. The signing of a Memorandum of Understanding (MOU) with France in 2006 to exchange practices and processes around high performance sport indicates not only a desire to improve performance, but also a recognition of the need to work with and learn from other elite sport systems.

Not only did the establishment of SPARC signal a growing recognition of the importance of elite sport to the government, but more significantly this was now demonstrated by the willingness to significantly increase crown funding for SPARC. However, support for elite sport continues to be balanced alongside recreational sport and physical recreation. From a relatively modest contribution of NZ$2.7 million in 2001–2002, government funding increased to over NZ$55 million in 2006. Resourcing of all three key areas has risen steadily since 2002 with elite sport funding increasing from NZ$22 million in 2003–2004 to over NZ$33 million in 2006–2007 (see Table 9.1). Increased investment by the crown into the sport sector (via SPARC) looks set to continue with the incumbent Labour government, in its 2005 election manifesto, committing to increased funding to sport and recreation of NZ$59.76 million in the 2008–2009 financial year (New Zealand Labour Party, 2005).

Significantly, the increased funding from government has had a flow-on effect to a number of other organisations in the sports sector. Funding to NSOs has increased significantly, from NZ$13,358,624 in 2001–2002 to NZ$32,552,342 in 2005–2006 (Table 9.2). This has also impacted upon the resources allocated for high performance in NSOs, with targeted high performance funding increasing from NZ$7,123,440 in 2001–2002 to NZ$11,491,300 in 2004–2005. Since 2003–2004, SPARC's funding to NSOs has increased significantly and has been accompanied by increased funding to the Academies, RSTs and Local Government. This rapid increase in, and control of, funding by SPARC has drawn attention to the ability of NSOs, in particular, to retain autonomy without compromising their (often) major

Table 9.1 SPARC actual total funding (NZ$)

Financial year	Total (m)	Crown funding (Vote funding – sport and recreation)[1]	Winning in events that matter to New Zealanders (m)	Being the most active nation (m)	Having the most effective sport and recreation systems (m)
2001–2002	35.6	2,724	N/A	N/A	N/A
2002–2003	42.2	9,761	N/A	N/A	N/A
2003–2004	53.8	24,916	22.0	19.8	12.0
2004–2005	72.2	36,790	25.3	32.4	14.47
2005–2006	84.3	44,245	31.1	35.9	17.26
2006–2007[2]	87.3	51,088	33.2	37.9	18.2

Here m denotes million.
[1] Does not include funding from other government agencies.
[2] Figures for 2006–2007 are forecast figures from Statement of Intent 2006–2009.
Adapted from SPARC Annual Reports (2001–2002, 2002–2003, 2003–2004, 2004–2005, 2005–2006).

Table 9.2 Allocation of SPARC investment funds (NZ$ million)

	National sports organisations	Academies (north, central and south)	Regional Sports Trusts	Local government
2001–2002	13,358,624	3,647,328	6,592,760	N/A
2002–2003	15,634,406	3,925,068	7,077,053	N/A
2003–2004	18,740,318	4,624,744	8,123,750	925,058
2004–2005	22,334,055	4,271,395	11,538,301	1,975,704
2005–2006	32,552,342	5,251,718	12,760,334	2,743,983

Adapted from SPARC Annual Reports (2003–2004, 2004–2005, 2005–2006).

source of income. The increase in funding, accompanied by the introduction of a target driven environment, has led NSOs to adopt a strong business focus on elite sport development, at times almost to the detriment of other areas within their sport (such as recreational sport). As a senior NSO official stated: 'I try to run it as a business and the business being to produce some high performance product, we weren't running the business just so everyone was having a good time' (Interview, 27 October 2006).

SPARC's recently developed High Performance Strategy articulates the direction and focus of New Zealand elite sport from 2006 to 2012. Evident is the further prioritisation of specific sports and a continued emphasis on targeted and accountable funding. The growing importance of the Olympic Games, and to a lesser extent the Commonwealth Games, was reinforced with the acknowledgement that SPARC would target a large proportion of its high performance investment at sports with the ability to deliver multiple Olympic and Commonwealth medals (SPARC, 2006c, p. 1). Nine high performance sports (athletics, cycling, rowing, sailing, swimming, triathlon, cricket, netball and rugby) were identified as priority sports. Interestingly, none of the same criteria that were used in 2002 to identify the priority sports were used 4 years later, with the new criteria clearly focused upon high performance and the ability to win medals on the world stage. The nine sports were selected based upon the NSOs: importance to New Zealand; results at the most recent pinnacle event; results progress towards world best performance, anticipated medal winning performance at the next pinnacle event; depth of talent and the number of medals available at their pinnacle event (Olympic sports); and their ability to impact the performance of their world-class athletes and teams (SPARC, 2006b, p. 7). Cricket, netball and rugby were selected due to their importance to New Zealand and their potential to win in events that matter to New Zealand, but will only receive investment support if they can demonstrate a genuine need for that support.

Of the six other sports, all are Olympic sports, a change from the seven priority sports identified in 2002, of which only equestrian, rowing and yachting were Olympic Sports. These nine sports will receive up to 70 per cent of SPARC's high performance budget. Up to 5 per cent of SPARC's high performance investment will be targeted at athletes in the top 16 of Olympic events and in the top eight in non-Olympic global events. The remainder of SPARC's high performance investment (up to 25 per cent) will be 'contested' among other sports that have the ability to compete creditably in events that matter to New Zealand. Alongside an increased prioritisation on Olympic sports New Zealand's elite sport policy now focuses on sports where multiple medals are on offer, a departure from providing for as many elite athletes as possible, to an emphasis on ensuring depth rather than breadth across a range of sports in an effort to achieve elite sporting success.

While the emergence of a coordinated and focused approach to elite sport development is a relatively recent phenomenon in New Zealand, there has been a consistent view about what sporting variables or dimensions are most beneficial in helping to achieve elite sporting success. Green and Houlihan (2005) suggest that facility development, the emergence of 'full-time' competitors, coaching, and sports science and medicine, and competition opportunities are four key dimensions important in determining the character and adequacy of an elite sport system. Although all four dimensions have in some respect been identified as important for the New Zealand elite system, this has to be tempered by an acknowledgement that there has been a varying degree of importance and focus placed on them in the New Zealand context. Coaching, and sports science and medicine combined and the emergence of full-time athletes are two areas which have been consistently identified as important in New Zealand's elite sport system in order for the country to increase the likelihood of success on the international sporting stage. Given the relatively recent development of a coordinated and targeted elite sport policy environment through the establishment of SPARC, it is perhaps unsurprising that the evidence of change and development amongst the four dimensions is still emerging. Along with these four dimensions, talent identification has also been consistently highlighted, frequently alongside improved coaching systems and standards, as an area critical to the successful development of elite sport in New Zealand (Ministerial Taskforce, 2001).

Important dimensions of elite sport development

Talent identification

Recognition of the need for an effective talent identification system resulted in the establishment of the Talent Identification Taskforce, which concluded that the area of talent identification was under-resourced, ad hoc and based on a belief of 'hope' rather than on any systematic approach (Talent Identification Taskforce, 2003, p. 9). A key recommendation therefore was the need to establish a systematic and holistic long-term development process within which an ongoing identification strategy was embedded. The adoption of a more long-term view was explicitly stated when the Taskforce identified that the fruits of such a strategy would not be realised until 2016. Further recognition of the role and importance of talent identification is evident in SPARC's 2006–2009 Statement of Intent, where the implementation of a talent development framework was identified as a key action in achieving the goal of having athletes and teams winning in events that matter to New Zealand. Although recognising that all children have the right to develop physical literacy, a clear focus of the talent identification system is to build and develop the pool of potential elite athletes. The Taskforce reinforced the need to increase the pool of potential athletes as, 'with more athletes being identified and developed, New Zealand will increase its competitiveness on the world stage' (Talent Identification Taskforce, 2003, p. 23). As a way of assessing whether this goal is being achieved, the number of NSOs with long-term talent development strategies will be measured as a guide to its success (SPARC, 2006d). Although the decision as to whether a particular sport has a talent identification plan remains with the NSO, in order to continue to receive high performance funding from SPARC, NSOs are required to show evidence of a clear talent identification plan. As noted in the review of the 2006 Commonwealth Games, 'SPARC investment should target high performance plans of national sports organisations only if they have a robust talent development framework in place to ensure we are developing more athletes of world class potential' (SPARC, 2006c, p. 8).

Coaching, sports science and medicine

Consistent with other countries such as Australia and Canada (see Green and Houlihan, 2005), coaching has been identified as a critical ingredient in the development and success of elite sport in New Zealand (Sports Development Inquiry Committee, 1985; Ministerial Taskforce, 2001; SPARC, 2006c). Coaching was highlighted in the Graham Report as 'a key priority in advancing sport participation and elite level excellence' (2001, p. 75). A number of areas in coaching were identified as needing urgent attention including: inconsistent standards; a lack of a clearly defined career pathway; variable development and education of coaches; poor access to quality research advice and a lack of structured networking resource information and career structures (Ministerial Taskforce, 2001). The New Zealand Coaching Strategy (2004) continued the dual emphasis of SPARC on both elite and recreational sport by addressing both areas.

Perhaps unsurprisingly the strategy noted that coaching must be a significant point of difference when compared to the rest of the world if New Zealand is to compete on the international stage. The recent High Performance Strategy identified coach development as a key strategy in assisting SPARC to achieve their goal of having athletes and teams winning consistently in events that matter to New Zealanders. A number of programmes such as the Carded Coach Programme, Prime Minister's Coaching Scholarship Programme and Coach Performance Enhancement Grants have all been developed to both enhance and reward elite coaching, and has resulted in increased investment over the past 5 years. In trying to improve coaching, the New Zealand Coaching Strategy (2004) identified the following for attention: (a) improving the quality and quantity of time available for coaches to focus upon coaching activities, (b) the need for increased recognition and status of coaches and (c) improvement of the quality of coach education process is critical to developing a world-class coaching environment. Recognition of the need to attract overseas coaches to develop New Zealand coaches and address areas where sport-specific expertise is lacking is also clearly identified as a strategy to address immediate weaknesses in the New Zealand system. As a senior NSO official explained:

in terms of getting the coach development right, if there are real gaps or weaknesses in terms of coaching we will try and address that and if that means bringing in someone from overseas and making sure there is succession planning, and bring a Kiwi in underneath, we will.

(Interview, 24 October 2006)

Coaching is also seen as a critical area for NSOs in attempts to improve their elite athlete performance and as a way of retaining talented and elite athletes in New Zealand. Moreover, the need to learn from overseas and 'buy in skills' is recognised as a valuable method of enhancing New Zealand coaches and, in turn, elite athletes:

Good coaching is a huge emphasis of our organisation and we run a national coaching school every year with 110 coaches in a live-in type of situation where we have overseas experts, and I mean the best overseas experts ... it's definitely a key strategy of ours to make sure coaching is improving. Athletes are only as good as the coaching they are getting.

(Interview, senior NSO official, 24 October 2006)

Yet, despite this, not all NSOs have been able to implement effective coaching strategies or systems. For some sports, the development of coaching has proven problematic, often due to insufficient resources, despite an acknowledgement that it is a core activity if they are to succeed on the international sporting stage:

Coaching has always been talked about and given lip service and we are still trying to sort the coaching programme out. We haven't got coaching sorted. I mean the coaching budget is NZ$50k per year and that is to employ someone as a coaching programmes manager. What could you do with that?

(Interview, senior NSO official, 27 October 2006)

Alongside coaching, the value of sport science to the elite sport system has been identified by SPARC as an area that requires further investment and development. The early establishment of the New Zealand Academy of Sport in 2000 indicated early recognition of the importance and value placed upon sports science. As noted earlier, investment in the Academies has increased from NZ$3,647,328 in 2001–2002 to NZ$5,251,718 in 2005–2006. However, the establishment of the first Performance Analysis Unit as recently as 2006 indicates that sport science is still a developing area for elite sport in New Zealand. Recognition remains of the need for continual improvement and as acknowledged by a senior SPARC official there is a need for the services to be 'world class and not just services'. Part of the problem appears to be due to a lack of experience in knowing what it takes to produce world-class athletes:

We recognise that there is a real lack of capability in a lot of those service provision areas [sports science] and we need to encourage the local providers to step up a level ... I think that is part of our biggest challenge over the next two or three years to accelerate the development of all those critical people that make up the key support roles.

(Interview, senior SPARC official, 27 October 2006)

Competition opportunities and emergence of full-time athletes

New Zealand's geographic isolation and conflicting seasons with the northern hemisphere has led to a pragmatic realisation that New Zealand sporting competitions need to dovetail into more significant (often northern hemisphere) competition schedules if its elite athletes are to attend national competitions that do not conflict with larger internationals events. For some sports, this is more of an issue than for others especially where the sport is predominantly based in the northern hemisphere. Yet despite identification of this problem, the move to alter national calendars has at times been slow. For athletics, the dominance of northern hemisphere competitions at the elite level is clearly evident:

We are the flea on the tail of the dog down here. Athletics is totally Eurocentric as that's where the population and investors and sponsors come from so we have to fit around everything. So the northern and southern split and our summer season causes problems [but] we work around it. So that's totally what our competitions are about.

(Interview, senior NSO official, 27 October 2006)

For some NSOs, rearranging the local competition calendar is driven by the need to have top New Zealand athletes visible and competing on the national scene. The participation of New Zealand's elite athletes at national and local competitions is seen to not only raise the level of local competition, but also expose the 'up and coming' athletes to what is required to become an elite athlete:

We have totally restructured our national calendar [and it was] a great decision. So everything is driven off the international calendar. If you cannot get your elite athletes to the national competition it devalues the national competition.

(Interview, senior NSO official, 25 October 2006)

The achievement of success on the international sporting stage has increasingly been associated with the need for full-time athletes. In reviewing New Zealand's performance at the Melbourne Commonwealth Games, the variation in perform-ance levels between full-time and part-time athletes was raised. As part of this SPARC recognised that New Zealand athletes are unlikely to be successful at future international events unless they are able to prepare full-time for such events (SPARC, 2006c). Without full-time athletes, success at the elite level is increas-ingly difficult. As discussed by a senior SPARC official, 'when you put money into elite [sport] it's for results. You have to go after results [and] you need to effectively take on the world, have athletes train full-time [and] you have to zero your resources in' (Interview, 25 October 2006).

The increased investment in sport has had a direct impact upon athletes' ability to train and compete on the international stage on a full-time basis. The introduction of Performance Enhancements Grants (PEGs) of NZ$5 million per year is directed at athletes in the top 16 in Olympic sports and the top 8 in non-Olympic global sports, with the aim of providing financial support for elite athletes to enable them to dedicate more time to training and competition. Other programmes such as the Prime Minister's Athlete Scholarship Awards also assist talented and elite athletes (as determined by the NSOs' perform-ance standards) to train while achieving tertiary or vocational goals. This has enabled elite athletes outside the professional codes of rugby union, cricket and rugby league to progress towards full-time status and to earn a living from competing at an elite level. For swimming, this was particularly evident, as a senior NSO official acknowledged:

The financial environment for them [athletes] is now the best it has ever been … they can actually earn a reasonable living. The top ten or fifteen in the Commonwealth Games' team would earn about between NZ$30,000 and NZ$40,000 per year, plus they have all their expenses paid to travel around Europe.

(Interview, 24 October 2006)

A significant part of the shift towards more full-time athletes has occurred during the last 4–5 years and has involved a combination of increased investment from SPARC, increased marketability of athletes, enabling additional revenues of funding from the private sector, and NSOs now having the capacity to support their elite athletes through incentive funding.

Facilities

The lack of a clear national plan, and systematic planning and consultation, led to concerns regarding the provision of elite sporting facilities. The provision of sporting facilities for elite athletes has only recently been identified as an area of priority concern for SPARC, especially in the provision of world-class training facilities for key sports. The development of sporting facilities has traditionally remained the responsibility of local government, which has resulted in an ad hoc and unsystematic approach to the type, spread and quality of sport facilities in New Zealand. This has contributed to a situation where facilities have been built without any, or with little, consultation at a national level. The recent construction of New Zealand's only indoor cycling velodrome in Invercargill led to criticism regarding its geographic location, being the 'wrong place, right facility', and the impact of this on its use and accessibility for elite athletes. The lack of a national strategy was highlighted as a potential reason for this. The reliance on local government to provide facilities raises issues regarding divergent priorities between elite and grassroots sport. As discussed by a senior NSO official, recreational sport was more of a priority for local government. The ability of NSOs to have input into or influence on facility development was at times random and dependent upon each local authority:

It depends on the council and how amenable they are for consultation and how much they listen … in some cases there are facilities built that have probably been mistakes as they have not listened to requirements whether it's been, you know, cut costs by reducing the size then it hasn't really been a facility that has met our needs. I would not say we are at a stage in directing councils in what they are building but we do have some say.

(Interview, senior NSO official, 24 October 2006)

Although the government has purposefully remained removed from taking responsibility for providing sporting facilities, SPARC recently identified 'facilities' as a vital area for intervention. The High Performance Strategy recognised that New Zealand has a lack of world-class facilities to which athletes have priority access. This renewed interest in New Zealand's elite sporting facilities is signalled by the commitment to conduct an evaluation of high performance facilities, which is to be completed by June 2007. However, the outcome and future action in relation to this audit is unclear. Caution not to create dependency upon national level funding for sporting facilities was expressed by a senior SPARC official: 'we also need to ask ourselves what we are developing here as we should be doing everything we can to make them self-sustaining rather than needing continuous ongoing government funding' (Interview, 16 October 2006).

Two specific concerns have been raised in respect of New Zealand's sporting facilities. First, many are becoming old and require considerable maintenance, due largely to a number of facilities being developed around the same period. Second, there is a considerable spread of facilities and limited resources or funding to continue or support their maintenance. In part, this is characterised by a large number of local or club facilities and an increasing recognition of the need to rationalise facilities. As such, the development of, and priority regarding the type of facilities built has been left predominantly to local government. Major sporting events, however, can receive national government support. The America's Cup, and in more recent times the involvement of government in the development of facilities for the upcoming Rugby World Cup in 2011 are considered on a case-by-case basis for government investment. These types of events are however separated out and considered by a discrete major events group that evaluates the impact of the event on areas such as tourism and economic development rather than as a process for developing recreational or elite sport.

As noted earlier many of these dimensions, although identified as early as 1985, have only recently begun to be addressed within a coordinated elite sport policy framework. The lack of world-class facilities in particular has only recently been addressed at a national level and the potential outcome of this activity remains unclear. Considerably more emphasis has been placed upon the development of coaching and sport sciences and medicine as demonstrated both through the level of policy activity and the level of resources dedicated to these areas. Increased support for full-time athletes has been identified as critical for New Zealand's elite sporting success and over the past 5 years SPARC has invested increasingly large amounts of funding for this objective. Again, however, there is a recognition that further development is needed in all these areas if New Zealand is to be successful on the international stage. Yet, this has to be tempered against the availability of resources and the need for SPARC to also address other areas of sport including recreational sport and physical recreation.

Conclusion

Over the past 15 years, there has been rapid development and change in New Zealand sport policy. Striving for athletes and teams winning consistently in events that matter to New Zealanders was a key departure from previous government investment in New Zealand sport. A clear 'investment' ethos, as opposed to providing grants, has led to SPARC redirecting, reshaping and refocusing the elite sport policy sector in New Zealand. The establishment of a single crown entity responsible for elite, recreational sport and physical recreation, coupled with a significant increase in crown funding, has resulted in SPARC taking a lead role in coordinating, developing and shaping the direction of elite and recreational sport and physical recreation.

Three major themes have emerged over the past 15 years in respect of elite sport policy. The first theme is the increasingly business-focused environment in which NSOs, and other agencies funded by SPARC, are expected to operate in return for funding. Funding by SPARC is driven by the expectation of a 'return on investment' and the achievement of clearly identified goals and targets. Second is the increasing legitimisation and acceptance of government intervention into elite sport matters should NSOs be unable to perform or achieve the goals identified. Increased government intervention has, however, led to concerns regarding the levels of autonomy NSOs now enjoy regarding the ways in which their respective sports are developed. Increasingly, investment in NSOs is dependent upon certain programmes or processes being in place, without which funding may be withdrawn, or more direct intervention may occur to ensure the success of elite athletes. The third theme to emerge is the increasing prioritisation of Olympic sports and the narrowing of focus towards sports where multiple medals are on offer. This is demonstrated both through the criteria considered to become a priority sport, and the increased emphasis placed on the Olympic Games as a pinnacle event for New Zealand athletes.

Finally, as a relative newcomer to developing elite (Olympic) athletes, in comparison to countries such as Australia, it is not surprising to see evidence of policy learning from other elite sport systems. Given New Zealand's geographic isolation and relatively small investment in elite sport in comparison to nations such as the United Kingdom and Australia, policy learning and transfer has been based around the need to learn, adapt and be innovative in order to drive elite sport success. In such a target-led environment, the indicators of success for New Zealand's strong recent emphasis on elite success can only be medals and trophies on the international stage, most notably at the Olympic Games.

References

Anon. (2001) Winds of change, *Australian Leisure Management (Sydney, Australia.)*, 28, 18–20.

Collins, C. and Downey, J. (2000) Politics, government and sport, in C. Collins (ed.), *Sport in New Zealand Society*, Palmerston North: Dunmore Press.

Collins, C. and Stuart, M. (1994) Politics and sport in New Zealand, in L. Trenberth and C. Collins (eds.), *Sport Management in New Zealand. An Introduction*, Palmerston North: Dunmore Press.

DFSNZ (2006) *'Changing the Name' Annual Report 2005/06*, New Zealand: Author.

Green, M. and Houlihan, B. (2005) *Elite Sport Development: Policy Learning and Political Priorities*, London: Routledge.

Hindson, A., Cushman, G. and Gidlow, B. (1994) Historical and social perspectives on sport in New Zealand, in L. Trenberth and C. Collins (eds.), *Sport Management in New Zealand: An Introduction*, Palmerston North: Dunmore Press.

Knight, G. (2005) The disappointment games: Narratives of Olympic failure in Canada and New Zealand, *International Review for the Sociology of Sport*, 40(1), 25–51.

Ministerial Taskforce (2001) *Getting Set for an Active Nation: Report of the Sport, Fitness and Leisure Ministerial Taskforce*, Wellington, New Zealand.

New Zealand Labour Party (2005) *Labour Manifesto 2005*, Wellington, New Zealand.

New Zealand Sports Drug Agency (2005) *Implementing the Code Annual Report 2004/05*, New Zealand: Author.

Quiggan, J. (1998) Social democracy and market reform in Australia and New Zealand, *Oxford Review of Economic Policy*, 14(1), 76–94.

Sam, M. (2004) Sport policy development in New Zealand: Paradoxes of an integrative paradigm, *International Review for the Sociology of Sport*, 39(2), 205–222.

SPARC (2002a) *Our Vision, Our Direction*, Wellington, New Zealand: Author.

SPARC (2002b) *Results and Financial Statements*, New Zealand: Author.

SPARC (2003a) *Annual Report for Year Ended 30 June 2003*, New Zealand: Author.

SPARC (2003b) *Statement of Intent 2003–2004*, New Zealand: Author.

SPARC (2004) *Annual Report for Year Ended June 2004*, New Zealand: Author.

SPARC (2005a) *Annual Report for the Year Ended 30 June 2005*, New Zealand: Author.

SPARC (2005b) *Re-igniting the SPARC. Looking back at Athens – forward to Beijing*, New Zealand: Author.

SPARC (2006a) *Annual Report for the Year Ended 30 June 2006*, New Zealand: Author.

SPARC (2006b) *High Performance Strategy 2006–2012*, New Zealand: Author.

SPARC (2006c) *Melbourne 2006. A Review of New Zealand's Performance at the 2006 Melbourne Commonwealth Games*, New Zealand: Author.

SPARC (2006d) *Statement of Intent 2006–2009*, New Zealand: Author.

Sports Development Inquiry Committee (1985) *Sport on the Move, Report to the Minister of Recreation and Sport*, Wellington, New Zealand: Government Print.

Statistics New Zealand (2007) *National Population Estimates*, Available at http://www.stats.govt.nz/products-and-services/hot-off-the-press/national-population-estimates/national-population-estimates-march-2007-qtr-hotp.htm (accessed 20 May 2007).

Stothart, B. (2000) The development of sport administration in New Zealand: From kitchen table to computer, in C. Collins (ed.), *Sport in New Zealand Society*, Palmerston North: Dunmore Press.

Talent Identification Taskforce (2003) *Linking Promise to the Podium. Talent Identification and Development in New Zealand*, New Zealand: SPARC.

CHAPTER 10

United States

Emily Sparvero, Laurence Chalip and
B. Christine Green

Introduction

Throughout the world, government (especially federal/central government) has increased its involvement in elite sport development (Chalip et al., 1996; Green and Houlihan, 2005). Except in the United States, governments have created schemes to subsidise elite athletes and their National Governing Bodies (NGBs), have created national training centres, and have funded applied sport science. The United States stands in stark contrast to the trends in elite sport development that are most commonly observed throughout the rest of the developed world insomuch as the federal government has chosen to delegate elite sport development to sport organisations, and to keep itself out of sport.

Federal involvement in elite sport

There are only three federal policies that impact elite sport development in the United States. The first is an anti-trust exemption granted to professional baseball in 1922 (*Federal Baseball v. National League et al.* [*259 US 200 (1922)*]). That exemption is revealing because the federal government explicitly identifies a professional sport, including the development of its elite players, as outside normal federal jurisprudence. Although the exception has not been explicitly extended to other sports, it has been treated as a more general policy. For example, when the (now defunct) United States Football League brought an anti-trust suit against the National Football League (NFL), they were awarded damages of only $1, which was tripled under anti-trust law, as the court also ruled that the NFL was acting as a monopoly (*United States Football League v. NFL, 842 F.2d 1335, 1344* [*2d Cir. 1988*]). In effect, the courts determined that in professional sport, anti-trust provisions that are enforced uncompromisingly in other industries are not as pertinent.

The second federal policy that impacts elite sport development is Title IX of the Education Amendments of 1972 (P.L. 92-318). The original intent of this legislation was to prohibit discrimination in educational programmes and activities by recipients of federal funding. While this legislation was not formulated to address sports, it has made a significant impact through application to participation and hiring in school sport. The statute does not require that an individual be directly affected in order to bring suit, so advocates of women's sports development have successfully used Title IX to increase school-based sport opportunities for women.

The application of this education legislation to school athletics programmes highlights the importance of schools in elite sport development. Under Title IX, schools receiving federal public funding are required to comply with one of the following three criteria: (a) the percentages of male and female athletes must be substantially proportional to the percentages of male and female athletes enrolled; (b) the school must have a history and continuing practice of expanding athletic opportunities for the underrepresented sex; or (c) the institution must fully and effectively accommodate the interests and abilities of the underrepresented sex.

Title IX has had opposite effects on men's and women's sport development. The National Collegiate Athletic Association (NCAA), which has the primary responsibility for governance and oversight of university athletics in the United States, created a category of 'emerging sports' for women to assist schools in meeting Title IX compliance. Olympic sports including women's ice hockey, field hockey, and rowing began as emerging sports and are now well established in most universities. Several other Olympic sports are currently classified as emerging sports, including archery, badminton, equestrian, synchronised swimming, and team handball. Meanwhile, some universities have responded to Title IX by eliminating some Olympic sports for men in order to obtain percentages of participation that appear equal for both sexes. The elimination of these sports from university athletics departments affects the sport's potential for success in international competition because it shrinks the pool of programmes through which elite athletes are cultivated. Between 1981 and 1999, universities eliminated 171 men's wrestling teams, 84 men's tennis teams, and 56 men's gymnastics teams (US General Accountability Office, 2001). Despite the negative impact Title IX has had on men's sports, its positive effect on women's sport has been sufficient to retain support. Title IX was reaffirmed by the Bush administration in 2003.

The third federal policy addressing elite sport development is the Amateur Sports Act, passed in 1978 and amended in 1996 (Amateur Sports Act of 1978, P.L. No. 95-606; Omnibus Consolidated and Emergency Supplemental Appropriations Act, P.L. No. 105-277), which grants to the United States Olympic Committee (USOC) all rights and responsibilities associated with elite sport development, which it is to pursue through its NGBs. The USOC has the authority to certify, not certify, or decertify any NGB. (The fact that international legal tradition places the right of NGB certification in the hands of the appropriate International Federation (IF) is conveniently ignored by the Act.) The USOC is a private not-for-profit organisation, which is responsible for raising its own funds without recourse to federal assistance. The USOC is not subject to any federal oversight, although it must provide a copy of its annual report to Congress. There is, however, no Congressional committee or office assigned the task of reading the report. In fact, there is no federal agency with any responsibility for elite sport development, and there is no government level official whose portfolio encompasses sport.

Based on tax documents and its 2005 annual report to Congress, the USOC earned US$118.2 million in total revenue (the most recent year from which we could obtain sufficient data). The major expenses were member support, which includes direct financial assistance to athletes and grant payments to NGBs (US$50.7 million), the maintenance and operation of Olympic Training Centres (US$23.2 million), expenses related to logistic and operational support for international competition (US$3.8 million), and coaching development (US$392, 255). The USOC provides a minimum of $250,000 annually to each NGB and provides performance funding based on the number of medals won by the sport (Stotlar and Wonders, 2006). According to its federal mandate, the USOC has responsibility for grassroots sport development as well as elite sport development. However, the USOC's current distribution of funds underscores its commitment to the development of elite athletes, often at the expense of grassroots sport development (despite an explicit requirement in the Amateur Sports Act that the USOC and its NGBs should endeavour to foster and grow mass participation in Olympic sports). The problem was noted in several interviews conducted during research supporting this chapter. The President of a track club that has produced world record holders, including Olympic gold medallists said:

It seems to me that all the national organisations don't seem to be affecting the track club much. You know the really sad thing I see is … you have so many good athletes in high school, and they don't have an opportunity to train anywhere. There's no place really for them to train … . We can't work with these kids during high school [because of the rules for school sport] … There aren't many great coaches at the high school level … . Helping these kids in the summer is about all we can do. There aren't many programmes [for young runners] … . We were trying to get something going [but] haven't been successful at getting support financially.

This has both exacerbated and been exacerbated by the plethora of sport organisations in the United States. A former President of a summer swimming league described it this way:

We dropped our affiliation with USA Swimming [the sport's NGB] because we simply got nothing for our registration fee except insurance, which we could get cheaper through the AAU [Amateur Athletic Union] … . Summer league programmes like ours are built on intense volunteer effort. We recruit lots of kids into the sport; some of them eventually go into year-round programmes. Some of this country's best swimmers began in programmes like ours … . We didn't get any help from USA Swimming. We don't get anything from the AAU either … . Both organisations are more concerned with elites than [with] grass-roots programmes like ours.

The inattention to grassroots development caused by government inattention and the elite focus of the USOC and its NGBs has created social class barriers to sport participation and excellence. A mental health professional seeking to use sport in his work with disadvantaged urban youth summarised the problem:

The problem for these kids is often that the family has problems, or doesn't know where to get information, or how to fill out the right forms, or that kind of thing. In order for a kid to be in a programme, there has to be initiative from somebody, and these kids usually don't have parents or anyone else who can [provide initiative. So] you've got to do outreach, and it's outreach to extremely aversive kinds of areas. We're talking ghetto areas; dangerous areas sometimes. Nobody wants to live in these areas, including YMCAs and other kinds of organisations that could offer programmes. So there is nothing for these kids, especially in the summer. They are also poor, which limits their opportunities.

The federal government's delegation of sport development to the USOC was explicitly an effort to prevent federal intrusion into American sport development. In the legislative sessions immediately following poor performances by the American team at the Munich Olympics (in 1972), two bills were introduced in the Senate (S 1192 and S 1580) that proposed to create a federal agency to regulate Olympic sports, and a companion bill was introduced in the House of Representative (HR 5624). These led to a great deal of ideological concern. Senator Glenn Beall summarised the opposition in a speech on the Senate floor:

I am reluctant to believe that the way to attack this problem is to set up still another broad Federal instrument … that will inevitably grow even bigger in coming years – and which we will find consuming even more tax dollars … . I also object to the feature of this legislation that puts the Federal Government in the position of determining one sole 'charter' holder for each sport … . I do not believe we should be in the business of creating monopolies.

(1973, p. 32769)

A staff memorandum to President Nixon opined:

The Bills [currently before congress] go too far in trying to solve the problem … . If you are faced with one of the bills, you will be vetoing an inadequate bill which may be perceived by the American people as the answer. You could therefore be criticised as a non-supporter of the amateur athlete.

(Jones, 1973)

While still serving as Vice-President, Gerald Ford published a commentary in *Sports Illustrated*, the nation's most widely read sports weekly, stating: 'Completely regimented, state-supported, state-manipulated athletic programmes are not for us. It is a matter of style, as well as philosophy. The [Bills are] anathema [because they would create] too much federal control' (Ford, 1974, p. 18). The President's Commission on Olympic Sports, which formulated the recommendations that became the Amateur Sports Act was subsequently created by President Ford specifically to forestall any federal government encroachment into sport development (Chalip, 1995).

In fact, the federal government's refusal to become a sport policymaker is consistent with the ideological foundations of American governance. The traditional American political philosophy is that the powers and intervention of government must be limited in order for individual liberties to be protected. This is widely used as a rationale to limit or prevent social legislation (Quadagno and Street, 2005) and has long stood as a stumbling block to those who seek to extend the reach of federal control (Handler, 1992).

In American government, when the federal government does not take a direct hand in policy, each of the 50 states is free to formulate and implement its own policies. This has not happened in the case of elite sport except for some support of a limited number of sports (particularly baseball, basketball, American football, track and field, and swimming) in state funded universities. However, state funding has not been targeted at elite sport development; rather, it has been a consequence of political pressure from university lobbyists and alumni who seek to have facilities, coaching, and support services that will attract already competent athletes to represent the university (Shaw, 1972; Duderstadt, 2000; Sperber, 2001). The objective has never been to contribute to development of the nation's pool of elite athletes; rather, the objective has been to contribute to the brand equity of the university through its sporting successes. Further, state funding is not sufficient to maintain university sport, which typically depends on private donations, sponsorships, and a share of university revenues (Covell, 2001; Fulks, 2000). Private educational institutions at the secondary and postsecondary level (which include the nation's most prestigious educational institutions) receive negligible support from the state; rather, they are funded through private sources.

The lack of state policies for sport development trickles down to local level, where government provides some sport opportunities. Grassroots sport development, which is the base of the American sports pyramid, occurs through public schools and public parks-and-recreation departments. The locus varies by state, operating at county level in some jurisdictions, and at city level in other jurisdictions. Again, however, neither government system is mandated to serve a national sport development system. Rather, the school-based system is designed to feed athletes into the university system, and parks-and-recreation serves mass participation rather than elite sport development. In fact, when the National Recreation and Parks Association (the national professional association for parks and recreation) applied for membership in the USOC (as a community-based multi-sport organisation), they were denied. Nevertheless, in most parks and recreation departments, children's programmes in popular school sports – particularly baseball, basketball, soccer, swimming, and American football – are often designed to create and feed talent into local high schools and to provide training during the schools' off season.

Private enterprise is expected to fill any gaps in sport provision. There is no sport club tradition in the United States that is comparable to the kind found elsewhere in the world. Some sports are endeavouring to establish clubs in order to broaden their reach, and a few (especially swimming) have enjoyed a long and successful tradition of club-based competition, although club athletes typically leave their clubs to compete for their schools during the school season (if their school fields a team in their chosen sport). Other sports, particularly golf and tennis, have been associated with expensive country clubs, which have been concerned with sport for upper-class social capital, rather than elite national representation. Professional sport is offered through teams that are sometimes called 'clubs', but those are actually privately owned franchises, which do not operate as clubs in the same sense as the membership-based clubs that field professional teams in much of Europe and Australia. In recent years, some enterprising coaches have created for-profit businesses organised around a club-like system, particularly in volleyball and gymnastics. These businesses are typically attractive to clientele because they offer coaching and facilities outside the school season, which parents expect will help their children to obtain scholarships to compete for a university.

Relatively new sports for which equipment sales can be lucrative, such as boardsailing and disc-golf (which is contested at the World Games), have relied extensively on retailers and peer coaching for their development – a pathway that compensates for the lack of a sport club tradition in the United States. Retailers may offer instruction, trips, social events, and even a club – all designed to build sales by promoting interest in the sport. Peer coaching is then fostered through clinics provided by retailers and at events. Retail-driven development has become sufficiently lucrative that some sports with school or professional pathways (most notably, running and triathlon) now include retail-based clubs.

Much of the sport that is not provided by parks-and-recreation, the schools, or club-like businesses is provided through large multi-sport organisations that function as private not-for-profit enterprises. Nineteen are members of the USOC. The three best known are the YMCA, Boys and Girls Clubs of America, and Jewish Community Centres (JCCs). Each of these organisations has educational and social service missions that sport is provided to serve. None explicitly seeks to contribute to national elite sport development. Their membership in the USOC provides a channel for communication among the organisations, and may make an organisation eligible for a USOC or NGB grant if-and-when one is available. There is, however, no USOC oversight or policy direction entailed by membership.

Athlete pathways

Athletes have multiple pathways into and through sport, but there is no well-mapped pathway to elite status. As a result, several professional sports leagues have their own development systems. For example, professional baseball has, since its inception in the nineteenth century, had a minor league development system. Each professional team has three class A, one class AA, and one class AAA affiliate developing players who are recruited from school, recreation, or multi-sport organisations. Professional ice hockey also maintains a minor league development system, and the National Basketball Association (NBA) (professional basketball) and the NFL (professional American football) have each created development leagues.

Nevertheless, school-based sport remains the dominant pathway for athletes who compete in sports that are offered in school. It is important to note that which sports are included in high school programmes and which are not varies to some degree nationally, although American football is almost universally included. Baseball, basketball, swimming, and track and field are also widely included in high school programmes. Volleyball, soccer, tennis, wrestling, and gymnastics are also often included in school sport schedules, although not as widely. Other sports (e.g., ice hockey, field hockey, rowing) are included regionally in some school programmes. However, most sports are rarely, if ever, found in high school sport systems (e.g., archery, canoeing, shooting, team handball, most winter sports).

High school sports are the primary pathway to university sport. Universities offer a limited number of sports (called 'varsity sports') through their athletics departments, with some variation in which sports are included in any particular university's system. In addition to the varsity sports offered through university athletics departments, students also have opportunities to participate in 'club' sports. In the American university system, club sports are neither supported nor regulated by the athletics department or the NCAA. University club sports include those that are not part of the varsity sports system, but for which there is some student interest. These sports are typically not supported through athletics departments, but are instead enabled by university recreational sport systems (which are separate from athletics departments) or student affairs departments. Varsity sport participation is limited to athletes who have already attained a comparatively elite level. On the other hand, club sports are less selective. Varsity athletes (i.e., those in the athletics department) enjoy institutional support through provision of facilities, coaching, trainers, and the costs of attending competitions. On the other hand, university club sport participants must arrange their own coaching and facility access, and are also responsible for the costs of competing. Thus, whereas varsity sports (i.e., those in university athletics departments) can foster elite capability, university club sports are neither designed, supported, nor intended to do so.

The salience of school-based sport has four effects. First, athletes are typically channelled into sports for which there are opportunities to compete in school. School-based competition provides social recognition (Weiss, 2001; Eccles et al., 2003), and it is often thought to be a pathway to a university scholarship (i.e., to be funded to compete on a varsity team). Second, since elite levels of competition require training and competition beyond the school season, athletes must find opportunities outside of school to train and compete. However, since public money for sport facilities and coaching is channelled significantly (albeit not uniquely) through schools, opportunities in many sports are limited. Third, since the rules for university sport participation limit the number of years that a student can compete (to 4 years) and require a minimal level of academic performance, elite athletes seeking to compete beyond their school and university years or whose academic performance is poor are not served by the system. Fourth, sports that are not represented in school competitions must recruit athletes from other sports, and must then create elite training schemes for the athletes who are recruited. This has been the strategy for facility intensive sports, such as luge and skeleton, and for sports that have low cultural penetration, such as rugby (which recruits widely from former players of American football).

From the standpoint of elite sport development, the system is avowedly chaotic. Figure 10.1 provides a heuristic diagram of key organisations in American sport development and their relationships. As examination of Figure 10.1 illustrates, there is a wide array of organisations that are only weakly networked. Although the USOC sits nominally at the centre of the American system, it is closely connected only to its own NGBs, and is only weakly associated with other sport organisations, many of which lack network ties to one another. Thus, there is no 'system' for elite sport development. Each sport faces different challenges when developing its elite athletes. Although the USOC provides training centres that NGBs can use from time-to-time to prepare elite competitors, each sport must develop its own system. Sports in which athletes are unlikely to make a living as professionals and that are also not typically included in inter-university competitions are at a distinct disadvantage. The disadvantage is exacerbated by the media's focus on professional and university sport, with the result that the majority of sports (i.e., those not included in school or university leagues and without a well-financed professional league) struggle to find facilities and coaching, and find it difficult to attract or retain athletes.

It is heuristically useful, therefore, to consider the pathways to development with reference to school and professional opportunities. As Table 10.1 shows, the vast majority of Olympic sports are not supported by professional or university-based opportunities. Further, very few sports have professional outlets, although the opportunity to compete for significant purses and to obtain significant endorsements has created a pathway that is often viewed as a professional outlet – e.g., in triathlon, cycling, and track-and-field (although many of the opportunities for remunerated competition exist outside the United States, even for American athletes).

What Table 10.1 highlights, in particular, is that the American focus on professional and school-based sport systems leaves the majority of sports without a salient pathway for achievement of elite status. Further, for a few sports, the school and professional opportunities are redundant – particularly in baseball, basketball, soccer, tennis, and ice hockey. Since the objective of university and professional systems is to build brand

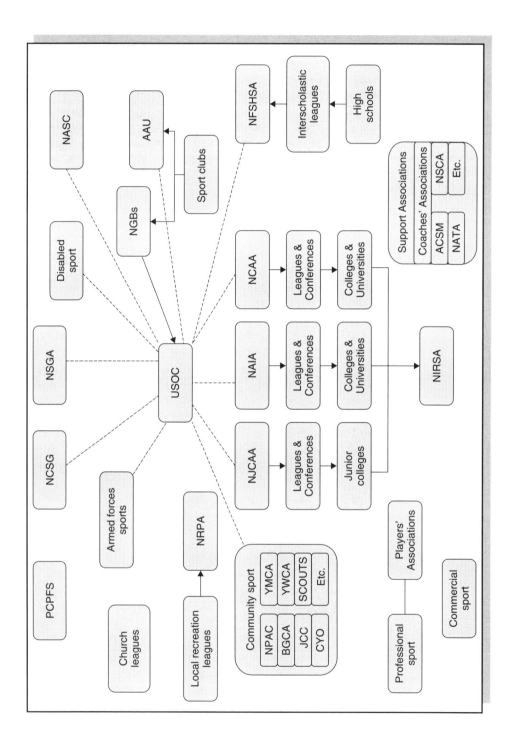

equity for the particular school or team via competitive success, there is little incentive to coordinate the two systems, which often find themselves vying with one another for the same athletes. It is not uncommon for highly skilled athletes to give up university scholarships to become professional, and universities place restrictions on athletes to discourage them from turning professional – e.g., by disallowing contact with agents. Some professional teams circumvent university restrictions by recruiting athletes while they are still in high school. For example, Freddy Adu became a professional soccer player (with DC United) at the age of 14. Similarly, professional circuits in individual sports, particularly tennis, include a number of teenage players who are being coached privately.

The vital point illustrated by Table 10.1 is that there are four development configurations that must be considered when examining elite sport development in the United States: (a) sports with a school and university base; (b) sports with a system for development of professional elites; (c) sports with both; and (d) sports with neither. Of course, sports within each quadrant also differ in the challenges they face when developing elite athletes. In particular, quality of coaching, availability of facilities, and level of cultural interest differentiate sport development challenges – even among sports appearing in the same quadrant. Since each sport is responsible for development of its own systems, sports do not share a common vision for athlete development. Nevertheless, for the reasons described so far, the challenges faced by sports within each quadrant are more similar than between quadrants.

Success of American athletes

It would be easy to be surprised by the lack of coordination in American sport development. After all, the United States

---

Figure 10.1   Key organisations in American sport development: AAU, Amateur Athletic Union; ACSM, American College of Sports Medicine; BGCA, Boys and Girls Clubs of America; CYO, Catholic Youth Organisation; JCC, Jewish Community Centres; NAIA, National Association of Intercollegiate Athletics; NASC, Native American Sports Council; NATA, National Athletic Trainers Association; NCAA, National Collegiate Athletic Association; NCSG, National Congress of State Games; NFSHSA, National Federation of State High School Athletics; NGB, National Governing Bodies; NIRSA, National Intramural Recreation Sports Association; NJCAA, National Junior College Athletic Association; NRPA, National Recreational and Parks Association; NSCA, National Strength and Conditioning Association; NSGA, National Senior Games Association; NPAC, National Police Athletic Clubs; PCPFS, President's Council on Physical Fitness and Sport; USOC, United States Olympic Committee; YMCA, Young Men's Christian Association; YWCA, Young Women's Christian Association

Table 10.1 School and professional system support for Olympic sports

	Little/no university presence	Significant presence in university sport systems
Little/no professional opportunity	*Summer sports* Archery Badminton Canoe/kayak Equestrian Men's field hockey Judo Modern pentathlon Sailing Shooting Synchronised swimming Table tennis Taekwondo Team handball Weightlifting *Winter sports* Biathlon Bobsled Curling Luge Speedskating	*Summer sports* Diving Fencing Gymnastics Rowing Softball Swimming Volleyball Water polo Wrestling Women's field hockey *Winter sports* Women's ice hockey
Significant professional opportunity	*Summer sports* Boxing Cycling Triathlon Marathon *Winter sports* Figure skating Snowboarding	*Summer sports* Athletics (track-and-field) Baseball Basketball Soccer Tennis *Winter sports* Men's ice hockey Skiing

has consistently dominated Olympic competition. Or has it? Figure 10.2 shows the percentage of summer Olympic medals earned by American athletes since World War II. Although the United States topped the medal table at 9 of the 15 most recent summer Olympic Games, its percentage of total medals has

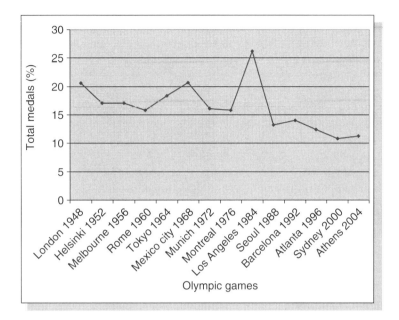

Figure 10.2 US medal performance in the summer Olympic Games

been declining. The jump in medals at the Los Angeles Olympics in 1984 illustrates the effect of the boycott by Warsaw Pact nations. Yet, despite the dismantling of communist-bloc sport systems since the end of the cold war (Riordan, 1993; Collins, 2004), the United States has barely maintained its relative level of international success. Whether this is due to the increasingly well coordinated sport development systems emerging elsewhere in the world, or is due to stagnation of the American system is not clear.

Results for the US team at the winter Olympic Games are shown in Figure 10.3. The winter results suggest that American winter sports have not been able to formulate a development strategy capable of generating a consistent level of success. Indeed, the US team has not topped the medals table at a winter Olympic Games, and has performed erratically.

It could be argued, nonetheless, that the United States is always a significant presence in international competition, particularly at the Olympic Games. But the United States is a large and wealthy country (almost 300 million people and a gross domestic product (GDP) that dwarfs any other – almost triple the next closest economy, according to the World Bank). Not surprisingly, higher population figures and a higher GDP are normally associated with higher levels of medal production (Bernard and Busse, 2004; Johnson and Ali, 2004). If one measures success in terms of Olympic gold medals per capita, the United States ranked 39th at the Athens Olympics. The United States earned one gold medal per 8.4 million people – far behind the top three: the Bahamas

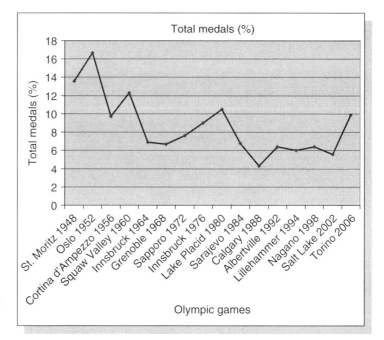

Figure 10.3 US medal performance in the winter Olympic Games

(one gold medal per 300,000), Norway (one gold medal per 900,000), and Australia (one gold medal per 1.2 million) (Standard and Poor's, 2004). Further, if one measures success with reference to GDP, the United States ranks 69th, with only 0.83 medals (gold + silver + bronze) per $100 billion (one thousand million) of GDP (Blustein, 2004). American performances at the winter Olympics have been even weaker – winning only 0.3 gold medals per 10 million people, or 0.23 total medals per $100 billion of GDP, ranking the United States as one of the world's weakest performers.

In part, the sub-par performance of American teams results from the narrow range of sports that enjoy university and/or professional opportunities. The United States has experienced its highest level of consistent success in summer Olympic sports that have one, the other, or both. Of the 102 medals won by the United States at the Athens Olympics, 27 were won by athletes in sports that have both university and professional opportunities (track-and-field, men's and women's basketball). The current dependence of American basketball performances on professional players was highlighted in Athens when American professional basketball stars declined to participate, rendering a team made up primarily of university players and professionals who are not starting players for their respective teams. As a result, the highly favoured American men's basketball team (which had dominated

Olympic basketball, particularly since professionals were allowed to play beginning in 1992) finished third (behind Argentina and Italy). On the other hand, the women basketball players rebounded from a third place Olympic finish in 1992 to dominate play and win gold in the following three Olympic Games which, not coincidentally, have taken place following the foundation of a professional American basketball league for women (the Women's National Basketball Association (WNBA), founded in 1996).

Unlike basketball, the US baseball team does not include stars from Major League Baseball, and typically fails to include the best Minor League Baseball players (in part, because the leagues are playing their normal season when the Olympics take place). Consequently, the American team only managed a bronze medal when playing at home in 1996. However, the Sydney Olympics (in 2000) began in September, after most lower-level minor league teams have completed their seasons. As a result, the team included some professional minor league players as well as university stars. The United States won the gold medal. But without professionals available for qualifying games in the lead-up to Athens (2004), the United States failed even to qualify to compete.

American athletes were also successful in summer sports with professional opportunities but lacking widespread representation at the university level (e.g., beach volleyball, boxing, cycling, triathlon, marathon), winning medals in each of the sports included in this quadrant. The United States has been particularly successful in beach volleyball, a sport that originated in Santa Monica, California in the 1920s. Since its inclusion on the Olympic programme in 1996, the American men have won two of three gold medals, and the women won the gold and bronze medals in 2004. At the winter Olympics, the United States' performance was improved by the inclusion of snowboarding on the Olympic programme. Snowboarding was developed in the United States during the 1960s, with professional snowboarders now making a living from the sport. Not coincidentally, 7 of the 25 US medals came in snowboarding.

Summer sports with university representation but without professional opportunities also fared well, accounting for 49 medals, of which 28 came in swimming and 9 came in gymnastics. Swimming has consistently been one of the leading medal-producing sports for the United States, in part because it is one of the few American sports for which school and university competitions are supported by a strong club system. There was widespread success in sports represented in this quadrant, as only diving and volleyball did not win medals.

Women's ice hockey is the only winter sport for which there is no professional opportunity but there is an opportunity to compete for some universities. Again, the value of a university system was demonstrated as the American team won medals in the past three Olympic Games. However, lacking any professional opportunities, the women's team performances have not maintained their pace, as the US team went from gold (in 1998) to silver (in 2002) to bronze (in 2006).

Of course, since the professional system is structured to create profits for franchise owners rather than to foster development of national elites, there is no guarantee that it will enable competitive success for the national team. Professional ice hockey for men is a good example. In fact, in recent years the number of American players in the National Hockey League (NHL) has hovered around 13 per cent (with more players coming from Canada, the Scandinavian countries, and the former Warsaw Pact than from the United States). So, despite the presence of some university-based programmes, the American men's team has managed only one medal – a silver in 2002 – since its fairytale win in 1980.

On the other hand, sports that lack university or professional opportunities produce few medals, or cannot qualify for Olympic competition. The United States has consistently failed to qualify in men's field hockey and men's team handball (except when qualification was automatic because the United States hosted the Olympics). The few successes for sports in this quadrant are not the result of any system for development of elite competitors. For example, the American competitor who won the silver medal in modern pentathlon in 2004 learned the event during her time as a student at Oxford University (in the United Kingdom). Both sailing and equestrian, which earned medals in 2004, have built their elite competitor base from private clubs that cater to wealthy patrons for whom skills are developed as a means to social capital, rather than as an intended pathway to national representation.

It is useful to note that some American successes in sports without a professional or a university opportunity have been enabled by the World Class Athlete Program (WCAP) of the US military. The programme was created in 1948 to enable soldiers to train and compete in international competitions. However, the WCAP is explicitly not a development programme, but was designed instead to serve a military morale function. It does not recruit athletes, but rather requires any soldier who wants to train to demonstrate that he or she has already achieved elite status. Further, while the soldier is training for elite competition, their first responsibility is to the military. For example, bobsled driver Shauna Rohbock competed at the Salt Lake City Olympics while supported through the WCAP, but was not able to continue training because she was deployed to Iraq the following year.

In summary, although the United States has enjoyed some success at summer and winter Olympic competitions, its performances have not been commensurate with the country's size or wealth. In fact, national performances continue to rely overwhelmingly on school, university, and professional systems which are not integrated into any coordinated fabric for sport development. In sports without a university or professional system, American competitive success depends substantially on athletes who obtain experience outside the United States, opportunities afforded by social clubs catering to the wealthy, or dispensation for an already international class athlete to train while in the US military. These have provided only haphazard and inconsistent development.

Research and development

Despite the differences among sports, they share a common challenge when seeking scientific support. A great deal of the advance in sport performances by athletes worldwide can be attributed to advances in the sport science upon which their coaching and care are based (Müller et al., 1999). American sports are challenged to keep pace. Although school, university, and professional sport systems are effective users of sport science knowledge, they are not producers of sport science knowledge.

There are some dedicated sport science facilities within the United States Olympic Training Centres (USOTCs), but these are not designed as significant research and development installations. The primary purpose of the USOTCs is to provide venues for elite athletes to come together for training. Some medical schools do occasionally dabble in sports medicine research, but there is no coordinated research scheme for sports medicine. The mass of American sport science research capacity resides in its universities, but outside of the athlete development system – primarily in departments variously called 'Kinesiology', 'Human Performance', or 'Physical Education'.

American universities rely extensively on research funding from foundations, corporations, or government. Universities typically charge 'overhead' to grants obtained from these sources, often taking 50 per cent or more of the funds off the top. Since the funding thus obtained helps to finance American universities, researchers are under increasing pressure to obtain grants that allow universities to take overhead. There are large grants available for health-based research through foundations, government agencies, and some corporations, but there is nothing comparable for sport-based research. The USOC, NGBs, NCAA, and professional leagues fund little research, and do not allow overhead to be taken when they do. As a result, American physiologists, bio-mechanists, and psychologists are under increasing pressure from their institutions to direct their research toward health and away from sport. Most already have. Since university sport is structured to develop athletes rather than knowledge, and because it exists separately from academic departments, there is no countervailing institutional encouragement for researchers to study sport.

Given the absence of a coordinated sport development strategy and the lack of any significant sport science funding body, the long-term outlook for American sport science is bleak. There is some government and foundation funding for research to reduce the use of drugs in sport, and substantial corporate funding for research to support development of commercial products (such as sports drinks), but none to support elite sport development. Although projects by sport scientists at the USOTCs and the individual commitments of some university faculty and students have helped to maintain a small stream of development-relevant sport science, there is no prospect for a significant or coordinated stream of sport science work formulated to enhance the foundation upon which American coaching or sport development are built.

Elite sport development amid the chaos

In order to obtain clearer insight into the ways that sport development proceeds in the presence or absence of university or professional opportunities, it is useful to explore specific examples. Descriptions are provided below of four sports – one from each quadrant in Table 10.1: basketball (professional and university pathways), rowing (university pathway), triathlon (professional pathway), team handball (no professional or university pathway). Data for these sections were obtained from archival materials and interviews with administrators for each sport.

Basketball

Thanks in large measure to its long history of professional play and the ubiquity of its presence in school and university sport programmes, basketball has enjoyed extensive media coverage and a high degree of cultural penetration. Facilities and coaching are widely available. There are many good players, so international teams are selected close to competitions, and trained together for only a short period of time, sometimes as few as 10 days.

There are 15 member organisations in USA Basketball (the sport's national governing body). There are additional organisations that provide opportunities to develop basketball skills, but that are not members of USA Basketball (e.g., public parks and recreation). The number and size of organisations contributing to basketball development reflect the sport's popularity and contribute to its cultural penetration, but also render a significant challenge when seeking to coordinate programmes or opportunities. Nevertheless, once a basketball player has attained sufficient skill to aspire to elite competition, it is expected that he or she will train and compete for a university or a professional team.

Participation in basketball typically begins at a young age. Children can learn the sport through an array of different organisations, including school, public recreation, the YMCA, Boys and Girls Clubs, and the JCCs. Most players who become elites have participated in a high school team. The Amateur Athletic Union (AAU) offers a parallel and complementary pathway. AAU programmes have experienced steady growth of between 3 and 7 per cent every year since the 1990s, with an estimated 170,000–190,000 boys and 160,000–180,000 girls playing on 28,000–32,000 AAU teams. Many athletes participate in AAU programmes during their school programme off season. Participation in AAU basketball increases exposure, thereby enhancing athletes' ability to obtain a university scholarship.

Because there are so many organisations offering an array of pathways in the sport, USA Basketball focuses primarily on providing international competition opportunities, which it sees as its appropriate role. It does not endeavour to identify or develop talent. In a year, on average, more than 300 men and women and 40 coaches participate in international events through USA Basketball. There are junior men's and women's teams, which are selected through USA Basketball's Youth Development Festival, a men's senior national team selected from NBA players who are willing to be available (many stars now demure), and a women's senior national team selected from WNBA and university teams. Selection of the men's senior national team has recently been altered such that teams are now selected by the team coach, rather than by a committee. It was hoped that this would improve the quality and thereby the success of the men's team. Coaches for the junior national teams are selected from leading high school and AAU coaches; coaches for the senior national men's and women's national teams are selected from among leading university and professional team coaches.

Reliance of the national team on professional players creates clashing demands. The NBA schedule runs from the fall to spring, which can conflict with preparation for international competition – a matter that is important so that players can learn to play together under international rules (which are different from NBA rules). Further, professional players have other commitments, such as those to their sponsors, which could cause them to sacrifice income (or even to breach a contract) in order to play for the national team.

The situation is even more difficult for women players. The WNBA plays its games from May to September to avoid conflict with the NBA's season. This typically conflicts with international competition. Further, some women on the senior team are attending university, so international competition can conflict with summer school classes that may be required for them to graduate or to retain their eligibility to compete for their university team. Some American women play in leagues overseas, which can lead to exhaustion as they try to juggle commitments to their professional team and the American national team.

USA Basketball is able to exert pressure for favourable competition times. The international community wants to see the highest level of competition, so they make an effort to accommodate the NBA's schedule. This ensures not only that American athletes will be able to represent their country, but it also allows foreign athletes who play in the NBA to return home to play for their own national teams.

Because basketball players are competing at elite levels outside of their participation in the national team, American athletes are not dependent on their NGB for financial support. Players from the men's and women's professional leagues receive no financial incentives for their participation, although USA Basketball covers players' expenses (e.g., food, travel, hotels) and insures players' professional contracts in case of injury. Even when players receive bonuses provided by the USOC's Operation Gold (which provides financial awards to athletes who win medals at the Olympics), they typically contribute their bonuses to charity. University players receive a small amount of funding while competing for the national team (approximately $150 per week). The amount they are allowed to receive is limited by the NCAA, which uses its authority over athletes' eligibility for university competition to restrict their right to earn money. High school athletes (who compete as members of the junior team) do not receive any payments beyond their expenses. One reason is that payment could make them ineligible for a scholarship to play university basketball.

Rowing

Rowing has long been a university sport for men, and has grown substantially as a university sport for women since passage of

Title IX. The sport is an attractive one to include for women because of the numbers of women who can be accommodated, which enables the sport to contribute significantly to universities' endeavours to meet Title IX gender equity requirements. Indeed, there are more universities offering rowing for women than for men. However, the sport is limited by the requirement that a large navigable body of water be available nearby – a requirement that makes the sport impractical for many universities.

The presence of the sport at university level has also encouraged creation of some high school programmes, as the availability of university scholarships and the presence of alumni from university rowing programmes have fostered some high school demand. Since universities typically recruit their athletes from high schools, rowers who have not competed in a high school programme find it difficult to obtain a university scholarship. Nevertheless, most parts of the country still lack any high school rowing. The sport has been slow to expand through high schools for four reasons: (a) limited availability of facilities; (b) the costs for equipment; (c) too few qualified coaches; and (d) the lack of a high school rowing tradition. USRowing (the sport's NGB) has sought to mitigate the negative effect that the small number of high school programmes has on scholarship opportunities by allowing university coaches to recruit during the first few days of the national championships for rowing clubs.

The sport has a modest but growing base of clubs. The growth in clubs has been encouraged by the presence of alumni from university rowing who seek to continue their careers as athletes or coaches after completing their 4 years of eligibility for university competition. Most clubs struggle to find adequate funding, and there is no national programme to help fund club development. Clubs typically rely on public recreation or the local authority responsible for waterways to enable storage of equipment and access to appropriate bodies of water. Coaching talent remains scarce – a matter that USRowing has been endeavouring to address through coaching clinics offered two or three times per year plus a coaching education programme that is supported through readings and DVDs. USRowing promotes club development through a Club-of-the-Year award, which is decided on the basis of six criteria: performance, community outreach, service to rowing, USRowing participation, technology (including communications), and safety. There is one winner nationally. The award is honorary, not remunerative.

The sport remains strongest in the north-eastern part of the country and has some strength in the northwest. Elsewhere, it is growing slowly, if at all. Wherever high school or university programmes exist, they have helped provide a nucleus for the sport's overall growth because school and university pro- grammes are far better funded than club programmes. As a result, USRowing is endeavouring to serve development of rowing in the schools by accommodating school teams in USRowing regattas whenever possible. (Otherwise, schools run their own regattas.) Since school rules differ from USRowing and international rules, school teams must race separately from club teams, even when USRowing is the organiser. Further, schools and universities emphasise sweeps, rather than sculls, so sculling remains predominantly for a set of club-only races. Schools have been reticent to incorporate sculling into their programmes because the skill and coaching requirements are so high, and the number of rowers who are served is compara- tively low.

Although American men and women are consistently among the best rowers in the world, USRowing recognises two funda- mental challenges to its continued growth and success: costs and training for elite competition. During the year, USRowing offers development camps for senior men and women and under-23 men and women at both lightweight and heavy- weight levels. Camps are offered during the summer months, usually lasting around six weeks. Athletes must apply for admis- sion to the camps and must cover their own costs. There are also camps for the national teams. Rowers are invited or selected for those camps.

In the absence of any professional opportunities, USRowing supports its most elite athletes – approximately 40 every year. Both men and women are supported, although a few more men than women typically earn support. For 2007, these elite ath- letes (based on performance in international competition) were awarded US$1,000 per month. They also obtained medical insurance coverage (separately) and could earn bonuses for winning performances at international events during the year. Rowers were not allowed to earn more than US$19,000 from stipend and bonuses combined. Although the supplemental income is helpful to rowers, it is insufficient for living and com- petition costs, so rowers must find means to supplement their incomes.

Costs remain an even more significant barrier to rowers work- ing their way into this top group. USRowing has sought to find means to reduce costs. It has negotiated a rebate programme to reduce the cost for clubs to purchase an outboard motor, and it has established a Task Force on Access, Affordability, and Diver- sity. Nevertheless, resources remain insufficient to foster the desired levels of growth and competitive excellence.

Triathlon

Triathlon is a sport largely driven through its events, as it is not a school or university sport, but provides opportunities to become professional through the prize money offered at many events. Participation in USA Triathlon-sanctioned events requires only that an athlete is a member of USA Triathlon (which is the NGB); it does not require club membership, although many participants do join clubs. Triathletes are eligible to become professional upon meeting the qualification standards set by USA Triathlon. Once qualified, they are eligible to compete for prize money in sanctioned events. The media presence afforded by professional triathlon events, particularly the Ironman World Championship and the ITC World Cup, is essential to promoting interest in the sport. While few professional triathletes can afford to live solely on their competitive earnings, professional opportunities for the participants help to fund elite competitors, and help to recruit promising athletes into the sport.

Since triathlon is not ensconced in the schools, it cannot rely on schools to promote the sport or to develop its athletes. However, many elite triathletes come to the sport from swimming, track, and cross-country running where they have competed via school sport structures. Many have exhausted their eligibility to compete at university level in their sport of choice. Rather than retiring at age 22, they choose to put their skills to use as a triathlete. Unlike sports that are developed through the schools, triathlon in the United States has no development pathway from entry as a child to professional status. That is not to say that opportunities do not exist at all levels. USA Triathlon supports its athletes through clubs, age group commissions, and national team programmes. It also offers training opportunities through elite camps and clinics, and sanctions more than 1,300 events every year.

USA Triathlon is increasingly concerned to develop athletes earlier in their careers. Although there is no systematic development system for school-aged children, local clubs are encouraged to provide opportunities for young triathletes. Youth (ages 7–15) and Junior (16–19) participation is one of the fastest growing divisions within the sport. Most youth participants compete in youth-only triathlons called 'Kids Triathlons'. The distances are short, and participants compete within one of four age groups (7–8, 9–10, 11–12, 13–15). Youth in the thirteen to fifteen age group and junior athletes can participate in Youth Elite Cup or Junior Elite Cup competitions, which are sprint events. Youth and Junior athletes have a number of camp-based training opportunities available to them through USA Triathlon. Like the Cup competitions, camps are designed for elite competitors.

The only relationship between Triathlon and the schools occurs via the university club sport system. There are approximately 72 university triathlon clubs affiliated to USA Triathlon. These clubs are not part of the NCAA. USA Triathlon operates a collegiate national championship for its university club members. It also supports a team of up to eight university triathletes who live and train at the USOTC in Colorado Springs during their summers away from school. These athletes may be selected from university triathlon clubs, but have also been selected on the basis of their performance in a single sport such as cross-country, track, or swimming at an NCAA competition.

Attracting and retaining young participants is an ongoing challenge, as the comparatively low costs and high visibility of school-based sports pull participants away. The problem is exacerbated by the sporadic nature of club development, the dependence of clubs on volunteer labour, and the high costs of participation. Club training requires pool rental, which can be difficult to obtain and expensive to purchase. Participants require increasingly expensive equipment, particularly a triathlon bike. Travel and accommodation costs for events are also significant. Not surprisingly, nearly half of USA Triathlon members report household incomes of over US$100,000. The majority of potential participants simply cannot afford to take part.

The reliance on individual and club-based training for athlete development has helped triathlon to skirt the age-related bias associated with sports that rely extensively on school and university systems. Triathletes can develop at their own pace without fear of being 'cut'. More than 50 per cent of triathletes are between the ages of 30 and 50 years. It is possible to take up the sport as an adult and advance to the professional level – something that would be inconceivable in most sports.

Team handball

Team handball lacks the institutional support of the other sports discussed in this chapter. The United States does field a team in team handball for elite international competition; however the sport has neither a strong base in American schools nor opportunities to compete at the professional level. While there is a national team, neither the men's team nor the women's team has been successful in Olympic competition. In fact, neither team was able to qualify for an Olympic Games after competing as hosts in 1996. Neither the men nor the women have ever managed an Olympic medal.

Lacking any school or professional presence in the United States, team handball has negligible cultural penetration. Because it does not follow the typical school-based sport development path, it relies on recruiting athletes from clubs (which exist only in a few large cities, such as Atlanta, Houston, and Los Angeles), other popular sports (such as basketball, volleyball, and soccer), and the US military. Athletes who wish to become members of the national team gain exposure by competing in club competitions.

In order to attract athletes into the sport, those who participate in high school or university sports are encouraged to attend open try-outs if they meet the physical requirements (women who are 180 centimetres or taller and men who are 193 centimetres or taller). Nearly all participants, including those selected for the national team, have come to team handball after successful careers in a school or university team sport. Team handball provides athletes who have completed their NCAA eligibility in their primary sport with the chance to continue elite participation, perhaps even at a higher level (e.g., Olympics, Pan-Am Games) because the pool of team handball athletes is small.

Although team handball is not part of the school or university sport system, it enjoys a strong presence at the military academies, particularly West Point and the Air Force Academy. The connection between the military and team handball continues beyond university, as team handball is supported by the military's World Class Athlete Program, and American soldiers stationed in Europe have formed teams to compete against local clubs. Consequently, the military remains a significant source of elite players.

As a sport that receives little funding and has a weak development system, it has adopted two different training strategies for national teams. The preferred strategy was to house the men's and women's teams at the USOTC in Colorado Springs, as was done from 1984 to 1988. The current training centre for the women's national team is located at the State University of New York at Cortland. Players have access to state-of-the-art athletic facilities at the university. They are eligible for on-campus housing if they are enrolled in classes, or live off campus if they are not. They are eligible for health insurance through the USOC, but are responsible for their own expenses, including travel to tournaments. The men's team has a more diffused training programme, as athletes live and train all over the country. Consequently, coaches for the men's team do not have the same level of control that coaches of the women's team enjoy.

The USOC would prefer to see the sport developed through schools as this would enable rapid cultural penetration. However, there is little indication that this could occur. Americans are largely unfamiliar with the sport, which receives little media attention and is often confused with a (very different) recreational sport of the same name. Further, the sport competes for facilities with already popular school sports like basketball and volleyball. The sport's problems have been exacerbated by the criticisms that have been levelled at its administration – driven, in part, by the sport's limited development. USA Team Handball, the organisation that functioned as the sport's NGB, was decertified by the USOC in 2006. Since that time, the USOC has assumed responsibility for governing the sport. They have chosen to focus on producing successful Olympic teams, rather than building a grassroots base.

The lack of grassroots development impedes efforts to popularise the sport, attract athletes, and build a successful national team. To foster development, national and club teams perform nearly 40 exhibition games each year to introduce Americans to the sport, and the USOC has produced a kit so that physical education teachers can introduce the sport in their classes. The kit has had no noticeable impact. Meanwhile, club development is hindered as the sport competes with established indoor sports, particularly volleyball and indoor soccer, for access to public facilities.

A few universities have supported club teams from time-to-time, but the presence and continuation of university club teams has depended on the presence of someone who has the experience and enthusiasm necessary to run the club. Since there are few university students who have played the sport, and fewer who have the skills to establish and maintain a club, the sport has struggled to establish university clubs. Further, since those clubs that have been established have relied on a student entrepreneur, they have often folded once the student graduates.

Observations and implications

The examples above illustrate the vital roles that university and professional sport play in American sport development. University sport provides facilities and coaching for elite athletes that might not otherwise be afforded. Professional sport provides an incentive and sometimes even a venue for athletes who have exhausted their eligibility for university competitions to train and compete. When both are present, they may compensate for the lack of a sport club tradition in the United States.

Nevertheless, from the standpoint of developing an elite corps of athletes, neither university nor professional sport is optimal. Athletes who compete professionally owe first fealty to the demands of their franchises and careers, not to national representation. Eligibility for university sport ends after 4 years, when most athletes are barely into their 20s – too soon for most to have honed themselves adequately for international competition. Further, professional and university sport systems seek the best athletes they can find, even if those athletes come from overseas, with the result that elites are as likely be trained for other national teams as for American teams (perhaps even more, as in ice hockey).

When both university and professional sports are available, there is no incentive to develop a club system to foster elite development, even if the lack of clubs hinders overall development. However, when a university or a professional option is missing, clubs are essential. In the absence of a university opportunity, clubs are necessary to develop talent; in the absence of a professional opportunity, clubs are essential to enable athletes to train and compete beyond their university years. That is why rowing and triathlon have each worked to establish clubs throughout the country.

Yet the absence of a sport club tradition makes them difficult to establish. American media and sporting traditions focus on school, university, and professional sport with the result that clubs are merely a sporting afterthought. Thus, when a sport lacks either, it also lacks the necessary cultural penetration to create specialist coaches, recruit skilled athletes, or stake a claim on facilities (as, e.g., in team handball). This is why all American sports seek to obtain a foothold in schools and universities, and why most harbour dreams of professionalisation.

It is a vicious cycle that American sport is unable to break: the university and professional systems inhibit the formation of a club network; formation of a club network requires the cultural penetration that university and/or professional sport enable. Government is unwilling to intervene. In this case, politics determine policy, as American antistatism continues to dictate that the federal government should take no role, and state governments have followed suit. Consequently, the American system remains different from others throughout the world – a fact in which most American policymakers and sport administrators take pride. American exceptionalism (Gutfield, 2002; Lockhart, 2003) is so well grounded in American sport policy that American sport managers borrow extensively from one another, but rarely from outside US borders.

Sport development in the United States provides a distinctive example of a laissez faire system. The seeming chaos may, in fact, represent market forces at work, although the dominant role of schools and universities depends substantially (though not uniquely) on government funding. Nevertheless, the social, cultural, and economic forces engendered by the system make it difficult to grow clubs and to sustain high-level national representation. What the system best illustrates is the challenge of building elite athletes in the absence of policy coordination.

References

Beall, G. (1973) In *Congressional Record*, Washington, DC: Government Printing Office, p. 32769.

Bernard, A.B. and Busse, M.R. (2004) Who wins the Olympic Games: Economic resources and medal totals, *Review of Economics and Statistics*, 86, 413–417.

Blustein, P. (2004) Winners with wallets: Richest nations tend to haul in most Olympic medals, *Washington Post*, 28 August, p. E1.

Chalip, L. (1995) Policy analysis in sport management, *Journal of Sport Management*, 9, 1–13.

Chalip, L., Johnson, A. and Stachura, L. (eds.) (1996) *National Sports Policies: An International Handbook*, Westport, CT: Greenwood Press.

Collins, M. (2004) Epilogue: Eastern European sport: Which ways from the current crossroads? *International Journal of the History of Sport*, 21, 833–843.

Covell, D. (2001) The role of corporate sponsorships in intercollegiate athletics, *Sport Marketing Quarterly*, 10, 245–247.

Duderstadt, J.J. (2000) *Intercollegiate Athletics and the American University: A University President's Perspective*, Ann Arbor, MI: University of Michigan Press.

Eccles, J.S., Barber, B.L., Stone, M. and Hunt, J. (2003) Extracurricular activities and adolescent development, *Journal of Social Issues*, 59, 865–889.

Ford, G. (1974) In defense of the competitive urge, *Sports Illustrated*, 8 July, pp. 16–23.

Fulks, D.L. (2000) *Revenues and Expenses of Division I and II Intercollegiate Athletics Programs: Financial Trends and Relationships*, Overland Park, KS: National Collegiate Athletic Association.

Green, M. and Houlihan, B. (2005) *Elite Sport Development: Policy Learning and Political Priorities*, New York: Taylor & Francis.

Gutfield, A. (2002) *American Exceptionalism: The Effects of Plenty on the American Experience*, Brighton, UK: Sussex Academic Press.

Handler, J.F. (1992) Postmodernism, protest, and the new social movements, *Law and Society Review*, 26, 697–731.

Johnson, D.K.N. and Ali, A. (2004) A tale of two seasons: Participation and medal counts at the summer and winter Olympic Games, *Social Science Quarterly*, 85, 974–993.

Jones, J. (1973) *Memo to The President.* Gerald R. Ford Library, Box 29, President's Commission on Olympic Sports: Records, May 24.

Lockhart, C. (2003) *The Roots of American Exceptionalism: History, Institutions and Culture*, New York: Palgrave Macmillan.

Müller, E., Zallinger, G. and Ludescher, F. (eds.) (1999) *Science in Sport*, New York: Taylor & Francis.

Quadagno, J. and Street, D. (2005) Ideology and public policy: Antistatism in American welfare state transformation, *Journal of Policy History*, 17, 52–71.

Riordan, J. (1993) The rise and fall of Soviet Olympic champions, *Olympika: The International Journal of Olympic Studies*, 2, 25–44.

Shaw, G. (1972) *Meat on the Hoof: The Hidden World of Texas Football*, New York: St. Martin's Press.

Sperber, M.A. (2001) *Beer and Circus: How Big-Time College Sports is Crippling Undergraduate Education*, New York: Henry Holt.

Standard and Poor's (2004) Bahamas leads medal tally at Athens 2004 Olympics. *Custom Index Solutions Research Report*, Available at http://www.sirca.org.au/20040830_CIS Research.pdf (retrieved 23 January 2007).

Stotlar, D.K. and Wonders, A. (2006) Developing elite athletes: A content analysis of US National Governing Body systems, *International Journal of Applied Sports Sciences*, 18, 121–144.

US General Accountability Office (2001) *Intercollegiate Athletics: Four-Year Colleges' Experiences Adding and Discontinuing Teams* (GAO No. 01-297), Washington, DC: US Government Printing Office.

Weiss, O. (2001) Identity reinforcement in sport, *International Review for the Sociology of Sport*, 36, 393–405.

Conclusion

Mick Green and Barrie Houlihan

Introduction

Our primary aim in this book was to build upon our knowledge and understanding of what has become known as 'a global sporting arms race' (Oakley and Green, 2001; UK Sport, 2006). Over the past decade, in particular, power struggles between nations to win medals and trophies on the international stage have clearly intensified. Alongside this intensification of effort, a growing body of evidence has emerged that suggests governments and national sporting organisations throughout the world spend increasing sums of money in their quest for international (Olympic) success (Green and Houlihan, 2005; De Bosscher et al., 2006; Jackson, 2006; UK Sport, 2006). This body of research also points to the requirement for a systematic and strategic approach to elite athlete development if nations are to realise their international sporting ambitions.

The framework developed by Green and Houlihan (2005) – indicating strong government intervention and support, substantial financial investment (governmental and/or Lottery funds), state-of-the-art elite-focused facilities, sophisticated coaching, sports science and sports medicine support, and a coherent competition calendar tailored to the requirements of elite performers – was either the point of reference or the point of departure for the authors of the nine country chapters. In other words, on the one hand, is there evidence to sustain the findings of Green and Houlihan (and others), which suggest that we are witnessing a trend towards homogeneity of the constituent parts that make up elite sport development systems? Or, on the other hand, are nations either constrained or bound by historical, cultural and/or institutional specificity in the ways in which elite athletes are identified, developed, funded and supported? In short, is there room within the global homogeneity thesis for diversity amongst nations? One way of addressing these questions, as indicated in Chapter 1, is to explore the argument that concerns regarding the extent of policy convergence between countries are provoked by pressures linked to globalisation, commercialisation and governmentalisation.

Common pressures for convergence

Globalisation

Any interrogation of globalisation as a guiding lens for developments in elite sport systems is inherently problematic as there is a tendency to concentrate on description of effects, for example, to describe similarities between elite development systems rather than to explore particular causes. Following this line of reasoning, evidence from the country studies points to the impact of globalisation in terms of its effects: all countries bar the United States exhibit many of the dimensions identified by Green and Houlihan (2005), indicating apparent convergence. Yet, this draws attention to at least two problems. Perhaps self-evidently, the first problem is that this does not tell us much about what has brought about change in different national contexts. If the cause is external, then what is the source? It is possible to argue that the source of change is/has been provoked by the Olympic movement or the global media but these are ultimately unconvincing because any pressure exerted is at best indirect and ultimately weak, particularly when viewed from the position of relatively affluent and successful 'sports powers'. One other possible explanation is that convergence stems from the 'coincidence' of similar domestic problems arising from political and economic globalisation. That is, countries have to position themselves globally, not just in relation to immediate neighbours or even regionally and, increasingly, countries also face pressures to compete for inward investment and markets on a global scale. The upshot is that countries face the domestic problem of creating and maintaining a regional/global profile at the same time as maintaining a distinct national identity. Hence, the paradox of using increasingly similar instruments to demonstrate national distinctiveness, for example, flags, anthems, participation in the Olympic Games, and national sporting 'heroes' brandishing medals and trophies on the winner's podium.

A second and perhaps more fundamental problem with the convergence thesis is the selection of variables. In this respect, Green and Houlihan (2005) suggest that four variables or dimensions are crucial for a strong elite development system: state-of-the-art facilities; financial support for full-time training; sophisticated sports science and medicine provision; and an elite-focused (increasingly Olympic-focused) competition structure. On this basis at least, then, there is a case to support the argument for convergence among most of the nine countries. However, such a conclusion could distract attention from the distinctiveness of different nations. For example, France, Poland and, perhaps to a lesser extent, Singapore exhibit far greater evidence of regulatory intervention than many other countries. As Bayle, Durand and Nikonoff argue in Chapter 6, 'France's machinery for centralised planning ensured a raft of legislative measures ... and regulations'. One effect of which was to effectively 'nationalise' the sports federations (national governing bodies, NGBs) 'in the name of the general interest and as a clear manifestation of the state's desire to play ... a supervisory role'. In Poland, Jolanta Żyśko explains 'that when it comes to shaping sport policies, in the Polish system it is the extent and depth of state intervention that stands out'. Key features of this interventionist model, according to Żyśko, include 'specific normative acts and the dominant and intervening role of public sports administration, notably of the central administration body – the Ministry of Sport' (Chapter 7).

Further distinctiveness is evident in the Norwegian case with the government's arm's length approach, and the persistence of 'social democratic' values within NIF/NOC, illustrated by restrictions on early-age entry to competitive events and the ban on using high altitude chambers for training. The reluctance of the Japanese government to embrace fully the principles of elite sport and to retain a historic 'concern with "physical education" or "social physical education"' is yet further confirmation of exceptionality among our nine cases (Yamamoto, Chapter 3). Thus although Sparvero, Chalip and Green (Chapter 10) argue for US exceptionalism, the case can also be made for (at least) modest exceptionalism elsewhere. Therefore, claims for convergence need to be made cautiously and due attention needs to be paid to the context within which apparently similar policy instruments are being used.

Commercialisation

We can view commercialisation in two forms – commodification and values. There appears to be evidence for the increasing commodification of athletes through both state and commercial sponsorship, albeit moderated in some countries by a concern for the athlete's post-sport career. This balancing act is arguably best exemplified in the case of France. In France, the state provides its elite athletes with 'contracts' which guarantee access to the labour market. According to Bayle, Durand and Nikonoff, these contracts provide not only a way to balance the demands of an athlete's sporting life, but also a means for ensuring 'professional activity at the end of [her/his] sporting career'. At the same time, the French state 'sponsors' its successful athletes with (tax-free) remuneration in the form of bonus payments for Olympic medals; just one of many countries to adopt this form of 'state sponsorship' of elite sport in the early twenty-first century.

The case of Norway provides yet another perspective to the different modes of the commodification of athletes. Grant-aid is provided for Norwegian elite athletes, but there is a far greater concern than in other countries for the overall well-being of its elite performers. As Augestad and Bergsgard (Chapter 8) note, the country's 'lifetime support programme' enables the athlete 'to fulfil a "double career"' because in Norway studying for a career after sport, alongside training for elite success, is seen as an important feature of its concept of the '24-hour athlete'. At the other extreme, while China provides what is termed, 'whole country support for the elite sport system', in reality the Chinese 'system' benefits only the most successful of its elite athletes. There is a dark side then, or as Fan Hong puts it, a 'brutal' approach to the treatment of the country's athletes: in 2004, 400,000 boys and girls trained at more than 3,000 sports schools, yet 95 per cent of these would leave school with no formal educational qualifications (Chapter 2).

Arguably, clearer examples of commercialisation can be seen in the growing adoption by countries of business-like values in approaches to funding elite sport. The manifestation of business-like values is evident in the establishment of performance targets, strategic planning, selectivity (of athletes and sports targeted for funding usually focused on the best medal prospects) and a growing trend of funding decisions based on the likelihood of achieving a return on investment. While there is evidence of business imperatives driving many countries' approaches to elite development, this has to be tempered by an acknowledgement of political (domestic) exigencies to focus on culturally significant sports and which can often override the turn towards business methods.

In New Zealand, in the context of broader market reform in the mid-1980s, Collins (Chapter 9) points to the government's concern to cultivate 'very hard-headed, cost effective, non-egalitarian policies'. Alongside the introduction of business concepts, the prioritisation of Olympic sports became part of the drive to target 'events that matter' to New Zealand, with seven 'priority sports' identified for increased funding (including cricket, netball, rowing, rugby and yachting). Sports organisations were no longer operating in an environment where they might expect an entitlement to government support, 'they were now required to show what the "investment" would return to SPARC [Sport and Recreation New Zealand]'. The case of Singapore is also significant in this respect. Within the context of strong government intervention, the development of sports excellence in Singapore has assumed a very prominent position in a very short period of time in the country's drive to raise its international profile. An important aspect of this rapid drive for international sporting success was the decision taken by the Singapore Sports Council in the early 1990s to 'focus on certain sports from which potential for success was greatest' (Teo, Chapter 4). The quest for rapid achievement is perhaps not surprising as it should be remembered that Singapore, 'as an independent nation', has yet to win an Olympic medal and its early focus on seven 'Core sports' was just one part (albeit significant) of the country's unabashed pursuit of Olympic glory.

Governmentalisation

It is hard to deny that governmentalisation (broadly meaning a focus on power relations conceived as the direction of conduct and the shaping of choice) (cf. Dean, 2007) has increased, either by direct management of elite sport systems (e.g., China, Singapore, France, New Zealand) or by close supervision and monitoring by governments of national sporting organisations (e.g., Japan, Poland). Perhaps the weakest example of governmentalisation is evident in increased state funding, either direct forms of funding or indirectly through lottery (lotto) mechanisms, but where the government is a relatively distant partner in the operations of sports organisations' development of elite performers (Norway is a good example here). In all cases, the significance of domestic institutional constraints is evident – most clearly in the United States (non-interventionism) but also in New Zealand (neoliberalism), Poland (state dependence), France and Singapore (regulation), Norway (social democratic culture), Germany (federalism), Japan (suspicion of state manipulation of sport) and China (one party centralist domination). Such 'constraints' can be viewed as a mix of deeply rooted culture (Norway, France, United States) and recent (post World War II) experience (Germany, Japan, Poland).

To take one prominent example, increasing governmentalisation through the establishment of a state-led apparatus for the delivery and management of sport is evident in Singapore. Through the Singapore Sports Council (SSC), the government has shaped, channelled and guided its national sporting organisations in such a way that they now operate within what Rose (1999, p. 22) terms a 'regulated freedom'. Teo's account of the trials and tribulations of the Singapore Athletics Association's (SAA) relationship with the Sports Council and the Committee on Sporting Singapore (CoSS), chaired by the Minister of Sport and 'tasked by the MCDS (Ministry of Community Development and Sports) to formulate a strategic blueprint for the future of Singapore sports policy', amply demonstrates this phenomenon. Enduring worries regarding the leadership and administrative capacities of the SAA were at the heart of the government's concerns. While national sport organisations (NSOs) were encouraged 'to set clear directions and goals for themselves', failure to comply with the SSC's Code of Governance for NSOs meant sanctions in terms of future funding arrangements. For the 'failing' SAA, its inability to meet a number of management-related targets resulted in its removal from the SSC's list of 'Core sports'. In short, the organisation had failed 'to modernise and had not adopted effective organisational administrative strategies befitting a Core sport' (Teo, Chapter 4). This scenario has clear overtones with the experience of the NSOs for athletics in Australia, Canada and the United Kingdom (Green and Houlihan, 2005, 2006).

Mechanisms for convergence and processes of learning

Intermingled with the broader pressures for convergence relating to globalisation, commercialisation and governmentalisation are the processes of policy learning, path dependency and the notion of 'policy determining politics'. In exploring these concepts as part of a cross-national analytic framework for an interrogation of policy convergence (cf. Klein and Marmor, 2006, p. 905), it is possible to gain a deeper understanding of elite sport developments in different domestic contexts. It is important here to emphasise the dynamic (temporal) nature of policy convergence (cf. Bennett, 1991; Pierson, 2000) in order to avoid the concept being used as a synonym for similarity. As Bennett (1991, pp. 219, 231) argues, 'To know that countries are alike tells us nothing about convergence. There must be movement over time toward some identified common point ... different processes may be observed, intermingling with each other, with some more relevant for some states at some times and for some dimensions of policy'.

While it is possible to argue that the range of policy instruments available for implementation of an elite-focused policy is remarkably similar in different social, cultural and political contexts (cf. Green and Oakley, 2001; UK Sport, 2006), it is also possible to argue that implementation relies (to a greater or lesser extent) on path dependent relationships – relationships irrevocably bound up with, and influenced by, processes of policy transfer, learning and lesson drawing. Indeed, one of the ways in which policy analysis might be improved by cross-national comparative research is where 'one hopes to draw lessons about why some policies appear promising and doable, promising and impossible, or doable but not promising' (Klein and Marmor, 2006, p. 905). The final conceptual perspective to be explored is whether 'policies determine politics' or, conversely, whether 'politics determine policy'? (cf. Lowi, 1972; Heinelt, 2005). The latter asserts that 'distinctive and durable national policymaking styles are causally linked to the policies of states' (Freeman, 1985, p. 469). The former, on the other hand, suggests that:

> Policy change is not only the result of windows of opportunity suddenly opening as the result of some upheaval in the economic or political climate. Policy change itself may open such windows by demonstrating that the previously unthinkable has become doable.
>
> (Klein and Marmor, p. 904)

Our chief concern then is to explore the evidence for policy convergence among the nine countries against a backdrop of intermingling pressures emerging from processes of globalisation, commercialisation and governmentalisation. More specifically, we consider how convergence might be defined and what mechanisms for convergence and processes of policy learning are evident. As part of this analysis, we seek to understand where countries look for lessons that might be applicable in their own locales. Finally, we explore factors that might inhibit convergence amongst nations, in particular, social, cultural and political specificities that may limit the extent to which countries are able to adopt (potentially fruitful) lessons from other jurisdictions.

Pierson (2000) argues that analysts' use of the concept of path dependence tends to fluctuate between a broader and narrower conception. The latter is helpful here. For Levi (1997, p. 28), this narrower view suggests that:

> Path dependence has to mean, if it is to mean anything, that once a country or region has started down a track, the costs of reversal are very high … the entrenchments of certain institutional arrangements obstruct an easy reversal of the initial choice.

This conception of path dependence in which previous steps in a particular direction bring about further movements in the same or similar direction invokes the idea of 'increasing returns' (Pierson, 2000, p. 252), which suggests that the likelihood of further steps along the same path increases with each move along that path. This is because the relative benefits of the current activity compared with other possible options increase over time. Put another way, the costs of exit from a particular path, and turning to an alternative route, rise. Increasing returns can also be viewed as self-reinforcing or offering positive feedback processes.

These ideas have particular resonance for elite sport policy development. For example, in Green and Houlihan's (2005) study, the case of Australia is instructive. So embedded are the institutional and administrative arrangements for elite sport development in Australia, that the federal government has been unable or unwilling to retrench from a position where it is highly supportive of elite sport policy. This is despite calls for at least the past 25 years for a re-thinking of the government's overt emphasis on elite development due to a perception that it is detrimental to mass participation programmes (cf. Commonwealth of Australia, 1999). Notwithstanding recent federal government rhetoric around extra funding for mass participation programmes (Department of Industry, Science and Resources, 2001), against a background of generalised concerns about rising obesity levels in the population, and in children and young people in particular, the political cost of retrenchment from support for elite development was just too great for this to be a viable path to take. In short, as Klein and Marmor (2006, p. 903) explain, 'history matters'.

As Kay (2005, p. 558) argues, 'Path dependency encapsulates the insight that policy decisions accumulate over time ... [and which] restricts options for future policymakers'. Several crucial decisions taken over the past 25–30 years point to a strong argument for path dependency in the case of Australia. First, the decision to prioritise elite (Olympic) athlete development in the early 1980s – prominent here was the establishment of the Australian Institute of Sport in 1981 – was crucial as it signalled a significant break with previous government thinking about sport priorities following poor performances by Australian athletes at the 1976 Montreal Olympic Games (Stewart et al., 2004). This event can be viewed not only as a significant exogenous shock, but also as the 'critical juncture' or triggering event, 'which set development along a particular path' (Pierson, 2000, p. 263).

Second, the establishment of the Australian Sports Commission in 1985 as the country's leading governmental sporting agency reinforced the institutionalisation of government commitment to elite development – despite continuing official federal rhetoric around support for mass participation (cf. Booth, 1995; Armstrong, 1997; Commonwealth of Australia, 1999). Third, the decision to bid for the right to host the 2000 Olympic Games and the subsequent award in 1993 of the Games to Sydney meant that the government was not about to divert from this path – or at least not consider divergence until after the Games. Fourth, the decision taken after the Sydney Games – when political support for elite sport might have been expected to be on the wane – to maintain relatively lower levels of funding for mass participation programmes than for elite development suggests that change is highly unlikely in the near future at least.

Undeniably, Australia's elite athletes have enjoyed considerable medal-winning success at recent Olympic Games, and in 2000 and 2004 in particular. Therefore, with little evidence of a strong voice for the mass participant in Australia, and with such strong public and media support for elite success, it is hard to conceive of conditions in which the federal government would turn from the path chosen some 25 years ago. In this case, the political 'costs' of switching from the path of elite athlete development are deemed to be too high and it appears that, in Australia, the quest for sustained excellence at the international level has been difficult to forgo once established (Green, 2007a). As Pierson (2000, p. 259) argues in a different but related context, as social and political actors 'make commitments based on existing institutions and policies, their cost of exit from established arrangements generally rises dramatically'. The dynamics of increasing returns and positive feedback is evident here as steps taken in a particular direction by the Australian federal government towards greater support for elite development triggered 'a self-reinforcing dynamic' (Pierson, 2000, p. 260). In other words, the generation of increased numbers of Olympic medals and the concomitant positive (political) symbolism that attaches itself to a successful Olympic nation means that, for Australia at least, retrenchment from this position has become politically unthinkable (Green, 2007a).

It may well be the case that such is the symbolic strength of sport generally and elite, international sport success especially for Australians, that we would be hard pressed to find such an enduring engagement with, and political support for, elite athlete development in other countries. Indeed, in none of the nine countries in this collection we have found evidence of such enduring, embedded and institutionalised path dependent relationships in respect of governmental support for elite athlete development. This is not to argue that governmental support for elite (Olympic) success is not evident. Nor is it to suggest that it is either a minor element of government sport policy or that mechanisms for putting in place structures, systems and institutions for elite sport are not growing. Rather, although governments in nations as diverse as Japan, Singapore and New Zealand, and to a lesser extent, Norway, have prioritised elite sport development in recent years, none displays evidence of the level of (elite sport) policy entrenchment evident in Australia. However, what the preceding chapters do reveal is that the policy mechanisms or instruments that make up the

increasingly systematic support frameworks for elite development are remarkably similar in eight of the nine countries
investigated for this study. In this respect, the one country that
stands out as remarkably different is the United States. For different reasons, the Chinese approach to forging an elite athlete
development system also stands out.

The impact of China's re-appearance on the Olympic stage in
1984 after an absence of 32 years was nothing short of remark-
able: Chinese athletes won 15 gold medals and the country finished fourth in the Olympic medals table (although it should be
recognised that both the Soviet Union and the German
Democratic Republic boycotted the 1984 Games). International
(and especially Olympic) success is a hugely symbolic expression of the country's attempts to 'develop elite sport and make
China a superpower in the world' (Hong et al., 2005, p. 511).
Chinese success on the international sporting stage has to be
seen, however, in the light of much wider and deeper political
and economic change in the country. From the late 1970s, China
initiated profound economic reform in its attempts to integrate
with the global economy and to 'catch up with the Western capitalist world through modernisation' (2005, p. 513). These glob-
alising pressures are heavily laced with a desire to pronounce to
the Western world the country's ideological and economic
superiority and national revival. Such is the importance placed
on Olympic success, especially at the 'home' Olympic Games in
Beijing in 2008, that central government control and management is paramount: this is just too important an issue to be left
to the market as the country gradually embraces capitalism.
However, policy change is already predicted post 2008. As the
deputy minister of the China General Administration of Sport
explained:

Before the Beijing Olympics elite sport has got mighty support from
both the state and the people ... After the games the situation will
change. The government will speed up the process of the commercialisation of sport and will require elite sport to stand on its own two feet.
(quoted in Hong et al., 2005, p. 526)

Although we might expect China to be investing heavily in
support systems for its elite athletes as it builds to the Beijing
Games in 2008, as Fan Hong explains in Chapter 2, what is perhaps surprising is the similarity of mechanisms employed by
(communist) China to those employed by liberal democratic
nations (see also Tan and Green, 2007). These mechanisms characterise China's 'whole country support for the elite sport system' – *Juguo tizhi* (Hong, Chapter 2). Notably: substantial and

sustained central government support and funding; the targeting of specific sports for extra support; the creation of national training centres; the search for, and employment of, the very best coaches and sport scientists; the restructuring of national competitions such that the focus is now on Olympic sports, rules and regulations; and the ongoing support for 'one of the most effective systems in the world for systematically selecting sports stars from a very young age' (Hong et al., 2005, p. 516). This gives some credence to the policy convergence thesis, where 'a common problem ... plays the role of independent variable' (Hoberg, 1986, p. 357). The common problem in our case being the search for *the* optimum system for the 'production' of (Olympic) medal-winning athletes (Oakley and Green, 2001). It also provides some support for the 'policies determine politics' argument.

On one level, we might agree that the evidence suggests the pre-eminence of the policy sector, and policy convergence around a number of mechanisms for supporting elite sport development. Given our earlier description of policy convergence, it is important to note that there has been movement over time in China as policy-makers have adapted its elite sport system from principles first used in the former Soviet Union (e.g., sports schools, the use of the armed forces and very early-age talent identification systems). At the same time, however, such is the overpowering influence of the state in China that it is difficult not to conclude that the political system dominates the type of policy choices available. As Pierson (2000, p. 259) notes from a path dependency perspective, 'Policies ... backed by the coercive power of the state, signal to actors what has to be done and what cannot be done'. As Fan Hong (Chapter 2) notes, such is the strength of the political/ideological discourse underpinning Olympic success in China that alternative voices arguing for the promotion of other forms of sport were silenced.

The case for path dependency resonates with this analysis. Indeed, Pierson (2000, p. 260) argues that, 'Once established, basic outlooks on politics, ranging from ideologies to understandings of particular aspects of governments or orientations toward political groups or parties are generally tenacious. They are path dependent'. In short, elite sport development in China is dominated to a large degree by the political system and the strength of the one party state system, albeit at the same time revealing a framework for elite sport development that includes many of the policy mechanisms used in the West. What is evident from this examination of nine countries is that the assumption that the same policy problems predetermine the same solutions or responses must always remain open to empirical investigation.

This is very clear in the chapter by Sparvero, Chalip and Green (Chapter 10), who reveal the reluctance of the US federal government to intervene in the development of elite athletes: 'In this case, politics determine policy, as American antistatism continues to dictate that the federal government should take no role and state governments have followed suit'. Sport development in the United States, argue Sparvero, Chalip and Green, is indicative of a laissez-faire system and, within this 'seeming chaos', elite sport development is dominated by market forces (professional sports) and the predominant role of schools, colleges and universities, which do not rely uniquely on government funding.

Paradoxically, perhaps, we can also demonstrate path dependency in this case. As Sparvero, Chalip and Green explain, 'the social, cultural, and economic forces engendered by the system make it difficult to grow clubs and to maintain high-level representation. What the system best illustrates is the challenge of building elite athletes in the absence of policy coordination'. It should come as no surprise then to find that 'American exceptionalism is so well grounded in American sport policy that ... sport managers borrow extensively from one another, but rarely from outside US borders'. We should be cautious then in our claims for increasing 'homogenisation of elite sports systems' (UK Sport, 2006, p. 3) and take heed of Bennett's (1991, p. 230) line of reasoning whereby 'Findings of convergence on some aspects of policy and divergence on others may be far more common than we realise'.

Thus, although increasing global competition is encouraging nations to adopt a more strategic approach to elite sport development, in the United States 'there is no "system" for elite sport development' (Sparvero, Chalip and Green). Whether the relative decline in the United States' dominance of the Olympic medals table since the 'home' Olympics in Los Angeles in 1984 is due to the increasingly sophisticated approaches adopted by nations as diverse as South Korea, the United Kingdom and Japan, 'or is due to stagnation of the American system is not clear' (Sparvero, Chalip and Green). What is clearer, however, is that the delegation of elite athlete development by the federal government to sport organisations and the US Olympic Committee means that 'The United States stands in stark contrast to the trends in elite sport development that are commonly observed throughout the rest of the developed world' (Sparvero, Chalip and Green).

In contrast to the United States, the case of Singapore is illustrative of policy convergence, as well as revealing the significance of our earlier concern to draw attention to the intermingling influences of globalisation, governmentalisation and, to a lesser extent, commercialisation. Lionel Teo's chapter illustrates well how, from the early 1990s, the country's 'omni-present *Sport for All* strategy has … been eclipsed by a sports excellence strategy'. Moreover, the Singapore government has 'embarked on a vigorous campaign to capitalise on the exten-sive global value of sport to the nation'. Nation building, national identity, and increasing global presence are at the heart of Singapore's attempts, through elite sport success, to establish itself as a vibrant independent sovereign state. Indeed, the Ministry of Community Development and Sports (2001, p. 5) states that:

The reason we are proposing the creation of an environment for sports excellence is not because others are doing it per se, but because it is one of the missing pieces that verbalises, illustrates and energises a matter of the heart: national pride and international respect.

In just over 10 years, then, the Singapore government has put in place a framework for elite athlete development that bears many of the hallmarks found in Green and Houlihan's (2005) study of Australia, Canada and the United Kingdom: substan-tial and sustained central government funding and Lottery money; the prioritisation of seven 'Core sports' for higher levels of support; specialised elite facilities, in particular, the creation of a dedicated Sports Institute and Sports School; the profes-sionalisation of coaching, and the establishment of sophisti-cated sports science and medicine support. Moreover, unlike the United States, Singapore has actively searched for lessons from abroad in its quest to become an international sporting superpower. Not only has the country sought advice through its Coaching Advisory Committee commissioning experts from the Australian Sports Commission and the Coaching Association of Canada, it has also searched extensively for the best foreign coaches, as well as talented foreign athletes, 'to enhance Singa-pore's chances of medal honours' at the Olympic Games (Teo, Chapter 4).

Given the relatively recent adoption of a sports excellence strategy in Singapore, it is difficult to draw conclusions with any certainty in respect of whether the path the government has embarked upon for the strategic and unambiguous pursuit of Olympic medals is one from which it may divert if Olympic glory is not realised in the near future. However, we do have some indication that the institutionalisation of an elite sport-focused policy in the early 1990s is not about to be abandoned quickly. Building on the principle of priority sports established in 1993, in 2006 an additional $SGD7 million was allocated 'specifically to nurture and prepare elite athletes for the 2008 and 2012 Olympic Games' (Teo, Chapter 4).

Moreover, as Singapore's Minister of Sport stated, in explaining the country's recent *Glory for the Nation* project: 'In this next stage, we're focussing our resources on the precious few whom we think really do have the potential to win an Olympic medal' (quoted in Tan, 2006, p. 55). Self-reinforcing pressures, positive feedback and increasing returns are all evident in the Singapore case. Buoyed by the country's best ever medal count in the 2002 Manchester Commonwealth Games (4 gold and 13 medals in total), increased funding in 2005 of some $SGD300 million for sports excellence up to 2010, and the establishment of a multi-million dollar organisational, administrative and institutional state-led infrastructure for sport, it would be difficult to foresee a future where the Singapore government diverted from its path to Olympic glory as it 'remains hopeful that the sports sector will equal or better its famed economic accomplishments' (Teo, Chapter 4).

In the case of New Zealand, Shane Collins (Chapter 9) charts the rapid change in the country's sport policy sector over the past 6 or 7 years. What is very clear again from this account is that, from the establishment of Sport and Recreation New Zealand (SPARC), the government's primary sporting agency, sport policy-makers in New Zealand have adopted many of the business model principles evident in the case of Singapore, as well as in many of the other countries explored in the preceding chapters, and in Green and Houlihan's study (2005, 2006). Accountability, performance targets, governance issues, annual and strategic planning, and return on investment are all now central to the realisation of SPARC's goals for elite sport. Priority sports, the setting of specific medal targets for different sports, and the establishment of a systematic, long-term approach to talent identification and development are also now vital components of the country's emergent system for elite sport development.

Evidence that the New Zealand government has introduced policies for developing and implementing an elite sport system that reveals convergence with other countries' systems, namely, evidence of policy movement over time rather than just similarity between systems, is amply demonstrated by Collins. From the publication of the report by the Sport, Fitness and Leisure Ministerial Taskforce in 2001 (Ministerial Taskforce, 2001), the funding of sport changed rapidly from a situation where NSOs enjoyed an entitlement to support, to a situation where today NSOs are now required to meet government-driven targets and to show what this investment would return to SPARC.

The significance of our earlier recognition of the intermingling influences of globalisation, commercialisation and governmentalisation is also apparent in New Zealand. It is possible to argue that at least one of the pressures for change in the sport policy sector can be attributed to 'some of the most radical economic reforms of any western country' during the 1980s (Collins, Chapter 9). As in other countries governed by neoliberal regimes, the New Zealand government introduced 'a systematic programme of commercialisation [and privatisation] within the public sector' (Collins, Chapter 9). These political changes had a direct impact on sport, according to Collins, with the *Sport on the Move* report reinforcing the need for a clear investment ethos as opposed to providing grants with few strings attached. Given our concern to chart processes of 'change', or movement over time, it is worth remembering that during the 1980s there was a residue of public and governmental hostility to allocating large amounts of public funding to a small number of international athletes.

Yet, despite the reservations of the 1980s, which were related to concerns that, in a democratic society, principles of social equity would be compromised by moves toward an elite focus, the seeds of a much more pragmatic and business-like approach to elite sport had been sown. And, as in nations as diverse as Australia, China, Singapore and the United Kingdom, the importance of (rapid) international sporting success was such that the New Zealand government adopted an increasingly 'hands-on' approach in its relationships with NSOs. No longer would NSOs have the autonomy to do as they wished with government grant-aid. As Collins explains, SPARC signalled its growing preparedness 'to become more … directly involved in the management of elite sport … if NSOs were unable to demonstrate effective elite sport systems more direct forms of intervention were now to be considered'. Today, such is the degree of legitimisation for elite success by the government that NSOs are in little doubt that failure to produce (Olympic) medal-winning athletes will result in punitive sanctions. The sanction of withdrawing funding to 'failing' NSOs is emerging as a common indicator, in a number of countries, of the growing governmentalisation of the elite sport sector.

From this evidence it is possible on one level to make the case that in New Zealand the development of elite sport policy provides support for the 'politics determine policy' thesis. Yet, even allowing for the influences of broader macro-political and economic change, once the commitment to support elite athlete development had been taken by the government, was there an alternative path available (or set of policy choices) to pursue other than the one eventually chosen? What we find is that the set of policy choices chosen, and the subsequent policy mechanisms used, closely mirror those found in many other countries: substantial government support and funding; prioritised sports for increased funding; the building of a systematic approach to talent identification and development; and the identification of coaching, sports science and sports medicine as important areas for future investment and support. Moreover, as in other nations, and especially in Singapore and the United Kingdom, the perception in New Zealand was that speed was of the essence under current international sporting conditions where 'simply maintaining performance in a climate of increased demand for success ... is a laudable achievement' (UK Sport, 2006, p. 15). It is also possible here then to make the argument that a similar policy problem (mediocre sporting performances at international-level competitions such as the Commonwealth Games and Olympic Games) shaped the path along which New Zealand politicians and policy-makers would travel in order to realise their ambitions for elite sport.

A major assumption underpinning path dependency accounts is that of dynamic analysis; that is, 'a historical interrogation of how the [potential] drivers of policy change unravel themselves over time' (Kay, 2005, p. 559). And, as Kay also notes, a key benefit of such an analysis is that 'different *rates* of policy change' (p. 559) can be traced. This is a significant insight regarding the charting of, and analysis into, elite sport policy development and policy change in New Zealand (and elsewhere). The rate of policy change in New Zealand has been swift and can be related to the salience of policy learning for the country's policy-makers. Indeed, Collins explains that, In New Zealand, 'learning and adapting policies and programmes from other sporting systems was ... recognised as a method through which the country could improve its elite sport system. More important at this juncture however is Collins' claim that 'SPARC identified the need to be smart, innovative *and adapt quickly*' (emphasis added).

An assessment of the three 'explanations'

Policy learning

While there is much evidence in the preceding accounts of countries' awareness of policy developments in different jurisdictions, it is often the case that the need for learning from abroad is precipitated in times of 'crisis', e.g., poor performance at an Olympic Games, or failure to win a Test series, or a major international championship in a culturally significant sport, such as cricket (Australia), rugby union (New Zealand) or skiing

(Norway). There are however significant departures from this thesis. In the case of Japan, 'learning' from other countries is conducted in a systematic and ongoing fashion. According to Yamamoto (Chapter 3), 'the establishment of an effective communication network involving actors across all levels of sport and the strategic utilisation of information have become *the* most distinctive features of the Japanese elite sport system'. Part of the reason for such a dedicated emphasis on 'intelligence gathering' is the geographical position of Japan and the concern that the country is remote from the dominant elite international sport communities located in Europe and North America (Yamamoto, Chapter 3).

In Singapore and in China, the use of 'imported' coaches (as well as athletes in the case of Singapore) is a significant feature of the ways in which these two countries utilise knowledge transfer from abroad. In the case of Singapore it is possible to argue that the government is pre-empting crisis as its rapid development of an elite sport system is designed to win Olympic medals for the first time. Whatever the motive, it is increasingly clear that countries are more than willing to utilise forms of policy learning and policy transfer as 'quick fixes' in the race for Olympic glory.

It is also the case that the prevalence of policy learning is most common in areas of greatest uncertainty. The emergence of systematic approaches for elite sport development is not only a relatively recent phenomenon for many countries. It is also the case that the realisation of elite sport success is determined by increasingly small margins where the difference between winning a gold medal and fourth place 'failure' can often be measured in fractions of a second or in millimetres. It is not surprising then that countries turn to tried and tested methods in other locales. It would be unwise, however, to ignore the possibilities for negative lessons to be drawn and also to understand that it is likely for some form of 'cultural adaptation' to take place before any lessons learnt can be put into practice (cf. Dolowitz and Marsh, 1996, 2000; Green, 2007b). The one country that remains impervious to the need to look for lessons outside its own borders is the United States. Such is the extent of American exceptionalism in this respect that it is hard to imagine a scenario that would provoke the country to search for different ways of supporting its elite athletes.

Path dependency

Many of those countries with a relatively embedded system for elite athlete development (China, France, Germany, Norway) as well as those countries that have constructed their elite systems more recently (Japan, Singapore, New Zealand) show little sign of adopting a different 'route' to international sporting success. This may be due of course to the argument that it is still too early in many countries to explore responses to 'policy fatigue' and/or 'policy failure'. Yet even where there have been signs of failure these have often been ignored or interpreted as 'evidence' of the need to go even faster and further down the path already set. Norway, for example, experienced poor performances at the summer Olympic Games in 1984 and then the winter Games in 1988. The response was not to divert from the path recommended in a NIF/NOC report following the disappointment in 1984. Rather, the decision taken was to go ahead with a centralised organisation that housed a unified set of resources for the support of athletes and various sports (Augestad and Bergsgard, Chapter 8).

It is clear therefore that more time is needed before we might be able to conclude with any degree of certainty that path dependency is deeply ingrained within the systems for elite sport development in the countries discussed in the preceding chapters. We can however make the case for some degree of 'soft' path dependency inasmuch as that most countries display evidence of: specialised sporting facilities, substantial state funding, full-time athletes and the adoption of 'business' planning models.

Policy determines politics

The evidence for the thesis that 'policy determines politics' is mixed. On the one hand it is possible to argue that, yes, the policy mechanisms and instruments that 'make up' elite sport development systems and approaches in countries with significantly different political systems and culture are remarkably similar: Norway (social democratic); China (communist); New Zealand (neoliberal); and France, Singapore and Poland (statist). On the other hand, the United States is a major exception to this argument and there is little evidence, according to Sparvero, Chalip and Green, that the country will shift from a strong example of the 'politics determining policy' scenario. However, many other countries' adoption of similar systems (and where we have categorised them as falling under the 'policy determines politics' rubric) is heavily moderated by domestic 'politics': for example, China (disregard for human rights), Norway (protection of children's rights and the moral/ethical decision not to use high altitude chambers) and Germany (commitment to federalism and subsidiarity).

To conclude, it is clear that increasing global competition is encouraging a growing number of nations to adopt a more strategic approach to the development of elite athletes in order to differentiate themselves from 'rival' countries. The countries discussed in the previous chapters provide strong evidence of strategic approaches based increasingly around a homogenous model of elite sport development but with subtle domestic variations. As the financial costs of constructing an elite sport development system rise inexorably, the question facing all nations today is 'to what extent do you wish to be part of this game?' (UK Sport, 2006, p. 16). It is not without a certain irony then that we are drawn to the conclusion that, to rephrase a Corinthian ideal, for countries to establish and then to sustain a successful elite sport development system in the early twenty-first century they have to 'Pay up! Pay up! And play the game!'.

References

Armstrong, T. (1997) Government policy, in W. Vamplew, K. Moore, J. O'Hara, R. Cashman and I.F. Jobling (eds.), *The Oxford Companion to Australian Sport* (2nd Revised edn), Oxford: Oxford University Press, pp. 188–190.

Bennett, C.J. (1991) Review article: What is policy convergence and what causes it?, *British Journal of Political Science*, 21, 215–233.

Booth, D. (1995) Sports policy in Australia: Right, just and rational?, *Australian Quarterly*, 67(1), 1–10.

Commonwealth of Australia (1999) *Shaping Up: A Review of Commonwealth Involvement in Sport and Recreation in Australia (Sport 2000 Task Force)*, Canberra: Commonwealth of Australia.

Dean, M. (2007) *Governing Societies: Political Perspectives on Domestic and International Rule*, Maidenhead: Open University Press.

De Bosscher, V., De Knop, P., Van Bottenburg, M. and Shibli, S. (2006) A conceptual framework for analysing sports policy factors leading to international sporting success, *European Sport Management Quarterly*, 6(2), 185–215.

Department of Industry, Science and Resources (2001). *Backing Australia's Sporting Ability: A More Active Australia*, Canberra: Australian Government Publishing Service.

Dolowitz, D. and Marsh, D. (1996) Who learns what from whom?: A review of the policy transfer literature, *Political Studies*, 44, 343–357.

Dolowitz, D. and Marsh, D. (2000) Learning from abroad: The role of policy transfer in contemporary policy-making,

Governance: An International Journal of Policy and Administration, 13(1), 5–24.

Freeman, G.P. (1985) National styles and policy sectors: Explaining structural variation, *Journal of Policy Studies*, 5(4), 467–496.

Green, M. (2007a) Olympic glory or grassroots development?: Sport policy priorities in Australia, Canada and the United Kingdom, 1960–2006, *The International Journal of the History of Sport*, 24(7), 921–953.

Green, M. (2007b) Policy transfer, lesson drawing and perspectives on elite sport development systems, *International Journal of Sport Management and Marketing*, 2(4), 426–441.

Green, M. and Houlihan, B. (2005) *Elite Sport Development: Policy Learning and Political Priorities*, London: Routledge.

Green, M. and Houlihan, B. (2006) Governmentality, modernisation and the 'disciplining' of national sporting organisations: Athletics in Australia and the UK, *Sociology of Sport Journal*, 23(1), 47–71.

Green, M. and Oakley, B. (2001) Elite sport development systems and playing to win: Uniformity and diversity in international approaches, *Leisure Studies*, 20(4), 247–267.

Heinelt, H. (2005) Do policies determine politics?, *School for Policy Studies Working Paper Series* (Paper Number 11), University of Bristol.

Hoberg, G. (1986) Technology, political structure and social regulation: A cross-national analysis, *Comparative Politics*, 18, 357–376.

Hong, F, Wu, P. and Xiong, H. (2005) Beijing ambitions: An analysis of the Chinese elite sports system and its Olympic strategy for the 2008 Olympic Games, *The International Journal of the History of Sport*, 22(4), 510–529.

Jackson, R. (2006) *Road to Excellence Business Plan*, Toronto: Canadian Olympic Committee and Canadian Paralympic Committee.

Kay, A. (2005) A critique of the use of path dependency in policy studies, *Public Administration*, 83(3), 553–571.

Klein, R. and Marmor, T.R. (2006) Reflections on policy analysis, in M. Moran, M. Rein and R.E. Goodin (eds.), *The Oxford Handbook of Public Policy*, Oxford: Oxford University Press.

Levi, M. (1997) A model, a method, and a map: Rational choice in comparative and historical analysis, in M.I. Lichbach and A.S. Zuckerman (eds.), *Comparative Politics: Rationality, Culture and Structure*, Cambridge: Cambridge University Press, 19–41.

Lowi, T. (1972) Four systems of policy, politics and choice, *Public Administration Review*, 33, 298–310.

Ministerial Taskforce (2001) *Getting Set for an Active Nation: Report of the Sport, Fitness and Leisure Ministerial Taskforce*, Wellington: The Taskforce.

Ministry of Community Development and Sports (2001) *Sporting Singapore Report: Summary Version*, Singapore: Ministry of Community Development and Sports.

Oakley, B. and Green, M. (2001) The production of Olympic champions: International perspectives on elite sport development systems, *European Journal for Sport Management*, 8(Special Issue), 83–102.

Pierson, P. (2000) Increasing returns, path dependence, and the study of politics, *American Political Science Review*, 94(2), 251–267.

Rose, N. (1999) *Powers of Freedom: Reframing Political Thought*, Cambridge: Cambridge University Press.

Stewart, B., Nicholson, M., Smith, A. and Westerbeek, H. (2004) *Australian Sport: Better by Design? The Evolution of Australian Sport Policy*. London: Routledge.

Tan, T-C. and Green, M. (2007) *A uniform system of elite sport development?: Interrogating China's drive for Olympic glory*, June, Paper presented at the China in the 21st Century: Culture, Politics and Business Workshop, Chinese Sport and the Beijing Olympic Games, Ireland: Irish Institute of Chinese Studies, University College Cork.

Tan, Y.H. (2006) Olympic gold beckons, *Today*, 15 November, 55.

UK Sport (2006) *Sports Policy Factors Leading to International Sporting Success*, London: UK Sport.

Index

Academic Sports Association of Poland, 172
Advisory Council of Health and Physical
    Education (ACHPE), 56, 59, 60, 71
Advisory Council on Sports and
    Recreation, 86
Amateur Athletic Union (AAU), 2, 261
Amateur Sports Act, 2, 244, 245, 247
American antistatism, 269, 284
American exceptionalism, 269, 289
Anti-trust exemption, 243
Army Sports Federation, 172
Artemis group, 159
Aréna, 159
Asian All-Stars Athletics Championships
    2004, 98, 104
Asian Athletics Association (AAA), 101
Asian Athletics Championships, 104
Asian Grand Prix Series 2005, 98, 104
Associations Act of 1989, 169
Athens Olympic Games 2004, 2, 54, 57, 61,
    63, 66, 68, 228
Athlete Career and Training Programme,
    97
Athlete Career Education Programme, 70
Athlete Career Transition Programme, 70
Athlete Development programmes, 97
Athlete–equipment system, 140
Athlete pathways, 249–253
Athlete Support System, 98
Athletes, rights and responsibilities,
    185–187
Athletics, 7, 8, 28, 29, 47, 98, 103, 128, 133,
    136, 150, 152, 158, 161, 187, 227,
    235, 278

Atlanta Olympic Games 1996, 34, 38, 60
Augsburg Theses, 141, 142
Australia, 6, 7, 8, 9, 11, 14, 66, 70, 102, 106,
    210, 233, 248, 278, 280, 281, 285, 287
Australian Sports Commission, 101, 280,
    285

Badminton, 29, 47, 89, 162, 244
Barcelona Olympic Games 1992, 34, 157, 255
Basic Plan for the Promotion of Sport, 57,
    60–61
Basketball, 28, 29, 37, 150, 157, 160, 183, 248,
    249, 251, 256, 257, 260–262
Beach volleyball, 44, 257
Beall, Glenn, 246
Beijing Olympic Games 2008, 2, 34, 37, 46,
    47, 61, 63, 72, 282
Boxing, 44, 47, 150, 257

Canada, 3, 6, 7, 9, 11, 66, 70, 210, 233, 285
Canoeing, 34, 195
Capable Olympic sports, 47
Carded Coach Programme, 234
Carding System, 98
Central sports federation, 117–118
Centres of Excellence (COE), 95–96, 152
Championship Sport Act, 169, 170, 171, 173,
    175, 185, 187
China, 60, 99, 104, 276, 282
    elite athlete development
        coaching and sports science research,
            42–43
        competition opportunities, 42
        resources, 38–39

China (*Continued*)
    selection and training, 40–42
    training facilities, 43–44
    elite sport system, 283
       beginning, 27–29
       consolidation, 29
       critique, 44–46
       development, 29–32
       Olympic strategy, 33–36
    Juguo tizhi, characteristics
       administrative system, for sport, 36–37
    Olympic medals in 2008, winning
       strategy
       athletes training, 47–48
       increase, in resources, 48–49
       preparation for competition, 49
       sports selection, 46–47
China General Administration of Sport,
    36–37, 282
China Sports Daily, 27
Club sports, 132, 148, 250, 266
Coach Performance Enhancement Grants,
    234
Coaches' Academy, of DOSB, 119, 123, 141
Coaching, 8
    in China, 42–43
    in France, 152
    in Germany, 128–129
    in Japan, 70–72
    in New Zealand, 233–235
    in Singapore, 100–102
    in United States, 263–264
Coaching Advisory Committee, 101, 285
Coaching Association of Canada, 101, 285
Code of Athlete Management (COAM), 107
Code of Governance (COG), 92, 278
Commercial sport sector, in Poland
    organisational structure, 175–176
    responsibilities, 167–170
    sport governance, changes in, 182–183
Commercialisation, 10–11, 275–277
Committee for Physical culture, 179–180
Committee on Sporting Singapore (CoSS),
    89, 277
Competitive Sports Division, 56, 68, 70
Convergence
    common pressures for, 9–13, 273–278
    and processes of learning, 278–288
Council for Coach, Instructor and Manager
    Training, 189

Council for Recreation and Sport, 222
Court of Arbitration for Sport (CAS), 10,
    174
Cricket, 219, 227, 231, 236, 288
Cross-country skiing, 196, 201, 205
Cultural Revolution, 29, 30, 32
Cycling, 44, 150, 183, 251, 257

Deng Yaping, 45
Deutscher Olympischer Sportbund (DOSB):
    see German Olympic Sports
    Confederation
Diet, 10, 199, 203, 204, 205
Diving, 34, 47, 257
Dreaming to be a Superpower, 45
Drug Free Sport New Zealand (DFSNZ),
    221
Dual development system, 136–139

Electricité de France, 159
Elite athlete, 63, 71, 75, 98, 103, 107, 149–156,
    198, 204, 228, 234, 236, 237, 275, 281
Elite athlete development, 3–9, 281–282,
    289
    characteristics, 4
    in China, 38–44
    coaching provision, 7–8
    elite facility development, 6–7
    full-time athletes, support for, 6
    international events, preparation for, 8
    in Japan, 56, 59, 60, 63
    sports science and medicine, 8
    in United States, 251
Elite sport policy development, 12, 13, 287
    in Japan, 56, 58–63
    lesson-drawing, 15
    in New Zealand, 225
    path dependency, 17–19
       tripartite categorization, 18
    policy learning, 14–15
    policy transfer, 15–16
    political characteristics, 19–20
    in Singapore, 84, 90, 92–104
Elite sports schools, 137
Equestrian, 227, 231, 244, 258

Fed Cup, 161
Federal Border Police (BGS), 138, 139
Federal Institute of Sports Science, 119,
    139, 140

Federal Ministry of the Interior (BMI), 124, 125–126, 130
Federal Performance Committee, 119
Federal Youth Games, 133
Federation Cup: *see* Fed Cup
Federation of Popular Sports and Athletics Clubs, 172
FIFA, 157, 158, 170, 174
Figure skating, 150, 162, 211
Football, 28, 29, 32, 37, 43, 150, 162, 167, 178, 183, 201
Ford, Gerald, 247
France, 14, 147, 275, 290
  financial support, for elite sport, 154–156
  'French model' of sport, 149–150
  organisation of elite sport, 151–153
  sports federation, 148
  support structures, for elite athletes, 153–154
  tensions, conflicts and future, 156–164
Freedom of Economic Activity Act, 174–175
French Basketball Federation, 157–158
French Championships, 160
French Tennis Federation (FFT), 158
Fukuoka Sports Talent Scout Project, 70, 73–74
Full-time athletes, 6
  in China, 28, 40, 41
  in Germany, 135–139
  in Japan, 67–69
  in New Zealand, 235–237
  in Singapore, 97–100
Fuzhou camp, 44
Fédération française de basketball (FFBB): *see* French Basketball Federation

German championship, 122
German Democratic Republic (GDR), 2, 117
German Gymnastics and Sports Federation, 118
German Hockey Federation, 133, 140, 141
German Olympic Sports Confederation, 116, 119, 121, 122, 123–125, 130
German Sports Aid Foundation, 119, 124, 135, 136
German Sports Confederation (DSB), 119, 130, 131, 135
German Swimming Federation, 142
Germany, 14, 18, 34
  top level sport system, 116

dimensions, 127–128
full-time athletes, support for, 135–139
historical roots and milestones, 117–120
principles and structures, 120–124
sports and training science, 139–142
sports facilities for, 128–131
state responsibility and competency, 124–127
talent spotting, 131–133
talent support, 133–135
Globalisation, 9, 10, 13, 273–275
Glory for the Nation, 108, 286
GlücksSpirale, 126, 127
Goh Chok Tong, 87
Golf, 150, 201, 227, 248
Governmental sport sector, in Poland
  organisational structure, 170–171
  responsibilities, 167–170
  sport governance, changes in, 179–182
Governmentalisation, 12, 277–278
Graham report, 225, 233
Great Leap Forward (GLF), 28
Group Lagardère, 158
Guangzhou camp, 44
Gymnastics, 28, 29, 31, 43, 44, 47, 69, 152, 162, 184, 201, 211, 248, 249

Haigen camp, 44
Haikou camp, 44
Handball, 150, 183
  see also Team handball
He Long, 30
Helsinki Olympic Games 1952, 28, 58
Helsinki World Championships 2005, 98
High Performance Athlete Programme, 107
High Performance Management Division (HPMD), 97
High Performance Strategy, 231, 233, 238
High Performance Unit (HPU), 220
Hillary Commission, 223, 224
Holmenkollen ski facility, 199
Hongta camp, 44
'Hovedlandsrennet', 206

IAAF World Indoor Championships, 104
IAAF Youth Athletics Championships, 104
Ice hockey, 150, 160, 249, 251, 257–258
Institute for Applied Coaching Science, 139
Institute for Applied Training Science in Leipzig (IAT), 140

Institute for Research and Further Development of Sports Equipment (FES), 139, 140
International Association of Athletics Federations (IAAF), 10, 96
International Football Federation: *see* FIFA
International Journal of the History of Sport, 45
International Olympic Committee (IOC), 58, 91, 151, 213
International Rugby Board (IRB), 158
Ironman World Championship, 265
Italian football federation, 157
ITC World Cup, 265

Japan, 277, 281, 289
  elite sport infrastructure
    athlete support and development, 67–72
    specialist facilities, 63–67
  elite sport policy, development of, 58–63
  elite sport system
    current structure, 54–58
    distinctive features, 76–78
    organisational structure, 55
    talent identification system, 72–74
    young athletes, competition opportunities for, 74–76
Japan Institute of Sports and Sciences (JISS), 54, 57
Japanese Olympic Committee (JOC), 54, 57, 61
Japan Top League (JTL), 62
Jiang Zemin, 35, 46
Johnson, Ben, 3
Juguo tizhi, 27, 36, 282
  administrative system, for sport, 36–38
Junior Elite Cup, 265

Katowice, 173
Kayaking, 153, 200
Kids Triathlons, 265
Kokutai, 57, 58, 73, 75–76
'Kretslag', 205

Lagardère, 159, 161
Lancel, 159
Laoweizhi, 28
LastMinute.com, 159
Lazio football club, 157

Lesson-drawing, 14, 15
Lillehammer Olympic Games 1994, 199, 207, 209
Liu Fuming, 48
Looking East Weekly, 45
Los Angeles Olympic Games 1984, 119
L'Equipe Magazine, 159

Manaudou, Laure, 159
Mao Zedong, 29, 30
Marathon, 103, 257
Masayo Imura, 72
Melbourne Commonwealth Games 2006, 228, 229, 236
MEXT (Ministry of Education, Culture, Sports and Technology), 54, 56, 60, 62, 63, 67, 73
Ministry of Community Development and Sports (MCDS), 89, 277, 285
Ministry of Community Development, Youth and Sports (MCYS), 107
Ministry of Recreation and Sport, 222
Montreal Olympic Games 1976, 2, 59, 225, 280
Motor sports, 150
Motorcycling, 150
Multi-million Dollar Award Programme, 88

Nagano winter Olympic Games 1998, 63, 160
Nasjonalanlegg, 199, 200
National Agency for the Advancement of Sports and Health (NAASH), 56
National Basketball Association (NBA), 158, 160, 249, 261–262
National Centre for the Development of Sport, 155
National Coaching Accreditation Programme (NCAP), 88, 100
National Coaching Plan, 100
National Collegiate Athletic Association (NCAA), 2, 244, 266
National Committee for Elite Sports, 151, 152
National Development Fund for Sport, 154
National Hockey League (NHL), 160
National Institute for Physical Sport and Education (INSEP), 152
National Olympic Committee for Germany (NOC), 119

National Programme for the Development of Sport 2006–2008, 152
National Recreation and Parks Association, 248
National Registry of Coaches (NROC), 101
National Skiing Federation, 206
National sport associations (NSAs), 88, 91–92
National Sports Organisations (NSOs), 221
Netball, 227, 231
Netherlands, the, 5
New Paper Big Walk, 96
New Zealand, 276, 277, 281, 286, 287, 288
    elite sport system
        business of, 225–232
        coaching, 233–235
        current structure, 219–221
        facilities, 237–239
        full-time athletes, 235–237
        sports science, 235
        talent identification, 232–233
    government intervention, 221–225
    High Performance Strategy, 231, 238
    priority sports selection, 227, 231
New Zealand Academy of Sport, 220, 221, 235
New Zealand Olympic Committee (NZOC), 221
New Zealand Sports Foundation (NZSF), 223
Nippon Revival Project, 61, 68
Norway, 195, 275, 276, 277, 281
    elite sport system, 195–198, 210–213
    focusing events, 206–208
    government and elite sport, 208–210
    infrastructure of elite sport, 198
        facility development, 198–200
        full-time competitors, 200–203
        sport science and medicine, 203–205
        squad system and competition opportunities, 205
    see also Olympiatoppen
Norwegian Olympic Committee and Confederation of Sports (NIF/NOC), 196, 200, 208
Norwegian Ski Federation, 205, 206

Olympiatoppen (OLT), 195, 202, 204, 207, 209, 211
    children, 212
    diet, 203

health section, 199
nutrition section, 199
public funding, 197
and sports federations, 196
Olympic Games, 7, 16, 63, 72, 108, 138, 153, 207, 231, 288
    Athens, 2, 54, 57, 61, 63, 66, 68, 228
    Atlanta, 34, 38, 60
    Barcelona, 34, 157, 255
    Beijing, 2, 34, 37, 46, 47, 61, 63, 72, 282
    Helsinki, 28, 58
    Lillehammer, 199, 207, 209
    Los Angeles, 119
    Montreal, 2, 59, 225, 280
    Rome, 148
    Seoul, 3, 34, 60, 64
    Sydney, 6, 34, 35, 161, 224, 257, 280
    Tokyo, 64, 70
Olympic squads, in Germany, 123
'Olympic strategy', 33–36, 38, 45, 46
Olympic training centres, 119, 123, 126, 129–131, 137, 138, 139, 140, 245
Oulmers affair, 157

Paris Judo Club, 158
Path dependency, 17–19, 278, 279, 280, 283, 284, 289–290
People's Action Party (PAP), 84
People's Daily, 31, 44
Performance Enhancement Grants (PEGs), 236
Physical Culture Act 1996, 169, 182
Physical Fitness Development Fund (PFDF), 177, 184
Ping-Pong diplomacy, 31–32
Poland, 13, 275, 277, 290
    elite sport
        athletes' rights and responsibilities, 185–187
        commercial sector, responsibilities, 167–170
        financing, 176–178
        governmental sector, responsibilities, 167–170
        infrastructure growth, 184–185
        organisational structure, 170–176
        sport competition, structure of, 187–188
        sport governance, changes in, 178–183
        voluntary sector, responsibilities, 167–170

Policy determines politics, 19, 278, 290–291
Policy learning, 14–15, 288–289
Policy transfer, 15–16
Polish Biathlon Association, 169
Polish Football Association, 169, 174
Polish Olympic Committee (POC), 170, 172
Polish Paralympics Committee, 172
Polish Skiing Association, 169
Polish sport associations, 169, 170, 172, 173–174, 175, 183, 184, 185, 187–188
Polish Sports Federation, 172
Potential Olympic sports, 47
Pressures for convergence, 9–13
  commercialisation, 10–12
  globalisation, 10
  governmentalisation, 12
Prime Minister's Athlete Scholarship Awards, 236
Prime Minister's Coaching Scholarship Programme, 234
Professional athlete, 150, 186
Provincial–federal rivalry, 6
Pyramid model, 86, 88

Racing Club de France, 159
Regional Committees for Performance Sport (LA-L), 122
Regulations for Children's Sport, 210, 211, 212
Research Institute for Physical Culture and Sport, 118, 139
Revitalisation sports, 227
Riksanlegg, 199
Rimejordet, Thor Ole, 203
Rome Olympic Games 1960, 148
Rowing, 34, 153, 227, 231, 244, 260, 262–264, 276
Rugby, 150, 158, 162, 219, 227, 231, 251

Safety of Mass Events Act of 1997, 169
Sailing, 6, 7, 89, 100, 150, 152, 167, 200, 258
Salt Lake City Games 2002, 160, 258
Sanya camp, 44
School Sports and Athletics Association, 172
School-based sport, 249, 250, 251, 266, 267
Sculling, 200, 264
Seoul Olympic Games 1998, 3, 34, 60, 64
Shengzhen camp, 44

Short track speed skating, 162
Singapore, 13, 21, 84, 276, 277, 281, 284, 285, 286, 287, 288, 289, 290
  elite sport policy
    developments and future directions, 105–108
    dimensions, 92–104
    key issues, 104–105
    National sport associations (NSAs), 88, 91–92
    Sports Community and Sporting Vision, 85
    sports excellence development, 86–91
Singapore Amateur Athletic Association (SAAA), 92, 93
Singapore Athletics Association (SAA), 84, 277
    coaching, sports science and sports medicine, 100–102
    elite level athletes, competition opportunities for, 102–104
    elite sport facilities, development of, 95–97
    full-time athletes, emergence of, 97–100
    organisation and administration, 92–95
Singapore National Olympic Council (SNOC), 86
Singapore Sports Council (SSC), 84, 276, 277
Skiing World Championships 1997, 199
Snowboarding, 150, 257
Soccer: see Football
Society of Strategic Research for the Development of Physical Education and Sport, 33
Société de bains de mer de Monaco, 159
South East Asia (SEA) Games, 87
SPARC (Sport and Recreation New Zealand), 219, 220, 221, 225, 226, 227, 228, 229, 231, 232, 235, 236, 238, 286
spexGLOW, 97, 98
spexTEAM, 97
Sporever, 159
Sport competition, 183, 187–188
Sport for All policy, 56, 59, 84, 87, 129, 208
Sport on the Move, 223, 224, 287
Sporting Culture Committee, 108
Sports Aid Fund, 88
Sports culture, in Singapore, 107–108
Sports facilities
  in Germany, 128–131

in Poland, 184
in Singapore, 95
Sports institute, in Singapore, 105–106
Sports Medicine and Sports Science
    Division (SMSSD), 102
Sports Promotion Lottery Law, 60
Sports science and medicine, 8
    in China, 42–43
    in Japan, 64–66
    in New Zealand, 233–235
    in Norway, 203–205
    in Poland, 188–190
    in Singapore, 100–102
    in United States, 259–260
Sports Science Research Committee, 64
SportsCOVER, 97
Squad system, 122–123
SSC–NSA relationship, 106–107
Standard Chartered Singapore Marathon, 96
State Physical Education and Sports
    Commission, 28, 36
Supranational policy actors, 9
Supranational provision, 10
Supranational redistribution, 10
Supranational regulation, 9–10
Surfing, 150
Swimming, 7, 8, 28, 29, 34, 44, 47, 89, 100,
    120, 133, 136, 152, 160, 167, 227, 231,
    237, 244, 248, 249, 257, 265
Sydney Olympic Games 2000, 6, 34, 35, 161,
    224, 257, 280

Table-tennis, 28, 29, 30, 31, 37, 43, 45, 100
Talent identification and development
    (TID), 16, 59, 286, 288
Talent Identification Taskforce, 233
Talent spotting system, 131–133
Talent support system, 131, 133–135
Team handball, 244, 260, 266–268
Team Lagardère, 158, 159
Tennis, 11, 150, 159, 161, 248, 249, 251
The Defeat in Seoul, 45
The Strategy of the Development of Sport Until
    2012, 168, 175
Title IX, 243–244, 263
Tokyo Asian Games 1958, 58
Tokyo Olympic Games 1964, 64, 70
Top level sport partner schools, 137–138
Top level sports system, in Germany, 116
    dimensions, 127

full-time athletes, support for, 135–139
    sports and training science, 139–142
    sports facilities for, 128–131
    talent spotting, 131–133
    talent support, 133–135
    historical roots and milestones, 117–120
    principles and structures, 120–124
    state responsibility and competency,
        124–127
Toppidrettssenteret, 198, 209
Toto, 56, 60, 61
Traditional Olympic sports, 47
Training centre system, 122, 123–124, 129
Training Doctor System, 64
Triathlon, 231, 253, 260, 265–266, 269
Turin winter Olympic Games 2006, 63
24-hour athlete, 202, 214, 276

UK Sport, 5, 17
UK Sport Institute (UKSI), 6, 7
Union of European Football Associations
    (UEFA), 158, 162
United Kingdom, 2, 5, 6, 7, 11, 12, 16, 18, 70,
    210, 278, 284, 285, 287, 288
United States, 2, 11, 16, 18, 27, 28, 31, 47, 58,
    66, 70, 158, 274, 277, 282, 284, 289,
    290
    athlete pathways, 249–253
    athletes' success, 253–259
    elite sport development
        basketball, 260–262
        rowing, 262–264
        team handball, 266–268
        triathlon, 265–266
    federal involvement, in elite sport, 243–249
    observations and implications, 268–270
    research and development, 259–260
United States Olympic Committee (USOC),
    244–245, 267
United States Olympic Training Centres
    (USOTCs), 259
University club sports, 250, 266
University of Saragossa, 157
USA Basketball, 260–262
USA Triathlon, 265–266
USRowing, 262–264

Varsity sports, 250
Vietnam SEA Games 2003, 98
Volleyball, 28, 150, 201, 248, 257, 268

Voluntary sport sector, in Poland
    organisational structure, 172–175
    responsibilities, 167–170
    sport governance, changes in, 183

Weak Olympic sports, 47
Weightlifting, 29, 44, 47, 89, 161, 162
Weimin, Yuan, 36
Windsurfing, 150
Winter Olympics, 3, 34–35, 74, 195, 200, 209,
    255, 257
World Anti-Doping Code, 16
World Class Athlete Program (WCAP),
    258, 267

Wrestling, 130, 153, 244, 249
Wu Shouzhang, 48

Xiang, Liu, 41
Xinhua News Agency, 45
Xinzhuan camp, 44

yachting, 227, 231
Youth Elite Cup, 265
Youth trains for the Olympics, 133

Zhao Yu, 45
Zhongshan camp, 44